Granular Computing and Big Data Advancements

Chao Zhang
Shanxi University, China

Wentao Li
Southwest University, China

A volume in the Advances in Systems Analysis, Software Engineering, and High Performance Computing (ASASEHPC) Book Series

Published in the United States of America by
IGI Global
Engineering Science Reference (an imprint of IGI Global)
701 E. Chocolate Avenue
Hershey PA, USA 17033
Tel: 717-533-8845
Fax: 717-533-8661
E-mail: cust@igi-global.com
Web site: http://www.igi-global.com

Library of Congress Cataloging-in-Publication Data

CIP Data Pending
ISBN: 979-8-3693-4292-3
eISBN: 979-8-3693-4293-0

British Cataloguing in Publication Data
A Cataloguing in Publication record for this book is available from the British Library.

Advances in Systems Analysis, Software Engineering, and High Performance Computing (ASASEHPC) Book Series

Vijayan Sugumaran
Oakland University, Rochester, USA

ISSN:2327-3453
EISSN:2327-3461

MISSION

The theory and practice of computing applications and distributed systems has emerged as one of the key areas of research driving innovations in business, engineering, and science. The fields of software engineering, systems analysis, and high performance computing offer a wide range of applications and solutions in solving computational problems for any modern organization.

The **Advances in Systems Analysis, Software Engineering, and High Performance Computing (ASASEHPC) Book Series** brings together research in the areas of distributed computing, systems and software engineering, high performance computing, and service science. This collection of publications is useful for academics, researchers, and practitioners seeking the latest practices and knowledge in this field.

Coverage

- Human-Computer Interaction
- Metadata and Semantic Web
- Parallel Architectures
- Virtual Data Systems

IGI Global is currently accepting manuscripts for publication within this series. To submit a proposal for a volume in this series, please contact our Acquisition Editors at Acquisitions@igi-global.com or visit: http://www.igi-global.com/publish/.

The (ISSN) is published by IGI Global, 701 E. Chocolate Avenue, Hershey, PA 17033-1240, USA, www.igi-global.com. This series is composed of titles available for purchase individually; each title is edited to be contextually exclusive from any other title within the series. For pricing and ordering information please visit http://www.igi-global.com/book-series/advances-systems-analysis-software-engineering/73689. Postmaster: Send all address changes to above address.

Titles in this Series

For a list of additional titles in this series, please visit: www.igi-global.com/book-series

Harnessing High-Performance Computing and AI for Environmental Sustainability
Arshi Naim (King Khalid University, Saudi Arabia)
Engineering Science Reference • copyright 2024 • 401pp • H/C (ISBN: 9798369317945) • US $315.00 (our price)

Recent Trends and Future Direction for Data Analytics
Aparna Kumari (Nirma University, Ahmedabad, India)
Engineering Science Reference • copyright 2024 • 350pp • H/C (ISBN: 9798369336090) • US $345.00 (our price)

Advancing Software Engineering Through AI, Federated Learning, and Large Language Models
Avinash Kumar Sharma (Sharda University, India) Nitin Chanderwal (University of Cincinnati, USA) Amarjeet Prajapati (Jaypee Institute of Information Technology, India) Pancham Singh (Ajay Kumar Garg Engineering College, Ghaziabad, India) and Mrignainy Kansal (Ajay Kumar Garg Engineering College, Ghaziabad, India)
Engineering Science Reference • copyright 2024 • 354pp • H/C (ISBN: 9798369335024) • US $355.00 (our price)

Advancements, Applications, and Foundations of C++
Shams Al Ajrawi (Wiley Edge, USA & Alliant International University, USA) Charity Jennings (Wiley Edge, USA & University of Phoenix, USA) Paul Menefee (Wiley Edge, USA) Wathiq Mansoor (University of Dubai, UAE) and Mansoor Ahmed Alaali (Ahlia University, Bahrain)
Engineering Science Reference • copyright 2024 • 564pp • H/C (ISBN: 9798369320075) • US $295.00 (our price)

IGI Global
PUBLISHER of TIMELY KNOWLEDGE

701 East Chocolate Avenue, Hershey, PA 17033, USA
Tel: 717-533-8845 x100 • Fax: 717-533-8661
E-Mail: cust@igi-global.com • www.igi-global.com

Table of Contents

Preface

In the dynamic landscape of today's information-driven world, the symbiosis between granular computing and big data stands out as a transformative force, steering advancements across diverse realms. At the core of this synergy lies the challenge of managing the exponential surge in digital information—a challenge that spans representation, processing, and interpretation at varying levels of granularity, as well as the collection, storage, and analysis of vast datasets that traditional methods grapple to navigate efficiently.

Granular Computing and Big Data Advancements, curated by Chao Zhang and Wentao Li, delves into this intersection, offering a comprehensive exploration of the latest methodologies, applications, and breakthroughs in the amalgamation of granular computing and big data. Bridging the gap between theoretical research and pragmatic implementations, this reference book aspires to equip researchers, academics, practitioners, and professionals with cutting-edge techniques, case studies, and real-world applications.

The primary goal of this book is to contribute to the evolving landscape of knowledge in this interdisciplinary domain. By presenting foundational principles, advanced techniques, and practical insights, it aims to facilitate the development of innovative solutions to complex data-related challenges, thereby playing a role in addressing the data deluge in our interconnected world.

The target audience for *Granular Computing and Big Data Advancements* spans a spectrum of individuals—from seasoned researchers and academics to practitioners and professionals—across fields such as granular computing, big data, data science, artificial intelligence, machine learning, and related disciplines. Graduate students, scholars, and industry experts seeking to deepen their understanding of theoretical foundations, methodologies, and practical applications will find this book particularly beneficial.

Key areas covered include the foundations and principles of granular computing, fundamental concepts and techniques of big data analytics, integration of granular computing and big data frameworks, granular computing approaches for data preprocessing and feature selection, big data processing and analytics techniques for large-scale datasets, hybrid granular computing and big data models and algorithms, granular computing-based machine learning and deep learning approaches for big data analysis, applications in various domains (e.g., healthcare, finance, manufacturing, cybersecurity), case studies and practical implementations of granular computing and big data solutions, and an exploration of challenges, opportunities, and future directions in granular computing and big data research.

We invite readers to embark on a journey through the pages of this book, exploring the rich tapestry of granular computing and big data advancements. May it serve as a valuable resource, inspiring new perspectives and fostering innovative solutions in the ever-evolving landscape of data-driven discovery.

ORGANIZATION OF THE BOOK

Chapter 1, authored by Binbin Sang, Lei Yang, Hongmei Chen, Weihua Xu, Yanting Guo, and Zhong Yuan, introduces the concept of Generalized Multi-Granulation Double-Quantitative Decision-Theoretic Rough Set (MS-GMDQ-DTRS) for handling knowledge acquisition in Multi-Source Information Systems (MsIS). The chapter begins with a foundation in Generalized Multi-Granulation Rough Set Model for MsIS (MS-GMRS) and proceeds to integrate it with double-quantitative decision-theoretic rough set models, showcasing improved fault tolerance capabilities. Experimental results on UCI datasets validate the enhanced fault tolerance in directly acquiring knowledge from MsIS.

Chapter 2, penned by Pengfei Zhang, Dexian Wang, and Tao Jiang, focuses on the integration of Multi-Source Information Fusion (MSIF) and Granular Computing (GrC). The chapter introduces solutions such as the multi-source homogeneous fusion model and heterogeneous data fusion method, highlighting their role in addressing uncertainty, fuzziness, and multi-source complexity. These approaches contribute to enhancing the efficiency and quality of information processing and decision support.

Chapter 3, authored by Qingbin Ji, provides a systematic review of Community Discovery in Complex Network Big Data. The chapter explores the theoretical basis of community discovery, categorizes community discovery methods, and introduces new tasks and applications in big data. Readers gain a comprehensive understanding of how community thinking can be introduced into big data analysis, thereby improving decision-making abilities.

Chapter 4, written by Qingzhao Kong, Wanting Wang, and Conghao Yan, emphasizes the efficiency of data mining through information granules. The chapter delves into numerical characteristics related to information granules, explores various granular structures induced by different learning rules, and develops a novel granular computing model based on three-way decision theory. The model is successfully applied in network security, showcasing its practical utility.

Chapter 5, authored by Jie Yang and Shuai Li, introduces a novel Sequential Three-Way Decisions model with Rough Fuzzy Sets (S3WDRFS). The chapter combines cost measure and three-way decisions theory to approximately describe uncertain knowledge in multi-granulation spaces. The proposed model establishes a method for optimal granularity selection, highlighting the monotonic decrease in decision cost with finer knowledge spaces.

Chapter 6, written by Tao Zhan, explores Multi-Granulation-Based Optimal Scale Selection in Multi-Scale Information Systems. The chapter introduces belief and plausibility functions within the context of multigranulation and presents a method for optimal scale selection. Analyses of optimistic and pessimistic multigranulation optimal scale selection reveal intrinsic connections between distinct methodologies.

Chapter 7, penned by Xiaoan Tang, delves into Fuzzy Hamacher Aggregation Functions and their applications to Multiple Attribute Decision Making. The chapter analyzes the application of Hamacher t-norm and t-conorm in fuzzy MADM, providing theoretical proof and a new method to compare alternatives with consideration of different parameters.

Chapter 8, authored by Baoli Wang, explores the concept of Knowledge Distance and its Relative Extensions. The chapter studies properties of knowledge distance, utilizes it to measure rough entropy of knowledge, and introduces relative knowledge distance based on relative cognition. The chapter's experimental analysis visually examines the structural characteristics of relative knowledge distance in hierarchical clustering.

Chapter 9, written by Dong Song, Ting Li, and Yuanlong Zhao, proposes a Feasibility Evaluation of Highwall Mining in Open-Pit Coal Mines based on Variable Weight Fuzzy Theory. The chapter presents a mathematical framework integrating AHP, FCE, and VWT to assess highwall mining feasibility, providing a quantitative assessment of the technology's feasibility in various technical conditions.

Chapter 10, authored by Zhikang Xu, Xiaodong Yue, and Ying Lv, introduces Trusted Fine-Grained Image Classification based on Evidence Theory and its Applications to Medical Image Analysis. The chapter integrates Dempster-Shafer Evidence Theory with deep learning to construct a trusted FGIC model, reducing uncertainty in fine-grained classification. Additionally, it explores the application of FGIC in medical image analysis for trusted classification.

IN CONCLUSION

As we bring this comprehensive reference book, *Granular Computing and Big Data Advancements*, to its conclusion, we reflect on the rich tapestry of insights and innovations presented by the distinguished authors. The amalgamation of granular computing and big data has proven to be a dynamic force, offering profound solutions and shaping the landscape of knowledge in various domains.

The chapters within this volume have traversed the intricate intersections of multi-source information systems, information fusion, community discovery in complex network big data, information granules, three-way decisions, optimal scale selection, fuzzy aggregation functions, knowledge distance, highwall mining feasibility, and trusted fine-grained image classification. Each contribution not only expands our theoretical understanding but also provides practical applications, paving the way for advancements in data science, artificial intelligence, and related disciplines.

The collaborative efforts of the authors, Chao Zhang, Wentao Li, Binbin Sang, Lei Yang, Hongmei Chen, Weihua Xu, Yanting Guo, Zhong Yuan, Pengfei Zhang, Dexian Wang, Tao Jiang, Qingbin Ji, Qingzhao Kong, Wanting Wang, Conghao Yan, Jie Yang, Shuai Li, Tao Zhan, Xiaoan Tang, Baoli Wang, Dong Song, Ting Li, Yuanlong Zhao, Zhikang Xu, Xiaodong Yue, and Ying Lv, have created a cohesive exploration of the latest advancements, methodologies, and applications in the merging realms of granular computing and big data.

Our hope is that this reference book not only serves as a valuable resource for researchers, academics, practitioners, and professionals but also inspires future endeavors in the field. By bridging the gap between theoretical research and practical implementations, this compilation contributes to the advancement of knowledge in the interdisciplinary domain and facilitates the development of innovative solutions to address the complex challenges posed by the data deluge in our interconnected world.

We extend our gratitude to the contributors for their exceptional scholarship and dedication, and to the readers for engaging with the diverse perspectives presented within these pages. May the insights gained from *Granular Computing and Big Data Advancements* foster continued exploration and progress in the ever-evolving landscape of data-driven discovery.

Chao Zhang
Shanxi University, China

Wentao Li
Southwest University, China

Chapter 1 Generalized Multi-Granulation Double-Quantitative Decision-Theoretic Rough Set of Multi-Source Information System

Binbin Sang
Chongqing Normal University, China

Weihua Xu
Southwest University, China

Lei Yang
Southwest Jiaotong University, China

Yanting Guo
Shenzhen University, China

Hongmei Chen
Southwest Jiaotong University, China

Zhong Yuan
Sichuan University, China

ABSTRACT

Traditionally, multi-source information system (MsIS) is typically integrated into a single information table for knowledge acquisition. Therefore, discovering knowledge directly from MsIS without information loss is a valuable research direction. In this chapter, the authors propose the generalized multi-granulation double-quantitative decision-theoretic rough set of multi-source information system (MS-GMDQ-DTRS) to handle this issue. First, they propose a generalized multi-granulation rough set model for MsIS (MS-GMRS) as the basis of other models. In this model, each single

DOI: 10.4018/979-8-3693-4292-3.ch001

information system is treated as a granular structure. Next, they combine MS-GMRS with double-quantitative decision-theoretic rough set to obtain two new models. They have better fault tolerance capability compared with MS-GMRS. Furthermore, they propose corresponding algorithms to calculate the approximation accuracy of the proposed models. Experiments are carried out on four datasets downloaded from UCI. Experimental results show that the two new models have better fault tolerance in directly acquiring knowledge from MsIS.

1. INTRODUCTION

As the information age continues to evolve, data form becomes more complex. This has promoted the development of some knowledge representation forms for complex data. Among these representation forms, multi-source information system (MsIS) (M. A. Khan & M. Banerjee,2008) is an important representative, which is a family of homogeneous single source information systems. In real-world applications, the MsIS is widely used in various fields, such as natural language processing (S. L. Sun, et al., 2017), extracting trips (F. L. Wang, et al., 2019), energy consumption prediction (J. Qin, et al., 2018), deep learning (W. S. Zhang, et al., 2018) and so on. In recent years, multi-source fusion (W. H. Xu, et al., 2016; W. H. Xu & J. H. Yu, 2017; B. B. Sang, et al., 2017; Y. Y. Huang, et al., 2018; J. T. Yao, et al., 2008), as a common method for dealing with MsIS, has been widely concerned, which can integrate infor- mation from MsIS into a single information table, acquire knowledge, and extract rules. This topic has attracted the attention of researchers because of its wide applications.

Integrating MsIS into a single information table is the most common multi-source fusion strategy. Then knowledge is acquired through the obtained information table. The integration method of MsIS is a necessary prerequisite for processing MsIS. In recent years, many multi-source fusion methods have been proposed. Particularly, Xu et al. proposed a multi-source fusion method based on information entropy (W. H. Xu, et al., 2016; B. B. Sang, et al., 2017) and information source selection principle (W. H. Xu & J. H. Yu, 2017). In these works, the multi-source fusion method uses a metric to select reliable information from a MsIS for integration into a single information table. In fact, the essence of this method is to integrate the description of objects from all information tables in MsIS into one classic information table. This is called integrating MsIS from the perspective of objects. It is worth noting that in the process of this integration, information loss will inevitably occur. Therefore, how to discover knowledge directly from MsIS without information loss motivates this study. In this paper, we focus on introduce the multi-granulation rough set theory into multi-source fusion.

Multi-granulation rough set is an important theory in granular computing. The concept of granular computing has been widely concerned since it was proposed by Zadeh (L. A. Zadeh, 1997). Recently, Yao (Y. Y. Yao, 2018) proposed three-way granular computing for processing information by integrating granular computing and three-way decision. From the perspective of granular computing, in the universe, an equivalence relation is a granular structure, multiple equivalence relations are multiple granular structures. In real-world applications, an object set needs to be described by multiple relations according to the user's needs or target of problem handling. To meet the actual needs, Qian et al. (Y. H. Qian, et al., 2010) proposed the theoretical framework of multi-granulation rough set (MGRS), which was used to process an information table with multiple granular structure. In recent years, the MGRS model has been widely extended and applied (J. H. Yu, et al., 2018; B. Z. Sun, et al., 2019; G. P. Lin, et al., 2012; G. P. Lin, et al., 2015; Y. H. Qian, et al., 2014, G. P. Lin, et al., 2016; X. Y. Che, et al., 2018). Yang et al. (X. Yang, et al., 2019) proposed a multi-level granular structure-based sequential three-way approach for solving multi-class decision issues. Attribute reduction based on single criterion is useless for complex problems. To address this issue, Li et al. (W. W. Li, et al., 2019) presented a multi-objective attribute reduction method. To solve linguistic information-based multiple attribute group decision making issue, Sun et al. (B. Z. Sun, et al., 2018) proposed three-way approach in the framework of decision-theoretic rough set.

Multi-granulation rough set theory provides a new way for information fusion. From the perspective of information fusion, the objective of the MGRS is to integrate information from one information table with multiple granular structures into the approximations of a target concept. In such an information table, the granular structure is usually composed of multiple attributes. Thus, an information fusion strategy based on the idea of multi-granulation is called fusing information from the perspective of attributes. In fact, each single information system in MsIS can be regarded as a granular structure. Inspired by the above, we argue that it is a feasible method to integrate MsIS based on multi- granulation rough set theory. It is worth pointing out that this method can directly generate approximations of a target concept in MsIS, thus avoiding information loss.

However the MGRS model is too strict or too loose in describing approximations, it does not take into account the situation that the minority is subordinate to the majority. To overcome this deficiency, Xu et al. (W. H. Xu, et al., 2012) proposed the theoretical framework of generalized multi-granulation rough set (GMRS), which is the extension of MGRS model. The key constituent of this model is to use an information level $\beta \in (0.5, 1]$ to control objects selection. By adjusting this parameter, the objects can be positively described in most classifications, and the objects that may be described below the corresponding level are deleted. So the GMRS model has better practicality. Based on this model, Qian et al. (J. Qian, et al., 2019) proposed a multiple thresholds-based generalized multi-granulation sequential three-way decision model for solving the issue of multi-granulation structure. Considering the advantages of the GMRS model, this paper exploits this model to deal with MsIS. Therefore, we build a new model, called generalized multi-granulation rough set model of MsIS (MS-GMRS), to acquire the knowledge of MsIS.

In order to improve the fault tolerance capability of the MS-GMRS model, we combine this model with double- quantitative decision-theoretic rough set (W. T. Li & W. H. Xu, 2015). Then we obtain two new models, called two kinds of generalized multi-granulation double-quantitative decision-theoretic rough set model for MsIS (MS-GMDQ-DTRS). Double- quantitative decision-theoretic rough set, as an important extension of Pawlak rough set theory, has been widely studied (W. H. Xu, et al., 2017; W. T. Li, et al., 2018). The Pawlak rough set theory (Z. Pawlak, 1982) is an important mathematical tool, which has been widely applied to attribute reduction (J. H. Dai, et al., 2013; J. H. Dai & Q. Xu, 2013; A. Ferone, 2018; M. S. Raza & U. Qamar, 2018; F. Min, et al., 2018), uncertainty measurement (J. H. Dai, et al., 2017; C. Z. Wang, et al., 2019), and decision theory (H. L. Dou, et al., 2016; X. Yang, et al., 2019), cost-sensitive leaning (Y. Fang & F. Min, 2019; M. Wang, et al., 2019; Y . X. Wu, et al., 2019; F. Min, et al., 2011; X.-A. Ma & X. R. Zhao, 2019; Y. B. Zhang, et al., 2019), rough data analysis (Y. H. Qian, et al., 2018) etc. However, the Pawlak rough set model has limitation, which is sensi- tive to noisy data. Since the degree of intersection between target set and knowledge granules is not considered, the Pawlak rough set model has no fault tolerant effect in processing information. To solve this issue, many meaningful works about the extension of Pawlak rough set model have been investigated. Among these extended models, double- quantitative decision-theoretic rough set model is an important representative, which is built by combining the graded rough set model (Y. Y. Yao & T. Y. Lin, 1996) and the decision-theoretic rough set model (Y. Y. Yao, 2007). These two rough set models have good fault tolerance, but their quantitative relations are different. In the graded rough set model, the absolute quantitative relation between target set and knowledge granules is considered, but the relative quantitative relation between them is neglected. In contrast, the decision-theoretic rough set model considers relative quantitative relation between target set and knowledge granules, while ignoring the absolute quantitative relation. To complement each other, it is necessary and valuable to combine the two quantitative models. In addition, in the decision-theoretic rough set, Yao et al. (Y. Y. Yao, 2007) offered an appropriate semantic explanation for decision-making process. This shows that the double-quantitative decision-theoretic rough set not only has strong fault tolerance, but has a reasonable decision-making process. This is the main reason why this model is exploited in this paper.

The main contributions of the work are four-folds. First, we build the generalized multi-granulation rough set model for MsIS and its relevant properties are investigated and proved. Second, based on the proposed model, we introduce the double-quantitative decision-theoretic rough set to obtain two new models, called two kinds of generalized multi-granulation double-quantitative decision-theoretic rough set model of MsIS. Meanwhile, the respective decision rules are presented. Third, we discuss the relations between the three models mentioned above and verify them through an illustrative case. Fourth, we respectively define the approximation accuracy of the three models and propose the corresponding algorithm, the objective is to compare the fault tolerance of the proposed models. Experiments on four data sets from UCI show that the fault tolerance capability of the proposed models.

The rest of the paper is organized as follows: Section 2 reviews the related work. Section 3 presents the MS-MRS model and proposes two MS-GMDQ-DTRS models based on it. Meanwhile, relevant properties and relations of the proposed models are investigated and proved. Section 4 presents an illustrative case for verifying the relevant properties and relations. Section 5 sets up the experiment and discusses the results. Section 6 concludes the work and outlines the future research.

2. PRELIMINARIES

In this section, we briefly introduce the some basic concepts of Pawlak rough set and some of its extended model.

2.1. Pawlak Rough Set

Let$IS = (U, AT, V, f)$ be an information system, where $U = x1, x2, ..., xn$ is a non-empty and finite set of objects, AT is a non-empty and finite set of attributes, $V = \cup_{a \in AT} V_a$, V_a, is the domain of attribute a, and $f: U \times AT \to V$ is an information function, $f(x, a) \in V_a (a \in AT)$. For any $A \subseteq AT$, an indiscernibility relation is $R_A = \{(x, y) \in U \times U | \forall a \in A, f_a(x) = f_a(y)\}$. The R_A is called an equivalence relation, which can generate a partition of U, denoted by $U/RA = \{[x]A | x \in U\}$. The $[x]A$ represents the equivalence class of x with respect to RA. The Pawlak approximation space is (U, R_A) briefly written as (U, R). For any $X \subseteq U$, the lower and upper approximations of X are

$$\underline{R}(X) = \{x \in U | [x]_R \subseteq X\}, \overline{R}(X) = \{x \in U | [x]_R \cap X \neq \emptyset\}.$$

The positive region, negative region, and boundary region of X are $POS(X) = \underline{R}(X), NEG(X) = (\overline{R}(X))^c$, and $BND(X) = \overline{R}(X) - \underline{R}(X)$. The approximation accuracy and roughness of X are $\alpha_R(X) = |\underline{R}(X)|/|\overline{R}(X)|$ and $\rho_R(X) = 1 - \alpha_R(X)$, where $|\cdot|$ represents cardinality of a set.

Let $DS = (U, AT \cup DT, V, f)$ be a decision system, where AT is a set of conditional attributes, DT is a set of decision attributes. The $U/DT = \{D_1, D_2, \ldots, D_m\}$ is the partition of the universe U on decision attributes. The lower and upper approximations of the partition U/DT are

$$\underline{R}(U/DT) = \underline{R}(D_1) \cup \underline{R}(D_2) \cup \ldots \cup \underline{R}(D_m), \overline{R}(U/DT) = \overline{R}(D_1) \cup \overline{R}(D_2) \cup \ldots \cup \overline{R}(D_m).$$

For U/DT, the approximation accuracy is

$$\alpha_R(U/DT) = \frac{\sum_{D_i \in U/DT} |\underline{R}(D_i)|}{\sum_{D_i \in U/DT} |\overline{R}(D_i)|}$$

2.2. Some Extended Rough Sets Models

(1) The graded rough set (GRS).

The GRS mainly describes the absolute quantitative relation between knowledge granules and basic concepts.

The upper and lower approximations with grade $k \in N$ are

$$\overline{R}_k(X) = \{x \in U \,\|\, [x]_R \cap X| > k\}, \underline{R}_k(X) = \{x \in U \,\|\, [x]_R| - |[x]_R \cap X| \le k\}.$$

The positive region, negative region, and boundary region of X are $POS(X) = \underline{R}_k(X)$, $NEG(X) = (\overline{R}_k(X))^c$, and $BND(X) = \overline{R}_k(X) - \underline{R}_k(X)$.

(2) The decision-theoretic rough set (DTRS).

The DTRS proposed a way about how to make decision under minimum Bayesian expectation risk. Based on the idea of three-way decisions, the DTRS describes the decision-making process with a state set Ω and an action set A. The $\Omega = \{X, Xc\}$, where X and Xc denote that $x \in X$ and $x \in Xc$, respectively. The $A = \{aP, aB, aN\}$, where aP, aB, and aN represent three actions about deciding $x \in POS(X), x \in BND(X)$, and $x \in NEG(X)$, respectively. Let λ_{PP}, λBP, and λNP denote the losses caused by take actions aP, aB, and aN, respectively, when $x \in X$. Let λPN, λBN, and λNN denote the losses caused by take the same when $x \in Xc$. Given the loss function, for any $x \in [x]R$, the expected loss for different actions are

$R(aP|[x]R) = \lambda PPP(X|[x]R) + \lambda PNP(Xc|[x]R)$,

$R(a_B|[x]_R) = \lambda_{BP}P(X|[x]_R) + \lambda_{BN}\, P(X^c|[x]_R)$,

$R(a_N\,|[x]_R) = \lambda_{NP}P(X|[x]_R) + \lambda_{NN}\, P(X^c|[x]_R)$,

where $P(X|[x]R) = |X \cap [x]R|/|[x]R|$ and $P(Xc|[x]R) = 1 - P(X|[x]R)$.
According to Bayesian decision procedure, minimum-risk decision rules are

(*P*) If $R(aP|[x]R) \leq R(aB|[x]R)$ and $R(aP|[x]R) \leq R(aN|[x]R)$, decide $x \in POS(X)$,

(*B*)If $R(aB|[x]R) \leq R(aP|[x]R)$and $R(aB|[x]R) \leq R(aN|[x]R)$, decide $x \in BND(X)$,

(*N*) If $R(aN|[x]R) \leq R(aP|[x]R)$ and $R(aN|[x]R) \leq R(aB|[x]R)$, decide $x \in NEG(X)$.

Taking into account the actual situations, there is an ordered relation between the decision cost values, i.e., $\lambda PP \leq \lambda BP < \lambda NP$ and $\lambda NN \leq \lambda BN < \lambda PN$. Then the above rules are re-expressed as

(*P*) If $P(X|[x]R) \geq \alpha and P(X|[x]R) \geq \gamma$, decide $x \in POS(X)$,

(*B*) If $P(X|[x]R) \leq \alpha and P(X|[x]R) \geq \beta$, decide $x \in BND(X)$,

(*N*) If $P(X|[x]R) \geq \beta and P(X|[x]R) \leq \gamma$, decide $x \in NEG(X)$,

where

$$\alpha = \frac{\lambda_{PN} - \lambda_{BN}}{(\lambda_{PN} - \lambda_{BN}) + (\lambda_{BP} - \lambda_{PP})}, \beta = \frac{\lambda_{BN} - \lambda_{NN}}{(\lambda_{BN} - \lambda_{NN}) + (\lambda_{NP} - \lambda_{BP})}, \gamma = \frac{\lambda_{PN} - \lambda_{NN}}{(\lambda_{PN} - \lambda_{NN}) + (\lambda_{NP} - \lambda_{PP})}.$$

If decision costs values meet the condition:

$(\lambda NP - \lambda BP)(\lambda PN - \lambda BN) > (\lambda BP - \lambda PP)(\lambda BN - \lambda NN)$, then we can get $0 \leq \beta < \gamma < \alpha \leq 1$. Then the rules of DTRS are

(P) If $P(X|[x]R) \geq \alpha$, decide $x \in POS(X)$,

(B) If $\beta < P(X|[x]R) < \alpha$, decide $x \in BND(X)$,

(N) If $P(X|[x]R) \leq \beta$, decide $x \in NEG(X)$.

In addition, according to the above rules, the upper and lower approximations of the DTRS model are

$$\overline{R}_{(\alpha,\beta)}(X) = \left\{x \in U \middle| P(X|[x]_R) > \beta\right\}, \underline{R}_{(\alpha,\beta)}(X) = \left\{x \in U \middle| P(X|[x]_R) \geq \alpha\right\}.$$

The positive region, negative region, and boundary region of X are

$$POS(X) = \underline{R}_{(\alpha,\beta)}(X), NEG(X) = \left(\overline{R}_{(\alpha,\beta)}(X)\right)^c, BNG(X) = \overline{R}_{(\alpha,\beta)}(X) - \underline{R}_{(\alpha,\beta)}(X)$$

(3) The double-quantitative decision-theoretic rough set (Dq-DTRS)

Both DTRS and GRS have strong fault tolerance, so they can not be ignored. By introducing absolute quantitative information in DTRS, two kinds of double-quantitative DTRS (Dq-DTRS) (i.e., DqI-DTRS and DqII-DTRS) are proposed, respectively.

i. The DqI-DTRS

The DqI-DTRS is made up of $(U, R(\alpha,\beta), Rk)$. For any $X \subseteq U$, the upper and lower approximations of X are

$$\overline{R}_{(\alpha,\beta)}(X) = \left\{x \in U \middle| P(X|[x]_R) > \beta\right\}, \underline{R}_k(X) = \left\{x \in U \middle| |[x]_R| - |[x]_R \cap X| \leq k\right\}.$$

The positive region, negative region, and upper and lower boundary region of X are

$$\begin{aligned} POS^I(X) &= \overline{R}_{(\alpha,\beta)}(X) \cap \underline{R}_k(X), \\ NEG^I(X) &= \left(\overline{R}_{(\alpha,\beta)}(X) \cup \underline{R}_k(X)\right)^c, \\ UBN^I(X) &= \overline{R}_{(\alpha,\beta)}(X) - \underline{R}_k(X), \\ LBN^I(X) &= \underline{R}_k(X) - \overline{R}_{(\alpha,\beta)}(X) \end{aligned}$$

Then, the following decision rules are

(PI)If $x \in X$ satisfies $P(X|[x]R) > \beta$ and $|[x]R| - |[x]R \cap X| \leq k$, then $x \in POSI(X)$,

(NI)If $x \in X$ satisfies $P(X|[x]R) \leq \beta$ and $|[x]R| - |[x]R \cap X| > k$, then $x \in NEGI(X)$,

(UbI) If $x \in X$ satisfies $P(X|[x]R) > \beta$ and $|[x]R| - |[x]R \cap X| > k$, then $x \in UBNI(X)$,

(LbI)If $x \in X$ satisfies $P(X|[x]R) \leq \beta$ and $|[x]R| - |[x]R \cap X| \leq k$, then $x \in LBNI(X)$.

ii. The DqII-DTRS

The DqII-DTRS is made up of $\left(U, \overline{R}_k, \underline{R}_{(\alpha,\beta)}\right)$. For any $X \subseteq U$, the upper and lower approximations of X are

$$\overline{R}_k(X) = \left\{x \in U \middle| |[x]_R \cap X| > k\right\}, \underline{R}_{(\alpha,\beta)}(X) = \left\{x \in U \middle| P(X|[x]_R) \geq \alpha\right\}.$$

Similarly, the positive region, negative region, and upper and lower boundary region of X are

$$POSII(X) = Rk(X) \cap R(\alpha,\beta)(X), NEGII(X) = (Rk(X) \cup R(\alpha,\beta)(X))c,$$

$$UBNII(X) = Rk(X) - R(\alpha,\beta)(X), LBNII(X) = R(\alpha,\beta)(X) - Rk(X).$$

Then, decision rules are

(PII) If $x \in X$ satisfies $P(X|[x]R) \geq \alpha$ and $|[x]R \cap X| \leq k$, then $x \in POSII(X)$,

(NII)If $x \in X$ satisfies $P(X|[x]R) < \alpha$ and $|[x]R \cap X| \leq k$, then $x \in NEGII(X)$,

$(UbII)$ If $x \in X$ satisfies $P(X|[x]R) < \alpha$ and $|[x]R \cap X| > k$, then $x \in UBNII(X)$

(*LbII*) If $x \in X$ satisfies $P(X|[x]R) \geq \alpha$ and $|[x]R \cap X| \leq k$, then $x \in LBNII(X)$.

(4) Generalized multi-granulation rough set (GMRS).

Given an information system $IS = (U, AT, V, f)$, for any $A \subseteq AT$, RA is an equivalence relation on U with respect to attribute set A, and U/RA is a partition of U with respect to RA. In the view of granular computing, the RA is seen as a granulation, expressed as A. The U/A is a granulation structure with respect to A. In many cases, U is partitioned by multiple equivalence relations $RAi(Ai \subseteq AT, i = 1, 2, ..., s)$, which are seen as multiple granulations (i.e., multi-granulation), expressed as $A_i \subseteq AT, i = 1, 2, \ldots, (s \leq 2^{|AT|})$ For any $X \subseteq U$,

$$\mathcal{S}_X^{A_i}(x) = \begin{cases} 1, \text{if}\left([x]_{A_i} \subseteq X, i \leq 2^{|AT|}\right); \\ 0, \text{otherwise}, \end{cases}$$

where A_i is called support feature function of x for X, which is used to describe the inclusion relation

between equivalence class $[x]Ai$ and X. The lower and upper approximations (W. H. Xu, X. T. Zhang, Q. R. Wang, 2012) of X for $\sum_{i=1}^{s} A_i$ are

$$\underline{GM}_{\sum_{i=1}^{s} A_i}(X)_\beta = \left\{x \in U | \frac{\sum_{i=1}^{s} c S_X^{A_i}(x)}{s} \geq \beta\right\},$$

$$\overline{GM}_{\sum_{i=1}^{s} A_i}(X)_\beta = \left\{x \in U | \frac{\sum_{i=1}^{s}\left(1 - \mathcal{S}_{\mathcal{X}^c}^{\mathcal{A}_i}(x)\right)}{s} > 1 - \beta\right\},$$

where β is an adjustable standard of information with respect to $\sum_{i=1}^{s} A_i$. The positive region, negative region, and boundary region of X are

$$POS(X) = \underline{GM}_{\sum_{i=1}^{s} A_i}(X)_\beta, NEG(X) = \left(\overline{GM}_{\sum_{i=1}^{s} A_i}(X)_\beta\right)^c,$$

$$BND(X) = \overline{GM}_{\sum_{i=1}^{s} A_i}(X)_\beta - \underline{GM}_{\sum_{i=1}^{s} A_i}(X)_\beta.$$

If $\beta = 0$, the GMRS model is degenerated into optimistic MGRS model, the lower and upper approximations (W. H. Xu, X. T. Zhang, Q. R. Wang, 2012) of X for $\sum_{i=1}^{s} A_i$ are

$$\underline{OM}_{\sum_{i=1}^{s} A_i}(X)_\beta = \left\{x \in U | \frac{\sum_{i=1}^{s} c S_X^{A_i}(x)}{s} \geq 0\right\},$$

$$\overline{OM}_{\sum_{i=1}^{s} A_i}(X)_\beta = \left\{x \in U | \frac{\sum_{i=1}^{s}\left(1 - \mathcal{S}_{\mathcal{X}^c}^{\mathcal{A}_i}(x)\right)}{s} > 1\right\}.$$

If $\beta = 1$, the GMRS model is degenerated into pessimism MGRS model, the lower and upper approximations (W. H. Xu, X. T. Zhang, Q. R. Wang, 2012) of X for $\sum_{i=1}^{s} A_i$ are

$$\underline{PM}_{\sum_{i=1}^{s} A_i}(X)_\beta = \left\{ x \in U | \frac{\sum_{i=1}^{s} c\, S_X^{A_i}(x)}{s} \geq 1 \right\},$$

$$\overline{PM}_{\sum_{i=1}^{s} A_i}(X)_\beta = \left\{ x \in U | \frac{\sum_{i=1}^{s} \left(1 - S_X^{A_i}(x)\right)}{s} > 0 \right\}.$$

3. MS-GMDQ-DTRS: GENERALIZED MULTI-GRANULATION DOUBLE-QUANTITATIVE DECISION-THEORETIC ROUGH SET MODEL OF MULTI-SOURCE INFORMATION SYSTEM

In this section, a MS-GMRS model is firstly proposed. To further improve the fault tolerance of this model, a pair of MS-GMDQ-DTRS models are developed by introducing the double-quantitative decision-theoretic rough set. The decision rules for this pair of models are given, respectively. We present relevant properties and relations of the proposed models.

3.1. MS-GMRS: Generalized Multi-Granulation Rough Set Model for Multi-Source Information System

In this subsection, we propose a generalized multi-granulation rough set model for MsIS (MS-GMRS) and its the relevant properties are studied. In order to evaluate the fault tolerance of this model, the approximation accuracy is defined. First, the definition of MsIS is introduced.

Definition 3.1 (G. P. Lin, J. Y. Liang, Y. H. Qian, 2015) A multi-source information system (MsIS) consists of multiple $ISi = (U, AT, Vi, fi)$. For any $i \in N^*$, the IS_i represents theith information system of the MsIS. Therefore, a MsIS can be defined as

$$MS = \{IS1, IS2, ..., ISs\}. \quad (1)$$

Similarly, a multi-source decision system (MsDS) consists of multiple

$$DSi = (U, AT \cup DT, Vi, fi).$$

For any $i \in N^*$, DS_i represents the *ith* decision system of the MsDS. Therefore, a MsDS can be defined as

$$MDS = \{DS1, DS2, ..., DSs\}. \tag{2}$$

Multiple single-source information systems (decision system) are grouped together to form a MsIS (MsDS) similar to an information box, as shown in Fig. 1, where $x1, x2, ..., xn$ are the objects in the U, $a1, a2, ..., am$ are the attributes in the $AT, IS1, IS2, ..., ISs$ are s single information systems that constitute a MsIS. Note: in this paper, the MsIS is isomorphic, i.e., all single information systems have the same set of attributes and objects, but in different single information systems, the value of the same object under the same attribute may be different.

Definition 3.2 Let $MS = \{IS1, IS2, ..., ISs\}$ be a MsIS, where $ISi = (U, AT, Vi, fi)$. In the MS-GMRS, for any $X \subseteq U$, the lower and upper approximations are defined by

$$\underline{MS - GM}_{MS}(X) = \left\{ x \in U | \frac{\sum_{i=1}^{s} MS - S_X^{SI_i}(x)}{s} \geq \varphi \right\}, \tag{3}$$

Figure 1. A multi-source information box

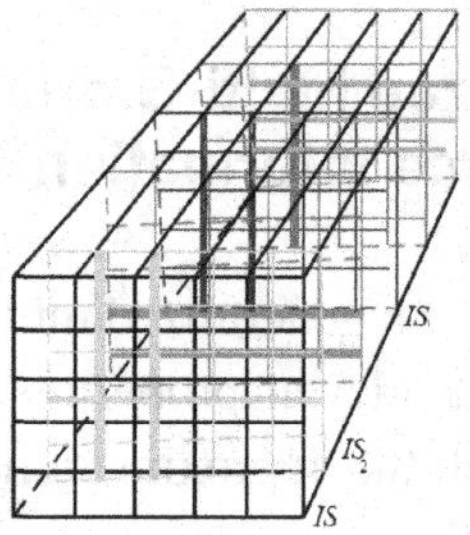

$$\overline{MS - GM}_{MS}(X) = \left\{ x \in U | \frac{\sum_{i=1}^{s} \left(1 - MS - S_{X^c}^{IS_i}(x)\right)}{s} > 1 - \varphi \right\}, \tag{4}$$

where $\phi \in (0.5, 1]$ is an adjustable information standard with respect to *MS*, *Xc* is a complement to *X*. Under*ISi*, the support feature functions of $x \in U$ with respect to *X* and *Xc* are

$$MS\text{-}S_{X^c}^{IS_i}(x) = \begin{cases} 1, & if([x]_{IS_i} \cap X = \varnothing); \\ 0, & if([x]_{IS_i} \cap X \neq \varnothing). \end{cases}$$

$$MS\text{-}S_{X}^{IS_i}(x) = \begin{cases} 1, & if([x]_{IS_i} \subseteq X); \\ 0, & otherwise. \end{cases}$$

$$MS\text{-}S_{X^c}^{IS_i}(x) = \begin{cases} 1, & if([x]_{IS_i} \cap X = \varnothing); \\ 0, & if([x]_{IS_i} \cap X \neq \varnothing). \end{cases}$$

Note that the$[x]ISi$represents the equivalence class of x with respect to AT in ISi. If X satisfies $MS - GMMS(X) = MS - GMMS(X)$, the X is a definable target set in MsIS. Conversely, the X is a rough target set. This model is called the generalized multi-granulation rough set model of MsIS (MS-GMRS). Then the positive region, negative region, and boundary region of X are

$$POS(X) = \underline{MS - GM}_{MS}(X),$$
$$NEG(X) = \left(\overline{MS - GM}_{MS}(X)\right)^c,$$
$$BND(X) = \overline{MS - GM}_{MS}(X) - \underline{MS - GM}_{MS}(X).$$

Here are two extreme forms of MS-GMRS model, namely pessimism multi-granulation rough set model of MsIS (MS-PMRS), and optimism multi-granulation rough set model of MsIS (MS-OMRS).

Definition 3.3 Let $MS = \{IS1, IS2, ..., ISs\}$be a MsIS, where $ISi = (U, AT, Vi, fi)$. In the MS-PMRS model, for any $X \subseteq U$, the lower and upper approximations are defined by

$$\underline{MS - PM}_{MS}(X) = \left\{ x \in U \middle| \wedge_{i=1}^{s}\left([x]_{IS_i} \subseteq X\right) \right\}$$

$$= \left\{ x \in U \middle| \frac{\sum_{i=1}^{s} MS - S_X^{IS_i}(x)}{s} \geq 1 \right\};$$

$$\overline{MS - PM}_{MS}(X) = \left\{ x \in U \middle| \vee_{i=1}^{s}\left([x]_{IS_i} \cap X \neq \varnothing\right) \right\}$$

$$= \left\{ x \in U \middle| \frac{\sum_{i=1}^{s}\left(1 - MS - S_{X^c}^{IS_i}(x)\right)}{s} > 0 \right\}.$$

The expression of the $POS(X), NEG(X)$, and $BND(X)$ of MS-PMRS model are the same as MS-GMRS model.

Definition 3.4 Let $MS = \{IS1, IS2, ..., ISs\}$ be a MsIS, where $ISi = (U, AT, Vi, fi)$. In the MS-OMRS model, for any $X \subseteq U$, the lower and upper approximations are defined by

$$\underline{MS-OM}_{MS}(X) = \left\{x \in U \middle| \wedge_{i=1}^{s}\left([x]_{IS_i} \subseteq X\right)\right\}\left\{x \in U \middle| \frac{\sum_{i=1}^{s} MS - S_X^{IS_i}(x)}{s} > 0\right\};$$

$$\overline{MS-OM}_{MS}(X) = \left\{x \in U \middle| \vee_{i=1}^{s}\left([x]_{IS_i} \cap X \neq \varnothing\right)\right\}$$

$$= \left\{x \in U \middle| \frac{\sum_{i=1}^{s}(1 - MS - S_{X^c}^{IS_i}(x))}{s} \geq 1\right\}.$$

The expression of the $POS(X), NEG(X)$, and $BND(X)$ of MS-OMRS model are the same as MS-GMRS model.

Proposition 3.1 Let $MS = \{IS1, IS2, ..., ISs\}$ be a MsIS, where $ISi = (U, AT, Vi, fi)$, for any $X \subseteq U, \phi \in (0.5, 1]$. The following conclusions hold:

(1) $\underline{MS-PM}_{MS}(X) \subseteq \underline{MS-GM}_{MS}(X) \subseteq \underline{MS-OM}_{MS}(X)$;
(2) $\overline{MS-OM}_{MS}(X) \subseteq \overline{MS-GM}_{MS}(X) \subseteq \overline{MS-PM}_{MS}(X)$.

Proof: (1) For any $x \in U$, one can prove $\underline{MS-PM}_{MS}(X) \subseteq \underline{MS-GM}_{MS}(X)$ through

$$x \in \underline{MS-PM}_{MS}(X) \Leftrightarrow \frac{\sum_{i=1}^{s} MS - S_X^{IS_i}(x)}{s} \geq 1.$$

As $\varphi \in (0.5, 1]$, $\frac{\sum_{i=1}^{s} MS - S_X^{IS_i}(x)}{s} \geq 1 \geq$. Then, $x \in \underline{MS-GM}_{MS}(X)$. Therefore,

$$\underline{MS-PM}_{MS}(X) \subseteq \underline{MS-GM}_{MS}(X).$$

Analogously,

$$x \in \underline{MS-GM}_{MS}(X) \frac{\sum_{i=1}^{s} MS - S_X^{IS_i}(x)}{s} \geq \varphi > 0 \Rightarrow x \in \underline{MS-OM}_{MS}(X).$$

Therefore, $\underline{MS-GM}_{MS}(X) \subseteq \underline{MS-OM}_{MS}(X)$.

(2) This conclusion can be proved similarly.

Proposition 3.2 Let $MS = \{IS1, IS2, ..., ISs\}$ be a MsIS, where $ISi = (U, AT, Vi, fi)$, for any $X \subseteq U$, $\phi \in (0.5, 1]$, the following properties are true.

$$(L_1)\underline{MS-GM}_{MS}(X^c) = \left(\overline{MS-GM}_{MS}(X)\right)^c; (U_1)\overline{MS-GM}_{MS}(X^c) = \left(\underline{MS-GM}_{MS}(X)\right)^c.$$

$$(L_2)\underline{MS-GM}_{MS}(X) \subseteq ;\ (U_2)X \subseteq \overline{MS-GM}_{MS}(X).$$

$$(L_3)\underline{MS-GM}_{MS}(\emptyset) = \emptyset;\ (U_3)\overline{MS-GM}_{MS}(\emptyset) = \emptyset.$$

$$(L_4)\underline{MS-GM}_{MS}(U) = ;\ (U_4)\overline{MS-GM}_{MS}(U) = U.$$

$$(L_5)X \subseteq Y \Rightarrow \underline{MS-GM}_{MS}(X) \subseteq \underline{MS-GM}_{MS}(Y);$$

$$(U_5)X \subseteq Y \Rightarrow \overline{MS-GM}_{MS}(X) \subseteq \overline{MS-GM}_{MS}(Y).$$

$$(L_6)\underline{MS-GM}_{MS}(X \cap Y) \subseteq \underline{MS-GM}_{MS}(X) \cap \underline{MS-GM}_{MS}(Y);$$

$$(U_6)\overline{MS-GM}_{MS}(X \cup Y) \supseteq \overline{MS-GM}_{MS}(X) \cup \overline{MS-GM}_{MS}(Y).$$

$$(L_7)\underline{MS-GM}_{MS}(X \cup Y) \supseteq \underline{MS-GM}_{MS}(X) \cup \underline{MS-GM}_{MS}(Y);$$

$$(U_7)\overline{MS-GM}_{MS}(X \cap Y) \subseteq \overline{MS-GM}_{MS}(X) \cap \overline{MS-GM}_{MS}(Y).$$

Proof: $(L_1)\forall X \subseteq U$,

$$x \in \overline{MS-GM}_{MS}(X) \Leftrightarrow \frac{\sum_{i=1}^{s}\left(1 - MS - S_{X^c}^{IS_i}(x)\right)}{s} > 1 - \varphi,$$

we have that

$x \in \left(\overline{MS - GM}_{MS}(X)\right)^c \Leftrightarrow \frac{\sum_{i=1}^{s}\left(1 - MS - S_{X^c}^{IS_i}(x)\right)}{s} \leq 1$

$- \varphi \Leftrightarrow \frac{\sum_{i=1}^{s} MS - S_{X^c}^{IS_i}(x)}{s} \geq \varphi \Leftrightarrow \underline{MS - GM}_{MS}(X^c)$. Therefore, the$(L_1)$ is proved. The (U_1) can be proved in the same way as (L_1).

(L_2) $\forall x \in \underline{MS - GM}_{MS}(X)$,

we have $\frac{\sum_{i=1}^{s} MS - S_X^{IS_i}(x)}{s} \geq \varphi > 0$.Obviously, $\exists i \leq s$ such that $[x]_{IS_i} \subseteq X$. So, $x \in X$ can be obtained. Therefore, the (L_2) is proved.

(U_2) Based on (L_1) and (L_2), we can get

$$\left(\overline{MS - GM}_{MS}(X)\right)^c = \underline{MS - GM}_{MS}(X^c) \subseteq X^c.$$

So $X \subseteq \overline{MS - GM}_{MS}(X^c)$ can be directly proved.

(L_3), (U_3), (L_4), and (U_4) can all be directly proved by Eqs. (3), (4).

$$(L_5)\forall x \in \underline{MS - GM}_{MS}(X) \Rightarrow \frac{\sum_{i=1}^{s} MS - S_X^{IS_i}(x)}{s} \geq \varphi.$$

$$X \subseteq Y \Rightarrow \sum_{i=1}^{s} MS - S_X^{IS_i}(x) \leq \sum_{i=1}^{s} MS - S_Y^{IS_i}(x) \Rightarrow \frac{\sum_{i=1}^{s} MS - S_Y^{IS_i}(x)}{s} \geq \varphi.$$

Then, we can get $x \in MS - GMMS(Y)$. Therefore, the$(L5)$ is proved. The $(U5)$ can be proved in the same way as $(L5)$.

$(L6)$ Based on the $(L5)$, we can get

$$X \cap Y \subseteq X \Rightarrow MS - GMMS(X \cap Y) \subseteq MS - GMMS(X)$$

and

$$X \cap Y \subseteq Y \Rightarrow MS - GMMS(X \cap Y) \subseteq MS - GMMS(Y).$$

Thus,

$$MS - GMMS(X \cap Y) \subseteq MS - GMMS(X) \cap MS - GMMS(Y)$$

is proved.

Similarly, (U6) can be proved.

(L7) can be directly certified according to (L5)-(U7) can be directly certified according to (U5).

For survey the classification ability of MS-GMRS model, the approximation accuracy is defined in MsDS. The specific definition is as follows.

Definition 3.5 Let $MDS = \{DS1, DS2, ..., DSs\}$ be a MsDS, where

$$DSi = (U, AT \cup DT, Vi, fi),\ U/DT = \{D1, D2, ..., Dn\}$$

is a set of decision classes. In MS-GMRS model, the approximation accuracy of U/DT is defined by

$$\alpha_{MDS}(U/DT) = \frac{\sum_{j=1}^{n} \left|\underline{MS - GM}_{MS}(D_j)\right|}{\sum_{j=1}^{n} \left|\overline{MS - GM}_{MS}(D_j)\right|}.$$

The following we design an algorithm for calculating the approximation accuracy of MS-GMRS model, which is Algorithm 1. The time complexity of this algorithm 1 is analyzed as: the time complexity of steps 3 - 13 is $O(m \times s)$, the time complexity of steps 15 - 22 is $O(m)$. Therefore, the time complexity of Algorithm 1 is $O((m \times s + m) \times n) = O(mns)$.

3.2. IMS-GMDQ-DTRS: The First Kind of Generalized Multi-Granulation Double-Quantitative Decision-Theoretic Rough Set for Multi-Source Information System

In this subsection, we proposed the first kind of generalized multi-granulation double-quantitative decision-theoretic rough set model of MsIS (IMS-GMDQ-DTRS) by introducing the DqI-DTRS model. The corresponding decision rules of this model are investigated.

Definition 3.6 Let $MS = \{IS1, IS2, ..., ISs\}$ be a MsIS, where $ISi = (U, AT, Vi, fi)$. In the IMS-GMDQ-DTRS model, for any $X \subseteq U$, the upper and lower approximations are defined by

$$\overline{MS - GM}^{I}_{MS}(X) = \left\{x \in U \middle| \frac{\sum_{i=1}^{s} MS - USI_X^{IS_i}(x)}{s} > 1 - \varphi\right\},$$

$$\underline{MS-GM^{I}_{MS}}(X) = \left\{ x \in U | \frac{\sum_{i=1}^{s} MS-LSI_X^{IS_i}(x)}{s} \geq \varphi \right\},$$

where $\phi \in (0.5, 1]$ is an adjustable information standard with respect to MS. Under *ISi*, the upper support feature function of $x \in U$ with respect to X is

$$MS\text{-}USI_X^{IS_i}(x) = \begin{cases} 1, & if P(X|[x]_{IS_i}) > \beta \ ; \\ 0, & otherwise. \end{cases}$$

```
Algorithm 1: The approximation accuracy is calculated in
MS-GMRS model

Input: MDS = {DS 1, DS 2, . . ., DS s}, U/D = {D1, D2, . .
., Dn}, ϕ.
Output: The approximation accuracy αMDS (U/DT).
begin
for g = 1: n do
for i = 1: m do
MS -US (i) ← 0; /* It represents MS-SDgDSix*/
MS -LS (i) ← 0; /* It represents 1-MS-SDgcDSix*/
for j = 1: s do
if [xi]DSj ⊆ Dg then
MS -LS (i) ← MS -LS (i) + 1;
end
if [xi]DIj ∩ Dg -:/ ∅ then
MS -US (i) ← MS -US (i) + 1;
end
end
end
MS -GMMS (Dg) ← ∅; MS -GMMS (Dg) ← ∅;
for i = 1: m do
if MS -LS (i)
MS -GMMS (Dg) ← MS -GMMS (Dg) ∪ {xi};
end
if MS -US (i)
MS -GMMS (Dg) ← MS -GMMS (Dg) ∪ {xi};
end
end
```

```
24 end
return: αMDSU/DT←∑k=1nMS-GM¯MSDg∑k=1nMS-GM¯MSDg.

25 end
```

Under ISi, the lower support feature function of $x \in U$ with respect to X is

$$MS\text{-}LSI_X^{IS_i}(x) = \begin{cases} 1, & if \left|[x]_{IS_i}\right| - \left|[x]_{IS_i} \cap X\right| \le k \ ; \\ 0, & otherwise. \end{cases}$$

If X satisfies $\overline{MS-GM}_{MS}^{I}(X) = \underline{MS-GM}_{MS}^{I}(X)$, X is a definable target set in MsIS. Conversely, X is a rough target set. The positive region, negative region, upper and lower boundary region of this model are

$$POS^I(X) = \overline{MS-GM}_{MS}^{I}(X) \cap \underline{MS-GM}_{MS}^{I}(X) \ ;$$
$$NEG^I(X) = \left(\overline{MS-GM}_{MS}^{I}(X) \cup \underline{MS-GM}_{MS}^{I}(X)\right)^c \ ;$$

$$UBN^I(X) = \overline{MS-GM}_{MS}^{I}(X) - \underline{MS-GM}_{MS}^{I}(X) \ ;$$
$$LBN^I(X) = \underline{MS-GM}_{MS}^{I}(X) - \overline{MS-GM}_{MS}^{I}(X).$$

Here are two extreme forms of IMS-GMDQ-DTRS model, namely the first kind of pessimism multi-granulation double-quantitative decision-theoretic rough set model of MsIS (IMS-PMDQ-DTRS), and the first kind of optimism multi-granulation double-quantitative decision-theoretic rough set model of MsIS (IMS-OMDQ-DTRS).

Definition 3.7 Let $MS = \{IS1, IS2, ..., ISs\}$ be a MsIS, where $ISi = (U, AT, Vi, fi)$. In the IMS-PMDQ-DTRS, for any $X \subseteq U$, the upper and lower approximations are defined by

$$\overline{MS-PM}_{MS}^{I}(X) = \left\{ x \in U \middle| \vee_{i=1}^{s}(P(X|[x]\_\{IS\_\{i\}\})> \beta) \right\}$$

$$= \left\{ x \in U \middle| \frac{\sum_{i=1}^{s} MS-USI_X^{IS_i}(x)}{s} > 0 \right\} \ ;$$

$$\underline{MS-PM}_{MS}^{I}(X) = \left\{ x \in U \middle| \wedge_{i=1}^{s}\left(\left|[x]_{IS_i}\right| - \left|[x]_{IS_i} \cap X\right| \le k\right) \right\}$$

$$= \left\{ x \in U \middle| \frac{\sum_{i=1}^{s} MS-LSI_X^{IS_i}(x)}{s} \ge 1 \right\}.$$

The expression of the positive region, negative region, upper and lower boundary region of this model are the same as IMS-GMDQ-DTRS model.

Definition 3.8 Let $MS = \{IS1, IS2, ..., ISs\}$ be a MsIS, where $ISi = (U, AT, Vi, fi)$. In the IMS-OMDQ-DTRS model, for any $X \subseteq U$, the upper and lower approximations are defined by

$$\overline{MS - OM^{I}_{MS}}(X) = \left\{ x \in U \middle| \wedge_{i=1}^{s}(P(X|[x]\_\{IS\_\{i\}\}) > \beta) \right\}$$

$$= \left\{ x \in U | \frac{\sum_{i=1}^{s} MS - USI_X^{IS_i}(x)}{s} \geq 1 \right\};$$

$$\underline{MS - OM^{I}_{MS}}(X) = \left\{ x \in U \middle| \vee_{i=1}^{s}\left(\left|[x]_{IS_i}\right| - \left|[x]_{IS_i} \cap X\right| \leq k\right) \right\}$$

$$= \left\{ x \in U | \frac{\sum_{i=1}^{s} MS - LSI_X^{IS_i}(x)}{s} > 0 \right\}.$$

The expression of the positive region, negative region, upper and lower boundary region of this model are the same as IMS-GMDQ-DTRS model.

Proposition 3.3 Let $MS = \{IS1, IS2, ..., ISs\}$ be a MsIS, where $ISi = (U, AT, Vi, fi)$, for any $X \subseteq U, \phi \in (0.5, 1]$. The following conclusions hold:

(1) $\underline{MS - PM^{I}_{MS}}(X) \subseteq \underline{MS - GM^{I}_{MS}}(X) \subseteq \underline{MS - OM^{I}_{MS}}(X)$;

(2) $\overline{MS - OM^{I}_{MS}}(X) \subseteq \overline{MS - GM^{I}_{MS}}(X) \subseteq \overline{MS - PM^{I}_{MS}}(X)$.

Proof: According to Eqs. (12), (13), (17), (18), (19), (20), the above properties are easily verified.

In what follow, we introduce the decision rules of the proposed models.

Rules 3.1 Let $MS = \{IS1, IS2, ..., ISs\}$ be a MsIS, where $ISi = (U, AT, Vi, fi)$. For any $X \subseteq U$, the decision rules of IMS-GMDQ-DTRS are

(P^I) If $\left|IS_i : P\left(X | [x]_{IS_i}\right) > \beta\right| > s(1 - \varphi), \left|IS_i : \left|[x]_{IS_i}\right| - \left|[x]_{IS_i} \cap X\right| \leq k\right| \geq s$, then $x \in POS^I(X)$;

(N^I) If $\left|IS_i : P\left(X | [x]_{IS_i}\right) > \beta\right| \leq s(1 - \varphi), \left|IS_i : \left|[x]_{IS_i}\right| - \left|[x]_{IS_i} \cap X\right| \leq k\right| < s$, then $x \in NEG^{\textrml}(X)$;

(UB^I) If $\left|IS_i : P\left(X | [x]_{IS_i}\right) > \beta\right| > s(1-\varphi), \left|IS_i : \left|[x]_{IS_i}\right| - \left|[x]_{IS_i} \cap X\right| \le k\right| < s$, then $x \in UBN^I(X)$;

(LB^I) If $\left|IS_i : P\left(X | [x]_{IS_i}\right) > \beta\right| \le s(1-\varphi), \left|IS_i : \left|[x]_{IS_i}\right| - \left|[x]_{IS_i} \cap X\right| \le k\right| \ge s$, then $x \in LBN^I(X)$.

Considering the idea of pessimism, the decision rules of IMS-PMDQ-DTRS model can be deduced, which are

(P^I) If $\left|IS_i : P\left(X | [x]_{IS_i}\right) > \beta\right| \ge 1, \left|IS_i : \left|[x]_{IS_i}\right| - \left|[x]_{IS_i} \cap X\right| \le k\right|$

$= s$, then $x \in POS^I(X)$;

(N^I) If $\left|IS_i : P\left(X | [x]_{IS_i}\right) \le \beta\right|$

$= s, \left|IS_i : \left|[x]_{IS_i}\right| - \left|[x]_{IS_i} \cap X\right| \le k\right| \ge 1$, then $x \in NEG^I(X)$;

(UB^I) If $\left|IS_i : P\left(X | [x]_{IS_i}\right) > \beta\right| \ge 1, \left|IS_i : \left|[x]_{IS_i}\right| - \left|[x]_{IS_i} \cap X\right| \le k\right| \ge 1$, then $x \in UBN^I(X)$;

(LB^I) If $\left|IS_i : P\left(X | [x]_{IS_i}\right) \le \beta\right| = s, \left|IS_i : \left|[x]_{IS_i}\right| - \left|[x]_{IS_i} \cap X\right| \le k\right|$

$= s$, then $x \in LBN^I(X)$.

Similarly, according to the idea of optimism, the decision rules of IMS-OMDQ-DTRS model can be obtained, which are

(P^I) If $\left|IS_i : P\left(X | [x]_{IS_i}\right) > \beta\right|$

$= s, \left|IS_i : \left|[x]_{IS_i}\right| - \left|[x]_{IS_i} \cap X\right| \le k\right| \ge 1$, then $x \in POS^I(X)$;

(NI)If $\left|IS_i : P\left(X | [x]_{IS_i}\right) > \beta\right|$

$= s, \left| IS_i : \left| [x]_{IS_i} \right| - \left| [x]_{IS_i} \cap X \right| \leq k \right| \geq 1$, then $x \in POS^I(X)$;

(UBI) If $\left| IS_i : P\left(X | [x]_{IS_i}\right) > \beta \right| = s, \left| IS_i : \left| [x]_{IS_i} \right| - \left| [x]_{IS_i} \cap X \right| > k \right|$

$= s$, then $x \in UBN^I(X)$;

(LBI) If $\left| IS_i : P\left(X | [x]_{IS_i}\right) \leq \beta \right| \geq 1, \left| IS_i : \left| [x]_{IS_i} \right| - \left| [x]_{IS_i} \cap X \right| \leq k \right| \geq 1$, then $x \in LBN^I(X)$.

Definition 3.9 Let $MDS = \{DS1, DS2, ..., DSs\}$ be a MsDS, where

$DSi = (U, AT \cup DT, Vi, fi)$, $U/DT = \{D_1, D_2, \ldots, D_n\}$

is a set of decision classes. In IMS-GMDQ-DTRS model, the approximation accuracy of U/DT is defined by

$$\alpha_{IMDS}(U/DT) = \frac{\sum_{j=1}^{n} \left| \underline{MS - GM}^{I}_{MS}(D_j) \right|}{\sum_{j=1}^{n} \left| \overline{MS - GM}^{I}_{MS}(D_j) \right|}.$$

In order to calculate the approximation accuracy of IMS-GMDQ-DTRS model, we design Algorithm 2. The time complexity is similar to that of Algorithm 1.

3.3. IIMS-GMDQ-DTRS: The Second Kind of Generalized Multi-Granulation Double-Quantitative Decision-Theoretic Rough Set for Multi-Source Information System

This subsection introduces the second kind of generalized multi-granulation double-quantitative decision-theoretic rough set model (IIMS-GMDQ-DTRS). Then the decision rules of this model are investigated.

Definition 3.10 Let $MS = \{IS_1, IS_2, \ldots, IS_s\}$ be a MsIS, where $IS_i = (U, AT, V_i, f_i)$. In the IIMS-GMDQ-DTRS model, for any $X \subseteq U$, the upper and lower approximations are defined by

$$\overline{MS - GM}^{II}_{MS}(X) = \left\{ x \in U \middle| \frac{\sum_{i=1}^{s} MS - USII_X^{IS_i}(x)}{s} > 1 - \varphi \right\},$$

$$\underline{MS-GM}^{II}_{MS}(X) = \left\{x \in U \mid \frac{\sum_{i=1}^{s} MS-LSII^{IS_i}_X(x)}{s} \geq \varphi\right\},$$

where $\phi \in (0.5, 1]$ is an adjustable information standard with respect to MS. Under IS_i, the upper support feature function of $x \in U$ with respect to X is

$$MS\text{-}USII^{IS_i}_X(x) = \begin{cases} 1, & if \left|[x]_{IS_i} \cap X\right| > k ; \\ 0, & otherwise. \end{cases}$$

Under IS_i, the lower support feature function of $x \in U$ with respect to X is

$$MS\text{-}LSII^{IS_i}_X(x) = \begin{cases} 1, & if P(X \mid [x]_{IS_i}) \geq \alpha ; \\ 0, & otherwise. \end{cases}$$

If X satisfies $\overline{MS-GM}^{II}_{MS}(X) = \underline{MS-GM}^{II}_{MS}(X)$, X is a definable target set in MsIS. Conversely, X is a rough target set. The positive region, negative region, upper and lower boundary region of this model are

$$POS^{II}(X) = \overline{MS-GM}^{II}_{MS}(X) \cap \underline{MS-GM}^{II}_{MS}(X) ;$$
$$NEG^{II}(X) = \left(\overline{MS-GM}^{II}_{MS}(X) \cup \underline{MS-GM}^{II}_{MS}(X)\right)^c ;$$

$$UBN^{II}(X) = \overline{MS-GM}^{II}_{MS}(X) - \underline{MS-GM}^{II}_{MS}(X) ;$$
$$LBN^{II}(X) = \underline{MS-GM}^{II}_{MS}(X) - \overline{MS-GM}^{II}_{MS}(X).$$

Here are two extreme forms of IIMS-GMDQ-DTRS model, namely the second kind of pessimism multi-granulation double-quantitative rough set model of MsIS (IIMS-PMDQ-DTRS), and the second kind of optimism multi-granulation double-quantitative rough set model of MsIS (IIMS-OMDQ-DTRS).

Definition 3.11 Let $MS = \{IS_1, IS_2, \ldots, IS_s\}$ be a MsIS, where $IS_i = (U, AT, V_i, f_i)$. In the IIMS-PMDQ-DTRS model, for any $X \subseteq U$, the upper and lower approximations are defined by

$$\overline{MS-PM^{II}_{MS}}(X) = \left\{ x \in U \middle| \vee_{i=1}^{s}(|[x]\_\{IS\_\{i\}\} \cap X| > k) \right\}$$

$$= \left\{ x \in U | \frac{\sum_{i=1}^{s} MS-USII_X^{IS_i}(x)}{s} > 0 \right\};$$

$$\underline{MS-PM^{II}_{MS}}(X) = \left\{ x \in U \middle| \wedge_{i=1}^{s}\left(P\left(X | [x]_{IS_i}\right) \geq \alpha\right) \right\}$$

$$= \left\{ x \in U | \frac{\sum_{i=1}^{s} MS-LSII_X^{IS_i}(x)}{s} \geq 1 \right\}.$$

The positive region, negative region, upper and lower boundary region of this model are the same as IIMS-GMDQ- DTRS model.

Definition 3.12 Let $MS = \{IS_1, IS_2, \ldots, IS_s\}$ be a MsIS, where $IS_i = (U, AT, V_i, f_i)$. In the IIMS-OMDQ-DTRS model, for any $X \subseteq U$, the upper and lower approximations are defined by

$$\overline{MS-OM^{II}_{MS}}(X) = \left\{ x \in U \middle| \wedge_{i=1}^{s}\left(\left|[x]_{IS_i} \cap X\right| > k\right) \right\}$$

$$= \left\{ x \in U | \frac{\sum_{i=1}^{s} MS-USII_X^{IS_i}(x)}{s} \geq 1 \right\}$$

$$\underline{MS-OM^{II}_{MS}}(X) = \left\{ x \in U \middle| \vee_{i=1}^{s}\left(P\left(X | [x]_{IS_i}\right) \geq \alpha\right) \right\}$$

$$= \left\{ x \in U | \frac{\sum_{i=1}^{s} MS-LSII_X^{IS_i}(x)}{s} > 0 \right\}.$$

The positive region, negative region, upper and lower boundary region of this model are the same as IIMS-GMDQ- DTRS model.

Proposition 3.4 Let $MS = \{IS_1, IS_2, \ldots, IS_s\}$ be a MsIS, where $IS_i = (U, AT, V_i, f_i)$, for any $X \subseteq U, \phi \in (0.5, 1]$. The following conclusions hold:

(1) $\overline{MS - PM^{II}_{MS}}(X) \subseteq \overline{MS - GM^{II}_{MS}}(X) \subseteq \overline{MS - OM^{II}_{MS}}(X)$;
(2) $\overline{MS - OM^{II}_{MS}}(X) \subseteq \overline{MS - GM^{II}_{MS}}(X) \subseteq \overline{MS - PM^{II}_{MS}}(X)$.

Proof: According to Eqs. (22), (23), (27), (28), (29), (30), the above properties are easily verified.

The following the decision rules of the proposed models are presented.

Rules 3.2 Let $MS = \{IS_1, IS_2, \ldots, IS_s\}$ be a MsIS, where $IS_i = (U, AT, V_i, f_i)$, for any $X \subseteq U$. The decision rules of IIMS-GMDQ-DTRS are

(P^{II}) If $\left|IS_i : \left|[x]_{IS_i} \cap X\right| > k\right| > s(1 - \varphi), \left|IS_i : P\left(X | [x]_{IS_i}\right) \geq \alpha\right| \geq s$, then $x \in POS^{II}(X)$;

(N^{II}) If $\left|IS_i : \left|[x]_{IS_i} \cap X\right| > k\right| \leq s(1 - \varphi), \left|IS_i : P\left(X | [x]_{IS_i}\right) \geq \alpha\right| < s$, then $x \in NEG^{II}(X)$;

(UB^{II}) If $\left|IS_i : \left|[x]_{IS_i} \cap X\right| > k\right| > s(1 - \varphi), \left|IS_i : P\left(X | [x]_{IS_i}\right) \geq \alpha\right| < s$, then $x \in UBN^{II}(X)$;

(LB^{II}) If $\left|IS_i : \left|[x]_{IS_i} \cap X\right| > k\right| \leq s(1 - \varphi), \left|IS_i : P\left(X | [x]_{IS_i}\right) \geq \alpha\right| \geq s$, then $x \in LBN^{II}(X)$.

Combining the idea of pessimism, the decision rules of IIMS-PMDQ-DTRS model can be deduced, which are

(P^{II}) If $\left|IS_i : \left|[x]_{IS_i} \cap X\right| > k\right| \geq 1, \left|IS_i : P\left(X | [x]_{IS_i}\right) \geq \alpha\right| = s$, then $x \in POS^{II}(X)$;

(N^{II}) If $\left|IS_i : \left|[x]_{IS_i} \cap X\right| \leq k\right| = s, \left|IS_i : P\left(X | [x]_{IS_i}\right) \geq \alpha\right| \geq 1$, then $x \in NEG^{II}(X)$;

(UB^{II}) If $\left|IS_i : \left|[x]_{IS_i} \cap X\right| > k\right| \geq 1, \left|IS_i : P\left(X | [x]_{IS_i}\right) \geq \alpha\right| \geq 1$, then $x \in UBN^{II}(X)$;

(LB^{II}) If $\left|IS_i : \left|[x]_{IS_i} \cap X\right| \leq k\right| = s, \left|IS_i : P\left(X | [x]_{IS_i}\right) \geq \alpha\right| = s$, then $x \in LBN^{II}(X)$.

Similarly, based on the idea of optimism, the decision rules of IIMS-OMDQ-DTRS model can be obtained, which are

(P^{II}) If $\left|IS_i:\left|[x]_{IS_i} \cap X\right| \leq k\right| = s, \left|IS_i:P\left(X|[x]_{IS_i}\right) \geq \alpha\right| \geq 1$, then $x \in POS^{II}(X)$;

(N^{II}) If $\left|IS_i:\left|[x]_{IS_i} \cap X\right| \leq k\right| \geq 1, \left|IS_i:P\left(X|[x]_{IS_i}\right) < \alpha\right| = s$, then $x \in NEG^{II}(X)$;

(UB^{II}) If $\left|IS_i:\left|[x]_{IS_i} \cap X\right| \leq k\right| = s, \left|IS_i:P\left(X|[x]_{IS_i}\right) < \alpha\right|$

$= s$, then $x \in UBN^{II}(X)$;

(LB^{II}) If $\left|IS_i:\left|[x]_{IS_i} \cap X\right| \leq k\right| \geq 1, \left|IS_i:P\left(X|[x]_{IS_i}\right) \geq \alpha\right| \geq 1$, then $x \in LBN^{II}(X)$

.

Definition 3.13 Let $MDS = \{DS_1, DS_2, \ldots, DS_s\}$ be a MsDS, where

$DS_i = (U, AT \cup DT, V_i, f_i), U/DT = \{D_1, D_2, \cdots, D_n\}$

is a set of decision classes. In IIMS-GMDQ-DTRS model, the approximation accuracy of U/DT is defined by

$$\alpha_{IIMDS}(U/DT) = \frac{\sum_{j=1}^{n}\left|\underline{MS-GM}^{II}_{MS}(D_j)\right|}{\sum_{j=1}^{n}\left|\overline{MS-GM}^{II}_{MS}(D_j)\right|}.$$

The following the Algorithm 3 is designed to calculate the approximation accuracy of IIMS-GMDQ-DTRS model, and its time complexity is similar to that of Algorithm 1.

3.4. The Relations Between Models

In this subsection, we discuss the inner relations between the MS-GMRS model and a pair of MS-GMDQ-DTRS models. Further, the relations between the decision regions of two MS-GMDQ-DTRS models are explored.

(1) The inner relations between the proposed models.

a. When $\beta = 0, k = 0$, the IMS-GMDQ-DTRS model degenerates to MS-GMRS model, i.e.,

$$(\overline{MS\text{-}GM}^{\mathrm{I}}_{MS}(X), \underline{MS\text{-}GM}^{\mathrm{I}}_{MS}(X)) \stackrel{\beta=0,k=0}{\rightarrow} (\overline{MS\text{-}GM}_{MS}(X), \underline{MS\text{-}GM}_{MS}(X)).$$

Since $\beta = 0, k = 0$, the upper support feature function $MS - USI^{IS_i}_{X}(x)$ degenerates to $1 - MS - S^{IS_i}_{X^c}(x)$, and the lower support feature function $MS - LSI^{IS_i}_{X}(x)$ degenerates to $MS - S^{IS_i}_{X}(x)$. Therefore, we have

$$\overline{MS - GM}^{I}_{MS}(X) = \overline{MS - GM}_{MS}(X) \text{ and } \underline{MS - GM}^{I}_{MS}(X) = \underline{MS - GM}_{MS}(X).$$

So the relation a. holds. That is to say, IMS-GMDQ-DTRS model is an extension of MS-GMRS model.

When $\beta > 0, k > 0$, the fault tolerance capability of the IMS-GMDQ-DTRS model is higher than that of the MS- GMRS model, i.e., $\alpha_{IMDS}(U/DT) \geq \alpha_{MDS}(U/DT)$. Since for any $X \in U/DT$, according to Eqs. (3), (4), (12), (13), we can get

$$\overline{MS - GM}^{I}_{MS}(X) \subseteq \overline{MS - GM}_{MS}(X), \underline{MS - GM}^{I}_{MS}(X) \supseteq \underline{MS - GM}_{MS}(X).$$

According to Eqs. (11), (21), it is easy to get $\alpha_{IMDS}(U/DT) \geq \alpha_{MDS}(U/DT)$. The higher the approximation accuracy of the model, the stronger the fault tolerance capability of the model. Thus the fault tolerance of IMS-GMDQ-DTRS model is superior to MS-GMRS model.

b. When $\alpha = 1, k = 0$, the IIMS-GMDQ-DTRS model also degenerates to MS-GMRS model, i.e.,

$$(\overline{MS\text{-}GM}^{\mathrm{I}}_{MS}(X), \underline{MS\text{-}GM}^{\mathrm{I}}_{MS}(X)) \stackrel{\beta=0,k=0}{\rightarrow} (\overline{MS\text{-}GM}_{MS}(X),$$
$$\underline{MS\text{-}GM}_{MS}(X)) \stackrel{\alpha=1,k=0}{\leftarrow} (\overline{MS\text{-}GM}^{\mathrm{II}}_{MS}(X), \underline{MS\text{-}GM}^{\mathrm{II}}_{MS}(X)).$$

$$(\overline{MS\text{-}GM}^{\mathrm{II}}_{MS}(X), \underline{MS\text{-}GM}^{\mathrm{II}}_{MS}(X)) \stackrel{\alpha=1,k=0}{\rightarrow} (\overline{MS\text{-}GM}_{MS}(X), \underline{MS\text{-}GM}_{MS}(X)).$$

Because $\alpha = 1, k = 0$, the upper support feature function

$$MS - USII^{IS_i}_{X}(x)$$

degenerates to $1 - MS - S^{IS_i}_{X^c}(x)$, and the lower support feature function

$$MS - LSII^{IS_i}_{X}(x)$$

also degenerates to $MS - S_X^{IS_i}(x)$. Thus, we have

$$\overline{MS - GM^{II}_{MS}}(X) = \overline{MS - GM_{MS}}(X) \text{ and } \underline{MS - GM^{II}_{MS}}(X) = \underline{MS - GM_{MS}}(X).$$

So the relation *b*. holds. Similarly, IIMS-GMDQ-DTRS model is also an extension of MS-GMRS model.

When $\alpha\langle 1,k\rangle 0$, the fault tolerance capability IIMS-GMDQ-DTRS model is higher than that of the MS-GMRS

model, i.e., $\alpha_{IIMDS}(U/DT) \geq \alpha_{MDS}(U/DT)$. Since for any $X \in U/DT$, according to Eqs. (3), (4), (22), (23), we obtain the conclusion that

$$\overline{MS - GM^{II}_{MS}}(X) \subseteq \overline{MS - GM_{MS}}(X), \underline{MS - GM^{II}_{MS}}(X) \supseteq \underline{MS - GM_{MS}}(X).$$

Based on Eqs. (11), (31), we obtain the conclusion that $\alpha_{IIMDS}(U/DT) \geq \alpha_{MDS}(U/DT)$. Similarly, the fault tolerance of IIMS-GMDQ-DTRS model is also better than that of MS-GMRS model.

c. When $\alpha = 1$, $\beta = 0$, $k = 0$, two MS-GMDQ-DTRS models degenerate to MS-GMRS model.

When $\alpha = 1, \beta = 0, k = 0$, based on the relations **a.** and **b.**, these three models are equivalent, i.e.,

$$(\overline{MS\text{-}GM^{\mathrm{I}}_{MS}}(X), \underline{MS\text{-}GM^{\mathrm{I}}_{MS}}(X)) \overset{\beta=0,k=0}{\rightarrow} (\overline{MS\text{-}GM_{MS}}(X),$$
$$\underline{MS\text{-}GM_{MS}}(X)) \overset{\alpha=1,k=0}{\leftarrow} (\overline{MS\text{-}GM^{\mathrm{II}}_{MS}}(X), \underline{MS\text{-}GM^{\mathrm{II}}_{MS}}(X)).$$

For the same reason as **a.** and **b.**, the IMS-PMDQ-DTRS model degenerates to MS-PMRS model and IMS-OMDQ- DTRS model degenerates to MS-OMRS model. The IIMS-PMDQ-DTRS model degenerates to MS-PMRS model and IIMS-OMDQ-DTRS model degenerates to MS-OMRS model.

When $\alpha\langle 1,\beta\rangle 0, k > 0$, the fault tolerance capability of two MS-GMDQ-DTRS models are higher than that of the MS-GMRS model, i.e.,

$$\alpha_{IMDS}(U/DT) \geq \alpha_{MDS}(U/DT) \text{ and } \alpha_{IIMDS}(U/DT) \geq \alpha_{MDS}(U/DT).$$

Based on the conclusions of **a.** and **b.**, the conclusion can be easily proved. Therefore, the fault tolerance capability of two MS- GMDQ-DTRS models are superior to MS-GMRS model in MsDS.

(2) The relations between the decision regions of two MS-GMDQ-DTRS models.

Based on DTRS model, if loss function satisfies

$$(\lambda_{NP} - \lambda_{BP})(\lambda_{PN} - \lambda_{BN}) > (\lambda_{BP} - \lambda_{PP})(\lambda_{BN} - \lambda_{NN}),$$

we have $0 \leq \beta < \alpha \leq 1$. We discuss the relations between different regions in two MS-GMDQ-DTRS models under different conditions of α and β while k keeps unchanged.

a. When $\alpha + \beta = 1$, the relations of the decision regions are

(I) $POS^{I}(X) = NEG^{II}(X^c)$;
(II) $NEG^{I}(X) = POS^{II}(X^c)$;
(III) $UBN^{I}(X) = UBN^{II}(X^c)$;
(IV) $LBN^{I}(X) = LBN^{II}(X^c)$.

Proof: First, by considering the support feature function, we can get

$$P\left(X | [x]_{IS_i}\right) > \beta \Leftrightarrow P\left(X^c | [x]_{IS_i}\right) < 1 - \beta, \left|[x]_{IS_i}\right| - \left|[x]_{IS_i} \cap X\right| \leq k \Leftrightarrow \left|[x]_{IS_i} \cap X^c\right| \leq k.$$

Due to $\beta = 1 - \alpha$, $P\left(X | [x]_{IS_i}\right) > \beta \Leftrightarrow P\left(X^c | [x]_{IS_i}\right) < \alpha$ can be obtained. So we can get

$$\left|IS_i : P\left(X | [x]_{IS_i}\right) > \beta\right| > s(1 - \varphi) \Leftrightarrow \left|IS_i : P\left(X^c | [x]_{IS_i}\right) < \alpha\right| > s(1 - \varphi)$$

$$\Leftrightarrow \left|IS_i : P\left((X^c) | [x]_{IS_i}\right) \geq \alpha\right| < s$$

and

$$\left|IS_i : \left|[x]_{IS_i}\right| - \left|[x]_{IS_i} \cap (X)\right| \leq k\right| \geq s\varphi \Leftrightarrow \left|IS_i : \left|[x]_{IS_i} \cap (X^c)\right| \leq k\right| \geq s\varphi$$

$$\Leftrightarrow \left|IS_i : \left|[x]_{IS_i} \cap (X^c)\right| > k\right| \leq s(1 - \varphi).$$

So we can get

$$\overline{MS - GM}^{I}_{MS}(X) \cap \underline{MS - GM}^{I}_{MS}(X) \Leftrightarrow \left(\overline{MS - GM}^{I}_{MS}(X^c) \cup \underline{MS - GM}^{II}_{MS}(X^c)\right)^c.$$

Therefore, $POS^{I}(X) = NEG^{II}(X^c)$ is certified. The proof of **(II)**, **(III)**, and **(VI)** are similar to that of **(I)**.

b. When $\alpha + \beta < 1$, the relations of the decision regions are

(I) $POS^{I}(X) \supseteq NEG^{II}(X^c)$;
(II) $NEG^{I}(X) \subseteq POS^{II}(X^c)$;
(III) $UBN^{I}(X) \supseteq UBN^{II}(X^c)$;
(IV) $LBN^{I}(X) \subseteq LBN^{II}(X^c)$.

Proof: Similarly, based on the support feature function, we can get

$$P\left(X|[x]_{IS_i}\right) > \beta \Leftrightarrow P\left(X^c|[x]_{IS_i}\right) < 1-\beta, \left|[x]_{IS_i}\right| - \left|[x]_{IS_i} \cap X\right| \le k \Leftrightarrow \left|[x]_{IS_i} \cap X^c\right| \le k.$$

Then for

$$\left|IS_i{:}P(X|[x]_{\{IS_i\}} > \beta\}\right| > s(1-\varphi) \Leftrightarrow \left|IS_i{:}P\left(X^c|[x]_{IS_i}\right) < 1-\beta\right| > s(1-\varphi)$$

and

$$\left|IS_i{:}\left|[x]_{IS_i}\right| - \left|[x]_{IS_i} \cap X\right| \le k\right| \ge s\varphi \Leftrightarrow \left|IS_i{:}\left|[x]_{IS_i} \cap (X^c)\right| \le k\right| \ge s$$

are obtained. Simultaneously,

$$\left|IS_i{:}P\left(X^c|[x]_{IS_i}\right) < 1-\beta\right| > s(1-\varphi) \Leftrightarrow \left|IS_i{:}P\left(X^c|[x]_{IS_i}\right) \ge 1-\beta\right| < s$$

and

$$\left|IS_i{:}\left|[x]_{IS_i} \cap (X^c)\right| \le k\right| \ge s\varphi \Leftrightarrow \left|IS_i{:}\left|[x]_{IS_i} \cap (X^c)\right| > k\right| \le s(1-\varphi)$$

hold. Since $\alpha < 1-\beta$,

$$\left|IS_i{:}P\left((X^c)|[x]_{IS_i}\right) \ge \alpha\right| < s\varphi \Rightarrow \left|IS_i{:}P\left(X^c|[x]_{IS_i}\right) \ge 1-\beta\right| < s$$

and

$$\left|IS_i{:}\left|[x]_{IS_i} \cap (X^c)\right| > k\right| \le s(1-\varphi) \Leftrightarrow \left|IS_i{:}\left|[x]_{IS_i} \cap (X^c)\right| > k\right| \le s(1-\varphi)$$

hold. So we get

$$\overline{MS-GM}^{I}_{MS}(X) \cap \underline{MS-GM}^{I}_{MS}(X) \Leftarrow \left(\overline{MS-GM}^{II}_{MS}(X^c) \cup \underline{MS-GM}^{II}_{MS}(X^c)\right)^c.$$

Thus the $POS^{I}(X) \supseteq NEG^{II}(X^{c})$ is certified. The (II), (III), and (VI) may be proofed similarly as (I).

c. When $\alpha + \beta > 1$, the relations of the decision regions are

(I) $POS^{I}(X) \subseteq NEG^{II}(X^{c})$;
(II) $NEG^{I}(X) \supseteq POS^{VII}(X^{c})$;
(III) $UBN^{I}(X) \subseteq UBN^{II}(X^{c})$;
(IV) $LBN^{I}(X) \supseteq LBN^{II}(X^{c})$.

Proof: Similarly, according to the support feature function, we can get

$P\left(X|[x]_{IS_i}\right) > \beta \Leftrightarrow P\left(X^{c}|[x]_{IS_i}\right) < 1-\beta, \left|[x]_{IS_i}\right| - \left|[x]_{IS_i} \cap X\right| \le k \Leftrightarrow \left|[x]_{IS_i} \cap X^{c}\right| \le k.$

Next, for

$$\left|IS_i: P\left(X|[x]_{IS_i}\right) > \beta\right| > s(1-\varphi) \Leftrightarrow \left|IS_i: P\left(X^{c}|[x]_{IS_i}\right) < 1-\beta\right| > s(1-\varphi),$$

$$\left|IS_i: \left|[x]_{IS_i}\right| - \left|[x]_{IS_i} \cap X\right| \le k\right| \ge s\varphi \Leftrightarrow \left|IS_i: \left|[x]_{IS_i} \cap (X^{c})\right| \le k\right| \ge s$$

can be obtained. Simultaneously,

$$\left|IS_i: P\left(X^{c}|[x]_{IS_i}\right) < 1-\beta\right| > s(1-\varphi) \Leftrightarrow \left|IS_i: P\left(X^{c}|[x]_{IS_i}\right) \ge 1-\beta\right| < s,$$

and $\left|IS_i: \left|[x]_{IS_i} \cap X^{c}\right| \le k\right| \ge s\varphi \Leftrightarrow$

$|IS_i : |[x]IS_i \cap (X)| > k| \le s(1-\phi)$. Since $\alpha > 1-\beta$, the $|IS_i : P(X|[x]IS_i) \ge 1-\beta| < s\phi \Rightarrow |IS_i : P((X)|[x]IS_i) \ge \alpha| <$

$s\phi$ and $|IS_i : |[x]IS_i \cap (X)| > k| \le s(1-\phi) \Leftrightarrow |IS_i : |[x]IS_i \cap (X)| > k| \le s(1-\phi)$ can be obtained. So we can get

$(X^{c}))^{c}$. Therefore, $POS^{I}(X) \subseteq NEG^{II}(X^{c})$ is certified. The proof of (II), (III), and (VI) is similar to that of (I).

Intuitively, the relations between the decision regions of two MS-GMDQ-DTRS models in different cases are shown in Table 1.

Table 1. The decision regions relations of two MS-GMDQ-DTRS models

$\alpha + \beta = 1$ 1	$POS^{I}(X) = NEG^{II}(X^c)$	$NEG^{I}(X) = POS^{II}(X^c)$)	$UBN^{I}(X) = UBN^{II}(X^c)$	$LBN^{I}(X) = LBN^{II}(X^c)$
$\alpha + \beta <$	$POS^{I}(X) \supseteq NEG^{II}(X^c)$	$NEG^{I}(X) \subseteq POS^{II}(X^c$	$UBN^{I}(X) \supseteq UBN^{II}(X^c)$	$LBN^{I}(X) \subseteq LBN^{II}(X^c)$
$\alpha + \beta > 1$	$POS^{I}(X) \subseteq NEG^{II}(X^c)$	$NEG^{I}(X) \supseteq POS^{II}(X^c)$	$UBN^{I}(X) \subseteq UBN^{II}(X^c)$	$LBN^{I}(X) \supseteq LBN^{II}(X^c)$

4. CASE STUDY

In this section, the conclusions of **3.4** are verified by an case of car detection. The fault tolerance between the proposed models is compared by calculating the approximation accuracy values of the proposed models. There are four automobile evaluation factories that evaluate 10 cars in terms of fuel consumption, machinery, appearance, and safety performance. Then the evaluation grade is divided into upper, middle, and lower. Finally, each car is evaluated as a high quality car or a general car. Therefore, the MsDS is constituted by evaluation results.

Let $MDS = \{DS_1, DS_2, DS_3, DS_4\}$ be a MsDS, where $DS_i = (U, AT \cup d, V_i, f_i)$. The $U = \{x_1, x_2, x_3, x_4, x_5, x_6, x_7, x_8, x_9, x_{10}\}$ stands for ten cars. The $AT = \{a_1, a_2, a_3, a_4\}$, where a_1 stands for fuel consumption, a_2 stands for machinery, a_3 stands for appearance, and a_4 stands for safety performance. The $V^i = \{0, 1, 2\}$, where "0" stands for lower grade, "1" stands for middle grade, and "2" stands for upper grade. The d is decision attribute which stands for quality of car. The $D^i = \{0, 1\}$, where "0" stands for general car and "1" stands for high quality car. The decision class $X = \{x_1, x_2, x_4, x_6, x_8\}$ is selected as the target set. Let $k = 1, \varphi = 0.65$. DS_1, DS_2, DS_3, DS_4 are the test results of four automobile evaluation factories. The MsDS is shown as Table 2.

Table 3 lists the equivalence classes of each object under each source.

4.1. Verification of 3.4 (1)

(1) Verification the conclusion 3.4 (1)-a

Table 2. A multi-source decision system

	a_1	a_2	a_3	a_4		a_1	a_2	a_3	a_4		a_1	a_2	a_3	a_4		a_1	a_2	a_3	a_4	d
x_1	1	2	2	1		1	2	2	1		1	2	1	1		1	2	2	1	1
x_2	1	2	1	1		1	2	2	1		1	2	1	1		1	2	1	1	1
x_3	1	1	2	1		1	1	1	1		1	2	1	1		1	1	2	1	0

	a_1	a_2	a_3	a_4		a_1	a_2	a_3	a_4		a_1	a_2	a_3	a_4		a_1	a_2	a_3	a_4	d
x_4	0	1	1	1		1	1	1	1		0	1	2	1		0	1	2	0	1
x_5	2	1	1	2		0	1	1	1		1	1	1	1		2	2	1	1	0
x_6	0	1	1	0		0	1	1	1		0	1	2	1		1	1	2	0	1
x_7	1	1	2	1		2	2	1	1		1	2	1	1		1	2	1	1	0
x_8	1	1	1	0		2	2	1	1		1	1	1	1		1	1	1	0	1
x_9	2	1	1	0		2	2	1	1		2	1	2	1		2	1	2	1	0
x10	1	1	1	0		1	1	1	1		2	1	2	1		0	1	2	0	0

Table 3. Statistical results of equivalence classes under each source

U	[x]DS 1	[x]DS 2	[x]DS 3	[x]DS 4
x1	x1	x1, x2	x1, x2, x3, x7	x1
x2	x2	x1, x2	x1, x2, x3, x7	x2, x7
x3	x3, x7	x3, x4, x10	x1, x2, x3, x7	x3
x4	x4	x3, x4, x10	x4, x6	x4, x10
x5	x5	x5, x6	x5, x8	x5
x6	x6	x5, x6	x4, x6	x6
x7	x3, x7	x7, x8, x9	x1, x2, x3, x7	x2, x7
x8	x8, x10	x7, x8, x9	x5, x8	x8
x9	x9	x7, x8, x9	x9, x10	x9
x10	x8, x10	x3, x4, x10	x9, x10	x4, x10

According to Eqs. (3), (4), the upper and lower approximations of *X* in MS-GMRS model are

$MS\text{-}GM_{\mathrm{MS}}(X) = \{x_1, x_2, x_3, x_4, x_5, x_6, x_7, x_8, x_{10}\}$, $\underline{MS\text{-}GM}_{\mathrm{MS}}(X) = \{x_1, x_6\}$.

Assume β = 0.4, k = 1, according to Eqs. (12), (13), the upper and lower approximations of *X* in the IMS-GMDQ- DTRS model are

$$\overline{MS - GM}_{MS}(X) = \{x_1,x_2,x_3,x_4,x_5,x_6,x_7,x_8,x_{10}\}, \underline{MS - GM}_{MS}(X) = \{x_1,x_6\}.$$

The above results show that

$$\overline{MS - GM}^{\mathrm{I}}_{MS}(X) \subseteq \overline{MS - GM}_{MS}(X), \underline{MS - GM}^{\mathrm{I}}_{MS}(X) \supseteq \underline{MS - GM}_{MS}(X)$$

Assume β = 0, k = 0, according to Eqs. (12), (13), the upper and lower approximations of *X* in the IMS-GMDQ- DTRS model are

$$\overline{MS - GM}^{\mathrm{I}}_{MS}(X) = \{x_1,x_2,x_3,x_4,x_5,x_6,x_7,x_8,x_{10}\}, \underline{MS - GM}^{\mathrm{I}}_{MS}(X) = \{x_1,x_6\}.$$

This indicates

$$\overline{MS-GM}^{\mathrm{I}}_{MS}(X) = \overline{MS-GM}_{MS}(X), \underline{MS-GM}^{\mathrm{I}}_{MS}(X) = \underline{MS-GM}_{MS}(X).$$

(2) Verification the conclusion 3.4 (1)-b

Assume $\alpha = 0.6, k = 1$, according to Eqs. (22), (23), the upper and lower approximations of X in the IIMS- GMDQ-DTRS model are

$$\overline{MS-GM}^{\mathrm{II}}_{MS}(X) = \{x_1, x_2\}, \underline{MS-GM}^{\mathrm{II}}_{MS}(X) = \{x_1, x_6\}.$$

The results show that

$$\overline{MSGM}^{\mathrm{II}}_{MS}(X) \subseteq \overline{MS-GM}_{MS}(X), \underline{MS-GM}^{\mathrm{II}}_{MS}(X) \supseteq \underline{MS-GM}_{MS}(X).$$

Assume $\alpha = 1, k = 0$, according to Eqs. (22), (23), the upper and lower approximations of X in the IIMS-GMDQ- DTRS model are

$$\overline{MS-GM}^{\mathrm{II}}_{MS}(X) = \{x_1, x_2, x_3, x_4, x_5, x_6, x_7, x_8, x_{10}\}, \underline{MS-GM}^{\mathrm{II}}_{MS}(X) = \{x_1, x_6\}.$$

This indicates

$$\overline{MS-GM}^{\mathrm{II}}_{MS}(X) = \overline{MS-GM}_{MS}(X), \underline{MS-GM}^{II}_{MS}(X) = \underline{MS-GM}_{MS}(X).$$

(3) Verification the conclusion 3.4 (1)-c.

When $\alpha = 1, \beta = 0, k = 0$, according to the calculation results of (1) and (2), the upper and lower approximations of the proposed models are equal, i.e.,

$$\overline{MS-GM}^{\mathrm{I}}_{MS}(X) = \overline{MS-GM}_{MS}(X) = \overline{MS-GM}^{II}_{MS}(X),$$
$$\underline{MS-GM}^{I}_{MS}(X) = \underline{MS-GM}_{MS}(X) = \underline{MS-GM}^{II}_{MS}(X).$$

That is say that two MS-GMDQ-DTRS models degenerate to MS-GMRS model, that is, the conclusion 3.4 (1)-c is verified.

4.2. Verification of 3.4 (2)

In the Bayesian decision procedure, the expert gives the loss function values for three cases in Table 4.λ

Table 4. Three cases of loss function

	α = 0.6, β= 0.4	α = 0.6, β= 0.3	α = 0.7, β= 0.4
aP : accept	λPP = 0, λPN = 22	λ PP = 0, λPN = 9	λPP = 0, λPN = 13
aB : defer	λBP = 12, λBN = 4	λ BP = 2, λBN = 6	λBP = 3, λBN = 6
aN : reject	λNP = 18, λNN = 0	λNP = 16, λNN = 0	λNP = 12, λNN = 0

(1) When $\alpha + \beta = 1, \alpha = 0.6, \beta = 0.4$,
we verify the conclusion 3.4 (2)-a.

According to Eqs. (12), (13), (16), the upper and lower approximations and decision regions of X in the IMS- GMDQ-DTRS model are

$$\overline{MS - GM}^{I}_{MS}(X) = \{x_1,x_2,x_4,x_5,x_6,x_7,x_8,x_{10}\}, \underline{MS - GM}^{I}_{MS}(X) = \{x_1,x_2,x_4,x_5,x_6,x_8\} ;$$

$$POS^{I}(X) = \{x_1,x_2,x_4,x_5,x_6,x_8\}, NEG^{I}(X) = \{x_3,x_9\},$$

$$UBN^{I}(X) = \{x_7,x_{10}\}, LBN^{I}(X) = \varnothing.$$

According to Eqs. (22), (23), (26), the upper and lower approximations and decision regions of X^c in the IIMS- GMDQ-DTRS model are

$$\overline{MS - GM}^{II}_{MS}(X^c) = \{x_3,x_7,x_9,x_{10}\}, \underline{MS - GM}^{II}_{MS}(X^c) = \{x_3,x_9\} ;$$

$$POS^{II}(X^c) = \{x_3,x_9\}, NEG^{II}(X^c) = \{x_1,x_2,x_4,x_5,x_6,x_8\},$$

$$UBN^{II}(X^c) = \{x_7,x_{10}\}, LBN^{II}(X^c) = \varnothing.$$

The above results show that

$POS^{I}(X) = NEG^{II}(X^c)$, $NEG^{I}(X) = POS^{II}(X^c)$, $UBN^{I}(X) = UBN^{II}(X^c)$, $LBN^{I}(X)$

$= LBN^{II}(X^c)$.

Thus the conclusion 3.4 (2)-a is verified.

(2) When $\alpha + \beta < 1$, $\alpha = 0.6$, $\beta = 0.3$, we verify the conclusion 3.4 (2)-b.

According to Eqs. (12), (13), (16), the upper and lower approximations and decision regions of X in the IMS- GMDQ-DTRS model are

$$\overline{MS - GM}^{I}_{MS}(X) = \{x_1,x_2,x_3,x_4,x_5,x_6,x_7,x_8,x_{10}\}, \underline{MS - GM}^{I}_{MS}(X) = \{x_1,x_2,x_4,x_5,x_6,x_8\} ;$$

$$POS^{I}(X) = \{x_1, x_2, x_4, x_5, x_6, x_8\}, NEG^{I}(X) = \{x_9\},$$

$$UBN^{I}(X) = \{x_3, x_7, x_{10}\}, LBN^{I}(X) = \varnothing.$$

According to Eqs. (22), (23), (26), the upper and lower approximations and decision regions of X^c in the IIMS- GMDQ-DTRS model are

$$\overline{MS - GM}^{II}_{MS}(X^c) = \{x_3, x_7, x_9, x_{10}\}, \underline{MS - GM}^{II}_{MS}(X^c) = \{x_3, x_9\} \ ;$$

$$POS^{II}(X^c) = \{x_3, x_9\}, NEG^{II}(X^c) = \{x_1, x_2, x_4, x_5, x_6, x_8\},$$

$$UBN^{II}(X^c) = \{x_7, x_{10}\}, LBN^{II}(X^c) = \varnothing.$$

The results indicate that

$^{I}(X) \supseteq NEG^{II}(X^c)$, $NEG^{I}(X) \subseteq POS^{II}(X^c)$, $UBN^{I}(X) \supseteq UBN^{II}(X^c)$, $LBN^{I}(X) \subseteq LBN^{II}(X^c)$.

Thus the conclusion 3.4 (2)-b is verified.

(3) When $\alpha + \beta > 1, \alpha = 0.7, \beta = 0.4$, we verify the conclusion 3.4 (2)-c.

According to Eqs. (12), (13), (16), the upper and lower approximations and decision regions of X in the IMS- GMDQ-DTRS model are

$$\overline{MS - GM}^{I}_{MS}(X) = \{x_1, x_2, x_4, x_5, x_6, x_7, x_8, x_{10}\}, \underline{MS - GM}^{I}_{MS}(X) = \{x_1, x_2, x_4, x_5, x_6, x_8\} \ ;$$

$$POS^{I}(X) = \{x_1, x_2, x_4, x_5, x_6, x_8\}, NEG^{I}(X) = \{x_3, x_9\},$$

$$UBN^{I}(X) = \{x_7, x_{10}\}, LBN^{I}(X) = \varnothing.$$

According to Eqs. (22), (23), (26), the upper and lower approximations and decision regions of X^c in the IIMS- GMDQ-DTRS model are

$$\overline{MS - GM}^{II}_{MS}(X^c) = \{x_3, x_7, x_9, x_{10}\}, \underline{MS - GM}^{II}_{MS}(X^c) = \{x_9\} \ ;$$

$$POS^{II}(X^c) = \{x_9\}, NEG^{II}(X^c) = \{x_1, x_2, x_4, x_5, x_6, x_8\},$$

$$UBN^{II}(X^c) = \{x_3, x_7, x_{10}\}, LBN^{I}(X^c) = \varnothing.$$

The above results show that

$POS^{I}(X) \subseteq NEG^{II}(X^c)$, $NEG^{I}(X) \supseteq POS^{II}(X^c)$, $UBN^{I}(X) \subseteq UBN^{II}(X^c)$, $LBN^{I}(X) \supseteq LBN^{II}(X^c)$.

Thus the conclusion 3.4 (2)-c is verified.

4.3. The comparison of approximation accuracy

In this subsection, we verify that the fault tolerance capability of the two MS-GMDQ-DTRS models is better than the MS-GMRS model.

(1) The approximation accuracy of the MS-GMRS mode is calculated.

According to Eqs. (3), (4), the upper and lower approximations of X and X^c in the MS-GMRS model are

$$\overline{MS-GM}_{MS}(X) = \{x_1, x_2, x_3, x_4, x_5, x_6, x_7, x_8, x_{10}\}, \underline{MS-GM}_{MS}(X) = \{x_1, x_6\};$$

$$\overline{MS-GM}_{MS}(X^c) = \{x_2, x_3, x_4, x_5, x_7, x_8, x_9, x_{10}\}, \underline{MS-GM}_{MS}(X^c) = \{x_9\}.$$

Based on Eq. (11), the approximation accuracy of MS-GMRS is $\alpha_{MDS}(U/d) = 0.1765$.

(2) When $\alpha = 0.6, \beta = 0.4$, the approximation accuracy of the two MS-GMDQ-DTRS models are calculated. According to Eqs. (12), (13), the upper and lower approximations of X and X^c in the IMS-GMDQ-DTRS model are

$$\overline{MS-GM}^{I}_{MS}(X) = \{x_1, x_2, x_4, x_5, x_6, x_7, x_8, x_{10}\}, \underline{MS-GM}^{I}_{MS}(X) = \{x_1, x_2, x_4, x_5, x_6, x_8\};$$

$$\overline{MS-GM}^{I}_{MS}(X^c) = \{x_2, x_3, x_4, x_5, x_7, x_8, x_9, x_{10}\}, \underline{MS-GM}^{I}_{MS}(X^c) = \{x_3, x_4, x_5, x_7, x_8, x_9, x_{10}\}.$$

Based on Eq. (21), the approximation accuracy of IMS-GMDQ-DTRS model is $\alpha_{IMDS}(U/d) = 0.8125$.

Similarly, according to Eqs. (22), (23), the upper and lower approximations of X and X^c in the IIMS-GMDQ-DTRS model are

$$\overline{MS-GM}^{II}_{MS}(X) = \{x_1, x_2\}, \underline{MS-GM}^{II}_{MS}(X) = \{x_1, x_6\};$$

$\overline{MS-GM}^{II}_{MS}(X^c) = \{x_3,x_7,x_9,x_{10}\}, \underline{MS-GM}^{II}_{MS}(X^c) = \{x_3,x_9\}.$

Based on Eq. (31), the approximation accuracy of IIMS-GMDQ-DTRS model is $\alpha_{IIMDS}(U/d) = 0.6667$.

The above results indicate that $\alpha_{IMDS}(U/d) > \alpha_{MDS}(U/d)$ and $\alpha_{IIMDS}(U/d) > \alpha_{MDS}(U/d)$. Therefore, when $\alpha + \beta = 1$, the conclusion that the fault tolerance capability of the two MS-GMDQ-DTRS models is better than the MS-GMRS model is verified.

(3) When $\alpha = 0.6$, $\beta = 0.3$, the approximation accuracy of the two MS-GMDQ-DTRS models are calculated. According to Eqs. (12), (13), the upper and lower approximations of X and X^c in the IMS-GMDQ-DTRS model are

$\overline{MS-GM}^{I}_{MS}(X) = \{x_1,x_2,x_3,x_4,x_5,x_6,x_7,x_8,x_{10}\}, \underline{MS-GM}^{I}_{MS}(X) = \{x_1,x_2,x_4,x_5,x_6,x_8\}$;

$\overline{MS-GM}^{I}_{MS}(X^c) = \{x_2,x_3,x_4,x_5,x_7,x_8,x_9,x_{10}\}, \underline{MS-GM}^{I}_{MS}(X^c) = \{x_3,x_4,x_5,x_7,x_8,x_9,x_{10}\}.$

Based on Eq. (21), the approximation accuracy of IMS-GMDQ-DTRS model is $\alpha_{IMDS}(U/d) = 0.7647$.

Similarly, according to Eq. (22), (23), the the upper and lower approximations of X and X^c in the IIMS-GMDQ- DTRS model are

$\overline{MS-GM}^{II}_{MS}(X) = \{x_1,x_2\}, \underline{MS-GM}^{II}_{MS}(X) = \{x_1,x_6\}$;

$\overline{MS-GM}^{II}_{MS}(X^c) = \{x_3,x_7,x_9,x_{10}\}, \underline{MS-GM}^{II}_{MS}(X^c) = \{x_3,x_9\}.$

Based on Eq. (31), the approximation accuracy of IIMS-GMDQ-DTRS model is $\alpha_{IIMDS}(U/d) = 0.6667$.

The above results show that $\alpha_{IMDS}(U/d) > \alpha_{MDS}(U/d)$ and $\alpha_{IIMDS}(U/d) > \alpha_{MDS}(U/d)$. Therefore, when $\alpha + \beta <$

1 this conclusion is also verified.

(4) When $\alpha = 0.7$, $\beta = 0.4$, the approximation accuracy of two MS-GMDQ-DTRS models are calculated. According to Eqs. (12), (13), the upper and lower approximations of X and X^c in the IMS-GMDQ-DTRS model are

$\overline{MS-GM}^{I}_{MS}(X) = \{x_1,x_2,x_4,x_5,x_6,x_7,x_8,x_{10}\}, \underline{MS-GM}^{I}_{MS}(X) = \{x_1,x_2,x_4,x_5,x_6,x_8\}$;

$\overline{MS-GM}^{I}_{MS}(X^c) = \{x_2,x_3,x_4,x_5,x_7,x_8,x_9,x_{10}\}, \underline{MS-GM}^{I}_{MS}(X^c) = \{x_3,x_4,x_5,x_7,x_8,x_9,x_{10}\}.$

Based on Eq. (21), the approximation accuracy of IMS-GMDQ-DTRS model is $\alpha_{IMDS}(U/d) = 0.8125$.

Similarly, according to Eq. (22), (23), the the upper and lower approximations of X and X^c in the IIMS-GMDQ- DTRS model are

$$\overline{MS - GM}^{II}_{MS}(X) = \{x_1, x_2\}, \underline{MS - GM}^{II}_{MS}(X) = \{x_1, x_6\} ;$$

$$\overline{MS - GM}^{II}_{MS}(X^c) = \{x_3, x_7, x_9, x_{10}\}, \underline{MS - GM}^{II}_{MS}(X^c) = \{x_9\}.$$

Based on Eq. (31), the approximation accuracy of IIMS-GMDQ-DTRS model is $\alpha_{IIMDS}(U/d) = 0.5$.

The above results show that $\alpha_{IMDS}(U/d) > \alpha_{MDS}(U/d)$ and $\alpha_{IIMDS}(U/d) > \alpha_{MDS}$ (U/d). Therefore, when $\alpha + \beta >$

1, this conclusion is also verified.

5. EXPERIMENTAL ANALYSIS

In this section, a series of experiments are conducted to show two MS-GMDQ-DTRS models are superior to MS- GMRS model in terms of fault tolerance by calculating the approximation accuracy. In this experiment, four data sets were downloaded from UCI, which are shown in Table 5. In this paper, all algorithms are coded in MATLAB. The specific operating environment (including hardware and software) is shown in Table 6.

Table 5. Specific information about the data sets

No.	Name	Objects	Attributes	Decision Classes	Number of Sources
1	Liver Disorders	345	7	2	10
2	Balance Scale	625	4	3	10
3	Wireless Indoor Localization	2000	7	4	10
4	Abalone	4177	8	3	10

Table 6. Specific information about the operating environment

Name	Model	Parameter
CPU	Intel(R) Core(TM) i7-8700	3.20 GHz
Platform	MATLAB	R2016b

Name	Model	Parameter
System	Windows 10	64 bit
Memory	DDR3	16.0 GB;1600 Mhz
Hard DSsk	MQ01ABD050	500 GB

In machine learning databases, multi-source data set is not easily available directly. The following two methods are proposed to construct multi-source data set by adding noise.

In the original decision system, the value of object x under attribute a is denoted as DS (x, a). The corresponding value of the ith decision system is denoted as $DS_i(x, a)$. First, generate q numbers $(n_1, n_2, \ldots, n_q)$ that satisfy the normal distribution. The first method is to add white noise by

$$DSi(x,a) = \begin{cases} DS(x,a) + n_i, if 0 \leq |n_i|, \\ DS(x,a) \; otherwise. \end{cases}$$

Similarly, the second method is to add random noise by

$$DSi(x,a) = \begin{cases} DS(x,a) + r_i if 0 \leq |r_i| \\ DS(x,a) \; otherwise. \end{cases}$$

We randomly select 40% of the original data to add white noise, the remaining 20% to add random noise, and the rest is unchanged. Then, through the above approach, a MsIS can be obtained. The process of generating MsDS is

Figure 2. The generation process of multi-source decision system

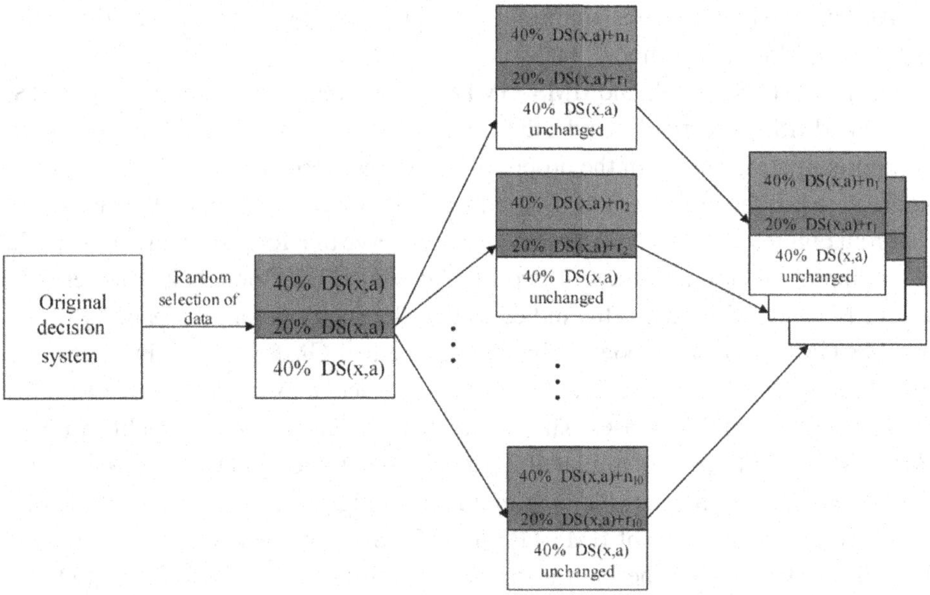

Table 7. The approximation accuracy of liver disorders data set

				IMS					IIMS		
NO	MS	$\beta = 0.4$	$\beta = 0.3$	$\beta = 0.2$	$\beta = 0.1$	$\beta = 0$	$\alpha = 0.6$	$\alpha = 0.7$	$\alpha = 0.8$	$\alpha = 0.9$	$\alpha = 1.0$
1	0.3168	**0.9438**	0.8742	0.8092	0.7691	0.7691	0.9146	0.7979	0.6690	0.5784	0.5784
2	0.2321	**0.7691**	0.6755	0.6295	0.6044	0.5946	0.7199	0.5518	0.4510	0.3894	0.3641
3	0.2256	**0.7199**	0.6360	0.6004	0.5524	0.5524	0.6807	0.5303	0.4538	0.3351	0.3351
4	0.2707	**0.8904**	0.8008	0.7490	0.7221	0.7035	0.8474	0.6916	0.5844	0.5227	0.4773
5	0.2278	**0.7670**	0.6780	0.6360	0.6108	0.6032	0.7066	0.5413	0.4473	0.3846	0.3647
6	0.2946	**0.9335**	0.8525	0.7829	0.7429	0.7373	0.9057	0.7710	0.6330	0.5421	0.5286
7	0.2212	**0.6953**	0.6197	0.5822	0.5451	0.5451	0.6466	0.5052	0.4215	0.3272	0.3272
8	0.2432	**0.8174**	0.7397	0.6911	0.6450	0.6450	0.7590	0.6205	0.5181	0.4066	0.4066
9	0.3244	**0.9904**	0.8996	0.8565	0.7908	0.7908	0.9856	0.8345	0.7518	0.6079	0.6079
10	0.2897	**0.9416**	0.8217	0.7679	0.7234	0.7234	0.9208	0.7228	0.6139	0.5116	0.5116

shown in Figuew 2. Every time we generate a MsDS, we have to re-randomly select the noise-added data once in the original data. The experiment generates ten MsDSs on the basis of each data set in Table 5.

For each data set in Table 5, the approximation accuracy of the proposed models are calculated by Algorithms 1-3, respectively. Let $\phi = 0.65$, $k = 1, \beta \in [0, 0.5)$, $\alpha \in (0.5, 1]$, the experimental results are shown in Tables 7, 8, 9,

10. The maximum values are highlighted in bold-face. In order to facilitate the expression, MS-GMRS model, IMS-

GMDQ-DTRS model, and IIMS-GMDQ-DTRS model are abbreviated as MS, IMS, and IIMS, respectively. Under different α, β, more detailed change trend lines of the approximate accuracy of the proposed models are shown in Figs. 3, 4, 5. In each figure, x-axis is the number of MsDS and y-axis is value of approximation accuracy.

From Figures 3, 4, under different α, β, we observe that for each data sets in Table 5, the approximation accuracy of two MS-GMDQ-DTRS models are higher than that of MS-GMRS model. This indicates that the fault tolerance capability of the two MS-GMDQ-DTRS models is better than the MS-GMRS model. Furthermore, from Figure 3, we find a rule that the approximate accuracy of IMS-GMDQ-DTRS model decreases as β decreases. This shows that the fault tolerance capability of the IMS-GMDQ-DTRS model is related to β and is monotonic. When $\beta = 0.4$, the fault tolerance capability reaches the maximum. From Figure 4, we also find a rule that the approximate accuracy of IIMS-GMDQ-DTRS model decreases as α increases. This also indicates that the fault tolerance capability of the IIMS-GMDQ-DTRS model is monotonic with α.When$\alpha = 0.6$, the fault tolerance capability reaches the maximum. From Figure 5, for each data set in Table 5, when $\alpha = 0.6$, $\beta = 0.4$, we find that the approximation accuracy of IMS- GMDQ-DTRS model is the highest. This indicates that when the fault tolerance capability of all models reaches its maximum, the IMS-GMDQ-DTRS model is higher than that of the other two models. Therefore, from the perspective of fault tolerance, the IMS-GMDQ-DTRS model should be preferred to deal with the classification and decision- making of multi-source data set.

Table 8. The approximation accuracy of balance scale data set

				IMS					IIMS		
NO.	**MS**	**$\beta = 0.4$**	**$\beta = 0.3$**	**$\beta = 0.2$**	**$\beta = 0.1$**	**$\beta = 0$**	**$\alpha = 0.6$**	**$\alpha = 0.7$**	**$\alpha = 0.8$**	**$\alpha = 0.9$**	**$\alpha = 1.0$**
1	0.0939	**0.8564**	0.7383	0.6542	0.6542	0.6542	0.4867	0.3669	0.2148	0.2148	0.2148
2	0.1008	**0.8827**	0.8266	0.7021	0.6891	0.6891	0.5430	0.4959	0.2705	0.2459	0.2459
3	0.2301	**0.8939**	0.7924	0.6862	0.6513	0.6464	0.6990	0.6344	0.5170	0.4320	0.4184
4	0.3416	**0.7654**	0.6458	0.5254	0.5072	0.4911	0.6378	0.6247	0.5433	0.4685	0.4528
5	0.0923	**0.8785**	0.8079	0.6619	0.6614	0.6614	0.5521	0.4794	0.2220	0.2181	0.2181
6	0.1096	**0.8439**	0.7740	0.6397	0.6109	0.6109	0.5778	0.5056	0.3093	0.2389	0.2389
7	0.1058	**0.7742**	0.7051	0.5900	0.5690	0.5685	0.4975	0.4420	0.2655	0.2101	0.2101

				IMS					IIMS		
NO.	MS	$\beta = 0.4$	$\beta = 0.3$	$\beta = 0.2$	$\beta = 0.1$	$\beta = 0$	$\alpha = 0.6$	$\alpha = 0.7$	$\alpha = 0.8$	$\alpha = 0.9$	$\alpha = 1.0$
8	0.0968	**0.8539**	0.7942	0.6703	0.6636	0.6636	0.5129	0.4692	0.2425	0.2306	0.2306
9	0.1230	**0.9187**	0.8118	0.6839	0.6609	0.6604	0.6219	0.5085	0.3195	0.2722	0.2703
10	0.0989	**0.7758**	0.6983	0.6009	0.5859	0.5859	0.5080	0.4100	0.2692	0.2103	0.2103

Table 9. The approximation accuracy of wireless indoor localization data set

				IMS					IIMS		
NO.	MS	$\beta = 0.4$	$\beta = 0.3$	$\beta = 0.2$	$\beta = 0.1$	$\beta = 0$	$\alpha = 0.6$	$\alpha = 0.7$	$\alpha = 0.8$	$\alpha = 0.9$	$\alpha = 1.0$
1	0.2871	**0.6978**	0.6773	0.6264	0.5849	0.4923	0.6164	0.5935	0.5045	0.4703	0.3438
2	0.3371	**0.7558**	0.6843	0.6409	0.5852	0.4817	0.6228	0.5957	0.5459	0.4964	0.3967
3	0.2593	**0.6172**	0.6005	0.5397	0.4781	0.3541	0.5846	0.5654	0.4711	0.4006	0.3019
4	0.2792	**0.6430**	0.6219	0.5666	0.4998	0.3730	0.5763	0.5480	0.4507	0.3998	0.3177
5	0.3370	**0.7527**	0.7247	0.6469	0.6026	0.4893	0.6854	0.6573	0.5507	0.4922	0.3920
6	0.2956	**0.6742**	0.6485	0.5803	0.5309	0.4175	0.6570	0.6282	0.5306	0.4570	0.3560
7	0.2637	**0.6549**	0.6350	0.5572	0.4881	0.3704	0.5609	0.5072	0.4306	0.3863	0.3081
8	0.2619	**0.6308**	0.6057	0.5684	0.4934	0.3699	0.5910	0.5655	0.4860	0.4113	0.3168
9	0.3515	**0.7109**	0.6860	0.6359	0.5646	0.4256	0.6197	0.5955	0.5325	0.4334	0.3481
10	0.2685	**0.6113**	0.5917	0.5917	0.4766	0.3580	0.5766	0.5514	0.4523	0.4004	0.3040

Table 10. The approximation accuracy of Abalone data set

				IMS					IIMS		
NO.	MS	$\beta = 0.4$	$\beta = 0.3$	$\beta = 0.2$	$\beta = 0.1$	$\beta = 0$	$\alpha = 0.6$	$\alpha = 0.7$	$\alpha = 0.8$	$\alpha = 0.9$	$\alpha = 1.0$
1	0.0798	**0.5431**	0.4216	0.3532	0.2989	0.2691	0.2937	0.1937	0.1588	0.1068	0.1016
2	0.0799	**0.5422**	0.4226	0.3605	0.3046	0.2726	0.2954	0.2051	0.1617	0.1082	0.1018
3	0.0805	**0.5692**	0.4361	0.3612	0.3065	0.2720	0.3152	0.2119	0.1653	0.1091	0.1028
4	0.0847	**0.5587**	0.4450	0.3808	0.3215	0.2918	0.2941	0.2016	0.1666	0.1157	0.1113
5	0.0796	**0.5415**	0.4241	0.3546	0.3002	0.2696	0.2923	0.1966	0.1556	0.1068	0.1012
6	0.0796	**0.5440**	0.4275	0.3599	0.3068	0.2722	0.3022	0.2060	0.1628	0.1075	0.1020
7	0.0796	**0.5411**	0.4278	0.3579	0.3050	0.2705	0.2982	0.2027	0.1567	0.1071	0.1014
8	0.0805	**0.5512**	0.4317	0.3620	0.3062	0.2722	0.3040	0.2104	0.1645	0.1091	0.1028
9	0.0800	**0.5547**	0.4291	0.3596	0.3055	0.2710	0.3040	0.2061	0.1626	0.1081	0.1024
10	0.0811	**0.5325**	0.4239	0.3600	0.3052	0.2761	0.2852	0.1895	0.1592	0.1083	0.1043

Figure 3. The approximation accuracies of MS-GMRS and IMS-GMDQ-DTRS

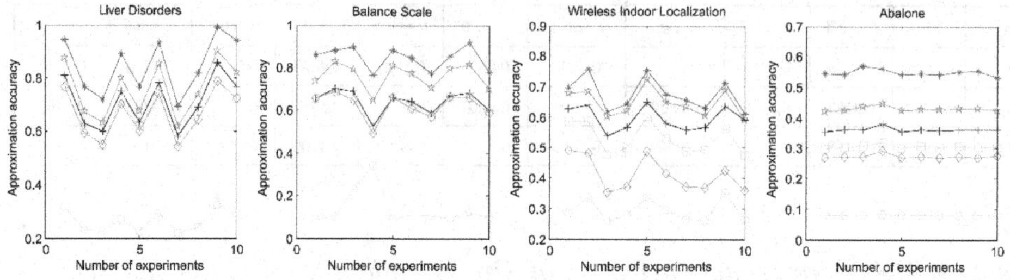

Figure 4. The approximation accuracies of MS-GMRS and IIMS-GMDQ-DTRS

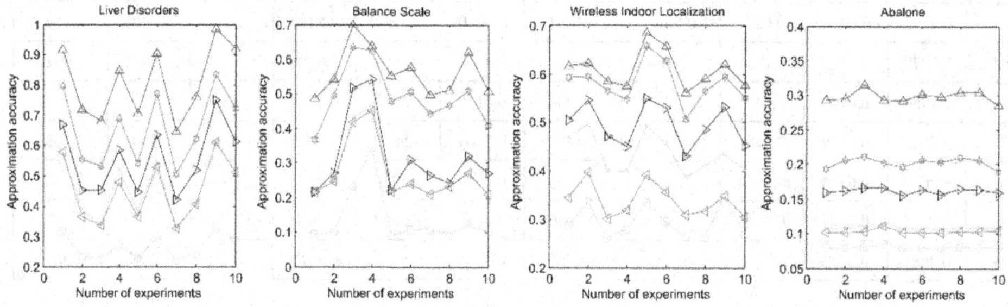

Figure 5. The approximation accuracies of MS-GMRS, IMS-GMDQ-DTRS (β = 0.4), and IIMS-GMDQ-DTRS (α = 0.6)

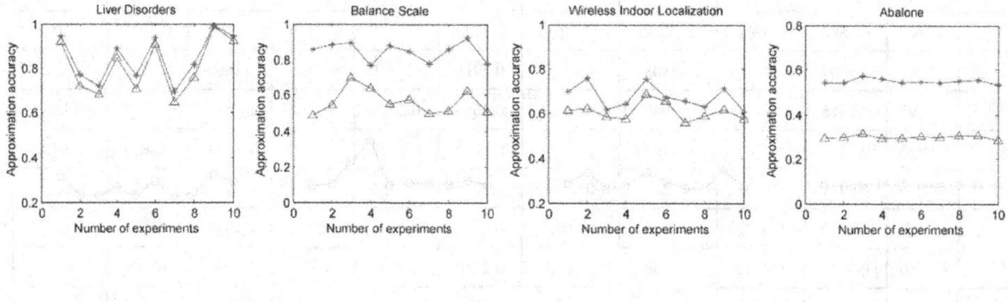

ACKNOWLEDGMENT

The chapter was supported by grants from the National Natural Science Foundation of China (No. 62306054), the Nature Science Foundation Project of Chongqing Science and Technology Bureau (Nos. CSTB2023NSCQ-MSX1010), the Science and Technology Research Program of Chongqing Municipal Education Commission (No. KJQN202300549), the Chongqing Normal University Foundation Project (No. 22XLB019).

REFERENCES

Che, X. Y., Mi, J. S., & Chen, D. G. (2018). Information fusion and numerical characterization of a multi-source information system. *Knowledge-Based Systems*, 145, 121–133. 10.1016/j.knosys.2018.01.008

Dai, J. H., Hu, H., Wu, W. Z., Qian, Y. H., & Huang, D. B. (2013). Maximal discernibility pairs based approach to attribute reduction in fuzzy rough sets. *IEEE Transactions on Fuzzy Systems*, 219, 151–167.

Dai, J. H., Wei, B. J., Zhang, X. H., & Zhang, Q. L. (2017). Uncertainty measurement for incomplete interval-valued information systems based on α-weak similarity. *Knowledge-Based Systems*, 136, 159–171. 10.1016/j.knosys.2017.09.009

Dai, J. H., & Xu, Q. (2013). Attribute selection based on information gain ratio in fuzzy rough set theory with application to tumor classification. *Applied Soft Computing*, 13(1), 211–221. 10.1016/j.asoc.2012.07.029

Dou, H. L., Yang, X. B., Song, X. N., Yu, H. L., Wu, W. Z., & Yang, J. Y. (2016). Decision-theoretic rough set: A multi-cost strategy. *Knowledge-Based Systems*, 91, 71–83. 10.1016/j.knosys.2015.09.011

Fan, B. J., Tsang, E. C. C., Xu, W. H., & Yu, J. H. (2017). Double-quantitative rough fuzzy set based decisions. *Information Sciences*, 378, 264–281. 10.1016/j.ins.2016.05.035

Fang, Y., & Min, F. (2019). Cost-sensitive approximate attribute reduction with three-way decisions. *International Journal of Approximate Reasoning*, 104, 148–165. 10.1016/j.ijar.2018.11.003

Ferone, A. (2018). Feature selection based on composition of rough sets induced by feature granulation. *International Journal of Approximate Reasoning*, 101, 276–292. 10.1016/j.ijar.2018.07.011

Huang, Y. Y., Li, T. R., Luo, C., Fujita, H., & Horng, S. J. (2018). Dynamic fusion of multi-source interval-valued data by fuzzy granulation. *IEEE Transactions on Fuzzy Systems*, 26(6), 3403–3417. 10.1109/TFUZZ.2018.2832608

Khan, M. A., & Banerjee, M. (2008). Formal reasoning with rough sets in multiple-source approximation systems. *International Journal of Approximate Reasoning*, 49(2), 466–477. 10.1016/j.ijar.2008.04.005

Li, W. T., Pedrycz, W., Xue, X. P., Xu, W. H., & Fan, B. J. (2018). Distance-based double-quantitative rough fuzzy sets with logic operations. *International Journal of Approximate Reasoning*, 101, 206–233. 10.1016/j.ijar.2018.07.007

Li, W. T., & Xu, W. H. (2015). Double-quantitative decision-theoretic rough set. *Information Sciences*, 316, 54–67. 10.1016/j.ins.2015.04.020

Li, W. W., Jia, X. Y., Wang, L., & Zhou, B. (2019). Multi-objective attribute reduction in three-way decision-theoretic rough set model. *International Journal of Approximate Reasoning*, 105, 327–341. 10.1016/j.ijar.2018.12.008

Lin, G. P., Liang, J. Y., & Qian, Y. H. (2015). An information fusion approach by combining multi-granulation rough sets and evidence theory. *Information Sciences*, 314, 184–199. 10.1016/j.ins.2015.03.051

Lin, G. P., Liang, J. Y., Qian, Y. H., & Li, J. J. (2016). A fuzzy multi-granulation decision-theoretic approach to multi-source fuzzy information systems. *Knowledge-Based Systems*, 91, 102–113. 10.1016/j.knosys.2015.09.022

Lin, G. P., Qian, Y. H., & Li, J. J. (2012). NMGRS: Neighborhood-based multi-granulation rough sets. *International Journal of Approximate Reasoning*, 53(7), 1080–1093. 10.1016/j.ijar.2012.05.004

Ma, X.-A., & Zhao, X. R. (2019). Cost-sensitive three-way class-specific attribute reduction. *International Journal of Approximate Reasoning*, 105, 153–174. 10.1016/j.ijar.2018.11.014

Min, F., He, H. P., Qian, Y. H., & Zhu, W. (2011). Test-cost-sensitive attribute reduction. *Information Sciences*, 181(22), 4928–4942. 10.1016/j.ins.2011.07.010

Min, F., Zhang, Z. H., & Dong, J. (2018). Ant colony optimization with partial-complete searching for attribute reduction. *Journal of Computational Science*, 25, 170–182. 10.1016/j.jocs.2017.05.007

Pawlak, Z., Rough sets. (1982). International Journal of Computer &. *Information Sciences*, 11, 34–356.

Qian, J., Liu, C. H., & Yue, X. D. (2019). Multi-granulation sequential three-way decisions based on multiple thresholds. *International Journal of Approximate Reasoning*, 105, 396–416. 10.1016/j.ijar.2018.12.007

Qian, Y. H., Liang, J. Y., Yao, Y. Y., & Dang, C. Y. (2010). MGRS: A multi-granulation rough set. *Information Sciences*, 180(6), 949–970. 10.1016/j.ins.2009.11.023

Qian, Y. H., Liang, X. Y., Wang, Q., Liang, J. Y., Liu, B., Skowron, A., Yao, Y. Y., Ma, J. M., & Dang, C. Y. (2018). Local rough set: A solution to rough data analysis in big data. *International Journal of Approximate Reasoning*, 97, 38–63. 10.1016/j.ijar.2018.01.008

Qian, Y. H., Zhang, H., Sang, Y. L., & Liang, J. Y. (2014). Multi-granulation decision-theoretic rough sets. *International Journal of Approximate Reasoning*, 55(1), 225–237. 10.1016/j.ijar.2013.03.004

Qin, J., Liu, Y., & Grosvenor, R. (2018). Multi-source data analytics for AM energy consumption prediction. *Advanced Engineering Informatics*, 38, 840–850. 10.1016/j.aei.2018.10.008

Raza, M. S., & Qamar, U. (2018). Feature selection using rough set-based direct dependency calculation by avoiding the positive region. *International Journal of Approximate Reasoning*, 92, 175–197. 10.1016/j.ijar.2017.10.012

Sang, B. B., Guo, Y. T., Shi, D. R., & Xu, W. H. (2017). Decision-theoretic rough set model of multi-source decision systems. *International Journal of Machine Learning and Cybernetics*, 9, 1–14.

Sun, B. Z., Ma, W. M., & Chen, X. T. (2019). Variable precision multi-granulation rough fuzzy set approach to multiple attribute group decision-making based on λ-similarity relation. *Computers & Industrial Engineering*, 127, 326–343. 10.1016/j.cie.2018.10.009

Sun, B. Z., Ma, W. M., Li, B. J., & Li, X. N. (2018). Three-way decisions approach to multiple attribute group decision making with linguistic information- based decision-theoretic rough fuzzy set. *International Journal of Approximate Reasoning*, 93, 424–442. 10.1016/j.ijar.2017.11.015

Sun, S. L., Luo, C., & Chen, J. Y. (2017). A review of natural language processing techniques for opinion mining systems. *Information Fusion*, 36, 10–25. 10.1016/j.inffus.2016.10.004

Wang, C. Z., Huang, Y., Shao, M. W., & Chen, D. G. (2019). Uncertainty measures for general fuzzy relations. *Fuzzy Sets and Systems*, 360, 82–96. 10.1016/j.fss.2018.07.006

Wang, F. L., Wang, J. X., Cao, J. Z., Chen, C., & Ban, X. G. J. (2019). Extracting trips from multi-sourced data for mobility pattern analysis: An app-based data example. *Transportation Research Part C, Emerging Technologies*, 105, 183–202. 10.1016/j.trc.2019.05.02832764848

Wang, M., Lin, Y., Min, F., & Liu, D. (2019). Cost-sensitive active learning through statistical methods. *Information Sciences*, 501, 460–482. 10.1016/j.ins.2019.06.015

Wu, Y. X., Min, X. Y., Min, F., & Wang, M. (2019). Cost-sensitive active learning with a label uniform distribution model. *International Journal of Approximate Reasoning*, 105, 49–65. 10.1016/j.ijar.2018.11.004

Xu, W. H., & Guo, Y. T. (2016). Generalized multi-granulation double-quantitative decision-theoretic rough set. *Knowledge-Based Systems*, 105, 190–205. 10.1016/j.knosys.2016.05.021

Xu, W. H., Li, M. M., & Wang, X. Z. (2016). Information fusion based on information entropy in fuzzy multi-source incomplete information system. *International Journal of Fuzzy Systems*, 19, 1–17.

Xu, W. H., & Yu, J. H. (2017). A novel approach to information fusion in multi-source datasets: A granular computing viewpoint. *Information Sciences*, 378, 410–423. 10.1016/j.ins.2016.04.009

Xu, W. H., Zhang, X. T., & Wang, Q. R. (2012). A generalized multi-granulation rough set approach. *International Conference on Intelligent Computing*, 681–689.

Yang, X., Li, T. R., Fujita, H., & Liu, D. (2019). A sequential three-way approach to multi-class decision. *International Journal of Approximate Reasoning*, 104, 108–112. 10.1016/j.ijar.2018.11.001

Yang, X., Li, T. R., Liu, D., & Fujita, H. (2019). A temporal-spatial composite sequential approach of three-way granular computing. *Information Sciences*, 486, 171–189. 10.1016/j.ins.2019.02.048

Yao, J. T., Raghavan, V. V., & Wu, Z. (2008). Web information fusion: A review of the state of the art. *Information Fusion*, 9(4), 446–449. 10.1016/j.inffus.2008.05.002

Yao, Y. Y. (2007). Decision-theoretic rough set models. *Lecture Notes in Computer Science*, 178, 1–12.

Yao, Y. Y. (2018). Three-way decision and granular computing. *International Journal of Approximate Reasoning*, 103, 107–123. 10.1016/j.ijar.2018.09.005

Yao, Y. Y., & Lin, T. Y. (1996). Generalization of rough sets using modal logics. *Intelligent Automation & Soft Computing*, 2(2), 103–120. 10.1080/10798587.1996.10750660

Yu, J. H., Zhang, B., Chen, M. H., & Xu, W. H. (2018). Double-quantitative decision-theoretic approach to multi-granulation approximate space. *International Journal of Approximate Reasoning*, 98, 236–258. 10.1016/j.ijar.2018.05.001

Zadeh, L. A. (1997). Toward a theory of fuzzy information granulation and its centrality in human reasoning and fuzzy logic. *Fuzzy Sets and Systems*, 90(2), 111–127. 10.1016/S0165-0114(97)00077-8

Zhang, W. S., Zhang, Y. J., Zhai, J., Zhao, D. H., Xu, L., Zhou, J. H., Li, Z. W., & Yang, S. (2018). Multi-source data fusion using deep learning for smart refrigerators. *Computers in Industry*, 95, 15–21. 10.1016/j.compind.2017.09.001

Zhang, Y. B., Miao, D. Q., Wang, J. Q., & Zhang, Z. F. (2019). A cost-sensitive three-way combination technique for ensemble learning in sentiment classification. *International Journal of Approximate Reasoning*, 105, 85–97. 10.1016/j.ijar.2018.10.019

Chapter 2
Multi-Source Information Fusion Models and Methods Based on Granular Computing

Pengfei Zhang
https://orcid.org/0000-0002-7090-0325
Chengdu University of Traditional Chinese Medicine, China

Dexian Wang
Chengdu University of Traditional Chinese Medicine, China

Tao Jiang
Chengdu University of Traditional Chinese Medicine, China

ABSTRACT

The advantages of the theory of multi-source information fusion (MSIF) lie in its provision of an effective approach to integrate, analyse, and utilize information from multiple diverse sources, facilitating improved decision-making, problem-solving, and information analysis. Granular computing (GrC) is a theoretical, technical, and methodological approach within the current field of intelligent information processing and granularity modelling, aiming to simulate human-like problem-solving. Combining both approaches can enhance the efficiency and quality of fusion. This chapter presents several solutions that combine multi-source information fusion with GrC, including the multi-source homogeneous fusion model and heterogeneous data fusion method. The introduction of these methods contributes to improved handling of uncertainty, fuzziness, and multi-source complexity issues, thereby enhancing the capabilities of information processing and decision support.

DOI: 10.4018/979-8-3693-4292-3.ch002

INTRODUCTION

Problem Background

A huge challenge is presented by the diversity and complexity of data types that have resulted from the rapid development of artificial intelligence and the Internet, especially for multi-source complex data processing involving multi-valued data, multi-information source data, and heterogeneous data. It is worthwhile to research how to ingeniously integrate and mine the complex data that has been gathered from various sources so that each information source can be used in combination with the others. Multi-source information fusion (MSIF), also known as multi-sensor information fusion, originated in the 1970s and is a comprehensive interdisciplinary subject. In reality, combining information from multiple sources is how humans and other animals in nature come to have an understanding of what is objective. Throughout the entire cognitive process, humans and animals first perceive objective objects from a variety of perspectives using their various senses (such as smell, hearing, touch, and taste) or specific functions, resulting in a large amount of complementary and redundant information. Then, the brain processes the perceived information in accordance with predetermined rules, leading to a unified cognition of the actual objects. This process of MSIF can help us understand things more comprehensively and accurately, thereby making smarter and more effective decisions.

Obviously, MSIF is a straightforward and simple concept. However, many practical considerations, such as the type and number of information sources, the distribution or scheduling of sensors, the computing and communication capabilities of the fusion system, efficient fusion algorithms, etc., must be made in order to create a multi-source information fusion system that is truly useful. Up to now, MSIF is still not a very mature development direction, and it has great development prospects in basic theory and application fields. There are three constraints on the development of MSIF: (1) The uncertainty of homogeneous/heterogeneous information of data types; (2) The inherent complexity introduced by multi-source information and multi-tasking; (3) There is currently no mathematics Tools to uniformly describe such complex problems. Therefore, it is very necessary to seek in-depth and effective theories and methods to describe and deal with MSIF problems.

Granular Computing (GrC) is a theory, technology and method for simulating human thinking in the current field of intelligent information processing and granular modelling research. From the perspective of computational intelligence, GrC is a natural model for simulating human thinking and solving large-scale complex problems. It replaces exact solutions with feasible and satisfactory approximate solutions to achieve the purpose of simplifying problems and improving problem-solving efficiency. By granularizing complex data and using information granules as the fundamental unit of computation in place of samples at the level of data analysis and processing, GrC increases computational efficiency. GrC and MSIF are two techniques that mimic how the human brain processes complex information in its entirety. MSIF emphasizes the thorough processing of various information sources or heterogeneous data, whereas GrC concentrates on the representation of the fundamental granular structure of the information system and complex problem solving.

The research significance of this work is to utilize the idea of MSIF combined with the technical methods related to GrC to synthesize the complex data from multiple sources to obtain potential, novel, correct and useful knowledge, so as to obtain more accurate and stable results.

A Brief Review of MSIF

The term "fusion", which is based on the comprehensive definition of multi-source knowledge, started to appear in publications in the late 1970s. Since then, MSIF theories and technology have advanced quickly as a separate discipline and have been successfully used in systems for tracking and identifying multiple targets, strategic warning and defense systems, and military command automation systems. Additionally, MSIF is gradually spreading to various civilian industries such as remote sensing monitoring, medical diagnosis, electronic commerce, wireless communication, and defect diagnostics (Llinas & Waltz, 1990; Hall, 1992; Hall, 2001).

Every year, the amount of data created worldwide is growing at a rate of 30%. Everything around us generates data through social media interchange, which is then relayed by a variety of networks, sensors, and mobile devices. With the entire understanding of information in a Big Data context, data acquisition is no longer constrained to a single data source. There are many sources for the storing and description of data. The links between data samples from diverse data sources, which express information between data samples from various perspectives, imply a variety of knowledge structure information (Zhang et al., 2021).

A multiple-metric learning approach was suggested by Zhang et al. (Zhang et al., 2013) to jointly learn a set of ideal homogeneous or heterogeneous metrics in order to combine the data gathered from various sensors for joint classification. In 2018, Che (Che et al., 2018) employed evidence theory, probability theory and information entropy to address the information fusion and numerical characterization of uncertain data in a multi-source information systems. Due to the fact that the Bayesian network is one of the most effective models in the field of probabilistic knowledge representation and reasoning and can effectively address the uncertainty problem of fault diagnosis, the authors (Cai et al., 2014) proposed a multi-source information fusion based fault diagnosis methodology using Bayesian network to improve the diagnostic accuracy of ground-source heat pump (GSHP) systems, especially for multiple-simultaneous faults.

The outcomes of the fusion will be irrational due to the ambiguity or dispute. Additionally, data may be gathered as complex numbers that can't be handled by current techniques. Zhang & Xiao (Zhang & Xiao, 2022) used the complex evidence theory (CET) to address the aforementioned problems. CET is an extension of the Dempster-Shafer evidence theory, in which the complex mass function (CMF) is used to simulate the mass function.

An MSIF model is proposed (Zhang et al., 2023) for outlier identification in order to identify the objects that deviate from the predicted ones following fusion, often known as anomalies or outliers. This two-stage methodology combines the fusion of data from several sources with the outlier identification of the merged data. The first step merges several information sources into a single information source based on the lowest uncertainty technique and uses information sets to establish uncertainty criteria for information source values. The second stage creates knowledge granules using the Gaussian kernel approach for possibility modeling based on the fused data.

Many scholars have studied the techniques of MSIF from different fields such as safety risk assessment (Guo & Zhang, 2021; Wang et al. 2022), heterogeneous network embedding (Li et al., 2020), Fault detection (Li et al., 2018) and so on.

A Brief Review on the Combination GrC and MSIF

Granular computing (GrC) was proposed by Zadeh (Zadeh,1979), its core concept is dividing information into various "granules" in accordance with certain relationships, and then to process the information granules to retrieve the information in the data (Zadeh,1998).

GrC and MSIF are two techniques to simulate the human brain for the comprehensive processing of complex information. GrC emphasizes the representation of the fundamental granular structure of information systems and complex problem solving, whereas MSIF emphasizes the thorough processing of various information sources or heterogeneous data. In recent years, many scholars have successfully applied the idea of GrC to the field of MSIF (Wei & Liang, 2019; Zhang et al., 2021; Xu et al., 2023). Multi-source data differs from general complex data in that the relationship between the information or data is more complex, the data scale is larger, and knowledge acquisition is more challenging. Therefore, this idea of information granulation is more suitable for knowledge acquisition and data analysis of complex data, such as stock credit scoring (Saberi et al., 2013), medical diagnosis (Wang et al., 2019; Li et al., 2020) and fault diagnosis (Lu et al. 2020) and other fields.

Rough set theory, evidence theory, and information entropy theory are the main theoretical foundations for the intersection research between GrC and MSIF. For example, Qian et al. proposed a fusion model of optimistic and pessimistic multi-granulation rough sets (Qian et al., 2010), and based on this, studied a fusion model of multi-granulation decision-theoretic rough sets (Qian et al., 2014). In order to establish uncertainty measurement indicators for the roughness of ordered information systems and the quality of approximate classification, Xu et al. proposed optimistic and pessimistic multi-granularity dominant rough set models to deal with the multi-granulation fusion problem of partially ordered data (Xu et al., 2012; Xu et al., 2017). Li & Zhang used information entropy to handle the information fusion method of a multi-source incomplete information system (Li & Zhang, 2017). Sang et al. proposed a decision rough set model based on conditional entropy, decision support and average fusion of multi-source data (Sang et al., 2018). Guo et al. considered a dual-weighted multi-source information fusion method by introducing the internal uncertainty and external correlation of information sources (Guo et al., 2017). Che et al. constructed a decision fusion model based on multi-granulation variable precision rough sets, aiming to achieve multi-source real-valued data fusion (Che et al., 2018). Moreover, Zhang and his collaborators studied the development of MSIF in granular computing from different perspectives, including hybird data processing and uncertainty measurement (Li et al., 2019a, 2019b; Xie et al., 2019; Zeng et al., 2020, Zhang et al., 2021), medical diagnosis (Wang et al., 2019; Li et al., 2020), feature selection (Yuan, et al., 2021a; Wang et al., 2021; Liu et al., 2022; Wang et al., 2022a; Deng et al., 2022; Yang et al., 2022; Yuan et al., 2021b; Zhang et al., 2023b; Deng et al., 2023), multi-view fusion and clustering (Wang et al., 2022b; Wang et al., 2023), outlier detection (Zhang et al., 2023a), multi-granularity fusion (Zhang et al., 2022), and others (Yang & Zhang., 2021; Yang & Zhang., 2023).

The Contribution of This Chapter

In order to obtain a consistent explanation or description of the measured object and to improve the performance of the information system, MSIF is based on multiple (homogeneous or heterogeneous) information sources combined in space or time in accordance with a specific standard. Fusion models typically combine data, feature, and decision information from three levels, starting at the fusion level. In this chapter, we introduce the approaches of MSIF in GrC from three perspectives, namely multi-source homogeneous fusion, heterogeneous attribute fusion and multi-granulation rough set fusion model. The following are the main contributions of this chapter.

1. The introduction of a unified description and modeling approach for multi-source homogeneous information systems. The neighborhood granularity structure is built using the neighborhood rough set model, and the uncertainty measures are built using the granularity calculation concept. A Sup-Inf fusion function is created based on the proposed uncertainty measure to fuse a multi-source isomorphic information system into a single-source information system while taking into account the uncertainty of the fusion of multiple information sources.

2. In order to handle categorical, numerical, and heterogeneous data, a feature selection method is created using the neighborhood rough set model as a unifying framework. The notion of neighborhood combination entropy (NCE) is introduced first. It may represent the likelihood of neighboring granule pairs that can probably be distinguished from one another. Then, under the condition of taking decision attributes into consideration, the conditional neighborhood combination entropy (cNCE) based on NCE is proposed. Additionally, some characteristics and connections between cNCE and NCE are derived.

According to the above literature analysis, we formally summarize some basic concepts and definitions used in the chapter. In Section 2, some basic concepts are introduced. In Section 3, the multi-source homogenous fusion model is proposed. Based on neighborhood combination entropy, the heterogenous attribute fusion method is presented in Section 4. Finally, the conclusions of this chapter and future work are given.

BASIC CONCEPTS AND DEFINITIONS

Single-Source Information System (SsIS)

Definition 2.1: (Zhang et al., 2021) Let (U, A, V, f) be a SsIS, where U is a non-empty finite object set and A is a non-empty finite attribute set. V is named an union of attribute domain, $V = \sum_{a \in A} V_a$,where V_a is the attribute domain of a. An information function $f \cdot U \times A \rightarrow V$ that satisfies any $a \in A$ and $x \in U$, with $a(x) \in V_a$. If $A = C \cup \{d\}$, then $(U, C \cup \{d\}, V, f)$ is called the decision information system (DIS), where C is the conditional attribute set, and d is the decision attribute set.

For ease of use, $(U, C \cup \{d\}, V, f)$ is shortened to $(U, C \cup \{d\})$. For each $R \subseteq C$, $IND(R)$ is named indiscernibility relation on U, indicated as

$$IND(R) = \{(x, y) \in U \times U \mid \forall a \in R, a(x) = a(y)\}$$

.

Obviously, $IND(R)$is an equivalence relation on U. For convenience, $IND(R)$can be written R.According to the equivalence relation, then lower and upper approximates of $X(X \subseteq U)$is defined as

$$\underline{R}(X) = \{x \in U:[x]_R \subseteq X\} \text{ and}$$

$$\overline{R}(X) = \{x \in U:[x]_R \cap X \neq \phi\}$$

.

respectively, where $[x]_R = \{y \in U:xRy\}$ that contains $X$is referred to as equivalence class. For any $X \subseteq U$,, the universe Ucan be divided into positive (POS), boundary (BND) and negative (NEG) regions, as follows.

$$\begin{cases} POS(X) = \underline{R}(X) \\ BND(X) = \overline{R}(X) - \underline{R}(X). \\ NEG(X) = U - \overline{R}(X) \end{cases}$$

Neighborhood Rough Set (NRS)

Definition 2.2: (Zhang et al., 2022c) Let $U = \{x_1, x_2, \cdots, x_n\}$be a nonempty set and $|U| = n$. Given $P \subseteq C$, for any $x, y, z \in U$, a distance function $d_P{:}d_P(x,y) \to \mathfrak{R}^+$,$\mathfrak{R}^+$is the set of nonnegative real numbers, and it satisfies the following conditions:

(1) $d_P(x,y) \geq 0 \cdot d_P(x,x) = 0$(Nonnegative)
(2) $d_P(x,y) = d_P(y,x)$(Symmetry)
(3) $d_P(x,y) \leq d_P(x,z) + d_P(y,z)$(Triangle Inequality)

$\forall P \subseteq A$, the Minkowski distance, can be used to express the distanced_P, i.e.,

$$d_P^p(x,y) = \sqrt[p]{\sum_{a \in P} |a(x) - a(y)|^p}.$$

More specifically, if $p = 1$, then $d_P^p$is the Manhattan distance;$p = 2$, it becomes the Euclidean distance; and it becomes the Chebyshev distance when $p = \infty$.

Definition 2.3: (Zhang et al., 2022c)$\forall x, y \in U, P \subseteq C$. Given a parameter $\delta \geq 0$,the neighborhood class (denoted as$N_P^\delta(x)$) of xw.r.t. P can defined as

$N_P^\delta(x) = \{y : \Delta_p(x,y) \leq \delta\}$.

Then, N_P^δ is called neighborhood relation on U, the neighborhood matrix $(N_P^\delta)_M = (r_{ij}^P)_{n\times n}$, where if $\Delta_p(x,y) \leq \delta$, then $r_{ij}^P = 1$; otherwise, $r_{ij}^P = 0$. For a neighborhood relation, we have:

(1) $r_{ij}^P = 1$(Reflexivity)
(2) $r_{ij}^P = r_{ji}^P$(Symmetry)

It is clear that the neighborhood relation is a type of similarity relation and that it fulfills reflexivity and symmetry.

Definition 2.4: (Kryszkiewicz, 1998) Let $(U, C \cup \{d\}, V, f, \delta)$ be a single-source neighborhood information system. Given$P \subseteq C$and$\delta \geq 0$. The neighborhood lower and upper approximations of X, indicated by$\underline{N_P^\delta}(X)and\overline{N_P^\delta}(X)$, respectively. Namely,

$$\underline{N_P^\delta}(X) = \{x \in U : N_P^\delta(x) \subseteq X\}, \quad \overline{N_P^\delta}(X) = \{x \in U : N_P^\delta(x) \cap X \neq \varnothing\}.$$

MULTI-SOURCE HOMOGENEOUS INFORMATION FUSION MODEL

In this section, we consider how to fuse multiple information sources into a single information source, which not only reduces the number of information sources, but also helps to fuse effective information from multiple information sources.

Definition 3.1: Suppose

$$MsHoIS = \{HoIS_i | HoIS_i = (U, A, V_i, f_i), i = 1, 2, \cdots, m\}$$

is a multi-source homogeneous information system (HsHoIS), which satisfies the following conditions:

(1) $U$is sample (object) set, and it is non-empty finite set;
(2) $HoIS_i$ expresses the i-th information source, and m is the number of information source;
(3)$A$is the attribute set of $HoIS_i$;
(4) V_a is the value of attribute and $a \in A$;
(5) For any $x \in U$and$a \in A$, $f_i : U \times A \to V_i$ is the information function, $a_i(x) \in V_i$is the homogenous data in i-th $HoIS_i$.

Moreover, an HsHoIS can also be written as

$$(U, HsHoIS) = (HoIS_1, HoIS_2, \cdots, HoIS_m)$$

Definition 3.2: Let

$$MsHoIS = \{HoIS_i | HoIS_i = (U, A, V_i, f_i), i = 1, 2, \cdots, m\}$$

be a HsHoIS. If there exist a missing value $* \in V_a$ in $HoIS_i$, then it can be called the incomplete homogenous information subsystem, denoted as $IHoIS_i$. Then, a MsHoIS can described as

$$(U, HsHoIS) = (IHoIS_1, IHoIS_2, \cdots, HoIS_m)$$

,

where $IHoIS_1$ and $IHoIS_2$ express the first information and the second information source are incomplete in this MsHoIS.

Definition 3.3: Given the

$$MsHoIS = \{HoIS_i | HoIS_i = (U, A, V_i, f_i), i = 1, 2, \cdots, m\},$$

for any $x, y \in U$ and $a \in A$, the distance between x and y can be defined by

$$d_a(x,y) = \begin{cases} 0, \text{if } a_i(x) = a_i(y); \\ 1, \text{if } x \neq y, a_i(x) = * \vee a_i(y) = *; \\ 0, \text{if } x \neq y, a_i(x) \neq * \wedge a_i(y) \neq * \wedge a_i(x) = a_i(y); \\ \frac{|a_i(x) - a_i(y)|}{4\sigma_a}, \text{if } x \neq y, a_i(x) \neq * \wedge a_i(y) \neq * \wedge a_i(x) \neq a_i(y), a \text{ is numeric }; \\ \begin{cases} 0 & a_i(x) = a_i(y) \\ 1 & otherwise \end{cases}, \text{if } x \neq y, a_i(x) \neq * \wedge a_i(y) \neq *, a \text{ is categorical,} \end{cases}$$

where σ_a is the standard deviation of the numeric attribute a.

Definition 3.4: Given the

$$MsHoIS = \{HoIS_i | HoIS_i = (U, A, V_i, f_i), i = 1, 2, \cdots, m\}.$$

For any $x, y \in U$ and $a \in P \subseteq A$, the homogeneous Euclidean distance metric (HEDM) on attribute a of i-th information source $HoIS_i$ can be denoted as

$$HEDM_P^i(x,y) = \begin{cases} \sqrt{\frac{1}{l}\sum_{l=1}^{l} \omega_{a_l} \times d_{a_l}^2(x,y)}, & a \text{ is numeric ;} \\ \begin{cases} 0 & x = y \\ 1 & otherwise \end{cases}, & a \text{ is categorical,} \end{cases}$$

where l is the number of attribute, and $|P| = l$; ω_{a_l} is the weight of the attribute a_l; $d_{a_l}^2(x,y)$ is the distance between samples x and y w.r.t. attribute a_l.

Definition 3.5: Given the

$$MsHoIS = \{HoIS_i | HoIS_i = (U, A, V_i, f_i), i = 1, 2, \cdots, m\}.$$

If $P \subseteq A$, for any $x, y \in U$ and $\delta \in [0,1]$, a neighborhood relation (NR) of i-th information source $HoIS_i$ can be denoted as

$$N_P^\delta = \{(x,y) \in U \times U : HEDM_P^i(x,y) \leq \delta\}.$$

Moreover, the NR of U is written as a relation matrix

$$(NBR_P^i)_M = (NBR_M^i(x,y))_{n \times n},$$

where $(NBR_P^i)_M = \begin{cases} 1, & HEDM_P^i(x,y) \leqslant \delta, \\ 0, & \text{else.} \end{cases}$

Definition 3.6: If $P \subseteq A$, for any $\delta \in [0,1]$, the neighborhood information entropy of i-th information source $HoIS_i$ can be denoted as

$$NIE_i^\delta(P) = -\sum_{i=1}^{n} \frac{1}{n} \log_2\left(\frac{|N_P^\delta(x_i)|}{n}\right).$$

The Infimum-Measure Approach in MsHIS

In this section, an unsupervised fusion approach based on neighborhood information entropy is proposed for multi-source homogeneous data.

At first, we introduce a basic framework (Yager, 2004) to view and implement the multi-source data fusion process. Let s be a solution, and some elements from S. Whether a solution is approved by an information source or not might be viewed as a "vote". Then, $Sup_i(s)$denotes a support for solution $s$from ith information source. $F$is the function that combines the support from each information source. Subsequently, we have,

$$Sup(s) = Sup_{s \in S}(F_1(s), F_2(s), \ldots, F_m(s)),$$

where $Sup_i(s)$is named the supremum-total support for s. Similarly,

$$Inf(s) = Inf_{s \in S}(F_1(s), F_2(s), \ldots, F_m(s)),$$

where $Inf_i(s)$is named the infimum-total support for s.

As we all know, the greater the information entropy, the greater the uncertainty, and the same is true for neighborhood information entropy. In order to reduce uncertainty, we hope to reduce the neighborhood information entropy as much as possible. The specific performance is the degree of support for neighborhood classes in neighborhood learning. Given this, we can obtain the following definition of infimum-measure approach.

Definition 4.1: Let $\delta \in [0,1]$, for any $a \in A_i$,the neighborhood information entropy with the minimum value of attribute a will be selected as the attribute of the new information system, it is denoted as

$$\mathrm{InfN}^{\delta}(a) = \mathrm{Inf}(F(I_1(a)), F(I_2(a)), \ldots, F(I_m(a))),$$

where $F = NIE_i^{\delta}(\{a\})$.

Multi-Source Homogeneous Information Fusion Algorithm Based on Infimum-Measure (MsHIF)

In this section, we use the minimum uncertainty measurement principle to fuse multi-source homogeneous data. The algorithm is described as follows.

Algorithm 1: The algorithm of MsHIF

Input: An MsHoIS $MsHoIS = \{HoIS_i \mid HoIS_i = (U, A, V_i, f_i), i = 1, 2, \cdots, m\}$, $\delta \in [0,1]$
Output: The single-source information system (U, N)
1: Normalize the original information sources by max-min approach, i.e., $Norm(a(x_j)) = \frac{a(x_j) - \min_{a(x_j)}}{\max_{a(x_j)} - \min_{a(x_j)}}$, where $\max_{a(x_j)}$ and $\min_{a(x_j)}$ are the maximum and minimum information source values, respectively.
2: Compute the distance of each information source by **Definition 3.3** and **Definition 3.4**.
3: Compute the neighborhood relation and relation matrix by **Definition 3.5**.
4: Compute neighborhood information entropy of each information source by **Definition 3.6**.
5: Compute *k*th attribute all information sources by **Definition 4.1**, $A \leftarrow \varnothing$; $N \leftarrow N \cup \{a_k\}$. Obtain the total neighborhood information entropy of each information source about attribute a, and select the attribute corresponding to the smallest neighborhood information entropy as the attribute of the fused single-source information system.

In the above-stated decision steps of the MsHIF method, let l denotes the number of all attributes, n denotes the number of all objects, $m$denotes the number of information sources. The complexity of Steps 1 to 5 is shown as follows:

$O(nml)$, $O(n^2ml)$, $O(nml)$, $O(nml)$, $O(ml)$.

Based on the above analysis, the overall complexity of the presented MsHIF method is $O(n^2ml)$.

Example

Table 1 shows an MsHoIS, where

$MsHoIS = \{IHoIS_1, HoIS_2, HoIS_3, IHoIS_4\}$,

"*" refers to the missing value, $U = \{x_1, x_2, x_3, x_4, x_5, x_6\}$shows six samples, $A = \{a_1, a_2, a_3, a_4\}$represents attribute set. $IHoIS_1$,$HoIS_2$,$HoIS_3$and $IHoIS_4$indicates four information sources, where $IHoIS_1$and $IHoIS_4$are incomplete.

Table 1. An MsHoIS

U	$IHoIS_1$				$HoIS_2$				$HoIS_3$				$IHoIS_4$			
	a_1	a_2	a_3	a_4	a_1	a_2	a_3	a_4	a_1	a_2	a_3	a_4	a_1	a_2	a_3	a_4
x_1	4	1.8	140	6300	6	3.8	150	6000	4	3.8	150	6200	6	*	150	6300
x_2	6	3.2	200	5000	6	3.1	190	6000	8	3.1	190	5000	*	3.2	200	5000
x_3	6	2.8	168	*	6	3.1	170	4800	6	3.0	170	4800	6	3.8	168	5000

continued on following page

Table 1. Continued

U	$IHoIS_1$				$HoIS_2$				$HoIS_3$				$IHoIS_4$			
	a_1	a_2	a_3	a_4	a_1	a_2	a_3	a_4	a_1	a_2	a_3	a_4	a_1	a_2	a_3	a_4
x_4	*	2.8	172	5500	8	4.9	200	4100	8	5.0	180	4800	*	2.8	172	5500
x_5	4	*	208	5700	4	4.1	295	6000	4	2.2	295	6000	4	3.5	180	5000
x_6	4	2.2	110	5200	4	2.2	110	5200	4	2.2	150	5500	4	2.2	110	*

From Table 1, $IHoIS_1$ is the first information source, taking this subsystem as an example, calculate the distance between x_1 and x_2 w.r.t. four attributes (a_1, a_2, a_3, a_4) as follows.

$$d_{a_1}(x_1, x_2) = 0.51;$$

$$d_{a_2}(x_1, x_2) = 0.71\ ;$$

$$d_{a_3}(x_1, x_2) = 0.45$$

and

$$d_{a_4}(x_1, x_2) = 0.72$$

.

Subsequently, the HEDM matrix $((HEDM_P^1)_M)$ of the first information source $IHoIS_1$ can be calculated as follows.

$$(HEDM_P^1)_M = \begin{pmatrix} 0 & 0.30 & 0.31 & 0.31 & 0.29 & 0.17 \\ 0.30 & 0 & 0.26 & 0.27 & 0.30 & 0.25 \\ 0.31 & 0.26 & 0 & 0.35 & 0.38 & 0.31 \\ 0.31 & 0.27 & 0.35 & 0 & 0.36 & 0.29 \\ 0.29 & 0.30 & 0.39 & 0.36 & 0 & 0.32 \\ 0.17 & 0.25 & 0.31 & 0.29 & 0.31 & 0 \end{pmatrix}.$$

Let $\delta = 0.25$. According to **Definition 3.5**, we have

$$(NBR_p^1)_M = \begin{pmatrix} 1 & 0 & 0 & 0 & 1 & 1 \\ 0 & 1 & 0 & 0 & 0 & 1 \\ 0 & 0 & 1 & 0 & 0 & 0 \\ 0 & 0 & 0 & 1 & 0 & 0 \\ 0 & 0 & 0 & 0 & 1 & 0 \\ 1 & 1 & 0 & 0 & 0 & 1 \end{pmatrix}.$$

By the idea of neighborhood, then

$$N_P^{0.25}(x_1) = \{x_1, x_6\}; N_P^{0.25}(x_2) = \{x_2, x_6\}; N_P^{0.25}(x_3) = \{x_3\};$$

$$N_P^{0.25}(x_4) = \{x_4\}; N_P^{0.25}(x_5) = \{x_5\} \text{and } N_P^{0.25}(x_6) = \{x_1, x_6\}.$$

Hence, the neighborhood granular structure of attribute set Pcan be denoted as

$$S_1^{0.25}(P) = (\{x_1, x_6\}, \{x_2, x_6\}, \{x_3\}, \{x_4\}, \{x_5\}, \{x_1, x_6\})$$

.

According to **Definition 3.6**, we can obtain the following values of neighborhood information entropy, it is shown as in Table 2.

Table 2. The neighborhood information entropy of information sources for different attributes

$IHoIS_1$	$HoIS_2$	$HoIS_3$	$IHoIS_4$
1.5	1.5	1.5	1.3
2.3	2.3	1.5	1.9
2.3	1.5	0.7	1.3
1.9	1.5	2.3	1.8

From Table 2, for attribute

a_1, $IHoIS_1(a_1) = 1.5$, $IHoIS_1(a_2) = 2.3$, $IHoIS_1(a_3) = 2.3$, $IHoIS_1(a_4) = 1.9$;

$HoIS_2(a_1) = 1.5$, $IHoIS_2(a_2) = 2.3$, $IHoIS_2(a_3) = 1.5$, $IHoIS_2(a_4) = 1.5$;

$HoIS_3(a_1) = 1.5$; $HoIS_3(a_2) = 1.5$, $HoIS_3(a_3) = 0.7$, $HoIS_3(a_4) = 2.3$;

$IHoIS_4(a_1) = 1.3$; $IHoIS_4(a_2) = 1.9$; $IHoIS_4(a_3) = 1.3$; $IHoIS_4(a_4) = 1.8$.

We have

$\mathrm{InfN}^{0.25}(a_1) = (F(IHoIS_1(a_1), HoIS_2(a_1), IHoIS_3(a_1), IHoIS_4(a_1))) = 1.3,$

then attribute$a_1$of the fourth information source can be selected as the attribute a_1 of the fused information system. Similarly, we have

$\mathrm{InfN}^{0.25}(a_2) = (F(IHoIS_1(a_2), HoIS_2(a_2), IHoIS_3(a_2), IHoIS_4(a_2))) = 1.5;$

$\mathrm{InfN}^{0.25}(a_3) = (F(IHoIS_1(a_3), HoIS_2(a_3), IHoIS_3(a_3), IHoIS_4(a_3))) = 0.7;$

$\mathrm{InfN}^{0.25}(a_4) = (F(IHoIS_1(a_4), HoIS_2(a_4), IHoIS_3(a_4), IHoIS_4(a_4))) = 1.5$

.

Let (U, N)be a new information fusion after fusion. Then,

$(U, N) = (V_{a_1}^{IHoIS_4}, V_{a_2}^{HoIS_3}, V_{a_3}^{HoIS_3}, V_{a_4}^{HoIS_2}).$

Table 3. The new information fusion after fusion(U, N)

a_1	a_2	a_3	a_4
6300	3.8	150	6000
5000	3.1	190	6000

continued on following page

Table 3. Continued

a_1	a_2	a_3	a_4
5000	3.0	170	4800
5500	5.0	180	4100
5000	2.2	295	6000
*	2.2	150	5200

Therefore, the new information system after fusion(U,N) can be obtained, as shown in Table 3. Table 3 fuses the information with the minimum neighborhood entropy among all information sources, which not only reduces the number of information sources, but also facilitates the complementation and integration of information.

HETEROGENEOUS ATTRIBUTE FUSION METHODS

In this section, we continue to study data from the perspective of neighborhoods, mainly dealing with the redundancy and fusion issues of categorical data, numerical data, and heterogeneous data. According to the idea of neighborhood decision information system, the concept of neighborhood heterogeneous decision information system (NHDIS) is proposed as follows.

Definition 5.1: Given an $NDIS = (U, N \cup \{d\}, V, f)$, if $N = N^{num} \cup N^{cat}$ (N^{num} and N^{cat} are the numerical and categorical data, respectively), for any $P \subseteq N$ and $\delta \geq 0$, then an NHDIS can be denoted as the six-tuple $NHDIS^{\delta} = (U, N \cup \{d\}, V, f, \delta)$.

The heterogeneous distance (HD) function is used to determine the separation between two samples in order to deal with heterogeneous data. Following, we determine the distance between numerical samples in an NHDIS using the Chebyshev distance. The 0-1 approach is used to determine distances for categorical data.

Definition 5.1: Given $NHDIS^{\delta} = (U, N \cup \{d\}, V, f, \delta)$, and $N = N^{num} \cup N^{cat}$. If

$$P_1 \subseteq N^{num}, P_2 \subseteq N^{cat} \text{ and } P = P_1 \cup P_2 \subseteq N,$$

then for each $x, y \in U$, the HD between x and y w.r.t. P is denoted by

$$\mathrm{HD}_P(x,y) = \max_{a \in P}\{\mathrm{HD}_{\{a\}}(x,y)\},$$

where

$$\mathrm{HD}_{\{a\}}(x,y) = \begin{cases} \mathrm{overlap}_{\{a\}}(x,y), & a \in P_1 \\ \mathrm{rn\_diff}_{\{a\}}(x,y), & a \in P_2 \end{cases}, \text{ and } \mathrm{overlap}_a(x,y)$$

$$= \begin{cases} 0, & a(x) = a(y) \\ 1, & \text{otherwise}, \end{cases}$$

$$rn\_diff_a(x,y) = |a(x) - a(y)|$$

.

Moreover, $(HD_P)_M = (HD_P(x,y))_{n \times n}$ is called heterogeneous distance matrix.

Definition 5.2: Given $NHDIS^\delta = (U, N \cup \{d\}, V, f, \delta)$ and $P \subseteq N$. If $P_1 \subseteq P$ and $P_2 \subseteq P$ are the numerical and categorical attributes, respectively. Then, the neighborhood granule of the object x induced by P_1, P_2, and $P_1 \cup P_2$ can be defined by

(1) $N^\delta_{P_1}(x) = \{x \mid HD_{P_1}(x,y) \leq \delta, y \in U\}$;
(2) $N^\delta_{P_2}(x) = \{x \mid HD_{P_2}(x,y) = 0, y \in U\}$;
(3) $N^\delta_{P_1 \cup P_2}(x) = \{x \mid HD_{P_1}(x,y) \leq \delta \wedge HD_{P_2}(x,y) = 0, y \in U\}$, and ^ is the "and" operator.

Then, the heterogenous neighborhood of x w.r.t. P can be calculated by

$$N^\delta_P(x) = N^\delta_{P_1 \cup P_2}(x) = N^\delta_{P_1}(x) \cap N^\delta_{P_2}(x).$$

In addition,

$N^\delta_{P_1}(x) = \bigcap_{a_1 \in P_1} N^\delta_{\{a_1\}}(x)$, $N^\delta_{P_2}(x) = \bigcap_{a_2 \in P_2} N^\delta_{\{a_2\}}(x)$, we have $N^\delta_P(x) = \bigcap_{a \in P} N^\delta_{\{a\}}(x)$.

Neighborhood Measures and Its Properties

In this subsection, several uncertainty measures based on neighborhoods are proposed.

Definition 5.3: Given $NHDIS^\delta = (U, N \cup \{d\}, V, f, \delta)$ and $\delta \geq 0$. If $P \subseteq N$, then the neighborhood combination entropy (NCE) w.r.t. P can be denoted as

$$NCE^\delta(P) = \frac{1}{n} \sum_{i=1}^{n} \frac{C_n^2 - C^2_{|N^\delta_P(x)|}}{C_n^2}.$$

Suppose $P, Q \subseteq N$, the NCE w.r.t. neighborhood relation $N^\delta_{P \cup Q}(x)$ can be denoted as

$$NCE^\delta(P,Q) = \frac{1}{n} \sum_{i=1}^{n} \frac{C_n^2 - C_{|N^\delta_{P \cup Q}(x)|}}{C_n^2}.$$

If the input variable is P and decision attribute is D, then the above equation can be written as

$$\text{NCE}^{\delta}(P,Q)=\frac{1}{n}\sum_{i=1}^{n}\frac{C_n^2-C_{|N_P^{\delta}(x)\cap[x]_D|}}{C_n^2}.$$

Definition 5.4: Given $P,Q \subseteq N$, the conditional neighborhood combination entropy of Q can be defined as

$$CNCE^{\delta}(Q|P)=\frac{1}{n}\sum_{i=1}^{n}\frac{C^2_{|N_P^{\delta}(x)|}-C^2_{|N_{P\cup Q}^{\delta}(x)|}}{C_n^2}.$$

Especially, if $P$is the input variable, and $D$is the decision attribute and

$D = \{d_1,d_2,\cdots,d_l\}$, then $N_{P\cup D}^{\delta}(x)=N_P^{\delta}(x)\cap D_x$,

we have

$$CNCE^{\delta}(P\cup D)=\frac{1}{n}\sum_{i=1}^{n}\frac{C^2_{|N_P^{\delta}(x)|}-C^2_{|N_P^{\delta}(x)\cap D_x|}}{C_n^2}.$$

Proposition 5.1: Given $P,Q \subseteq N$,we have

$CNCE^{\delta}(Q|P)=CNCE^{\delta}(P\cup Q)-NCE^{\delta}(P)$.

Proof: According to **Definition 5.4**, we have

$$\begin{aligned}CNCE^{\delta}(Q|P)&=\frac{1}{n}\sum_{i=1}^{n}\frac{C^2_{|N_P^{\delta}(x_i)|}-C^2_{|N_{P\cup Q}^{\delta}(x_i))|}}{C_n^2}\\&=\frac{1}{n}\sum_{i=1}^{n}\frac{C_n^2+C^2_{|N_P^{\delta}(x_i)|}-C_n^2-C^2_{|N_{P\cup Q}^{\delta}(x_i))|}}{C_n^2}\\&=\frac{1}{n}\sum_{i=1}^{n}\frac{C_n^2-C^2_{|N_{P\cup Q}^{\delta}(x_i)|}}{C_n^2}-\frac{1}{n}\sum_{i=1}^{n}\frac{C_n^2-C^2_{|N_P^{\delta}(x_i)|}}{C_n^2}\\&=CNCE^{\delta}(P\cup Q)-NCE^{\delta}(P).\end{aligned}$$

This completes the proof.

Definition 5.5: Given $NHDIS^{\delta} = (U,N\cup\{d\},V,f,\delta)$ and $\delta \geq 0$. If $P \subseteq N$, then the neighborhood combination granulation is defined as

$$NCG^{\delta}(P) = \frac{1}{n}\sum_{i=1}^{n}\frac{C^2_{|N^{\delta}_p(x))|}}{C^2_n},$$

where $\frac{C^2_{|N^{\delta}_p(x))|}}{C^2_n}$ refers to the probability of pairs of elements in term of neighborhood class within the total number of pairs of elements on the universe U.

Corollary 5.1: Given $P \subseteq N$,we have

$$0 \leq NCG^{\delta}(P) \leq 1.$$

Proof: Obviously.

Corollary 5.2: Given $P \subseteq N$, we have

$$NCE^{\delta}(P) + NCG^{\delta}(P) = 1.$$

Proof: According to **Definitions 5.3 and 5.5**, then

$$\begin{aligned} & NCE^{\delta}(P) + NCG^{\delta}(P) \\ & = \frac{1}{n}\sum_{i=1}^{n}\frac{C^2_{|N^{\delta}_p(x_i))|}}{C^2_n} + \frac{1}{n}\sum_{i=1}^{n}\frac{C^2_n - C^2_{|N^{\delta}_p(x_i)|}}{C^2_n} \\ & = \frac{1}{n}\sum_{i=1}^{n}\left(\frac{C^2_{|N^{\delta}_p(x_i))|}}{C^2_n} + \frac{C^2_n - C^2_{|N^{\delta}_p(x_i)|}}{C^2_n}\right) \\ & = \frac{1}{n}\cdot n = 1 \end{aligned}$$

.

This completes the proof.

An Attribute Selection Algorithm

Definition 6.1: Given $NHDIS^{\delta} = (U, N \cup \{d\}, V, f, \delta)$ and $P \subseteq A$. P is a reduction if and only if the following two conditions are both true:

(1) $CNCE^{\delta}(D|P) \leq CNCE^{\delta}(D|N)$;

(2) $\mathrm{CNCE}^{\delta}(D|P - \{a\}) > \mathrm{CNCE}^{\delta}(D|P), \forall a \in P$

In **Definition 6.1**, (1) indicates that the CNCE of the reduction set P cannot be lower than the CNCE of all attribute; and (2) limits the minimality of the reduction set.

Definition 6.2: Given $NHDIS^{\delta} = (U, N \cup \{d\}, V, f, \delta)$and $\delta \geq 0$. For any $a \in P \subseteq N$, then the inner significance of a w.r.t. P is denoted by

$$\mathrm{Sig}_{\mathrm{in}}(a,P,D) = \mathrm{CNCE}^{\delta}(D|P - \{a\}) - \mathrm{CNCE}^{\delta}(D|P).$$

In **Definition 6.2**, for any $a \in P$, if a is inner significance w.r.t. P, then

$$\mathrm{Sig}_{\mathrm{in}}(a,P,D) > 0,$$

otherwise, $\mathrm{Sig}_{\mathrm{in}}(a,P,D) \leq 0$. Moreover, the core of attribute set of $P$is denoted

$$\mathrm{Core}_P = \{a \in P | \mathrm{Sig}_{\mathrm{in}}(a,P,D) > 0\}.$$

Definition 6.3: Given $NHDIS^{\delta} = (U, N \cup \{d\}, V, f, \delta)$and $\delta \geq 0$. For any $a \in (N - P)$, then the outer significance of a w.r.t. P is denoted by

$$\mathrm{Sig}_{\mathrm{out}}(a,P,D) = CNCE^{\delta}(D|P) - CNCE^{\delta}(D|P \cup \{a\}).$$

In **Definition 6.3**, for $a \in (N - P)$, if $a$is outer significance w.r.t. P, then $\mathrm{Sig}_{\mathrm{out}}(a,P,D) > 0$,otherwise, $\mathrm{Sig}_{\mathrm{out}}(a,P,D) \leq 0$.

In this paper, a heuristic algorithm for attribute selection is proposed, which takes the two attribute significances as heuristic functions. In other words, an attribute reduction algorithm based on conditional neighborhood combination entropy (ARCNCE) is designed

Algorithm 2: The algorithm of ARCNCE

Input: A $NHDIS^{\delta} = (U, N \cup \{d\}, V, f, \delta)$, $\delta \in [0,1]$
Output: A reduct RED
1: Initialize $Core_P = \varnothing$,$RED = \varnothing$;
2: Compute $\mathrm{Sig}_{\mathrm{in}}(a,P,D)$by **Definition 6.2**. If $\mathrm{Sig}_{\mathrm{in}}(a,P,D) > 0$,then $Core_N \leftarrow Core_N \cup \{a\}$;
3:$RED \leftarrow Core_N$;
4: Compute $\mathrm{Sig}_{\mathrm{out}}(a,RED,D)$by **Definition 6.3**;
5: Select $a_0 = \arg\max\{\mathrm{Sig}_{\mathrm{out}}(a,RED,D), a \in (N - RED)\}$;
6: $RED \leftarrow RED \cup \{a_0\}$;
7: Compute $CNCE(D|RED) \leq CNCE(D|N)$;
8: for any $a \in RED$, compute $CNCE(D|RED - \{a\}) \leq CNCE(D|RED)$;
9:$RED \leftarrow RED - \{a\}$.

In Algorithm 2, let$m$denotes the number of all attributes, n denotes the number of all objects, . The complexity of Steps 1 to 3 is $O(n^2m^2)$, which is to obtain the indispensable attributes; The complexity of Steps 4 to 6 is $O(n^2m^2)$, which is to obtain the best candidate attribute from the remaining attribute set $N - RED$ to the selected attribute subset RED until relative reduct RED is obtained. The complexity of Steps 7 to 9 is $O(n^2|RED|^2)$, which is to delete redundant attributes from the relative reduct *RED*. Therefore, the worst search complexity is $O(n^2 m^2)$in Algorithm 2.

Example

In this subsection, an example will be given to fuse heterogeneous attributes and how to obtain reduction result. In Table 2, it represents a NHDIS, where

$$U = \{x_1, x_2, x_3, x_4, x_5, x_6\} N^{num} = \{a_1, a_2, a_3\}, N^{cal} = \{a_4, a_5\}.$$

Table 4. The original NHDIS

U	a_1	a_2	a_3	a_4	a_5	d
x_1	0.8	3.8	150	1	2	Y
x_2	0.6	3.1	190	1	1	Y
x_3	0.4	3	170	2	2	N
x_4	0.6	5	180	2	2	Y
x_5	0.1	4.5	295	2	1	N
x_6	0.3	2.2	150	1	3	N

First, we normalize the numerical data of the original data of Table 4. According to max-min method, the normalized results are shown on Table 5.

Table 5. The normalized NHDIS

U	a_1	a_2	a_3	a_4	a_5	d
x_1	1	0.57	0	1	2	Y
x_2	0.71	0.32	0.28	1	1	Y
x_3	0.43	0.29	0.14	2	2	N
x_4	0.61	1	0.21	2	2	Y
x_5	0	0.82	1	2	1	N
x_6	0.29	0	0	1	3	N

Then, let $P_1 = \{a_1, a_2, a_3\}, P_2 = \{a_4, a_5\}$ and $\delta = 0.3$. For numerical data, by **Definition 5.1**, we have

$$M\left(HD_{P_1}\right) = \begin{bmatrix} 0 & 0.2857 & 0.5714 & 0.4286 & 1.0000 & 0.7143 \\ 0.2857 & 0 & 0.2857 & 0.6786 & 0.7241 & 0.4286 \\ 0.5714 & 0.2857 & 0 & 0.7143 & 0.8621 & 0.2857 \\ 0.4286 & 0.6786 & 0.7143 & 0 & 0.7931 & 1.0000 \\ 1.0000 & 0.7241 & 0.8621 & 0.7931 & 0 & 1.0000 \\ 0.7143 & 0.4286 & 0.2857 & 1.0000 & 1.0000 & 0 \end{bmatrix}_{6\times 6}$$

$$\Rightarrow M\left(N_{P_1}^{0.3}\right) = \begin{bmatrix} 1 & 1 & 0 & 0 & 0 & 0 \\ 1 & 1 & 1 & 0 & 0 & 0 \\ 0 & 1 & 1 & 0 & 0 & 1 \\ 0 & 0 & 0 & 1 & 0 & 0 \\ 0 & 0 & 0 & 0 & 1 & 0 \\ 0 & 0 & 1 & 0 & 0 & 1 \end{bmatrix}_{6\times 6}$$

For categorical data, we can directly obtain the neighborhood relation matrix (namely, δ=0), then

$$M\left(N_{P_2}^{0}\right) = \begin{bmatrix} 1 & 0 & 0 & 0 & 0 & 0 \\ 0 & 1 & 0 & 0 & 0 & 0 \\ 0 & 0 & 1 & 1 & 0 & 0 \\ 0 & 0 & 1 & 1 & 0 & 0 \\ 0 & 0 & 0 & 0 & 1 & 0 \\ 0 & 0 & 0 & 0 & 0 & 1 \end{bmatrix}_{6\times 6}.$$

Finally, by **Definition 5.2**, we have

$$M(N_{P_1 \cup P_2}^{\delta}) = M(N_{P_1}^{0.3}) \wedge M(N_{P_2}^{0}) = \begin{bmatrix} 1 & 0 & 0 & 0 & 0 & 0 \\ 0 & 1 & 0 & 0 & 0 & 0 \\ 0 & 0 & 1 & 0 & 0 & 0 \\ 0 & 0 & 0 & 1 & 0 & 0 \\ 0 & 0 & 0 & 0 & 1 & 0 \\ 0 & 0 & 0 & 0 & 0 & 1 \end{bmatrix}_{6\times 6}.$$

Algorithm 2 is used to reduce the NHDIS in Table 2, and the process of calculation is described as follows. At first, we perform Steps 1-3, for any $a \in N$, we can calculate its inner significance $\mathrm{Sig}_{\mathrm{in}}(a, N, D)$.Then,

$\mathrm{Sig}_{\mathrm{in}}(a_1, N, D) = 0, \mathrm{Sig}_{\mathrm{in}}(a_2, N, D) = 0.0222 > 0,$

$\mathrm{Sig}_{\mathrm{in}}(a_3, N, D) = 0, \mathrm{Sig}_{\mathrm{in}}(a_4, N, D) = 0$ and $\mathrm{Sig}_{\mathrm{in}}(a_5, N, D) = 0.$

Hence, we can obtain the core attribute set $P = \{a_2\}$. Next, we perform Steps 4-6 to calculate the outer significance $\text{Sig}_{\text{out}}(a, N, D)$ $(a \in N - P)$. We find the best candidate attribute from $N - P$, and add the corresponding attribute to reduction P. By calculation,$a_4$anda_1 satisfy the condition, so the reduction set of features is further obtained $P = \{a_2, a_4, a_1\}$. Finally, we perform Steps 7-9, and it is found that there are no redundant attributes in the candidate reduction set $P = \{a_2, a_4, a_1\}$. Hence, the final reduction set as $P = \{a_2, a_4, a_1\}$.

CONCLUSION

This chapter gives two solutions for multi-source information fusion, namely multi-source homogeneous information fusion model and heterogeneous attribute fusion method. Both methods make use of the concept of neighborhoods. The first method creates uncertainty metrics in accordance with the minimum uncertainty method, which can effectively fuse multiple sources of information. The second method creates a new neighborhood combinatorial entropy by combining categorical and numerical attributes and uses it to select attributes.

The main contribution of this chapter is by combining the ideas of multi-source information fusion and granular computing. Neighborhood rough set is one of the important methodologies in granular computing, and the two proposed methods help to extend the application scenarios of granular computing and promote the development of multi-source information fusion in granular computing.

In future work, the following aspects can be focused on (1) multimodal data fusion. Most of the existing data are in the form of multimodal, how to granularize the multimodal data with the help of the idea of granular computing, and then design the model of multisource information fusion for integration and fusion is worthy of research; (2) multi-granulation fusion. Constructing a multi-granulation fusion mechanism can be studied from a multi-scale, hierarchical perspective.

REFERENCES

Cai, B., Liu, Y., Fan, Q., Zhang, Y., Liu, Z., Yu, S., & Ji, R. (2014). Multi-source information fusion based fault diagnosis of ground-source heat pump using Bayesian network. *Applied Energy*, 114, 1–9. 10.1016/j.apenergy.2013.09.043

Che, X., Mi, J., & Chen, D. (2018). Information fusion and numerical characterization of a multi-source information system. *Knowledge-Based Systems*, 145, 121–133. 10.1016/j.knosys.2018.01.008

Deng, Z., Li, T., Deng, D., Liu, K., Zhang, P., Zhang, S., & Luo, Z. (2022). Feature selection for label distribution learning using dual-similarity based neighborhood fuzzy entropy. *Information Sciences*, 615, 385–404. 10.1016/j.ins.2022.10.054

Deng, Z., Li, T., Liu, K., Zhang, P., & Deng, D. (2023). Feature selection based on probability and mathematical expectation. *International Journal of Machine Learning and Cybernetics*, 1–15.

Fan, W., & Xiao, F. (2022). A complex Jensen–Shannon divergence in complex evidence theory with its application in multi-source information fusion. *Engineering Applications of Artificial Intelligence*, 116, 105362. 10.1016/j.engappai.2022.105362

Guo, K., & Zhang, L. (2021). Multi-source information fusion for safety risk assessment in underground tunnels. *Knowledge-Based Systems*, 227, 107210. 10.1016/j.knosys.2021.107210

Guo, Y., Tsang, E. C., & Xu, W. (2017, July). A weighted multi-granulation decision-theoretic approach to multi-source decision systems. In *2017 International Conference on Machine Learning and Cybernetics (ICMLC)* (Vol. 1, pp. 202-210). IEEE. 10.1109/ICMLC.2017.8107765

Hall, D. (1992). *Mathematical Techniques in Multisenor Data Fusion*. Artech House Publisher.

Hall, D. (2001). *Handbook of Multisenor Data Fusion*. CRC Press. 10.1201/9781420038545

Kryszkiewicz, M. (1998). Rough set approach to incomplete information systems. *Information Sciences*, 112(1-4), 39–49. 10.1016/S0020-0255(98)10019-1

Li, B., Pi, D., Lin, Y., Khan, I. A., & Cui, L. (2020). Multi-source information fusion based heterogeneous network embedding. *Information Sciences*, 534, 53–71. 10.1016/j.ins.2020.05.012

Li, H., Huang, H. Z., Li, Y. F., Zhou, J., & Mi, J. (2018). Physics of failure-based reliability prediction of turbine blades using multi-source information fusion. *Applied Soft Computing*, 72, 624–635. 10.1016/j.asoc.2018.05.015

Li, M., & Zhang, X. (2017). Information fusion in a multi-source incomplete information system based on information entropy. *Entropy (Basel, Switzerland)*, 19(11), 570. 10.3390/e19110570

Li, Z., Zhang, P., Ge, X., Xie, N., & Zhang, G. (2019b). Uncertainty measurement for a covering information system. *Soft Computing*, 23(14), 5307–5325. 10.1007/s00500-018-3458-5

Li, Z., Zhang, P., Ge, X., Xie, N., Zhang, G., & Wen, C. F. (2019a). Uncertainty measurement for a fuzzy relation information system. *IEEE Transactions on Fuzzy Systems*, 27(12), 2338–2352. 10.1109/TFUZZ.2019.2898158

Li, Z., Zhang, P., Xie, N., Zhang, G., & Wen, C. F. (2020). A novel three-way decision method in a hybrid information system with images and its application in medical diagnosis. *Engineering Applications of Artificial Intelligence*, 92, 103651. 10.1016/j.engappai.2020.103651

Liu, K., Li, T., Yang, X., Yang, X., Liu, D., Zhang, P., & Wang, J. (2022). Granular cabin: An efficient solution to neighborhood learning in big data. *Information Sciences*, 583, 189–201. 10.1016/j.ins.2021.11.034

Llinas, J., & Waltz, E. (1990). *Multisensor Data Fusion*. Artech Housse publisher.

Lu, C., Xu, P., & Cong, L. H. (2020). Fault diagnosis model based on granular computing and echo state network. *Engineering Applications of Artificial Intelligence*, 94, 103694. 10.1016/j.engappai.2020.103694

Saberi, M., Mirtalaie, M. S., Hussain, F. K., Azadeh, A., Hussain, O. K., & Ashjari, B. (2013). A granular computing-based approach to credit scoring modeling. *Neurocomputing*, 122, 100–115. 10.1016/j.neucom.2013.05.020

Sang, B., Guo, Y., Shi, D., & Xu, W. (2018). Decision-theoretic rough set model of multi-source decision systems. *International Journal of Machine Learning and Cybernetics*, 9(11), 1941–1954. 10.1007/s13042-017-0729-x

Wang, D., Li, T., Deng, P., Wang, H., & Zhang, P. (2022b). Dual graph-regularized sparse concept factorization for clustering. *Information Sciences*, 607, 1074–1088. 10.1016/j.ins.2022.05.101

Wang, D., Li, T., Deng, P., Zhang, F., Huang, W., Zhang, P., & Liu, J. (2023). A generalized deep learning clustering algorithm based on non-negative matrix factorization. *ACM Transactions on Knowledge Discovery from Data*, 17(7), 1–20. 10.1145/3584862

Wang, D., Li, T., Huang, W., Luo, Z., Deng, P., Zhang, P., & Ma, M. (2023). A multi-view clustering algorithm based on deep semi-NMF. *Information Fusion*, 99, 101884. 10.1016/j.inffus.2023.101884

Wang, G., Li, T., Zhang, P., Huang, Q., & Chen, H. (2021). Double-local rough sets for efficient data mining. *Information Sciences*, 571, 475–498. 10.1016/j.ins.2021.05.007

Wang, P., Zhang, P., & Li, Z. (2019). A three-way decision method based on Gaussian kernel in a hybrid information system with images: An application in medical diagnosis. *Applied Soft Computing*, 77, 734–749. 10.1016/j.asoc.2019.01.031

Wang, T., Liu, R., & Qi, G. (2022). Multi-classification assessment of bank personal credit risk based on multi-source information fusion. *Expert Systems with Applications*, 191, 116236. 10.1016/j.eswa.2021.116236

Wang, Z., Chen, H., Yuan, Z., Yang, X., Zhang, P., & Li, T. (2022a). Exploiting fuzzy rough mutual information for feature selection. *Applied Soft Computing*, 131, 109769. 10.1016/j.asoc.2022.109769

Wei, W., & Liang, J. (2019). Information fusion in rough set theory: An overview. *Information Fusion*, 48, 107–118. 10.1016/j.inffus.2018.08.007

Xie, X., Li, Z., Zhang, P., & Zhang, G. (2019). Information structures and uncertainty measures in an incomplete probabilistic set-valued information system. *IEEE Access : Practical Innovations, Open Solutions*, 7, 27501–27514. 10.1109/ACCESS.2019.2897752

Xu, W., Huang, X., & Cai, K. (2023). Review of multi-source information fusion methods based on granular computing. *Journal of Data Acquisition & Processing*, 38(2), 245–261.

Xu, W., Li, W., & Zhang, X. (2017). Generalized multigranulation rough sets and optimal granularity selection. *Granular Computing*, 2(4), 271–288. 10.1007/s41066-017-0042-9

Xu, W., Sun, W., Zhang, X., & Zhang, W. (2012). Multiple granulation rough set approach to ordered information systems. *International Journal of General Systems*, 41(5), 475–501. 10.1080/03081079.2012.673598

Yager, R. R. (2004). A framework for multi-source data fusion. *Information Sciences*, 163(1-3), 175–200. 10.1016/j.ins.2003.03.018

Yang, F., & Zhang, P. (2021). Using 2-tuple Linguistic Model for Multi-source Set-valued Information Fusion. In *2021 16th International Conference on Intelligent Systems and Knowledge Engineering (ISKE)* (pp. 557-560). IEEE.

Yang, F., & Zhang, P. (2023). MSIF: Multi-source information fusion based on information sets. *Journal of Intelligent & Fuzzy Systems*, 44(3), 4103–4112. 10.3233/JIFS-222210

Yang, X., Chen, H., Li, T., Zhang, P., & Luo, C. (2022). Student-t kernelized fuzzy rough set model with fuzzy divergence for feature selection. *Information Sciences*, 610, 52–72. 10.1016/j.ins.2022.07.139

Yuan, Z., Chen, H., Xie, P., Zhang, P., Liu, J., & Li, T. (2021a). Attribute reduction methods in fuzzy rough set theory: An overview, comparative experiments, and new directions. *Applied Soft Computing*, 107, 107353. 10.1016/j.asoc.2021.107353

Yuan, Z., Chen, H., Zhang, P., Wan, J., & Li, T. (2021b). A novel unsupervised approach to heterogeneous feature selection based on fuzzy mutual information. *IEEE Transactions on Fuzzy Systems*, 30(9), 3395–3409. 10.1109/TFUZZ.2021.3114734

Zadeh, L. A. (1979). Fuzzy sets and information granularity. *Fuzzy sets, fuzzy logic, and fuzzy systems: Selected papers*, 433-448.

Zadeh, L. A. (1998). Some reflections on soft computing, granular computing and their roles in the conception, design and utilization of information/intelligent systems. *Soft Computing*, 2(1), 23–25. 10.1007/s005000050030

Zeng, J., Li, Z., Zhang, P., & Wang, P. (2020). Information structures and uncertainty measures in a hybrid information system: Gaussian kernel method. *International Journal of Fuzzy Systems*, 22(1), 212–231. 10.1007/s40815-019-00779-8

Zhang, G., Li, Z., Zhang, P., & Xie, N. (2021). Information structures and uncertainty in an image information system. *Journal of Intelligent & Fuzzy Systems*, 40(1), 295–317. 10.3233/JIFS-191628

Zhang, P., Li, T., Luo, C., & Wang, G. (2022a). AMG-DTRS: Adaptive multi-granulation decision-theoretic rough sets. *International Journal of Approximate Reasoning*, 140, 7–30. 10.1016/j.ijar.2021.09.017

Zhang, P., Li, T., Wang, G., Luo, C., Chen, H., Zhang, J., Wang, D., & Yu, Z. (2021). Multi-source information fusion based on rough set theory: A review. *Information Fusion*, 68, 85–117. 10.1016/j.inffus.2020.11.004

Zhang, P., Li, T., Wang, G., Wang, D., Lai, P., & Zhang, F. (2023a). A multi-source information fusion model for outlier detection. *Information Fusion*, 93, 192–208. 10.1016/j.inffus.2022.12.027

Zhang, P., Li, T., Yuan, Z., Deng, Z., Wang, G., Wang, D., & Zhang, F. (2023b). A possibilistic information fusion-based unsupervised feature selection method using information quality measures. *IEEE Transactions on Fuzzy Systems*, 31(9), 2975–2988. 10.1109/TFUZZ.2023.3238803

Zhang, P., Li, T., Yuan, Z., Luo, C., Liu, K., & Yang, X. (2022c). Heterogeneous feature selection based on neighborhood combination entropy. *IEEE Transactions on Neural Networks and Learning Systems*.35925855

Zhang, P., Li, T., Yuan, Z., Luo, C., Wang, G., Liu, J., & Du, S. (2022b). A data-level fusion model for unsupervised attribute selection in multi-source homogeneous data. *Information Fusion*, 80, 87–103. 10.1016/j.inffus.2021.10.017

Zhang, Y., Zhang, H., Nasrabadi, N. M., & Huang, T. S. (2013). Multi-metric learning for multi-sensor fusion based classification. *Information Fusion*, 14(4), 431–440. 10.1016/j.inffus.2012.05.002

Chapter 3
Community Discovery in Complex Network Big Data

Qingbin Ji
https://orcid.org/0000-0002-5591-6783
North University of China, China

ABSTRACT

Community structure is a topological property of complex networks, and community discovery is the foundation of community structure study. Community discovery technology could serve as an important tool to provide strong theoretical support for big data analysis, research, and application, thereby aiding people's prediction and decision-making behavior. The authors aim to provide a systematic review of the fundamental and application of community structure theory in complex network big data studies, with a particular focus on the promoting role of community discovery in specific re-search fields. This chapter mainly consists of three parts: 1) first introduced the theoretical basis of community discovery, 2) second introduced community discovery methods categorizing from technology, and 3) last introduced new tasks and application of community discovery in big data. By reading this chapter, readers should gain a comprehensive understanding of how to introduce community thinking in big data analysis and contribute to improving decision-making ability.

INTRODUCTION

The 2021 Nobel Prize in Physics recognized the fundamental role of complex systems in natural sciences and awarded for groundbreaking contributions to understanding complex physical systems (The Nobel Committee for Physics, 2021).

DOI: 10.4018/979-8-3693-4292-3.ch003

In the past two or three decades, the study on complex systems has stepped into big data, mainly, at least in part, to the development of information technology leading to a rapid improvement in people's ability to produce, collect, and manage massive amounts of data. For example, Facebook alone generated 4 petabytes of data per day (Souravlas et al., 2021). This trend has a significant impact on complex decision making, and brought new challenges to the storage, management, and mining of complex big data.

New tools and methods need to be developed to extract valuable insights from massive datasets, thus rising to a new paradigm of big data (Vespignani, 2018), one of which analyzing and understanding big data from the perspective of networks. Complex network is an abstract model for understanding complex systems in the real world, such as social networks, the Internet, food network, and metabolic network, et al (Strogatz, 2001). There are many suggested methods for analyzing complex network structures, including community structure. It has become one of the conditions for composing to cite the concept of community structure in related fields (Molontay & Nagy, 2019).

Community discovery is the foundation of community structure study, as only, at least in some certain, by identifying underly communities in the network can we accurately and effectively analyze and understand the functions of the network with its structure (Yang & Leskovec, 2012), and these functions play an important role in decision-making of complex. Community discovery is a typical interdisciplinary research field with numerous participating scholars, research paths, and technical methods. Scholars have conducted thorough discussions on community discovery issues from different perspectives, promoting in-depth research in different fields. Nowadays, with the widespread introduction of complex networks in big data analysis, community discovery technology has been extended to application fields by concepts like community, such as subgraph (Mcguire & Nguyen, 2014; Pulgar-Rubio et al., 2017). Currently, there is limited literature definitely on the relationship between community discovery and complex decision-making, at least not as much as we have found. But we believe that community discovery, as a fundamental tool and key problem, can provide strength support for complex decision-making study.

The following will be a review of these studies and the latest work. The remaining part of this article is organized as follows. The first section introduced the theoretical basis of community discovery, including the basic concepts of community discovery and the historical origins of community discovery study. The second section introduced community discovery methods, focusing on using technology and limited to using only network topology. The third part introduced the application of community discovery in big data, categorizing from the perspective of completing new tasks and modern technology, especially to deep leaning. Finally, there is a summary.

THEORETICAL BASIS OF COMMUNITY DISCOVERY

By abstracting the individuals of complex systems as nodes and the connections between individuals as edges, complex systems can be modeled as *complex networks* (Newman, 2010), abbreviated as *networks*. The study object of community discovery is complex networks, which is a fundamental task in the field of network science, and graph theory is the mathematical foundation of network science research[1].

Before the emergence of network science, problems like community discovery had appeared in various forms in different disciplines, especially in the fields of graph partition, social network analysis, and cluster analysis. Many concepts and methods related to community discovery have migrated from these three fields.

In 2002, Girvan and Newman (Girvan & Newman, 2002) first introduced the concept of community structure. *Community structure* refers to the natural presence of modules (or clusters, groups) in complex networks with a higher degree of aggregation called *communities*. The connections between nodes within these modules are closer than the connections between nodes between modules. A simple network with four natural communities indicates that the internal nodes of the four natural communities circled by dashed lines are more tightly connected (Ji et al, 2020), as shown in Figure 1.

Figure 1. Demonstration of a simple network with four natural communities

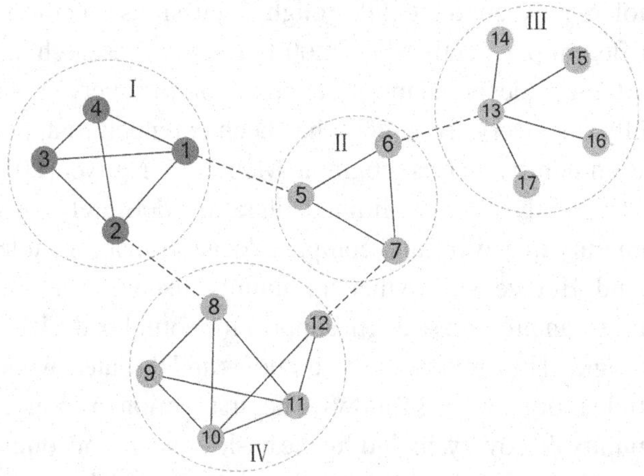

Natural communities exist in society, such as families, villages, towns, countries, governments, enterprises, work groups, and friend circles, which can all be considered as natural communities. Community modules also appear in many other network systems, such as users with similar purchasing interests in online shopping websites

(Zhao et al, 2021), articles on related topics in citation networks (Jin et al, 2019), and components in infectious disease transmission networks (Marcel & Jones, 2010), et al. By analyzing and identifying community modules, we can gain a meso-level understanding of the structure and behavior of networks, which can help analyze network characteristics and reduce the difficulty of studying complex systems. For example, identifying communities and their borders can more effectively distinguish the roles of nodes in social networks (Zhao et al, 2021), identifying semantic communities can improve the interpretability of machine learning in the context of natural language processing (Jin et al, 2019), and observing the different dynamic processes that occur in the network at the community level can better explain the complex behavior of real systems (Yan, 2022).

Figure 2. Karate network with two ground-truth communities

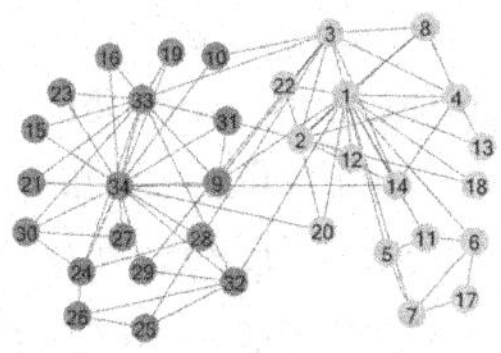

Note. Each community is represented in distinct colors.

Community structure is currently a popular topic in network science research. But communities in complex networks are often implicated under the topology of the network. The Karate network (Zachary, 1977) has two ground-truth communities represented in distinct colors, as shown in Figure 2. Although the nodes have been optimized and arranged, it is still difficult to directly find out the communities in such a small network with only our eyes. Community discovery techniques are needed to explore and reveal the community structure of the network.

Concepts

In mathematics, a *graph* is a complex composed of sets of nodes and edges, both of which can have multiple properties, from which various types of networks can be derived. As a simple form of graph, an unweight undirected network[2] is denoted by $G = (V, E)$, where $V = \{i \mid i = 1, 2, \ldots\}$ is a set of nodes and $E = \{(i, j) \mid i, j \in E\}$ is a set of edges. This kind of network is the main study object in this article, and even in community discovery.

Some topological properties are defined to describe the network structure. The total number of nodes in the network is denoted by $n = |V|$, known as the *order* of the network, and the total number of edges is denoted by $m = |E|$, as the *size* of the network. The adjacency matrix of network G is a real symmetric matrix with zero diagonal elements, which denoted by $A = (a_{ij})_{n\times n}$, where $a_{ij} = 1$ when $(i, j) \in E$; otherwise, $a_{ij} = 0$. Nodes i and j are *neighbors* to each other if $e\ (i, j) \in E$. The neighbors set of node i is denoted by $V(i) = \{j \mid e\ (i, j) \in E\}$, and $V[i] = \{i\} \cup V(i)$ is the *closed* neighbors set of node i. The *degree* of node i is defined as $d_i = \sum_{j\in V} a_{ij} = | V(i) |$, and the degree of network G is defined as $d = \sum_{i\in V} d_i = 2m/n$. For directed network, there are in-degree $d_i^{in} = \sum_{j\in V} a_{ji}$ and out-degree $d_i^{out} = \sum_{j\in V} a_{ij}$ of node i, respectively. The *network density* of network G is defined as $\rho = 2m/(n(n-1)) = d/(n\text{-}1)$, and the *node network density* of node i is defined as the network density of the subgraph $G[V[i]]$, which is the neighbor subgraph of node i (Ji et al, 2020).

More complex topological indices are developed to capture the properties of complex networks. For example, a *path* is an ordered sequence of nodes, $\{i,j,\ldots\}$, where adjacent nodes i,j are neighbors to each other. If there is at least one path between any pair of nodes in a network, it is said that the network is *connected*; otherwise, the network *disconnected*. The *shortest path* between two nodes in a network refers to the path with the least number of edges connecting the two endpoints. The *distance* between nodes refers to the number of edges on the shortest path between two endpoints. The *average path length* of a network, also known as the *characteristic path length* or *average distance*, refers to the average distance between any two nodes, denoted as L.

In addition, most real-world network systems, also known as complex networks, generally share some more complex topological properties, such as:

- *Sparsity*, referring to the phenomenon that the actual number of edges in a real complex network is much smaller than the maximum possible number of edges, which can be characterized by a dense power law, $m(t) \sim n^{\alpha}\ (t)$, $1 < \alpha < 2$, where $m(t)$ and $n(t)$ are the number of nodes and edges in the network evolution process, respectively.
- *Small world effect*, referring to the phenomenon where the characteristic path length L of complex networks is noticeably short. In the case of a fixed average degree, the characteristic path length of a complex network is generally scaled by the logarithm of the number of nodes n, or even smaller.
- *Scale-free* property. The degree distribution of complex networks has a right skewed distribution characteristics with the highest value on the left side of the mean degree, which usually has the characteristics of a power-law distribution, that is, $P(d) \sim d^{\gamma}$, $2 \leq \gamma \leq 3$, where $P(d)$ is the probability of the degree of a randomly selected node is exactly d.

- Community structure, characterizing the phenomenon of uneven edge distribution in complex networks at a mesoscopic level. It is believed that community structure is an organized manifestation of complex networks, and therefore, both regular and random graphs do not include communities.

A *partition* of network G refers to dividing all nodes of the network into k disjoint subsets of nodes, denoted by $P = \{V_m \mid m = 1,\ldots,k, k \geq 2, V_m \neq \emptyset, \cup_{m=1}^{k} V_m = V, V_m \cap_{m\neq n} V_n = \emptyset\}$. If $V_m \cap_{m\neq n} V_n \neq \emptyset$, it indicates there is overlap between subsets of nodes, that is communities have nodes in common, where the term "*cover*" usually instead of "partition".

There is currently no unified and consistent study on the definition of community. Four main primary of community definitions are found in literature.

1) The set of nodes with high similarity is called a community. Common techniques for measuring node similarity are *structural similarity*, which is the number of common neighbours that two nodes i,j have, denoted by $n_{ij} = |V(i) \cap V(j)|$. Rather than using the raw count n_{ij}, however, one typically normalizes it in some way, leading to measures such as cosine angle (Newman, 2012), $\delta_{ij} = n_{ij}(d_i d_j)^{-1/2}$, or uses another normalized metrics based on random walk theory (Zhang et al., 2018). In clustering analysis, the content information of nodes is constantly used to map nodes to high-dimensional space and then estimate similarity, such as emotional communities (Jin et al., 2019).
2) The node sets with larger intrinsic degrees are called communities by comparing the intrinsic and extrinsic degrees of the node sets, such as clique community (Palla et al., 2005), $\forall i \in V_m, d_i^{in} = |V_m| - 1$, strong community, $\forall i \in V_m, \exists d_i^{in} \geq d_i^{out}$, and weak community (Radicchi et al, 2004), $\exists \sum d_i^{in} \geq \sum d_i^{out}$. To meet the optimization conditions, one has set thresholds on such definitions, although these designs have certain degree of arbitrariness (Liu et al., 2020).
3) Some studies indirectly define communities by defining a quantitative indicator of community structure. For example, modularity-based methods usually transform community detection into optimization modeling and consider the partition that maximizes modularity as the community structure of the network (Newman & Girvan, 2004). Some more quantitative indicators can be found in (Yang & Leskovec, 2012).
4) Other studies directly start with community discovery methods and conclude that the results of the discovery are the communities. The label propagation (LPA) algorithms map the problem of community discovery to that of local stability in the label propagation process and output a set of nodes labeled with the same label as communities (Raghavan et al., 2007).

Overall, a *community* in a network $G = (V, E)$ refers to a connected node-induced subgraph of V_m to G, where V_m is a tightly connected set of nodes, $V_m \subset V$, $V_m \neq \varnothing$. *Community discovery*, also known as *community detection*, refers to the identification of tightly connected modules and module structures in a connected network, by using information encoded in the network topology.

Traditional Methods

Figure 3. Illustration of hierarchical clustering for karate network

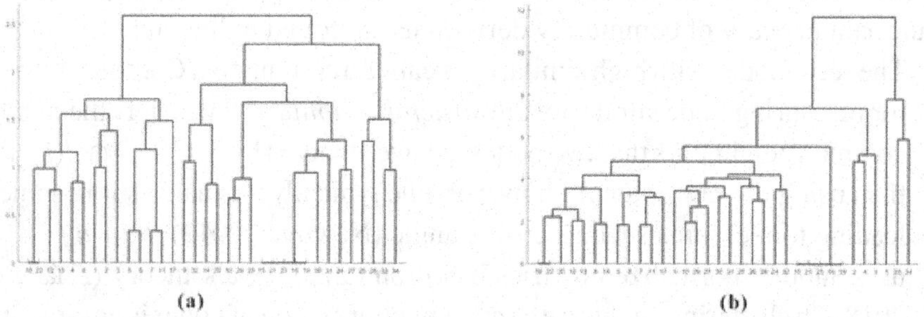

Note. Clustering by the technology of Single-linkage clustering: (a) evaluate similarity of nodes by cosine angle, and (b) evaluate dissimilarity of nodes by Euclidean distance.

Traditional community discovery methods include clustering detection and graph partitioning. Clustering methods include partition clustering and aggregation clustering, and the output result is a dendrogram. A horizontal slice at any level of this dendrogram can provide a community structure, as shown in Figure 3.

Hierarchical Clustering

These methods are bottom-up approaches, and the central principle is that: If we can derive a measure of how strongly nodes in a network are connected together, then by grouping the most similar nodes we can divided the network into multiple communities (Zhang et al., 2018).This grouping is done in a hierarchical manner, also known as hierarchical clustering, and has now developed into an entire family of techniques. Fig. 3 is an illustration of the results of hierarchical clustering of the Karate network using single link clustering technology. In the latest studies, techniques such as random walks (Zhang et al., 2018) and network embedding learning (Duan et al., 2020) are used to define node similarity. The shortcomings of such methods include: 1) The definition of structural similarity sometimes clearly does not conform to people's intuitive cognition: Two nodes that are connected to each other but do not have a common neighbor have $\delta_{ij} = 0$, but two pairs of nodes that are not connected but have common neighbors have $\delta_{ij} > 0$; 2) Although tightly connected community cores can be obtained, peripheral nodes are often lost, as shown in Figure 3 (b).

Partition Clustering

The partitioning clustering method is top-down, first treats all nodes as a module, and then continuously splits them. Common techniques include splitting methods and k-means clustering. The GN (Girvan-Newman) algorithm (Girvan & Newman, 2002; Newman & Girvan, 2004) is a typical splitting method that uses edge betweenness as a measure of edge centrality, with a time cost of $O(n^3)$. Green et al. (Green & Bader, 2013) and Sharmila et al. (Sharmila et al., 2020) improved the method, but the computation is still time-consuming. K-means clustering embeds each data point into a metric space, pre-allocates k centroids, and re-estimates the centroids in each iteration. When the position of the centroid stabilizes, output the clustering result (Bai et al, 2017; Cai et al, 2019). The main drawbacks of technology are: 1) Need to specify the number of output clusters; 2) Implied a dense network that does not conform to the sparse characteristics of complex networks.

Graph Partitioning

Most graph partitioning algorithms assume $k = 2$, which means dividing the network into two equal parts one time. But by continuously iterating into two parts, the graph can be divided into the final required number of groups, although it cannot be guaranteed that the required number of communities is a multiple of 2. The most widely used methods among them are the Kernighan-Lin (KL) algorithm and spectral bisection method.

KL algorithm is a greedy optimization algorithm that optimizes a profit function that represents the difference between the number of edges inside a module and the number of edges between modules and has a time complexity of $O(n^2 \log n)$, or $O(n^2)$ in sparse network. The quality of KL algorithm's output strongly depends on the initial partition, so currently, KL algorithm is commonly used to improve partitions found through other techniques.

Spectral graph partitioning theory is a method used for graph segmentation, focusing on the second smallest eigenvalue λ_2 of the Laplacian matrix, called algebraic connectivity (Pothen et al, 1990), of a graph: if $\lambda_2 > 0$, then the graph is connected; The smaller λ_2, the better the separation of the graph. Assuming the adjacency matrix as the feature matrix, there are two clusters C_1 and C_2 in G, define an objective function, or called *Cut Size*, $R = \sum_{i \in C_1, j \in C_2} a_{ij}$ and a n-dimensional index vector **s**: If

s belongs to cluster C_1, then element $s_i = 1$; otherwise $s_i = -1$. The Laplace matrix of A is $L = D - A$, where D is a n-th diagonal matrix with element $d_{ii} = d_i$. Then there is $R = ¼\sum_{ij}(1-s_i s_j)\, a_{ij} = ¼\, \mathbf{s}^T L\mathbf{s} = \sum_v a_v^2 \lambda_v$, where $\mathbf{s} = \sum_{v=1}^{n} a_v \mathbf{v}_v$, $a_v = \mathbf{v}_v^T\mathbf{s}$, λ_v and $\mathbf{v}_v$ are the eigenvalues and eigenvectors of the Laplacian matrix L of the matrix, respectively. When the second smallest eigenvalue λ_2 of L is significantly separated from other larger eigenvalues, partitioning the network based on the symbols of the eigenvector $\mathbf{v}_2$ elements can minimize the value R under the constraint of equal size of C_1 and C_2. The graph bisection method can only obtain two clusters at a time and requires a balanced size of the clusters.

METHODS FOR COMMUNITY DISCOVERY

Modern community discovery methods consider the specific properties of complex networks, such as large scale, sparsity, high clustering, and scale-free characteristics. The following is a brief review of these studies.

Modularity-Based Method

Newman et al. believe that community structure is an organized manifestation of complex networks, and by comparing it with randomly configured networks of the same configuration, the community structure of the network can be revealed. The concept of *modularity* (Newman & Girvan, 2004) was proposed to quantify the community structure strength of a network, defined as $Q(G,P) = \frac{1}{2m}\sum_{ij}\left(a_{ij} - \frac{d_i d_j}{2m}\right)\delta_{ij}$, where δ_{ij} represents whether nodes i and j belong to the same community in partition P. The precise solution to maximize modularity is an NP-hard problem, so optimization techniques are used to handle it (Blondel et al, 2008; Clauset et al, 2004). In recent studies, modularity is often combined with other techniques to design community detection algorithms or evaluate the quality of algorithm outputs (Du et al., 2021; Wei & Ahnertm 2020). However, the definition of modularity itself has resolution limitations, which prevent the discovery of sufficiently small communities, as shown in Figure 4. Nevertheless, modularity remains the most popular indicator of community strength.

Figure 4. Illustration of modularity-based method's resolution limitation

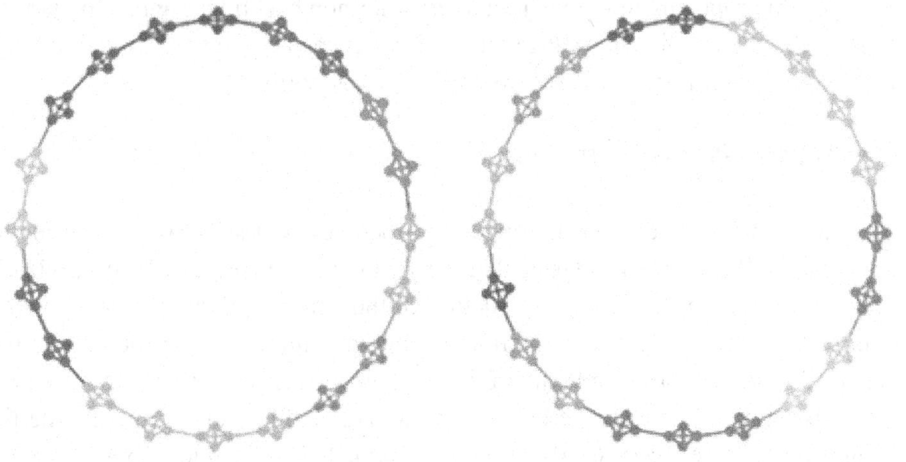

Note. Modularity-based methods cannot discover sufficiently small communities in a ring graph, where k = 20. (a) is a community structure recovered by the CNM algorithm (Clauset et al, 2004), with Q = 0.839 and k = 10; (b) is a community structure recovered by the BGLL method (Blondel et al, 2008), with Q = 0.826 and k = 11.

Spectral-Based Methods

This type of method assumes that if there are some obvious outlier eigenvalues in the eigenvalues spectrum of the network's feature matrix, it may contain information about community structure to achieve better community partitioning results. Newman (Newman, 2006) uses a modularity matrix as the feature matrix B. We consider p_{ij} is the probability for an edge to fall between every pair of vertices i,j, and there is $p_{ij} = d_i d_j/(2m)$ in configuration modal, which is the null model that compared to in modularity. Let $b_{ij} = a_{ij} - p_{ij}$, then modularity can be rewrite in $Q = \sum_{ij} (a_{ij} - p_{ij}) s_i s_j/(4m) = \mathbf{s}^T B\mathbf{s}/(4m)$. Write $\mathbf{s}$ as a linear combination of the normalized eigenvectors $\mathbf{u}_i$ of the modularity matrix B, thus there is $Q = \sum_i a_i^2 \beta_i/(4m)$, where β_i is the eigenvalue of B corresponding to the eigenvector $\mathbf{u}_i$. Assume that the eigenvalues are labeled in decreasing order $\beta_1 \geq \beta_2 \geq \ldots \geq \beta_n$ and the task of maximizing Q is one of choosing the quantities a_i^2 so as to place as much as possible of the weight in the in the terms corresponding to the largest (most positive) eigenvalues. Finally, extract the eigenvectors corresponding to the first k eigenvalues, maps them to a k-dimensional space, and then use standard clustering techniques to divide the network into k communities. Most focus of such study is on constructing different feature matrices (Jing et al., 2021). But when the network is very sparse, the eigenvalue spectrum of the matrix usually does not separate clearly, while constructing a dense feature matrix can greatly increase the computational cost, for example, Krzakala et al. (Krzakala et al., 2016) proposing to reconstruct a $2m$ order non backtracking matrix based on edge-edge relationships to replace the modularity matrix. Spectral-based methods, with their elegant form, still receive widespread attention.

Dynamics-Based Methods

These methods focus on the dynamic processes on the network. The method based on the Potts model suggests that the grid structure with energy minimization can characterize the community structure of the network, thereby modeling community detection as a Hamiltonian function energy minimization problem (Inaba et al., 2021), but the time complexity of these algorithms exceeds $O(n^2)$. Random walk methods estimate the distance between node pairs before clustering, and the time complexity often exceeds $O(n^3)$ (Yi et al., 2021). The technique of map equations, such as Infomap (Zeng & Yu, 2018), can represent the length of random walks using information entropy, but the time cost is still high. The original label propagation algorithm models community detection as a label propagation process, with the greatest advantage of being fast, but the output results are very unstable (Raghavan et al., 2007). Xu et al. (Xu et al., 2020) used two-step neighbor labels to determine node labels but lost the speed advantage of the original method. The most prominent advantage of dynamics-based methods is that it can be easily extended to directed and weighted networks.

Methods Based on Statistical Inference

The goal of these methods is to fit a network generation model containing community structure based on known data, and the fitted model is the discovered community structure. The most typical models include Stochastic Block Models (SBM) and Affiliation Graph Models (AGM). SBM can generate an n-order network A based on a given probability matrix Ψ, where node i is assigned a block C^i, and the elements $\Psi_{C^i C^j}$ represent the probability of edges between nodes i and j. Karrer et al. (Karrer & Newman, 2011) considered the heterogeneity of complex networks, while Mu et al. (Mu et al., 2022) combined SBM with spectral methods. AGM (Yang & Leskovec, 2013) is a bipartite graph $B\ (V, C, F)$, where V is the set of nodes and C is the community set, $F = \{F_{VC} \geq 0\}$ representing the membership relationship between nodes and communities. It can transform community discovery into the non-negative matrix factorization problem. The biggest drawback of statistical inference-based methods themselves may be that they must know the number of communities in advance, but it is possibly directly or indirectly deriving the number of communities by integrating other technologies.

Clique Percolation Method

The Clique Percolation Method (CMP) (Palla et al, 2005) models community discovery as a penetration problem of *k*-clique. *K*-clique refers to a fully connected subgraph in a network consisting of *k* nodes, and the set of all connected *k*-clique is called a *k*-clique community. Due to finding out all cliques in the network, the time complexity of the algorithm is too expensive. Currently, CMP are often used to compare the results with other overlapping community algorithms (Doluca & Oguz, 2021).

Overlapping Community Detection

Overlapping communities are commonly present in society, for example, a person's circle of friends and colleagues often intersect but are not the same. Moreover, there are factors that may connect two people who are somehow overlapping, such as a football fan and a fan of a specific football club. CMP is the earliest proposed overlapping community detection algorithm. Shen et al. (Shen et al., 2008) utilized hierarchical techniques to reveal the phenomenon of nested overlap in communities, and AGM can be naturally used for overlapping community detection (Yang & Leskovec, 2013). The extended LPA algorithm can discover overlapping communities (Mahabadi & Hosseini, 2020), and methods based maximal clique expansion are also commonly used for overlapping community detection (Yang et al, 2020). Currently, scholars often study overlapping and non-overlapping community discoveries within one framework (Ding et al., 2018; Luo et al., 2018).

In summary, existing community discovery studies have some challenges: 1) Many studies do not have a formal definition of communities, and directly discover modules in the network from the model and conclude that the output module is the community. This poses difficulties in theoretically analyzing the effectiveness of algorithms. 2) Lake of benchmark data and available test data. Artificial benchmark networks are certainly particularly useful to assess the performance of discovery algorithms, but these generative models usually cannot overall characterize the true characteristics of complex networks, and the cost of manually labeled the network is expensive. This inspires us to draw inspiration from machine learning.

COMMUNITY DISCOVERY IN BIG DATA

Complex networks from the perspective of big data have some unique properties. In this context, communities have new features, and community discovery is facing new tasks. Community discovery is no longer limited to using only network topology, but the convergence of data and topology may reveal more hidden features and intrinsic connections behind big data.

Local Community Detection

Most existing community discovery methods use global indices to discover global communities. When applied to large information technology networks and online social networks, the agnosticism of the entire network leads to only local methods to discover local communities. Due to the enormous size of real networks and the universality of methods, subgraph expansion-based methods have received widespread attention, and modeling ideas can often be applied to community discovery in multiple tasks simultaneously (Ding et al., 2018; Luo et al., 2018; Yang et al., 2020). The purpose of local community detection is to use the local topology information of the network to discover the largest and most tightly connected subgraphs in the network. A framework for local community discovery is illustrated as follows.

Since only knowing the partial structure of the network, local community detection research generally divides the original network G into two parts: the known part C and the unknown part U, where C is also known as the *running subgraph*. Let both C and U be node-induced subgraphs of network G, then there is $U = G - C$, and denote the nodes in C and U by V_C and V_U, respectively. Depending on whether connected to U, adjusting V_C is also divided into two parts: the internal set $\dot{V}_C$ and inner border ∂V_C^{in} . The nodes directly connected to C in U are called the one-step neighbors of C, abbreviated as *neighbors*, and the set of neighboring nodes of C is also called outer border ∂V_C^{out} of C. Then the inner and outer borders of C form its border $\partial V_C = \partial V_C^{in} \cup \partial V_C^{out}$. According to the context of local community detection, it is stipulated that the information in U can only be obtained by traversed layer by layer through the outer border ∂V_C^{out} of running subgraph C. Mark each iteration process with time $t = 0,1,2,...$, and a local discovery method generally includes three stages: 1) Initial stage. At time $t = 0$, find the community core as the initial subgraph C_0 from seed. b) Growth iteration stage. By traversing network from ∂V_C^{in} to ∂V_C^{out} and absorbing node passed in ∂V_C^{out}, C_{t-1} expands to C_t. c) End stage. Perform a post-processing and output the resulting subgraph, which is the community found.

Dynamic Community Detection

While analyzing rapidly evolving social networks, dynamic community detection tasks have received significant attention (He et al., 2018). It states that evolution is a fundamental feature of communities in social networks and can be tracked using timestamp-based community definitions. Currently, the dynamic incremental community evolution method is the focus of these studies (Li et al., 2021; Wang et al., 2018). The primary idea is that: Most of the structures of dynamic communities remain stable during the evolution process, and it can be measured to improve computational efficiency because of only a small portion of the topology structure that changed at time t based on identifying the community structure at time t-1.

The general process of dynamic community detection is as follows. The initial community structure of a dynamic network by using a local method. Then a dynamic community updating method is running to guide the community identification of the rest snapshots from initial community structure, which most crucial aspect is avoiding re-computing in each snapshot for efficiency. Finally, the community structure of this snapshot can be got by partially updating the founded community structure of the previous snapshot.

Wang et al. (Wang et al., 2018) addressed that dynamic events are a major factor, so the method must first identify the affected nodes of different dynamic events, and then rejudge the community affiliation of these affected nodes at each snapshot. Any dynamic event in social networks can be regarded as derived from a collection of four simple and basic changes: 1) a new node added, 2) an existing node removed, 3) a new edge added, and 4) an existing edge removed. When these events occur, only some local parts of the social networks are affected.

Due to the limited availability of real datasets with timestamps and the small size of the datasets, such methods can only be experimented on small networks and artificial networks, and the study results lack support for large-scale real network experiments.

Community Detection in Heterogeneous Networks

Modeling complex networks as hypergraphs, heterogeneous networks, or multipartite graphs can reduce information loss, such as paper collaboration networks: Nodes correspond to authorship, hyperedges connect multiple authors of the same paper, and the collaboration network can be modeled as a hyper-graph. Nodes can be divided into two types: authorship and paper. If the edge is only located between the authorship and paper, the cooperative network can be modeled as a bipartite graph; If citation relationships are still allowed between papers, such a collaborative network is called a heterogeneous network. In these scenarios, community detection in hypergraphs, multi-partite graphs, and heterogeneous networks are receiving increasing attention (Chien et al., 2018; Kaminski et al., 2020). However, in the graph theory system, theoretical research on such networks is not yet sufficient, and detecting communities in these networks still face many difficulties.

COMMUNITY DISCOVERY IN TOPOLOGICALLY INCOMPLETE NETWORKS (TIN)

Besides of the reasons mentioned above, data loss may occur during the construction of network topology, especially node context information. Meanwhile, in many real-world applications, only part of the network structure is available, and it is sometimes topologically incomplete, and usually disconnected (Xin et al., 2017). In other words, an observed network may miss too many edges to be connected, because the corresponding application usually has access to only a representative sample of the entire original network. For example, the topology of the Internet is inferred by aggregating paths or traceroutes, which miss some edges and then reveal only a part of the whole Internet.

Currently, the primary is to convert the input TIN into a connected one before running community detection methods. In this station, two approaches can be chosen: 1) Linear approach, all connected components are linked one by one according to the ascending order of the size of their components, where two nodes randomly selected from the two components respectively; 2) Star approach, each connected component is associated to the largest connected component respectively with a new-adding edge. Through this processing, existing community discovery methods can directly deal with TIN.

SUBGRAPH EXPANSION METHODS IN LOCAL COMMUNITY DETECTION

The subgraph expansion method has a complete suite of techniques, and its core idea is that the formation and stability of a community depend on its core members, so the community core can be used as a seed to continuously expand into a community by absorbing adjacent nodes. Subgraph expansion methods can be used for local community discovery, but their focus is different.

Luo et al. (Luo et al., 2018) defined three criterion of absorption node in initial based on fuzzy membership degree, but it requires manual setting of parameters and thresholds. Ding et al. (Ding et al., 2018) directly calculated the strength of the connection between the test node and the running subgraph, while Yang et al. (Yang et al., 2020) used the clique as the community core, but the computational costs of both were relatively high. The biggest difficulty of subgraph expansion methods lies in balancing local and global metrics: The method has higher time efficiency but unstable output results with local metrics, while no directions of effective optimization with global metrics. Only greedy strategies can be used and result in higher computational costs for the algorithm based on global index.

COMMUNITY DISCOVERY BASED ON DEEP LEARNING

Due to the full utilization of computing resources, community discovery based on deep learning has become a trend in the development of community detection (Cai et al., 2020; Su et al., 2022). The rapid development of social networks has led to an increase in available datasets that include both content and topology. These real networks are very sparse and often cannot cluster communities based alone on network topology. By utilizing learning techniques, it is possible to better utilize the high-dimensional nonlinear features and highly correlated features of nodes, neighborhoods, and subgraphs, and transform them into topological information of the network.

In conventional machine learning, community detection attempts to generate network embedding with few dimensions to reconstruct the original network. However, in a broad sense, the representation of a low dimensional space is linear. The fact that the real-world networks include nonlinear structures makes the traditional strategies less useful. Therefore, Our perspective shifts towards deep learning.

The Deep Learning-based (DL-based) community detection methods can be divided into three big families:

Auto-encoders Based (AE-Based) Community Detection. The deep neural network based auto-encoders are used to learn data coding in an unsupervised manner, and to improve spatial proximity by a proper pre-processing of the adjacency matrix. The embeddings provided have nonlinear properties and thus the auto-encoder is suitable for mapping data points into the low-dimensional space (Ivannikova et al., 2018). In these methods, topology and node content information can be considered as objective functions to be combined in a linear form, where the primary is mapping data points into the lower dimensional spaces. Compared with methods only using topology, these methods are more resilient to sparsity related to large-scale graphic data. In addition, in many real-world scenarios, considering that most nodes are unmarked and there is almost no prior knowledge of the community in the data, AE-Based methods are the best choice for unsupervised learning tasks. Because the high dimensionality of the feature space of the input data normally increases the number of trainable parameters, many approaches focus on reducing and sharing the trainable parameters to improve the efficiency of deep learning models.

Convolutional Neural Networks/Graph Neural Networks Based (CNN/GNN-Based) Community Detection. The CNNs are an attractive solution for community detection because they combine the convolution application to pooling, especially after introducing of Markov Random Fields (MRF). The MRF was converted to a convolutional layer, which was incorporated into CNN (He et al., 2018). GNNs technically combine graph mining and deep learning and thus they are capable of modeling and detecting the underlying relationships in graph-based data. The framework of GNN-Based methods usually consists of two parts: 1) auto-encoder, which captures the effect of the neighboring nodes to a specific target node and compactly encodes the topology structure of a network, and (2) a self-training clustering module, which performs clustering based on the learned representation and manipulates the latent representation according to the current clustering result (Wang et al., 2019). CNN/GNN-based community detection strategies are basically semi-supervised or supervised learning strategies. It should be noted that as the depth of the convolutional network is increased, performance declines.

Generative Adversarial Networks Based (GAN-Based) Community Detection. GANs are employing two competing deep neural networks: a generator and a discriminator. The latter discriminates if an input sample comes from the prior data distribution or from the generator and the former is trained to generate the samples in such a way that the discriminator is convinced that the samples come from a prior data distribution (Pan et al., 2020). Combining effective GANs with affiliation graph models can model densely overlapping community structures. Thus, the performance of GANs and the direct vertex-community membership representation of AGMs join forces to solve the dense overlapping issues (Jia et al., 2019). Most GANs compare the generated fake data, which are produced based on Gaussian distribution sampling to the real data. But some approaches like JANE (Yang et al., 2020) can be used to separate real and fake combinations of embeddings, topology information, and node features, where the fake attribute network is not based only on the Gaussian distribution.

In summary, DL-based can fully utilize data and computational resources and can compensate for the shortcomings of non-DL-based methods. But its most significant drawback may be that most machine learning methods assume the existence of a Gaussian distribution, but the community distribution in the real world is a power-law distribution. Combining topology information and node features, the Gaussian distribution can capture the semantic variations in latent space. Thus, the overall embedding results become more useful, and the performance of network analysis is highly improved. In addition, such methods often lack a trusted community definition and require a considerable number of computational resources.

SUMMARY

This article provides a systematic review of the application of community structure theory in complex network big data study rather than only focus on community discovery itself in other surveys, with a particular focus on the promoting role of community discovery technology in specific research areas.

Big data of semi-structured or unstructured would naturally be constructed into complex networks with structures. In this way, high-dimensional data can be mapped to graph space to use network analysis techniques to mine knowledge in big data. As a key technology, community discovery could serve as an important tool to provide strong theoretical support for big data analysis, research, and application, thereby aiding people's prediction and decision-making behavior. Meanwhile, the prosperity of big data research can also address the shortcomings of lacking reliable real datasets in community discovery study, and then make the two fields complementary and advancing together.

By reading this chapter, readers can gain a comprehensive understanding of how to introduce community thinking into big data analysis and contribute to improving decision-making skills.

REFERENCES

Bai, L., Cheng, X., Liang, J., & Guo, Y. (2017). Fast graph clustering with a new description model for community detection. *Information Sciences*, 388, 37–47. 10.1016/j.ins.2017.01.026

Blondel, V. D., Guillaume, J. L., Lambiotte, R., & Lefebvre, E. (2008). *Fast unfolding of communities in large networks*. 10.1088/1742-5468/2008/10/P10008

Cai, B., Wang, Y., Zeng, L., Hu, Y., & Li, H. (2020). Edge classification based on convolutional neural networks for community detection in complex network. *Physica A*, 556, 124826. 10.1016/j.physa.2020.124826

Cai, B., Zeng, L. N., Wang, Y. P., Li, H. J., & Hu, Y. M. (2019). Community detection method based on node density, degree centrality, and *k*-means clustering in complex network. *Entropy (Basel, Switzerland)*, 21(12), 1145. 10.3390/e21121145

Chien, E., Lin, C. Y., & Wang, I. H. (2018). Community detection in hypergraphs: optimal statistical limit and efficient algorithms. *International Conference on Artificial Intelligence and Statistics*. https://proceedings.mlr.press/v84/chien18a/chien18a-supp.pdf

Clauset, A., Newman, M. E. J., & Moore, C. (2004). Finding community structure in very large networks. *Physical Review. E*, 70(6 Pt 2), 066111. 10.1103/PhysRevE.70.06611115697438

Ding, X., Zhang, J., & Yang, J. (2018). A robust two-stage algorithm for local community detection. *Knowledge-Based Systems, 152*, 188-199. 10.1016/j.knosys.2018.04.018

Doluca, O., & Oguz, K. (2021). APAL: Adjacency propagation algorithm for overlapping community detection in biological networks. *Information Sciences*, 579, 574–590. 10.1016/j.ins.2021.08.031

Du, Y. J., Zhou, Q., Luo, J. X., Li, X. Y., & Hu, J. R. (2021). Detection of key figures in social networks by combining harmonic modularity with community structure-regulated network embedding. *Information Sciences*, 570, 722–743. 10.1016/j.ins.2021.04.081

Duan, Z., Sun, X., Zhao, S., Chen, J., Zhang, Y. P., & Tang, J. (2020). Hierarchical community structure preserving approach for network embedding. *Information Sciences*, 546, 1084–1096. 10.1016/j.ins.2020.09.053

Girvan, M., & Newman, M. E. J. (2002). Community structure in social and biological networks. *Proc Natl Acad, USA, 99*(12), 7821-7826. 10.1073/pnas.122653799

Green, O., & Bader, D. A. (2013). Faster betweenness centrality based on data structure experimentation. *Procedia Computer Science*, 18, 399–408. 10.1016/j.procs.2013.05.203

He, D. X., You, X. X., Feng, Z. Y., Jin, D., Yang, X., & Zhang, W. (2018). A Network-Specific Markov Random Field Approach to Community Detection. *Proceedings of the 32th AAAI Conference on Artificial Intelligence*. 10.1609/aaai.v32i1.11281

Inaba, K., Inagaki, T., Igarashi, K., Utsunomiya, S., & Takesue, H. (2021). Potts model solver based on hybrid physical and digital architecture. *Communications on Physics*, 5(1), 1–8. 10.21203/rs.3.rs-464366/v1

Ivannikova, E., Park, H., Hmlinen, T., & Lee, K. (2018). *Revealing community structures by ensemble clustering using group diffusion*. Elsevier. 10.1016/j.inffus.2017.09.013

Ji, Q. B., Li, D. Y., & Jin, Z. (2020). Divisive algorithm based on node clustering coefficient for community detection. *IEEE Access : Practical Innovations, Open Solutions*, 8, 142337–142347. 10.1109/ACCESS.2020.3013241

Jia, Y. T., Zhang, Q. Q., Zhang, W. N., & Wang, X. B. (2019). CommunityGAN: Community Detection with Generative Adversarial Nets. *Proceedings of the WWW '19: The World Wide Web Conference,* 784-794. 10.1145/3308558.3313564

Jin, D., Wang, K., Zhang, G., Jiao, P., & Huang, X. (2019). Detecting communities with multiplex semantics by distinguishing background, general and specialized topics. *IEEE Transactions on Knowledge and Data Engineering*, 32(11), 2144–2158. 10.1109/TKDE.2019.2937298

Jing, B., Li, T., Ying, N., & Yu, X. (2021). Community detection in sparse networks using the symmetrized Laplacian inverse matrix (slim). *Statistica Sinica*, 32(1), 1–22. 10.5705/ss.202020.0094

Kaminski, B., Pralat, P., & Theberge, F. (2020). Community Detection Algorithm Using Hypergraph Modularity. *International Workshop on Complex Networks and Their Applications*. Springer.

Karrer, B., & Newman, M. E. J. (2011). Stochastic blockmodels and community structure in networks. *Physical Review. E*, 83(1 Pt 2), 016107. 10.1103/PhysRevE.83.01610721405744

Krzakala, F., Moore, C., Mossel, E., Neeman, J., Sly, A., Zdeborova, L., & Zhang, P. (2013). Spectral redemption in clustering sparse networks. *Proceedings of the National Academy of Sciences of the United States of America*, 110(52), 20935–20940. 10.1073/pnas.131248611024277835

Li, W., Zhu, H., Li, S., Wang, H., & Jin, Q. (2021). Evolutionary community discovery in dynamic social networks via resistance distance. *Expert Systems with Applications*, 171, 114536. 10.1016/j.eswa.2020.114536

Liu, F., Xue, S., Wu, J., Zhou, C., Hu, W., Paris, C., Nepal, S., Yang, J., & Yu, P. S. (2020). Deep learning for community detection: progress, challenges and opportunities. http://arxiv.org/abs/2005.0822510.24963/ijcai.2020/693

Luo, W. J., Zhang, D. F., Jiang, H., Ni, L., & Hu, Y. M. (2018). Local community detection with the dynamic membership function. *IEEE Transactions on Fuzzy Systems*, 26(5), 3136–3315. 10.1109/TFUZZ.2018.2812148

Mahabadi, A., & Hosseini, M. (2020). SLPA-based parallel overlapping community detection approach in large complex social networks. *Multimedia Tools and Applications*, 80(5), 6567–6598. 10.1007/s11042-020-09993-1

Marcel, S., & Jones, J. H. (2010). Dynamics and control of diseases in networks with community structure. *PLoS Computational Biology*, 6(4), e1000736. Advance online publication. 10.1371/journal.pcbi.100073620386735

Mcguire, M. P., & Nguyen, N. P. (2014). Community structure analysis in big climate data. *2014 IEEE International Conference on Big Data (Big Data) IEEE*, 38-46. https://ieeexplore.ieee.org/document/7004442

Molontay, R., & Nagy, M. (2019). Two decades of network science: as seen through the co-authorship network of network scientists. *Proceedings of the 2019 IEEE/ACM international conference on advances in social networks analysis and mining*, 578-583. 10.1145/3341161.3343685

Mu, C., Mele, A., Hao, L., Cape, J., Athreya, A., & Priebe, C. E. (2022). On spectral algorithms for community detection in stochastic blockmodel graphs with vertex covariates. *IEEE Transactions on Network Science and Engineering*, (5). https://doi.org//arXiv.2007.0215610.48550

Newman, M. E. J. (2006). Finding community structure in networks using the eigenvectors of matrices. *Physical Review. E*, 74(3), 036104. 10.1103/PhysRevE.74.03610417025705

Newman, M. E. J. (2010). *Networks: An Introduction*. Oxford Univ. Press. 10.1093/acprof:oso/9780199206650.001.0001

Newman, M. E. J. (2012). Communities, modules and large-scale structure in networks. *Nature Physics*, 8(1), 25–31. 10.1038/nphys2162

Newman, M. E. J., & Girvan, M. (2004). Finding and evaluating community structure in networks. *Physical Review. E*, 69(2 Pt 2), 026113. 10.1103/PhysRevE.69.02611314995526

Palla, Derényi, Farkas, & Vicsek. (2005). Uncovering the overlapping community structure of complex networks in nature and society. *Nature, 435*(7043), 814-818. https://arxiv.org/PS_cache/physics/pdf/0506/0506133v1.pdf

Pan, S., Hu, R., Fung, S. F., Long, G., Jiang, J., & Zhang, C. Q. (2020). Learning Graph Embedding with Adversarial Training Methods. *IEEE Transactions on Cybernetics*, 2020(50), 2475–2487. 10.1109/TCYB.2019.293209631484146

Pothen, A., Simon, H. D., & Liou, K. P. (1990). Partitioning sparse matrices with eigenvectors of graphs. *SIAM Journal on Matrix Analysis and Applications*, 11(3), 430–452. 10.1137/0611030

Pulgar-Rubio, F., Rivera-Rivas, A. J., Pérez-Godoy, M. D., González, P., Carmona, C. J., & Del Jesus, M. J. (2017). Multi-objective evolutionary fuzzy algorithm for subgroup discovery in big data environments - A MapReduce solution. *Knowledge-Based Systems*, 2017(117), 70–78. 10.1016/j.knosys.2016.08.021

Radicchi, F., Castellano, C., Cecconi, F., Loreto, V., & Parisi, D. (2004). Defining and identifying communities in networks. *National Academy of Sciences, 101*(9), 2658-2663. http://arxiv.org/PS_cache/cond-mat/pdf/0309/0309488v2.pdf

Raghavan, U. N., Réka, A., & Kumara, S. (2007). Near linear time algorithm to detect community structures in large-scale networks. *Physical Review. E*, 76(3 Pt 2), 036106. 10.1103/PhysRevE.76.03610617930305

Sharmila, M., Chitra, P., Jeba, G. S., Priyanka, N., & Mirunalini, K. (2020). Community Detection in Social Networks based on Local Edge Centrality and Adaptive Thresholding. *2020 4th International Conference on Trends in Electronics and Informatics (ICOEI),* 751-756. 10.1109/ICOEI48184.2020.9142897

Shen, H., Cheng, X., Cai, K., & Hu, M. B. (2008). Detect overlapping and hierarchical community structure in networks. *Physica A Statal Mechanics & Its Applications, 388*(8), 1706-1712. 10.1016/j.physa.2008.12.021

Souravlas, S., Anastasiadou, S., & Katsavounis, S. (2021). A survey on the recent advances of deep community detection. *Applied Sciences (Basel, Switzerland),* 11(16), 7179. 10.3390/app11167179

Strogatz, S. H. (2001). Exploring complex networks. *Nature*, 410(6825), 268–276. 10.1038/3506572511258382

Su, X., Xue, S., Liu, F. Z., Wu, J., Yang, J., Zhou, C., Hu, W. B., Paris, C., Nepal, S., Jin, D., Sheng, Q. Z., & Yu, P. S. (2022). A comprehensive survey on community detection with deep learning. *IEEE Transactions on Neural Networks and Learning Systems*. Advance online publication. 10.1109/TNNLS.2021.313739635263257

The Nobel Committee for Physics. (2021). *Data snapshot: Scientific Background on the Nobel Prize in Physics 2021*. https://www.nobelprize.org/prizes/physics/2021/advanced-information

Vespignani, A. (2018). Twenty years of network science. *Nature*, 558(7711), 528–529. 10.1038/d41586-018-05444-y29941900

Wang, C., Pan, S., Hu, R., Long, G., Jiang, J., & Zhang, C. (2019). Attributed Graph Clustering: A Deep Attentional Embedding Approach. *Proceedings of the Twenty-Eighth International Joint Conference on Artificial Intelligence (IJCAI-19)*, 3670–3676. 10.24963/ijcai.2019/509

Wang, Z., Li, Z., Yuan, G., Sun, Y., Rui, X., & Xiang, X. (2018). Tracking the evolution of overlapping communities in dynamic social networks. *Knowledge-Based Systems, 157*, 81-97. 10.1016/j.knosys.2018.05.026

Wei, M., & Ahnert, S. E. (2020). Neutral components show a hierarchical community structure in the genotype-phenotype map of RNA secondary structure. *Journal of the Royal Society, Interface*, 20200608(171), 20200608. 10.1098/rsif.2020.0608

Xin, W., & Chaokun, B. (2017). Deep community detection in topologically incomplete networks. *Physica A*, 469, 342–352. 10.1016/j.physa.2016.11.029

Xu, G., Guo, J., & Yang, P. (2020). Tns-LPA: an improved label propagation algorithm for community detection based on two-level neighbourhood similarity. *IEEE Access*, 23526-23536. 10.1109/ACCESS.2020.3045085

Yan, C. (2022). Nestedness interacts with subnetwork structures and interconnection patterns to affect community dynamics in ecological multilayer networks. *Journal of Animal Ecology*, 91(4), 738–751. 10.1111/1365-2656.1366535061910

Yang, J., & Leskovec, J. (2012). Defining and evaluating network communities based on ground-truth. *Knowledge and Information Systems*, 42(1), 181–213. 10.1007/s10115-013-0693-z

Yang, J., & Leskovec, J. (2013). Overlapping community detection at scale: A nonnegative matrix factorization approach. *ACM International Conference on Web Search & Data Mining*. ACM. 10.1145/2433396.2433471

Yang, L., Wang, Y., Gu, J., Wang, C., Cao, X., & Guo, Y. (2020). JANE: Jointly Adversarial Network Embedding. *Proceedings of the Twenty-Ninth International Joint Conference on Artificial Intelligence (IJCAI-20)*, 1381–1387. 10.24963/ijcai.2020/192

Yang, Y., Shi, P., Wang, Y., & He, K. (2020). Quadratic optimization based clique expansion for overlapping community detection. http://arxiv.org/abs/2011.01640

Yi, Y., Jin, L. H., Yu, H., Juo, H. R., & Cheng, F. (2021). Density sensitive random walk for local community detection. *IEEE Access : Practical Innovations, Open Solutions*, 9, 27773–27782. 10.1109/ACCESS.2021.3058908

Zachary, W. W. (1977). An information flow model for conflict and fission in small groups. *Journal of Anthropological Research*, 33(4), 452–473. 10.1086/jar.33.4.3629752

Zeng, J., & Yu, H. (2018). A Distributed Infomap Algorithm for Scalable and High-Quality Community Detection. *Proceedings of the 47th International Conference on Parallel Processing*. 10.1145/3225058.3225137

Zhang, W., Kong, F., Yang, L., Chen, Y. F., & Zhang, M. Y. (2018). Hierarchical community detection based on partial matrix convergence using random walks. *Tsinghua Science and Technology*, 23(1), 35–46. 10.26599/TST.2018.9010053

Zhao, W., Luo, J., Fan, T., Ren, Y., & Xia, Y. (2021). Analyzing and visualizing scientific research collaboration network with core node evaluation and community detection based on network embedding. *Pattern Recognition Letters*, 144(10), 54–60. 10.1016/j.patrec.2021.01.007

ENDNOTES

1 In the field of community discovery, the terms "network" and "graph" are usual used together without distinction. Meanwhile, the terms "complex network" and "network" are also equivalent in common.

2 We only introduce unweight undirected networks for simplicity here but enough to illustrate the basic, although the community discovery can be deployed in any other type of network, such as weight or directed ones.

Chapter 4
Information Granule, Modeling, and Application From the Perspective of Granular Computing

Qingzhao Kong
Jimei University, China

Wanting Wang
https://orcid.org/0009-0004-3441-3441
Jimei University, China

Conghao Yan
Jimei University, China

ABSTRACT

By granulating the data in the information table and using information granules to analyze the data, the efficiency of data mining can be greatly improved. In this chapter, firstly, in order to better understand information granules, many numerical characteristics related to information granules are deeply discussed. Then, due to different learning rules, various granular structures can be induced. In addition, with the help of these granular structures, corresponding data mining models are constructed according to the needs of learning tasks. Specifically, based on the idea of three-way decision, a novel granular computing model is developed. What's more, the developed model can be successfully applied in network security.

DOI: 10.4018/979-8-3693-4292-3.ch004

INTRODUCTION

Due to limited cognitive abilities, when humans process a large amount of complex information, they often divide the large amount of complex information or data into several simpler blocks based on characteristics and performance of the data. Each separated block is considered as a granule. In fact, granules refer to blocks formed by individuals through equivalence, similarity, proximity, or functional relationships. This process of processing information is called information granulation. For example, there are various types of goods in shopping malls, and it is difficult to effectively manage them if they are not arranged in a certain way. So people divide the mall into several blocks based on the type, volume, and grade of goods placed on the shelves, and arrange the shelves accordingly. Each block will hold goods of the same type, volume, or grade.

In obtaining information granules, people generally granulate the data according to certain rules. The obtained information granules are summarized to form a set of information granules. Based on different rules, all information granules can have various relationships, which can lead to different granule structures. Because the learning tasks vary greatly, this inevitably leads to a variety of granular structures. Starting from the granular structure, a large number of granular computing models can be established based on actual data problems.

There is a type of model in granular computing that focuses on dealing with uncertainty. For example, rough set is a typical representative of this type of model, which focuses on dealing with the uncertainty of computational objects. Based on various practical backgrounds, people have proposed various rough set models. These models have played an important role in addressing various data issues.

Review of Information Granules

Information granules have been studied for a long time (Marek & Pawlak, 1976; Marek & Truszczynski, 1999; Pawlak, 1973, 1982). For any set of attributes, many information granules can be induced based on attribute features. Because these information granules can be interpreted, then these information granules are called descriptive information granules or definable information granules. While some information granules cannot be generated based on any set of attributes, and have no clear meaning. Such information granules are called undefined information granules (Yao, 2015; Kong & Chang, 2022b). Due to the existence of undefined information granules, there are always errors in the acquired knowledge. Analyzing or mining data mainly involves studying undefined information granules. For example, in rough set theory, definable information granules are usually used to describe and represent undefined information granules. Currently, the numerical characteristics of information granules have become a new research direction and hotspot.

Review of Granular Structure

Granular structure is usually composed of information granules induced from a dataset or an information table. Due to the influence of learning tasks and data characteristics, information granules with different relationships can be induced from the dataset, and the collection of these information granules forms various granular structures. Based on these granular structures, many granular computing models can be developed. For symbol datasets, granular structures such as partition, covering, multi-partition, and multi-covering can be induced (Pawlak, 1982; Zhu, 2009; Zhu & Wang, 2012; Qian, et al., 2010, 2014). For numerical data, the concept of neighborhood is proposed through the distance function (Randall Wilson & Martinez, 1997). From perspective of granular structure, all neighborhoods constitute a covering of all sample data. Of course, for mixed data, we can also obtain mixed granular structures (Hu, et al., 2008a). In addition, based on the idea of three-way decision, an information granule called a description set can be defined through the intersection of information granules (Kong, et al., 2022a). This type of information granule not only has good interpretability, but also has important practical applications.

Review of Modeling

For symbol datasets, Pawlak first proposed a rough set model based on a partition on the universe. Then, the partition is promoted to the covering, and the covering rough set model is proposed (Zakowski, 1983). From then on, covering rough sets have been widely studied. So far, dozens or even hundreds of covering rough set models have been proposed. In 2010, Qian (Qian, et al., 2010) first proposed a novel rough set model based on multiple partitions. The proposed model quickly attracted the attention of scholars, and the multi-granulation rough set model is currently a hot research topic in rough set theory. Later, some scholars extended multiple partitions to multiple coverings and introduced the multi-covering rough set models. For numerical data, neighborhood rough sets are proposed through the tool of neighborhood. Neighborhood rough sets are good at mining numerical data (Wang, et al., 2018; Barman & Patra, 2019). Recently, people have begun to pay attention to the problem of mining mixed data. By combining traditional Pawlak rough sets and neighborhood rough sets, people have constructed mixed rough sets to analyze mixed data, and achieved many important progress (Hu, et al., 2008b; Wei, et al., 2012; Zhang, et al., 2016; Yuan, et al., 2022). Of course, many other granular computing models can also be constructed based on information granules and granular structures to analyze data. For example, by utilizing the three-way decision approach, a new granular computing model can be introduced, which plays an important role in network security (Kong, et al., 2022a).

The Motives and Contribution of This Chapter

The study of information granules has a history of more than 40 years, and people have obtained many important conclusions about information granules. Based on information granules, many granular structures and granular computing models are explored. But to this day, there are the following issues that need to be studied.

1. People still have insufficient understanding of the numerical characteristics of information granules. For example, in a dataset or an information table, we have no knowledge of the number of induced and non-induced information granules, as well as the bases and dimensions of the induced and non-induced information granule spaces. These issues require further research.
2. Further research is needed to derive the granular structure from the dataset or information table. At present, the research on granular structures mainly focuses on partition, neighborhood, covering, and other aspects. We need to develop new granular structures based on constantly emerging practical problems.
3. Suitable granular computing models need to be introduced to address various novel learning tasks.

Based on the above analysis, the contributions of this chapter involves the following three aspects.

1. This chapter first introduces various numerical characteristics of information granules. The number of information granules, the base and dimension of the information granule space are given. In addition, the numerical characteristics of information granules related to rough set theory are also discussed.
2. Unlike traditional granular structures, here, based on the three-way decision idea, all attributes are divided into necessary attributes, reject attributes, and neutral attributes. A number of new information granules are developed and a novel granular structure is explored. This type of granular structure has good interpretability.
3. Next, a new granular computing model is defined based on this proposed granular structure. This granular computing model not only has good mathematical properties, but also can describe the samples in the dataset. Finally, the application of this model in network security is discussed.

Based on the above analysis, this chapter is organized as follows: In the second section, some basic concepts are briefly reviewed; In the third section, a detailed introduction is given to the numerical characteristics of information granules; In the fourth section, the information granules and granular structure constructed based on the idea of three-way decision are proposed; In the fifth section, a novel granular computing model is developed. And a detailed introduction is given to the application of the model in network security. Finally, a brief summary and outlook are provided on the content of this chapter.

BASIC KNOWLEDGE

Information Granules

The information table that can display the data visually is an important information system. In data mining, the collected samples and their labels are often gathered together to form an information table, and then the data in the information table is analyzed and reasoned. Usually, an information table can be marked by

$$I = (OB, AT, \{V_a | a \in AT\}, \{f_a | a \in AT\}) \tag{1}$$

where $OB = \{o_1, o_2, \cdots, o_n\}, AT = \{a_1, a_2, \cdots, a_m\}, V_a$ and f_a represent the universe, attribute set, attribute value of attribute a and information function about attribute a, respectively (Pawlak, 1981).

For each $A \subseteq AT$ and each $o \in OB$, the equivalence relation E_A, the equivalence class of o and a partition of the universe induced from E_A can be written as (Pawlak, 1991):

$$o E_A o' \Leftrightarrow \forall a \in A; (f_a(o) = f_a(o'))$$

$$[o]_A = \{o' \in OB | o E_A o'\};$$

$$OB/E_A = \{[o]_A | o \in OB\}.$$

Definition 2.1 (Yao, 2015; Kong & Chang, 2022b): In an information table shown by Eq. (1), for any $P \subseteq OB/E_A, \cup P$ is called an induced information granule or a defined information granule. The set composed of all induced information granules is called induced information granule space, and denoted as $\mathcal{IG}$, that is $\mathcal{IG} = \{\cup P | P \subseteq OB/E_A\}$.

Definition 2.2 (Yao, 2015; Kong & Chang, 2022b): In an information table shown by Eq. (1), for each $W \subseteq 2^{OB}/\mathcal{IG}$, we call $\cup W$ a non-induced information granule or an undefinable set. we use $\mathcal{NIG}$ to denote all the non-induced information granules, that is $\mathcal{NIG} = \{\cup W | W \subseteq 2^{OB}/\mathcal{IG}\}$.

Based on Definitions 2.1 and 2.2, the power set of the domain U can be divided into two categories: definable information granules and undefined information granules.

Definition 2.3 (Pawlak, 1982): In an information table shown by Eq. (1), $A \subseteq AT$ is a set of attributes. For each $W \subseteq OB$,

$$\underline{apr}_A(W) = \{o \in OB | [o]_A \subseteq W\},$$

$$\overline{apr}_A(W) = \{o \in OB | [o]_A \cap W \neq \emptyset\}$$

are respectively called the lower and upper approximations of W with respect to A. And

$$(\underline{apr}_A(W), \overline{apr}_A(W))$$

is called the rough set of W. Here,

$$(\underline{apr}_A(W), \overline{apr}_A(W))$$

can be regarded as a special information granule. Furthermore,

$$\mathcal{RS} = \{(\underline{apr}_A(W), \overline{apr}_A(W)) | W \subseteq OB\}$$

is the set of all rough sets, and called as the space of rough set.

Granular Structure

In the information table shown in Eq. (1), if $V_a=\{0,1\}$, where $f_a(o)=1$ means that o has the attribute a; $f_a(0)=0$ means that o does not have the attribute a. This type of information table is called a binary information table. We know that binary information table is a common type of information system. Because the induced granular structures will change with different information tables. Therefore, we mainly introduce the granular structures that can be induced from the binary information table.

In the binary information table,

$$g_j^{a_i} = \left\{o \in OB | f_{a_i}(o) = j\right\}, i = 1,2,\cdots,m; j = 0,1. \quad (2)$$

are the elementary information granules.

Based on these elementary information granules shown by Eq. (2), four kinds of granular structures can be explored as follows (Kong, et al., 2022b):

(1) The partition on the universe *OB* (Pawlak, 1982, 1991; Qian, et al., 2018; Kong & Chang, 2022b):

$$\mathrm{P}_{AT} = \left\{ g_{j_1}^{a_1} \cap g_{j_2}^{a_2} \cap \cdots \cap g_{j_m}^{a_m} (\neq \varnothing) \middle| j_i \in \{0,1\}, i = 1,2,\cdots,m \right\} \quad (3)$$

(2) The covering on the universe *OB* (Bonikowski, et al, 1998; Pomykala, 1987; Wang, et al., 2018; Yao & Yao, 2012; Zhu, 2009; Zhu & Wang, 2012):

$$C_{AT} = \left\{ g_0^{a_1}, g_1^{a_1}, g_0^{a_2}, g_1^{a_2}, \cdots, g_0^{a_m}, g_1^{a_m} \right\} \quad (4)$$

(3) The multi-partition on the universe OB(Qian, et al., 2010, 2014):

$$\mathscr{P}_{AT} = \left\{ \mathrm{P}_{a_1}, \mathrm{P}_{a_2}, \cdots, \mathrm{P}_{a_m} \right\} \quad (5)$$

where $\mathrm{P}_{a_i} = \{g_0^{a_i}, g_1^{a_i}\}, i = 1,2,\cdots,m.$

(4) The multi-covering on the universe *OB* (Lin et al., 2013):

$$\mathscr{C}_{AT} = \{C_0, C_1\} \quad (6)$$

where $C_0 = \{g_0^{a_1}, g_0^{a_2}, \cdots, g_0^{a_m}\}$, and $C_1 = \{g_1^{a_1}, g_1^{a_2}, \cdots, g_1^{a_m}\}$.

In order to better understand the four types of granular structures shown in Eq.s (3)-(6). In what follows, a specific binary information table is used to provide a detailed introduction to these four types of granular structures.

Example 2.1: Here is a binary information table

$$I = (OB, AT, \{V_a | a \in AT\}, \{f_a | a \in AT\}),$$

where $OB = \left\{o_1, o_2, \cdots, o_8\right\}, AT = \left\{a_1, a_2, a_3, a_4\right\}$. More details can be shown in Table 1 as follows.

Table 1. A binary information table

OB	a_1	a_2	a_3	a_4
o_1	1	1	0	0
o_2	0	1	0	1
o_3	0	0	1	1
o_4	1	1	0	0
o_5	0	1	0	1
o_6	0	0	0	1
o_7	1	0	0	1
o_8	1	1	1	0

By Eq. (2), all elementary granules can be computed as follows:

$$g_0^{a_1} = \{o_2, o_3, o_5, o_6\}, g_1^{a_1} = \{o_1, o_4, o_7, o_8\}; g_0^{a_2} = \{o_3, o_6, o_7\}, g_1^{a_2} = \{o_1, o_2, o_4, o_5, o_8\};$$

$$g_0^{a_3} = \{o_1, o_2, o_4, o_5, o_6, o_7\},\ g_1^{a_3} = \{o_3, o_8\};\ g_0^{a_4} = \{o_1, o_4, o_8\},\ g_1^{a_4} = \{o_2, o_3, o_5, o_6, o_7\}.$$

Then according to Eq.s (3)-(6), four types of granular structures will be presented as follows:

(1) The partition on the universe *OB*:

$$\mathrm{P}_{AT} = \{\{o_1, o_4\}, \{o_2, o_5\}, \{o_3\}, \{o_6\}, \{o_7\}, \{o_8\}\};$$

(2) The covering on the universe *OB*:

$$C_{AT} = \{g_0^{a_1}, g_1^{a_1}, g_0^{a_2}, g_1^{a_2}, g_0^{a_3}, g_1^{a_3}, g_0^{a_4}, g_1^{a_4}\}$$
$$= \{\{o_2, o_3, o_5, o_6\}\{o_1, o_4, o_7, o_8\}, \{o_3, o_6, o_7\}, \{o_1, o_2, o_4, o_5, o_8\},$$
$$\{o_1, o_2, o_4, o_5, o_6, o_7\}, \{o_3, o_8\}, \{o_1, o_4, o_8\}, \{o_2, o_3, o_5, o_6, o_7\}\}$$

(3) The multi-partition on the universe *OB*:

$$\mathscr{P}_{AT} = \{\mathrm{P}_{a_1}, \mathrm{P}_{a_2}, \mathrm{P}_{a_3}, \mathrm{P}_{a_4}\} = \{\{g_0^{a_1}, g_1^{a_1}\}, \{g_0^{a_2}, g_1^{a_2}\}, \{g_0^{a_3}, g_1^{a_3}\}, \{g_0^{a_4}, g_1^{a_4}\}\}$$
$$= \{\{\{o_2, o_3, o_5, o_6\}, \{o_1, o_4, o_7, o_8\}\}, \{\{o_3, o_6, o_7\}, \{o_1, o_2, o_4, o_5, o_8\}\},$$
$$\{\{o_1, o_2, o_4, o_5, o_6, o_7\}, \{o_3, o_8\}\}, \{\{o_1, o_4, o_8\}, \{o_2, o_3, o_5, o_6, o_7\}\}\}$$

(4) The multi-covering on the universe OB:

$$\mathscr{C}_{AT} = \{C_0, C_1\} = \{\{g_0^{a_1}, g_0^{a_2}, g_0^{a_3}, g_0^{a_4}\}, \{g_1^{a_1}, g_1^{a_2}, g_1^{a_3}, g_1^{a_4}\}\}$$
$$= \{\{\{o_2, o_3, o_5, o_6\}, \{o_3, o_6, o_7\}, \{o_1, o_2, o_4, o_5, o_6, o_7\}, \{o_1, o_4, o_8\}\},$$
$$\{\{o_2, o_3, o_5, o_6\}, \{o_1, o_2, o_4, o_5, o_8\}\}, \{\{o_3, o_8\}, \{o_2, o_3, o_5, o_6, o_7\}\}\}$$

The above are four common types of granular structures. Based on these granular structures, many granular computing models can be constructed, especially a large number of rough set models can be designed.

MAIN RESULTS

Here, we will mainly introduce the properties of information granules, granular computing models, and related applications.

Number Characteristics of Information Granules

The number characteristics of information granules are a very important aspect of their properties. There has been little research on this area before. Here we focus on the number characteristics of information granules (Kong & Chang, 2022a).

In an information table shown by Eq. (1), each subset of OB is an information granule. In the above analysis, all information granules can be divided into two parts: induced information granules and non-induced information granules. We know that the number of all subsets in OB is $2^{|OB|}$. In other words, the number of all information granules is $2^{|OB|}$. In granular computing, induced information granules play an important role in data analysis and knowledge discovery. For example, in all kinds of rough set models, induced information granules are used to approximate the non-induced information granules. So, we can't help but wonder how many induced and non-induced information granules exist in an information table?

Theorem 3.1: In the information table shown by Eq. (1),$A \subseteq AT$ is an attribute subset of AT, and OB/E_A is a partition of OB induced by attribute subset A. Then
(1) The number of all induced information granules is $2^{|OB/E_A|}$, that is,

$$|\mathscr{IG}| = 2^{|OB/E_A|}.$$

(2) The number of all non-induced information granules is $2^{|OB|} - 2^{|OB/E_A|}$, that is,

$$|\mathscr{NIG}| = 2^{|OB|} - 2^{|OB/E_A|}.$$

As we all know, on a real axis, there must be a rational number between any two irrational numbers. Similarly, is there any non-induced information granule between any two induced information granules with strict inclusion relation? How many non-induced information granules exist?

Theorem 3.2: In the information table shown by Eq. (1), OB/E_A is a partition of OB. W_1, W_2 are two induced information granules and $W_1 \subset W_2$. And there exists

$$\mathscr{P} = \{P_1, P_2, \cdots, P_s\} \subseteq OB/E_A$$

such that $\cup_{i=1}^{s} P_i = W_2/W_1$, where $|P_i| \geq 2$, $i=1,2,\ldots,s$. Then, the number of non-induced information granules between W_1 and W_2 is $(2^{|P_1|} - 2) \cdot (2^{|P_2|} - 2) \cdot \ldots \cdot (2^{|P_s|} - 2)$.

Because the induced information granules are closed under set intersection, union, and complement, we have the following definition.

Definition 3.1: In the information table shown by Eq. (1), $\mathscr{IG}$ is the induced information granule space. Then $\mathscr{BIG} \subseteq \mathscr{IG}$ is called a base of the induced information granule space $\mathscr{IG}$ under set intersection, union, and complement, if

(1) For each $V \in \mathscr{IG}$, there exists $\mathscr{BIG}' \subseteq \mathscr{BIG}$ such that V can be represented by the sets in $\mathscr{BIG}'$ through set intersection, union, and complement;

(2) For each $W \in \mathscr{BIG}$, we can not get a subset $\mathscr{BIG}'' \subseteq \mathscr{BIG}/\{W\}$ such that W is expressed by the sets in $\mathscr{BIG}''$ through set intersection, union, and complement.

Theorem 3.3: In the information table shown by Eq. (1), $A \subseteq AT$ is an attribute subset of AT, $OB/E_A = \{P_1, P_2, \cdots, P_s\}$ is a partition of OB, and $\mathscr{IG}$ is the induced information granule space induced from the information table. Then

$$(OB/E_A)/\{P_i\} = \{P_1, P_2, \cdots, P_{i-1}, P_{i+1} \cdots, P_s\}$$

is a base of the induced information granule space $\mathscr{IG}$ under set intersection, union, and complement, $i=1,2,\ldots,s$. And the dimension of induced information granule space $\mathscr{IG}$ is $s-1$.

Because the non-induced information granules are closed under set complement, we have the following definition.

Definition 3.2: In the information table shown by Eq. (1), $\mathscr{NIG}$ is the non-induced information granule space. Then $\mathscr{BNIG} \subseteq \mathscr{NIG}$ is called a base of the non-induced information granule space $\mathscr{NIG}$ under set complement, if

(1) For each $V \in \mathscr{NIG}$, there exists $V' \in \mathscr{BNIG}$ such that $V = \overline{V'}$ or $V = \overline{(V')}$;

(2) For each $W \in \mathscr{BNIG}$, there does not exist a non-induced information granule $W' \in \mathscr{BNIG}/\{W\}$ such that $W = \overline{W'}$.

Theorem 3.4: In the information table shown by Eq. (1), $A \subseteq AT$ is an attribute subset of AT, $OB/E_A = \{P_1, P_2, \cdots, P_s\}$ is a partition of OB, then

(1) $\mathcal{NIG} = \{W_1, \overline{W_1}, W_2, \overline{W_2}, \cdots, W_t, \overline{W_t}\}$, where W_i is the non-induced information granule, $\overline{W_i} = OB - W_i$, and $t = \frac{2^n - 2^s}{2}$;

(2) $\mathcal{BNIG} = \{W_1', W_2', \cdots, W_t'\}$ is a base of the non-induced information granule space $\mathcal{NIG}$ under set complement, where $W_i' = W_i$ or $\overline{W_i}$, $i=1,2,\ldots,t$. And the dimension of non-induced information granule space $\mathcal{NIG}$ is $\frac{2^n - 2^s}{2}$.

In rough set theory, for each subset of the universe, the subset can be described by its rough set. Then, how many rough sets are there in a rough set model?

Theorem 3.5: In the information table shown by Eq. (1), $A \subseteq AT$ is an attribute subset of AT, let

$$OB/E_A = \{P_1, P_2, \cdots, P_r, P_{r+1} \cdots, P_s\}$$

be the partition of OB induced by the information table, where $|P_i|>1$, $i=1,2,\ldots,r$; $|P_j|=1$, $j=r+1, r+2,\ldots,s$. Then the number of rough sets is

$$\sum_{j=0}^{s-r} \sum_{i=0}^{r} C_{s-r}^{j} \cdot C_r^i \cdot 2^{r-i}.$$

In what follows, we provide the definitions of intersection, union, and complement of rough sets, respectively.

Definition 3.3: For any two rough sets

$$(\underline{apr}_A(V), \overline{apr}_A(V), \text{ and } (\underline{apr}_A(W), \overline{apr}_A(W)) \in \mathcal{RS},$$

the intersection and union of

$$(\underline{apr}_A(V), \overline{apr}_A(V), \text{ and } (\underline{apr}_A(W), \overline{apr}_A(W))$$

are defined as follows:

$$(\underline{apr}_A(V), \overline{apr}_A(V)) \cap (\underline{apr}_A(W), \overline{apr}_A(W))$$

$$= ((\underline{apr}_A(V) \cap \overline{apr}_A(W)), (\underline{apr}_A(V) \cap \overline{apr}_A(W))),$$

$$(\underline{apr}_A(V), \overline{apr}_A(V)) \cup (\underline{apr}_A(W), \overline{apr}_A(W))$$

$$= ((\underline{apr}_A(V) \cup \overline{apr}_A(W)), (\underline{apr}_A(V) \cup \overline{apr}_A(W))),$$

Fan and Zhi (Fan & Zhi, 2001) point out that let

$$S = \left(V \cup \left\{ w \middle| ([w]_A \cap V \cap W = \varnothing) \wedge ([w]_A \cap V \neq \varnothing) \wedge ([w]_A \cap W \neq \varnothing) \right\}\right) \cap W,$$

$$T = \left(V - \left\{ w \middle| ([w]_A \subseteq V \cap W) \wedge ([w]_A \not\subseteq V) \wedge ([w]_A \not\subseteq W) \right\}\right) \cap W,$$

then we have

$$(\underline{apr}_A(S) \cap \overline{apr}_A(S)) = (\underline{apr}_A(V), \overline{apr}_A(V)) \cap (\underline{apr}_A(W), \overline{apr}_A(W)),$$

$$(\underline{apr}_A(T) \cap \overline{apr}_A(T)) = (\underline{apr}_A(V), \overline{apr}_A(V)) \cup (\underline{apr}_A(W), \overline{apr}_A(W)).$$

Definition 3.4: For each rough set $(\underline{apr}_A(W), \overline{apr}_A(W)) \in \mathcal{RS}$, the complement of $(\underline{apr}_A(W), \overline{apr}_A(W))$ is defined as follows:

$$\overline{(\underline{apr}_A(W), \overline{apr}_A(W))} = (\underline{apr}_A(\overline{W}), \overline{apr}_A(\overline{W})).$$

From Definitions 3.3 and 3.4, rough sets are closed under rough set intersection, union and complement. Then, we can define the base of rough set space under intersection, union and complement.

Definition 3.5: In the information table shown by Eq. (1), $\mathcal{RS}$ is the rough set space induced from the information table. Then $\mathcal{BRS} \subseteq \mathcal{RS}$ is called a base of the rough set space $\mathcal{RS}$ under rough set intersection, union, and complement, if

(1) For each $(\underline{apr}_A(V), \overline{apr}_A(V)) \in \mathcal{RS}$, there exists $\mathcal{BRS}' \subseteq \mathcal{BRS}$ such that $(\underline{apr}_A(V), \overline{apr}_A(V))$ can be represented by the rough sets in $\mathcal{BRS}'$ through intersection, union, and complement operations;
(2) For each $(\underline{apr}_A(W), \overline{apr}_A(W)) \in \mathcal{BRS}$, we can not get a subset $\mathcal{BRS}'' \subseteq \mathcal{BRS} / \{(\underline{apr}_A(W), \overline{apr}_A(W))\}$ such that $(\underline{apr}_A(W), \overline{apr}_A(W))$ is expressed by the rough sets in $\mathcal{BRS}''$ through intersection, union, and complement operations.

Theorem 3.6: In the information table shown by Eq. (1), $A \subseteq AT$ is an attribute subset of AT, $OB/E_A = \{P_1, P_2, \cdots, P_r, P_{r+1} \cdots, P_s\}$ be the partition of OB induced from an information table, where $|P_i|>1$, $i=1,2,\ldots,r$; $|P_j|=1$, $j=r+1,r+2,\ldots,s$. And $\mathscr{RS}$ is the rough set space induced from the information table. Let

$$\mathscr{BRS}' = \{(\varnothing,\{P_1\}),(\varnothing,\{P_2\}),\cdots,(\varnothing,\{P_r\})\},$$

$$\mathscr{BRS}'' = \{(\{P_1\},\{P_1\}),(\{P_2\},\{P_2\}),\cdots,(\{P_s\},\{P_s\})\}/\{(\{P_i\},\{P_i\})\}.$$

Then $\mathscr{BRS} = \mathscr{BRS}' \cup \mathscr{BRS}''$ is a base of the rough set space $\mathscr{RS}$ under rough set intersection, union, and complement, $i=1,2,\ldots,s$. And the dimension of rough set space $\mathscr{RS}$ is $s+r-1$.

MODELING

Many kinds of granular computing models can be established based on different granular structures. For example, based on Eq.s (2)-(6), Pawlak rough set, covering rough set, multi-partition rough set and multi-covering rough set can be developed respectively. These rough set models have been widely and deeply studied, and have been applied to many data problems. Since these four types of rough set models can be seen in many literature, they will not be elaborated here.

When constructing the four types of rough set models mentioned above, we believe that the importance of all attributes in the information table is the same. Therefore, we consider all attributes as a whole without distinction. But sometimes we need to divide the attributes of an information table into three parts according to some rules. For example, from the perspective of the importance of attributes, we can divide all attributes into three parts: the attributes that must have; the attributes that cannot have; and the attributes that is dispensable. Now, let us look at a specific example. When selecting scholarship winners, the candidates are required to meet the following conditions: excellent examination results and participation in social practice, no cheating records and no international student, and no requirement for history of major diseases and athletic ability. That is to say that excellent examination results and social practice are necessary for students to apply for scholarships; At the same time, this student is not an international student, and can't have any cheating records; While the attributes of athletic ability and history of major diseases have no impact on the selection of scholarships.

Based on the above description, an information table shown in Table 2 can be developed, where we take the students as the research objects and regard international student, excellent examination results, excellent athletic ability, social practice, history of major diseases and cheating records as the attributes.

Example 3.1: Let $I = (OB, AT, \{V_a | a \in AT\}, \{f_a | a \in AT\})$ be an information system, where

$$OB = \{o_1, o_2, o_3, o_4, o_5, o_6, o_7, o_8\}, AT = \{a_1, a_2, a_3, a_4, a_5, a_6\}.\ a_1, a_2, a_3, a_4, a_5$$

and a_6 respectively represent international student, excellent examination results, excellent athletic ability, social practice, history of major diseases and cheating records. In addition, $f_{a_i}(o_j) = 1$ means that o_j has the attribute a_i; $f_{a_i}(o_j) = 0$ means that o_j does not have the attribute a_i, i=1,2,3,4,5,6; j=1,2,3,4,5,6,7,8. More details can be shown in Table 2.

Table 2. An information system

OB	a_1	a_2	a_3	a_4	a_5	a_6
o_1	0	1	1	1	1	0
o_2	1	0	0	1	1	0
o_3	0	0	1	0	0	1
o_4	0	1	0	0	1	0
o_5	1	0	1	1	1	0
o_6	0	0	0	1	1	0
o_7	1	0	0	1	1	0
o_8	0	1	0	1	1	0

According to Table 2, here are some basic information granules, which are very important and will be used in the following sections. When these information granules are developed, we also explain what they mean, respectively.

(a) $g_{a_1} = \{o_2, o_5, o_7\}$ and $\overline{g_{a_1}} = \{o_1, o_3, o_4, o_6, o_8\}$, where g_{a_1} and $\overline{g_{a_1}}$ are sets of all international students and all non international students, respectively;

(b) $g_{a_2} = \{o_1, o_4, o_8\}$ and $\overline{g_{a_2}} = \{o_2, o_3, o_5, o_6, o_7\}$, where g_{a_2} and $\overline{g_{a_2}}$ are sets of all students with excellent examination results and all students without excellent examination results, respectively;

(c) $g_{a_3} = \{o_1, o_3, o_5\}$ and $\overline{g_{a_3}} = \{o_2, o_4, o_6, o_7, o_8\}$, where g_{a_3} and $\overline{g_{a_3}}$ are sets of all students with excellent athletic ability and all students without excellent athletic ability, respectively;

(d) $g_{a_4} = \{o_1,o_2,o_5,o_6,o_7,o_8\}$ and $\overline{g_{a_4}} = \{o_3,o_4\}$, where g_{a_4} and $\overline{g_{a_4}}$ are sets of all students who have participated in social practice and all students who have not participated in social practice, respectively;

(e) $g_{a_5} = \{o_3\}$ and $\overline{g_{a_5}} = \{o_1,o_2,o_4,o_5,o_6,o_7,o_8\}$, where g_{a_5} and $\overline{g_{a_5}}$ are sets of all students with a history of major illness and all students with a history of major illness, respectively;

(f) $g_{a_6} = \{o_5,o_7\}$ and $\overline{g_{a_6}} = \{o_1,o_2,o_3,o_4,o_6,o_8\}$, where g_{a_6} and $\overline{g_{a_6}}$ are sets of all students with cheating records and all students without cheating records, respectively.

So we got twelve basic information granules. According to the twelve basic granules, all the students who meet the requirements of applying for scholarship can be found as follows:

$$(g_{a_2} \cap g_{a_4}) \cap (\overline{g_{a_1}} \cap \overline{g_{a_6}})$$
$$= (\{o_1,o_4,o_8\} \cap \{o_1,o_2,o_5,o_6,o_7,o_8\}) \cap (\{o_1,o_3,o_4,o_6,o_8\} \cap \{o_1,o_2,o_3,o_4,o_6,o_8\}) = \{o_1,o_8\}$$

Let us consider another case, some students need to be selected to participate in the sports meeting. The requirements are excellent sports ability and no major disease history. Similarly, all students who meet the requirements can be presented as follows:

$$g_{a_3} \cap \overline{g_{a_5}}$$
$$= \{o_1,o_3,o_5\} \cap \{o_1,o_2,o_4,o_5,o_6,o_7,o_8\} = \{o_1,o_5\}$$

Inspired by Example 3.1, for a binary information table, and any $a \in A$, g_a is the set of all objects with attribute a; $\overline{g_a}$ is the set of all objects without attribute a. For $A_s, A_t \subseteq AT$, where $\varnothing \subseteq A_s, A_t \subseteq AT$, and $A_s \cap A_t = \varnothing$, then the attribute set AT can be divided into three disjoint parts: A_s, A_t, and $A_r = AT/(A_s \cup A_t)$. The attributes in A_s, A_t, and A_r are called indispensable attributes, rejected attributes and neutral attributes, respectively. Then all objects that have attributes in A_s, don't have attributes in A_t, and have no restrictions on attributes in A_r can be proposed as follows:

$$g_{A_sA_t} = \left(\cap_{a_i \in A_s} g_{a_i}\right) \cap \left(\cap_{a_j \in A_t} \overline{g_{a_j}}\right) \cap \left(\cap_{a_k \in A_r} \left(g_{a_k} \cup \overline{g_{a_k}}\right)\right)$$
$$= \left(\cap_{a_i \in A_s} g_{a_i}\right) \cap \left(\cap_{a_j \in A_t} \overline{g_{a_j}}\right)$$

Therefore, based on the granules $g_{A_sA_t}$, a granular structure can be shown:

$$\mathcal{G} = \left\{ g_{A_sA_t} (\neq \varnothing) \middle| \varnothing \subseteq A_s, A_t \subseteq A, A_s \cap A_t = \varnothing, A_s \cup A_t \neq \varnothing \right\}. \quad (7)$$

Definition 3.11: In the binary information table shown in Eq. (1), based on the granular structure shown in Eq. (7), for each $X \subseteq OB$,

$$OP_{A_s A_t}(X) = \left\{ o \in OB \middle| o \in g_{A_s A_t} \cap X \right\}$$

is called the approximation set of X with respect to $A_s A_t$. Meanwhile, $OP_{A_s A_t}$ is called the approximation operator with respect to $A_s A_t$.

Remark: *For each* $X \subseteq OB$, *we have the following results.*

(1) $OP_{A_s A_t}(X) = \varnothing$ means that each object with attributes in A_s but without attributes in A_t does not belong to X;

(2) $OP_{A_s A_t}(X) \neq \varnothing$,$OP_{A_s A_t}(X) \neq g_{A_s A_t}$ and $OP_{A_s A_t}(X) \neq X$ means that only part of the objects with attributes in A_s but without attributes in A_t belongs to X;

(3) $OP_{A_s A_t}(X) = g_{A_s A_t}$ means that all objects with attributes in A_s but without attributes in A_t belong to X;

(4) $OP_{A_s A_t}(X) = X$ means that each object in X has the attributes in A_s but does not have the attributes in A_t.

Definition 3.12: In the binary information table shown in Eq. (1), based on the granular structure shown in Eq. (7), for any $A_s, A_t \subseteq AT$, and $A_s \cap A_t = \varnothing$, if there exists $a_s \in A_s$ or $a_t \in A_t$ such that $g_{A_s/\{a_s\},A_t} = g_{A_s A_t}$ or $g_{A_s A_t/\{a_t\}} = g_{A_s A_t}$, then a_s and a_t are respectively called the reducible attributes of A_s and A_t; Otherwise, a_s and a_t are respectively called the reducible attributes of A_s and A_t. The ordered pair $\left(A_s^{Red}, A_t^{Red}\right)$ is called a reduction of $(A_s A_t)$, if $\left(A_s^{Red}, A_t^{Red}\right)$ satisfies two conditions:

(1) $g_{A_s^{Red} A_t^{Red}} = g_{A_s A_t}$;

(2) For each $a_s^{'} \in A_s^{Red}$, and each $a_t^{'} \in A_t^{Red}$, one can find that $g_{A_s^{Red}/\{a_s^{'}\},A_t^{Red}} \neq g_{A_s A_t}$ and $g_{A_s^{Red} A_t^{Red}/\{a_t^{'}\}} \neq g_{A_s A_t}$.

Remark: *In the binary information table shown in Eq. (1),* $A_s^{'} \subseteq A_s$ *and* $A_t^{'} \subseteq A_t$ *,then we have the following results.*

(1) For any $X \subseteq OB$, we have that $OP_{A_s A_t}(X) \subseteq OP_{A_s^{'} A_t^{'}}(X)$;

(2) If $a_s \in A_s^{'}$, $a_t \in A_t^{'}$ are both the reducible attributes of $A_s^{'}$ and $A_t^{'}$, then $a_s \in A_s^{'}$, $a_t \in A_t^{'}$ are both the reducible attributes of A_s and A_t.

Definition 3.13: In the binary information table shown in Eq. (1), based on the granular structure shown in Eq. (7), for any $X \subseteq OB$ and any $A_s, A_t \subseteq AT$ (where $A_s \cap A_t = \varnothing$), if there exists $a_s \in A_s$ or $a_t \in A_t$ such that

$$OP_{A_s/\{a_s\},A_t}(X) = OP_{A_s A_t}(X) \text{ or } OP_{A_s A_t/\{a_t\}}(X) = OP_{A_s A_t}(X),$$

then a_s and a_t are respectively called the reducible attributes of A_s and A_t with respect to X; Otherwise, a_s and a_t are respectively called the irreducible attributes of A_s and A_t with respect to X.

The ordered pair $\left(A_s^{Red_X}, A_t^{Red_X}\right)$ is called a reduction of (A_s, A_t) with respect to X, if $\left(A_s^{Red_X}, A_t^{Red_X}\right)$ satisfies two conditions:

(1) $OP_{A_s^{Red_X}, A_t^{Red_X}}(X) = OP_{A_s, A_t}(X)$;

(2) For each $a_s^{'} \in A_s^{Red_X}$, and each $a_t^{'} \in A_t^{Red_X}$, one can find that

$$OP_{A_s^{Red_X}/\{a_s^{'}\}, A_t^{Red_X}}(X) \neq OP_{A_s^{Red_X}, A_t^{Red_X}}(X) \text{ and } OP_{A_s^{Red_X}, A_t^{Red_X}/\{a_t^{'}\}}(X) \neq OP_{A_s^{Red_X}, A_t^{Red_X}}(X).$$

APPLICATIONS

Network security is now a hot research direction. With the increasing popularity of information technology, people not only enjoy the convenience brought by information technology, but also pay more attention to the security of information transmission. Therefore, it is particularly important to study various network security problems. There is a information security network shown in Figure 1. The information transceiver o_0 can send the information to detection station a_1. Then information detection station a_1 detects the information. Eventually, the detected information will be sent to information transceivers o_2, o_4, o_5, o_6, o_7. Meanwhile, the information transceiver o_0 can also send the information to detection station a_2. Then information detection station a_2 detects the information. Finally, the detected information will be sent to information transceivers $o_1, o_2, o_3, o_4, o_5, o_6, o_7, o_9$.

For the information security network shown in Figure 1, the following basic assumptions need to be satisfied:

(1) Any two information transceivers cannot share undetected information;

(2) The information send and received by any transceiver shall be detected by at least one information detection station.

In this information security network, the following questions often need to be solved (Kong, et al, 2022a).

(Q1) Which of the five message generators o_1, o_3, o_4, o_7, o_8 sends and receives information only through information detection stations a_1, a_2, a_3?

(Q2) Which of all message generators sends and receives information only through information detection stations a_2, a_2, a_3?

(Q3) Which of all message generators sends and receives information through information detection stations a_2, a_6 but not through a_5?

(Q4) If the information detection station a_2 is under maintenance and cannot work properly, what impact will it have on the conclusion of questions 3 listed above?

(Q5) Which of the five message generators o_0, o_1, o_2, o_5, o_7 sends and receives information through information detection stations a_1,a_2,a_6 but not through a_3,a_5?

(Q6) If the information detection station a_2 is under maintenance and cannot work properly, what impact will it have on the conclusion of questions 5 listed above?

Figure 1. An information security network

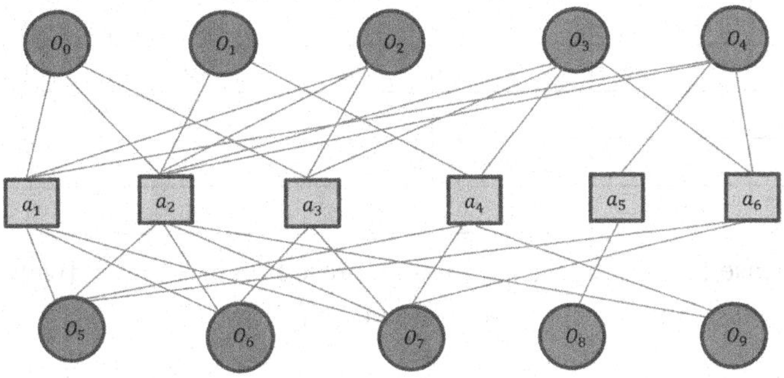

Next, we first use the given information security network to induce the corresponding granular computing model proposed in Definition 3.11 through three steps, and then answer the questions mentioned above by using this model.

Step 1: According to Figure 1, we can turn the information security network to an information table

$I = (OB,AT,\{V_a|a \in AT\},\{f_a|a \in AT\}),$

where

$OB = \{o_0,o_1,o_2,o_3,o_4,o_5,o_6,o_7,o_8,o_9\}, AT = \{a_1,a_2,a_3,a_4,a_5,a_6\}$;

$V = \cup_{a_j \in AT} V_{a_j}, V_{a_j} = \{0,1\}; f_{a_j}(o_i) = 1;$

means that the information sent by the information transceiver o_i will be checked by the information detection station a_j; $f_{a_j}(o_i) = 0$ means that the information sent by the information transceiver o_i won't be checked by the information detection station a_j, i=0,1,…,9, j=1,2,…,6. More details can be found in Table 3.

continued on following page

Table 3. Continued

Table 3. An information system based the information security

OB	a_1	a_2	a_3	a_4	a_5	a_6
o_0	1	1	1	0	0	0
o_1	0	1	0	1	0	0
o_2	1	1	1	0	0	0
o_3	0	1	1	1	0	1
o_4	1	1	0	0	1	1
o_5	1	1	0	1	0	1
o_6	1	1	1	0	0	0
o_7	1	1	1	1	0	1
o_8	0	0	1	0	1	1
o_9	0	1	1	1	0	1

Step 2: Based on the information table presented in Table 3, twelve basic information granules can be respectively shown as follow.

$$g_{a_1} = \{o_0, o_2, o_4, o_5, o_6, o_7\}, g_{a_2} = \left\{ o_0, o_1, o_2, o_3, o_4, o_5, o_6, o_7, o_9 \right\},$$
$$g_{a_3} = \{o_0, o_2, o_3, o_6, o_7, o_8, o_9\}, g_{a_4} = \{o_1, o_3, o_5, o_7, o_9\}, g_{a_5} = \{o_4, o_8\},$$
$$g_{a_6} = \{o_3, o_4, o_5, o_7, o_8, o_9\} ;$$

$$\overline{g_{a_1}} = \{o_1, o_3, o_8, o_9\}, \overline{g_{a_2}} = \{o_8\}, \overline{g_{a_3}} = \{o_1, o_4, o_5\},$$
$$\overline{g_{a_4}} = \{o_0, o_2, o_4, o_6, o_8\}, \overline{g_{a_5}} = \{o_0, o_1, o_2, o_3, o_5, o_6, o_7, o_9\}, \overline{g_{a_6}} = \{o_0, o_1, o_2, o_6\}.$$

Based on the structures of g_{a_i} and $\overline{g_{a_i}}$, g_{a_i} is the set of all the information transceivers that the information sent and received must be detected by the information detection station a_i; and $\overline{g_{a_i}}$ is the set of all the information transceivers that the information sent and received do not need to be detected by the information detection station a_i, i=1,2,3,4,5,6.

Step 3: First, let us answer the first question. Let

$$X_1 = \{o_1, o_3, o_4, o_7, o_8\}, A_{s_1} = \{a_1, a_2, a_3\}, A_{t_1} = \{a_4, a_5, a_6\},$$

then $g_{A_{s_1}A_{t_1}} = \{o_0, o_2, o_6\}$. So, we have that $OP_{A_{s_1}A_{t_1}}(X_1) = \varnothing$. From Remark 1, we know that among the five message generators o_1, o_3, o_4, o_7, o_8, there is no message generator in X_1 that can send and receive information only through information detection stations a_1, a_2, a_3.

Second, we will answer the second question. Let $X_2=OB$,

$$A_{s_2} = \{a_1,a_2,a_3\}, A_{t_2} = \{a_4,a_5,a_6\}, \text{ then } g_{A_{s_2},A_{t_2}} = \{o_0,o_2,o_6\}.$$

So, we have that $OP_{A_{s_2},A_{t_2}}(X_2) = g_{A_{s_2},A_{t_2}} = \{o_0,o_2,o_6\}$.From Remark 1, we know that among all the message generators, these three message generators o_0,o_2,o_6 can send and receive information only through information detection stations a_1,a_2,a_3.

Third, let us answer the third question. Let $X_3=OB$, $A_{s_3} = \{a_2,a_6\}, A_{t_3} = \{a_5\}$, we have that $g_{A_{s_3},A_{t_3}} = \{o_3,o_5,o_7,o_9\}$.Thus, we have that $OP_{A_{s_3},A_{t_3}}(X_3) = \{o_3,o_5,o_7,o_9\}$. Therefore, based on Remark 1, one can find that message generators o_3,o_5,o_7,o_9 send and receive information through information detection stations a_2,a_6 but not through converters a_5 in this information security network.

Fourth, let us answer the fourth question. According to Definition 3.13, a_2 is a reducible attribute of A_{s_3} and A_{t_3} with respect to X_3. Then, if the information detection station a_2 dose not work, it won't make any difference to the conclusion of question 3.

Fifth, let us deal with the fifth question. Let

$$X_4 = \{o_0,o_1,o_2,o_5,o_7\}, A_{s_4} = \{a_1,a_2,a_6\}, A_{t_4} = \{a_3,a_5\},$$

we have that $g_{A_{s_4},A_{t_4}} = \{o_5\}$. Thus, we have that $OP_{A_{s_4},A_{t_4}}(X_4) = \{o_5\}$. Therefore, based on Remark 1, one can find that only message generator o_5 in X_4 sends and receives information through information detection stations a_1,a_2,a_6 but not through converters a_3,a_5 in this information security network.

Finally, we will answer the last question. Since a_2 is a reducible attribute of A_{s_3} and A_{t_3},$A_{s_3} \subseteq A_{s_4}$ and $A_{t_3} \subseteq A_{t_4}$, then based on Remark 2, a_2 is also a reducible attribute of A_{s_4} and A_{t_4}. Therefore, if the information detection station a_2 dose not work, it won't make any difference to the conclusion of question 5.

CONCLUSION

First, starting from information granules, a detailed study is conducted on the numerical characteristics of information granules, including the number of information granules, the base and dimension of the different information granule spaces. Then, taking the binary information table as an example, we focus on examining various granular structures that can be induced from the binary information table. Specifically, based on the three-way decision theory, we study a new granular structure. According to this type of granular structure, a novel granular computing model is proposed. Moreover, this granular computing model proposed in this chapter can be successfully applied in network security.

Although research on information granules has been conducted for a long time and has achieved many excellent results. However, different actual scenarios often lead to various types of information granules. Therefore, it is necessary to construct appropriate information granules based on the constantly emerging data problems. In addition, with the increasing demand for data mining effectiveness, more efficient granular computing models need to be continuously developed.

ACKNOWLEDGMENT

This work is partially supported by the Natural Science Foundation of Fujian Province (No. 2020J01707), and the National Foundation Cultivation Program of Jimei University (No. ZP2020063).

REFERENCES

Bai, X. L., Yun, Z. Q., Xuan, D., Lai, T. H., & Jia, W. J. (2009). Optimal patterns for four-connectivity and full coverage in wireless sensor networks. *IEEE Transactions on Mobile Computing*, 9(3), 435–448.

Barman, B., & Patra, S. (2019). A novel technique to detect a suboptimal threshold of neighborhood rough sets for hyperspectral band selection. *Soft Computing*, 23(24), 13709–13719. 10.1007/s00500-019-03909-4

Bonikowski, Z., Brynirski, E., & Wybraniec, U. (1998). Extensions and intentions in the rough set theory. *Information Sciences*, 107(1-4), 149–167. 10.1016/S0020-0255(97)10046-9

Fan, S. D., & Zhi, T. Y. (2001). The algebraic property of rough sets [in Chinese]. *Journal of Shanxi University*, 24, 116–119.

Hu, Q. H., Liu, J. F., & Yu, D. R. (2008b). Mixed feature selection based on granulation and approximation. *Knowledge-Based Systems*, 21(4), 294–304. 10.1016/j.knosys.2007.07.001

Hu, Q. H., Yu, D. R., Liu, J. F., & Wu, C. X. (2008a). Neighborhood rough set based heterogeneous feature subset selection. *Information Sciences*, 178(18), 3577–3594. 10.1016/j.ins.2008.05.024

Kong, L. S., Ren, X. F., & Fan, Y. J. (2019). Study on assessment method for computer network security based on rough set. In *2009 IEEE International Conference on Intelligent Computing and Intelligent Systems*, Shanghai, China.

Kong, Q. Z., & Chang, X. E. (2022a). Number characteristics of information granules in information tables. *Journal of Engineering*, 12, 1208–1218.

Kong, Q. Z., & Chang, X. E. (2022b). Rough set model based on variable universe. *CAAI Transactions on Intelligence Technology*, 7(3), 503–511. 10.1049/cit2.12064

Kong, Q. Z., Xu, W. H., & Zhang, D. X. (2022b). A comparative study of different granular structures induced from the information systems. *Soft Computing*, 26(1), 105–122. 10.1007/s00500-021-06499-2

Kong, Q. Z., Zhang, X. W., Xu, W. H., & Long, B. H. (2022a). A novel granular computing model based on three-way decision. *International Journal of Approximate Reasoning*, 144, 92–112. 10.1016/j.ijar.2022.01.015

Lin, G. P., Liang, J. Y., & Qian, Y. H. (2013). Multigranulation rough sets: From partition to covering. *Information Systems*, 241, 101–118.

Marek, V. W., & Pawlak, Z. (1976). Information storage and retrieval systems: Mathematical foundations. *Theoretical Computer Science*, 1(4), 331–354. 10.1016/0304-3975(76)90077-3

Marek, V. W., & Truszczynski, M. (1999). Contributions to the theory of rough sets. *Fundamenta Informaticae*, 39(4), 389–409. 10.3233/FI-1999-39404

Pawlak, Z. (1973). Mathematical Foundations of Information Retrieval, Research Report CC. *PAS Reporter*, 101.

Pawlak, Z. (1981). Information systems, theoretical foundations. *Information Systems*, 6(3), 205–218. 10.1016/0306-4379(81)90023-5

Pawlak, Z. (1982). Rough sets. *International Journal of Computer Information Sciences*, 11(5), 341–356. 10.1007/BF01001956

Pawlak, Z. (1991). *Rough sets: theoretical aspects of reasoning about data*. Kluwer Academic Publishers. 10.1007/978-94-011-3534-4

Pomykala, J. A. (1987). Approximation operations in approximation space. *Bulletin of the Polish Academy of Sciences*, 9-10, 653–662.

Qian, Y. H., Liang, J. Y., Yao, Y. Y., & Deng, C. Y. (2010). MGRS: A multi-granulation rough set. *Information Sciences*, 180(6), 949–970. 10.1016/j.ins.2009.11.023

Qian, Y. H., Liang, X. Y., Wang, Q., Liang, J., Liu, B., Skowron, A., Yao, Y., Ma, J., & Dang, C. (2018). Local rough set: A solution to rough data analysis in big data. *International Journal of Approximate Reasoning*, 97, 38–63. 10.1016/j.ijar.2018.01.008

Qian, Y. H., Zhang, H., Sang, Y. L., & Liang, J. Y. (2014). Multi-granulation decision-theoretic rough sets. *International Journal of Approximate Reasoning*, 55(1), 225–237. 10.1016/j.ijar.2013.03.004

Randall Wilson, D., & Martinez, T. R. (1997). Improved heterogeneous distance functions. *Journal of Artificial Intelligence Research*, 6, 1–34. 10.1613/jair.346

Sun, M. F., Chen, J. T., Zhang, Y., & Shi, S. Z. (2012). A new method of feature selection for flow classification. *Physics Procedia*, 24, 1729–1736. 10.1016/j.phpro.2012.02.255

Wang, Q., Qian, Y. H., Liang, X. Y., Guo, Q., & Liang, J. (2018). Local neighborhood rough set. *Knowledge-Based Systems*, 153, 53–64. 10.1016/j.knosys.2018.04.023

Wei, W., Liang, J. Y., & Qian, Y. H. (2012). A comparative study of rough sets for hybrid data. *Information Sciences*, 190, 1–16. 10.1016/j.ins.2011.12.006

Yao, Y. Y. (2015). The two sides of the theory of rough sets. *Knowledge-Based Systems*, 80, 67–77. 10.1016/j.knosys.2015.01.004

Yao, Y. Y., & Yao, B. X. (2012). Covering based rough set approximations. *Information Sciences*, 200(1), 91–107. 10.1016/j.ins.2012.02.065

Yuan, Z., Chen, H. M., Li, T. R., Sang, B. B., & Wang, S. (2022). Outlier detection based on fuzzy rough granules in mixed attribute data. *IEEE Transactions on Cybernetics*, 52(8), 8399–8412. 10.1109/TCYB.2021.305878033750721

Zakowski, W. (1983). Approximations in the space (μ,π). *Demonstratio Mathematica*, 16(3), 761–769. 10.1515/dema-1983-0319

Zhang, X., Mei, C. L., Chen, D. G., & Li, J. H. (2016). Feature selection in mixed data: A method using a novel fuzzy rough set-based information entropy. *Pattern Recognition*, 56, 1–15. 10.1016/j.patcog.2016.02.013

Zhu, W. (2009). Relationship among basic concepts in covering-based rough sets. *Information Sciences*, 179(14), 2478–2486. 10.1016/j.ins.2009.02.013

Zhu, W., & Wang, F. Y. (2012). The fourth type of covering-based rough sets. *Information Sciences*, 201, 80–92. 10.1016/j.ins.2012.01.026

Chapter 5
A Novel Sequential Three-Way Decision With Rough Fuzzy Sets Based on Optimal Granularity Selection

Jie Yang
Zunyi Normal University, China

Shuai Li
Nanchang Hangkong University, China

ABSTRACT

By introducing the cost measure and three-way decisions theory into the multi-granulation spaces, the uncertain knowledge is approximately described, and the selection method of cost-sensitive optimal knowledge space is proposed. To choose the optimal cost knowledge space to describe a fuzzy concept, a sequential three-way decisions model with rough fuzzy sets (S3WDRFS) is established. It is found that decision cost in multi-granulation knowledge spaces will monotonically decrease with finer knowledge spaces. A selection method of cost-sensitive optimal knowledge space for approximating a fuzzy concept is achieved.

DOI: 10.4018/979-8-3693-4292-3.ch005

1. INTRODUCTION

As a general probabilistic rough set model, a three-way decision model (3WD) was proposed by Yao (2009) based on both probabilistic rough sets and decision theory. 3WD has attracted much attention in recent years, and a great of success in various fields is achieved, such as classification (Liu et al., 2019), clustering (Yu et al., 2015), email spam filtering (Jia et al., 2012), decision making (Liang et al., 2015), etc. The main idea of 3WD is dividing a domain into three disjoint regions by considering the minimum decision risk. Based on the idea of three-way decisions, 3WD not only considers decision risk factors, but also involves three decision actions, i.e., acceptance, rejection and deferment. Generally speaking, the object concepts in 3WD are usually accurate and crisp. For a decision-making problem, there are only two states which are opposite and disjoint each other for a precise concept. For example, in the decision-making problems of diagnosis analysis, there are only two states of Yes or No for a patient. That is, a patient either has the disease or does not have the disease.

However, in many real decision-making applications, the states of the object concept may be uncertain and fuzzy in practice. For a given pollution degree of river applicant, the evaluation results may not be described by two completely opposite states with Yes or No. That would be the case if a river is either a pollution-free river or a polluted river. As a matter of fact, the target concept is usual fuzzy rather than crisp in many real applications, and the membership degree represents the credibility that the objects belong to the concept or state. To address this problem, the rough fuzzy sets (Yao et al., 2008), as an extension of Pawlak's rough sets, is proposed to describe a fuzzy set (or an uncertain concept). In rough fuzzy sets, the lower and upper approximation fuzzy sets are considered as two boundary fuzzy sets of the target concept. Based on the idea of decisions-theoretic rough sets, (Sun, 2019) proposed a formal three-way decisions with rough fuzzy sets (3WDRFS) model and verify the validity of 3WDRFS by a credit card applicant decision-making problem. For more generalizations and applications of 3WDRFS, please refer to References.

Based on the granular computing theory, Yao first introduced the concept of sequential three-way decisions (S3WD), which implements the idea called progressive computing. In essence, sequential three-way decisions focus on solving problems by switching the granularity layer from coarser to finer gradually, which means the same problem could be processed in a hierarchical granular structure . Recently, a series of research on S3WD were developed. Yang and Li proposed a unified S3WD model and multilevel incremental algorithms for complex problem solving. Based on DTRS, Li presented a cost sensitive S3WD model for image processing. Qian proposed an attribute reduction algorithm for S3WD under dynamic granulation.

Hao presented the S3WD model for multi-scale information tables and constructed a new optimal scale selection method in a dynamic multi-scale decision table.

In real-world decision making, S3WD is a new approaches for simulating human's multi-granularity thinking to deal with complex problem. How to choose the most optimal granularity to make the right decision is a crucial issue. It is well-known that cost-sensitive learning is an important issue in machine learning and data mining . In the view of decision making, test cost and decision cost are the most popular types of cost. On the one hand, decision cost is a kind of misclassification cost and the analysis on the decision cost can improve the classification quality. It is well known that the decision cost of classical rough sets is only rooted in the boundary region, while the decision cost of decisions-theoretic rough fuzzy sets not only comes from the boundary region, but also comes from the negative or positive regions, because the membership degrees of these objects in the negative or positive regions are not completely equal to 1 or 0. On the other hand, test cost refers to the associated cost for obtaining a data item of an object. For example, in medical diagnosis, a blood test usually associates with the money or time spent on testing blood. By considering both test cost and decision cost in decisions-theoretic rough sets, Min et al formulated the attribute reduction as an optimal granularity selection problem, which aims to minimize the total cost of classification. Zhao proposed a confidence-level-based covering rough set model to select an optimal cost-sensitive granularity, which is more efficient than the fixed granularity approaches. Yang et al proposed a general framework for the study the decisions-theoretic rough sets in the view of multicost strategy. However, there are still several shortcomings in the current research about cost-sensitive learning as follows: (1) Lack of theoretical analysis on the change rules of decision cost in sequential three-way decisions model. (2) In real-world applications, the test cost includes many factors, i.e., time, money, technology, and it is hard to be evaluated exactly and objectively since each factor has different dimension, which influence decision making to a great extent. (3) Current researches in cost-sensitive learning only consider the total cost as the objective function, which is not true in many practical applications. For example, in the medical system, the economic condition of patients is taken into account, if a patient is very rich, maybe he will not care about the price of this detection method as long as it is accurate. On the contrary, if a patient is not very rich, maybe he will choose the detection method which is relatively cheap but the test results are relatively accurate, which is a popular detection method. Therefore, it is practically desirable for the user to select a satisfactory solution from a set of optimal solutions based on his or her own condition or preferences. (4) Lack of stepwise optimal granularity selection to make exemplary decision under the constraint condition. To solve the above problems, we propose a granulation optimization method to select the optimal cost-sensitive granularity base on sequential three-way decisions mode with rough fuzzy sets (S3WDRFS) model.

The main contribution of this paper has three aspects as follows: (1) we discuss the change regularities of decision cost of the S3WDRFS model and its three regions in a hierarchical granular structure in detail. (2) We present a cost-sensitive granularity optimization mechanism based on the qualitative heuristic function proposed. (3) Based on the cost-sensitive granularity optimization mechanism, we establish a stepwise optimal granularity selection method based on S3WDRFS.

The rest of this paper is organized as follows. Many preliminary concepts or definitions such as rough fuzzy sets, step fuzzy set, average membership degree, average fuzzy set, probabilistic rough fuzzy sets are briefly recalled in Section 2. In Section 3, the S3WDRFS model is presented and the relationship between S3WDRFS and S3WDRS is analyzed. In Section 4, the change regularities of decision cost with changing approximation spaces in S3WDRFS are presented. In Section 5, we propose an optimal qualitative cost-sensitive knowledge space selection based on S3WDRFS model. A case study for a relevant illustration is provided and simulation experiments are conducted to verify the effectiveness of the proposed method in Section 6. In Section 7, the conclusions are drawn.

2. PRELIMINARIES

In order to facilitate the description of this paper, many basic concepts are reviewed briefly in this section.

In this paper, we denote an decision system by $S = (U, C \cup D, V, f)$, *where* U is a non-empty finite domain, C is the set of condition attributes, D is the decision attribute, V is the set of all attribute values and f: $U \times C$ is an information function.

Definition 1 (Rough Sets) (Pawlak, 1982) Given an decision system $S = (U, C \cup D, V, f)$, $R \subseteq C$ and $X \subseteq U$, the lower and upper approximation sets of X are defined as follows,

$\underline{R}(X) = \{x \in U | [x]_R \subseteq X\}$ and $\overline{R}(X) = \{x \in U | [x]_R \cap X \neq \phi\}$,

where $[x]_R$ *denotes the equivalence class induced by the equivalence relation* U/R, namely, $U/R = \{[x]_R\} = \{[x]_1, [x]_2, \cdots, [x]_m\}$.

In this paper, a partition space U/R *is also called a knowledge space or granularity space. For simplicity, let* $[x]_R \triangleq [x]$ in case of confusion. If $\overline{R}(X) = \underline{R}(X)$, X is a definable set, otherwise X is a rough set. The universe U is divided by positive region, boundary region, negative region, then the three regions can be defined respectively as follows,

$POS_R(X) = \underline{R}(X)$, $BND_R(X) = \overline{R}(X) - \underline{R}(X)$ *and* $NEG_R(X) = U - \overline{R}(X)$.

Definition 2 (Rough Fuzzy Sets) (Dubois, and Prade, 1992) Given an decision system $S = (U, C \cup D, V, f)$, $R \subseteq C$ and X is a fuzzy set on U, then the lower and upper approximation sets of Xcan be defined as a pair of fuzzy sets, and its membership degree are defined as follows,

$\mu_{\underline{R}}(x) = \inf\{\mu(y) | y \subseteq [x]_R\}$ and $\mu_{\overline{R}}(x) = \sup\{\mu(y) | y \subseteq [x]_R\}$,

if $\underline{R}(X) = \overline{R}(X)$, then X *is a definable fuzzy set, otherwise* X is a rough fuzzy sets.

Definition 3 (Step Fuzzy Set) For any given information system $S = (U, C \cup D, V, f)$, C denotes an attribute set. $R \subseteq C$ and X is a fuzzy set on U. $U/R = \{[x]_1, [x]_2, \cdots, [x]_L\}$ is a partition space, where $[x]_i = \{x_{i1}, x_{i2}, \cdots, x_{it_i}\}(i = 1, 2, \cdots, L)$ and $t_1 + t_2 + \cdots + t_L = n$, X is a fuzzy set on U. If $\mu_X(x_{i1}) = \mu_X(x_{i2}) = \cdots = \mu_X(x_{it_i}) = c_i$ $(0 \le c_i \le 1, i = 1, 2, \cdots, L)$, then $X$is a step fuzzy set on U/R.

Definition 4 (Average Membership degree) Given an decision system $S = (U, C \cup D, V, f)$, $R \subseteq C$ and X is a fuzzy set on U, $U/R = \{[x]_1, [x]_2, ..., [x]_L\}$ is a partition space. $\forall x \in [x]_i$, where $i = 1, 2, \ldots, L$, $\overline{\mu}(x) = \overline{\mu}([x]_i) = \frac{\sum_{x \subseteq [x]_i} \mu(x)}{|[x]_i|}$, then we call $\overline{\mu}(x)$is the average membership degree.

In Definition 4, $\overline{\mu}(x)$ *can be understood as the probability that an object* $x \in [x]_i$ belongs to the fuzzy concept X by the given equivalence relation U/R.

Definition 5 (Average Fuzzy Set) Given an decision system $S = (U, C \cup D, V, f)$, $R \subseteq C$ and X is a fuzzy set on U, $U/R = \{[x]_1, [x]_2, \cdots, [x]_L\}$ is a partition space, where $[x]_i = \{x_{i1}, x_{i2}, \cdots, x_{it_i}\}(i = 1, 2, \cdots, L)$ and $t_1 + t_2 + \cdots + t_L = |U|$, X is a fuzzy set on U. If $\overline{\mu}_{X^*}(x_{i1}) = \overline{\mu}_{X^*}(x_{i2}) = \cdots = \overline{\mu}_{X^*}(x_{it_i}) = \overline{\mu}([x]_i) = \frac{\sum_{x \subseteq [x]_i} \mu(x)}{|[x]_i|}, i = 1, 2, \cdots, L$, where X^* is a fuzzy set on U, then we call X^* is the average fuzzy set of X.

Example 1. Given an decision system $S = (U, C \cup D, V, f), R \subseteq C$, $X = \frac{0.1}{x_1} + \frac{0.2}{x_2} + \frac{0.5}{x_3} + \frac{0.6}{x_4} + \frac{1}{x_5} + \frac{1}{x_6} + \frac{0.7}{x_7} + \frac{0.3}{x_8} + \frac{0.2}{x_9}$ is a fuzzy set on U; $U/R = \{\{x_1, x_2\}, \{x_3, x_4, x_5\}, \{x_6, x_7\}, \{x_8, x_9\}\}$, then

$$\underline{R}(X) = \frac{0.1}{x_1} + \frac{0.1}{x_2} + \frac{0.5}{x_3} + \frac{0.5}{x_4} + \frac{0.5}{x_5} + \frac{0.7}{x_6} + \frac{0.7}{x_7} + \frac{0.2}{x_8} + \frac{0.2}{x_9}$$

$$\overline{R}(X) = \frac{0.2}{x_1} + \frac{0.2}{x_2} + \frac{1}{x_3} + \frac{1}{x_4} + \frac{1}{x_5} + \frac{1}{x_6} + \frac{1}{x_7} + \frac{0.3}{x_8} + \frac{0.3}{x_9}$$

$$R(X^*) = \frac{0.15}{x_1} + \frac{0.15}{x_2} + \frac{0.7}{x_3} + \frac{0.7}{x_4} + \frac{0.7}{x_5} + \frac{0.85}{x_6} + \frac{0.85}{x_7} + \frac{0.25}{x_8} + \frac{0.25}{x_9}.$$

$$X = \frac{\mu_1}{x_1} + \frac{\mu_2}{x_2} + \cdots + \frac{\mu_N}{x_N}$$

Definition 6 (Probabilistic rough fuzzy sets)(Yao, 2009) Given an decision system $S = (U, C \cup D, V, f)$ *with a pair of threshold* $\alpha, \beta (0 \le \beta \le \alpha \le 1), R \subseteq C$ and X is a fuzzy set on U, the lower and upper approximation sets of $X$are defined as follows,

$\underline{R}^{(\alpha,\beta)}(X) = \{x \in U | \overline{\mu}([x]) \ge \alpha\}$ and $\overline{R}^{(\alpha,\beta)}(X) = \{x \in U | \overline{\mu}([x]) > \beta\}$

The universe U *is divided by positive region, boundary region, negative region, which can be defined as follows,*

$$POS_R^{(\alpha,\beta)}(X) = \{x \in U | \overline{\mu}([x]) \ge \alpha\} = \underline{R}^{(\alpha,\beta)}(X)$$

$$BND_R^{(\alpha,\beta)}(X)=\{x \in U|\beta < \overline{\mu}([x])< \alpha\} = \overline{R}^{(\alpha,\beta)}(X)-\underline{R}^{(\alpha,\beta)}(X)$$
$$NEG_R^{(\alpha,\beta)}(X)=\{x \in U|\overline{\mu}([x])\leq \beta\} = U-\overline{R}^{(\alpha,\beta)}(X).$$

3. SEQUENTIAL THREE-WAY DECISIONS WITH ROUGH FUZZY SETS

In order to obtain $\alpha and\ \beta$, a three-way decisions mode with rough fuzzy sets is proposed based on the decisions-theoretic rough sets theory according to the minimum expected overall decision risk. On one hand, 3WDRFS model brings new insight into the problem of parameter setting for the probabilistic rough fuzzy set. On the other hand, it also can provide an effective approach to a decision-making problem with fuzzy states in practice.

Definition 7 (Three-way decisions with rough fuzzy sets) (Sun, 2014) Given an decision system $S = (U, C \cup D, V, f)$, $R \subseteq C$ and let X is a fuzzy set on U. The action set $A = \{a_P, a_B, a_N\}$ represents three kinds of actions which are acceptation, rejection and deferred decisions. $\lambda_{PP}, \lambda_{BP}, \lambda_{NP}$ denote the losses incurred for taking actionsa_P, a_B, a_N, respectively. When an object belongs to target set X, and $\lambda_{PN}, \lambda_{BN}, \lambda_{NN}$ denote the losses incurred for taking these actions when an object does not belong to target set X. Thus, the expected losses associated with taking different actions with object x can be expressed as follows,

$$\Re(a_P|[x])=\lambda_{PP}\overline{\mu}([x])+\lambda_{PN}(1-\overline{\mu}([x]))$$

, (1)

$$R(a_B|[x])=\lambda_{BP}\overline{\mu}([x])+\lambda_{BN}(1-\overline{\mu}([x]))$$

, (2)

$$R(a_N|[x])=\lambda_{NP}\overline{\mu}([x])+\lambda_{NN}(1-\overline{\mu}([x]))$$

. (3)

Where, $\overline{\mu}([x]) = \frac{\sum_{y \subseteq [x]} \mu(y)}{|[x]|}$ *denotes the membership degree of the equivalence class* $[x]$ induced by equivalence relation U/R belong to object concept X, and $1 - \overline{\mu}([x])$ denotes the membership degree of the equivalence class $[x]$ induced by equivalence relation U/R belong to target set X^C. From the perspective of probability and statistics, $\overline{\mu}([x])$ can be understood as the probability that a randomly selected object $x \in [x]$ belong to target set X, and $1 - \overline{\mu}([x])$ also can be understood as the probability that a randomly selected object $x \in [x]$ not belong to target set X.

According to the Bayesian decision rule, the minimum-risk decision rules can be obtained as follows,

(P)If $R(a_P|[x]) \leq R(a_N|[x])$ *and* $R(a_P|[x]) \leq R(a_B|[x])$, decide $x \in POS(X)$;

(B)If $R(a_B|[x]) \leq R(a_N|[x])$ *and* $R(a_B|[x]) \leq R(a_P|[x])$, decide $x \in BND(X)$;

(N)If $R(a_N|[x]) \leq R(a_B|[x])$ *and* $R(a_N|[x]) \leq R(a_P|[x])$, decide $x \in NEG(X)$.

(P) $\overline{\mu}([x]) \geq \frac{(\lambda_{PN} - \lambda_{BN})}{(\lambda_{PN} - \lambda_{BN}) + (\lambda_{BP} - \lambda_{PP})}$ *and* $\overline{\mu}([x]) \geq \frac{(\lambda_{PN} - \lambda_{NN})}{(\lambda_{PN} - \lambda_{NN}) + (\lambda_{NP} - \lambda_{PP})}$

(B) $\overline{\mu}([x]) \leq \frac{(\lambda_{PN} - \lambda_{BN})}{(\lambda_{PN} - \lambda_{BN}) + (\lambda_{BP} - \lambda_{PP})}$ *and* $\overline{\mu}([x]) \geq \frac{(\lambda_{BN} - \lambda_{NN})}{(\lambda_{BN} - \lambda_{NN}) + (\lambda_{NP} - \lambda_{BP})}$

(N) $\overline{\mu}([x]) \leq \frac{(\lambda_{PN} - \lambda_{NN})}{(\lambda_{PN} - \lambda_{NN}) + (\lambda_{NP} - \lambda_{PP})}$ *and* $\overline{\mu}([x]) \leq \frac{(\lambda_{BN} - \lambda_{NN})}{(\lambda_{BN} - \lambda_{NN}) + (\lambda_{NP} - \lambda_{BP})}$

The decision rules can be re-expressed as follows:

(P)If $\overline{\mu}([x]) \geq \alpha$ *and* $\overline{\mu}([x]) \geq \gamma$, decide $x \in POS(X)$;

(B)If $\overline{\mu}([x]) \leq \alpha$ *and* $\overline{\mu}([x]) \geq \beta$, decide $x \in BND(X)$;

(N)If $\overline{\mu}([x]) \leq \alpha$ *and* $\overline{\mu}([x]) \leq \gamma$, decide $x \in NEG(X)$.

Combining with the above formulas (1), (2), (3), we can obtain the three parameters α, β, γ *respectively according to the minimum-risk decision rules (P`)-(N`),*

For rule(P`)

$$\alpha = \frac{(\lambda_{PN} - \lambda_{BN})}{(\lambda_{PN} - \lambda_{BN}) + (\lambda_{BP} - \lambda_{PP})} = \left(1 + \frac{\lambda_{BP} - \lambda_{PP}}{\lambda_{PN} - \lambda_{BN}}\right)^{-1} \tag{4}$$

For rule(B`)

$$\beta = \frac{(\lambda_{BN} - \lambda_{NN})}{(\lambda_{BN} - \lambda_{NN}) + (\lambda_{NP} - \lambda_{BP})} = \left(1 + \frac{\lambda_{NP} - \lambda_{BP}}{\lambda_{BN} - \lambda_{NN}}\right)^{-1} \tag{5}$$

For rule(N`)

$$\gamma = \frac{(\lambda_{PN} - \lambda_{NN})}{(\lambda_{PN} - \lambda_{NN}) + (\lambda_{NP} - \lambda_{PP})} = \left(1 + \frac{\lambda_{NP} - \lambda_{PP}}{\lambda_{PN} - \lambda_{NN}}\right)^{-1} \tag{6}$$

In other words, one can systematically determine the required threshold values from loss functions

$\frac{\lambda_{BP} - \lambda_{PP}}{\lambda_{PN} - \lambda_{BN}} < \frac{\lambda_{NP} - \lambda_{PP}}{\lambda_{PN} - \lambda_{NN}} < \frac{\lambda_{NP} - \lambda_{BP}}{\lambda_{BN} - \lambda_{NN}}$

$\frac{b}{a} > \frac{d}{c} \Rightarrow \frac{b}{a} > \frac{b+d}{a+c} > \frac{d}{c}$

$\alpha_I \beta_I$

$0 \leq \lambda_{PP} \leq \lambda_{BP} \leq \lambda_{NP} \leq 1$ and $0 \leq \lambda_{NN} \leq \lambda_{BN} \leq \lambda_{PN} \leq 1$ *are two reasonable assumptions for constructing a 3WDRFS model and it follows that* $0 < \alpha \leq 1, 0 \leq \beta \leq 1, 0 < \gamma \leq 1$. Furthermore, if $\frac{\lambda_{BP}}{\lambda_{NP}} + \frac{\lambda_{BN}}{\lambda_{PN}} \leq 1$, we have $0 \leq \beta < \gamma < \alpha \leq 1$ [25, 18]. The rules (P),(B) and (N) can be expressed as follows,

(P)if $\overline{\mu}([x]) \geq \alpha$, *decide* $x \in POS_R^{(\alpha,\beta)}(X)$;

(B)if $\beta \leq \overline{\mu}([x]) < \alpha$, *decide* $x \in BND_R^{(\alpha,\beta)}(X)$;

(N)if $\overline{\mu}([x]) < \beta$, *decide* $x \in NEG_R^{(\alpha,\beta)}(X)$.

Unlike rules in classical rough set, the rules (P),(B) and (N)obtained from the three regions are probably uncertain. According to the above analysis, the decision cost from the three regions can be defined as follows,

$$DC(NEG_R^{(\alpha,\beta)}(X)) = \sum_{x \in NEG_R^{(\alpha,\beta)}(X)} \overline{\mu}([x])\lambda_{NP},$$

$$DC(BND_R^{(\alpha,\beta)}(X)) = \sum_{x \in BND_R^{(\alpha,\beta)}(X)} \overline{\mu}([x])\lambda_{BP} + (1 - \overline{\mu}([x]))\lambda_{BN},$$

$$DC(POS_R^{(\alpha,\beta)}(X)) = \sum_{x \in POS_R^{(\alpha,\beta)}(X)} (1 - \overline{\mu}([x]))\lambda_{PN}.$$

Then, the decision cost $DC_R^{(\beta,\alpha)}(X)$ *can be defined as follows,*

$$DC_R^{(\alpha,\beta)}(X) = DC(NEG_R^{(\alpha,\beta)}(X)) + DC(BND_R^{(\alpha,\beta)}(X)) + DC(POS_R^{(\alpha,\beta)}(X))$$

$$= \sum_{x \in NEG_R^{(\alpha,\beta)}(X)} \overline{\mu}([x])\lambda_{NP} + \sum_{x \in BND_R^{(\alpha,\beta)}(X)} (\overline{\mu}([x])\lambda_{BP} + (1 - \overline{\mu}([x]))\lambda_{BN})$$

$$+ \sum_{x \in POS_R^{(\alpha,\beta)}(X)} (1 - \overline{\mu}([x]))\lambda_{PN}.$$

The decision cost $DC_R^{(\beta,\alpha)}(X)$ *comes from three regions: positive region, boundary region and negative region. The semantic of* $DC(POS_R^{(\alpha,\beta)}(X))$ is the decision cost when we obtain (P) rule. Similar semantic could be applied to $DC(BND_R^{(\alpha,\beta)}(X))$ and $DC(NEG_R^{(\alpha,\beta)}(X))$

In this paper, for convenience, supposing the cost of correct classification is 0, then $\lambda_{PP} = \lambda_{NN} = 0$, *and we have* $\alpha = \frac{\lambda_{PN} - \lambda_{BN}}{\lambda_{PN} - \lambda_{BN} + \lambda_{BP}}$, $\beta = \frac{\lambda_{BN}}{\lambda_{BN} + \lambda_{NP} - \lambda_{BP}}$ in 3WDRFS model. In order to make an appropriate decision search by considering both the decision cost and test cost, based on the 3WDRFS, we propose a definition of sequential three-way decisions with rough fuzzy sets (S3WDRFS) as follows,

Definition 8 (Sequential three-way decisions with rough fuzzy sets) Given an decision system $S = (U, C \cup D, V, f)$, $R_1 \subseteq R_2 \subseteq \ldots \subseteq R_M \subseteq C$ and let X is a fuzzy set on U. Then the sequential three-way decisions with rough fuzzy sets can be denotes by the following series:

$GL_i = (U, R_i \cup D, V, f)$,

$GS = (GL_1, GL_2, \ldots, GL_M)$,

where, GL_i *denotes the ith granularity layer based on the equivalence relation* U/R_i., and GS denotes a hierarchical granular structure

With respect to a series of attribute sets $(R_1, R_2, \ldots, R_M)$, *we have a sequence of decision cost descriptions of S3WDRFS model,*

$DC = (DC_{R_1}^{(\beta,\alpha)}(X), DC_{R_2}^{(\beta,\alpha)}(X), \ldots, DC_{R_M}^{(\beta,\alpha)}(X))$,

with increasing information contents. However, this simplified series of attributes sets is one of the results with respect to the construction of hierarchical granular structure. In order to solve different problems, different hierarchical granular structures can be obtained by ranking the attributes by its importance, test cost, etc.

Figure 1. Process of calculation of decision cost in S3WDRFS model

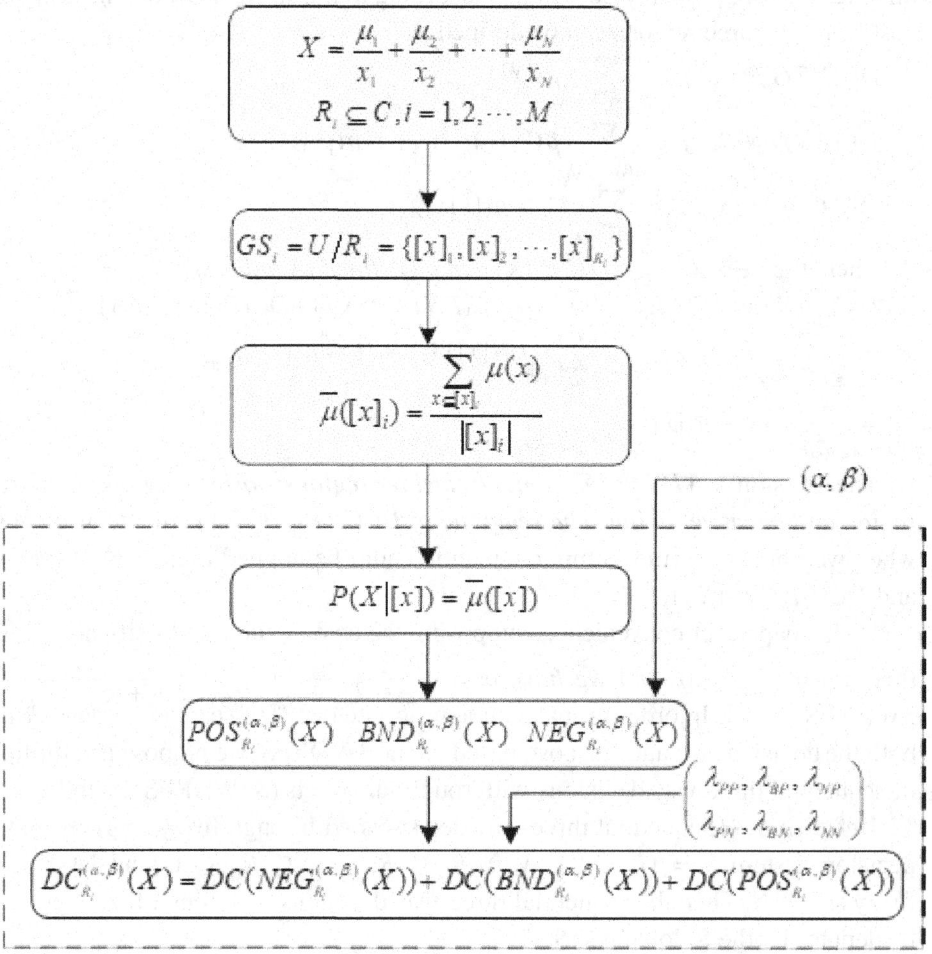

Figure 1 presents the process of calculation of decision cost in S3WDRFS model, where dotted line frame presents the process of calculation of decision cost in sequential three-way decisions with probabilistic rough sets (S3WDPRS) model. It is obviously that when the target concept X *is accurate and crisp inFigure 1, namely, the membership degree of each object is 1 or 0, then S3WDRFS model degenerates to S3WDRS model. Therefore, S3WDRFS model is more versatile than S3WDRS model. When* $\alpha=\beta=0.5$in Figure 1, S3WDRFS model degenerate to 0.5-sequential three-way decisions with rough fuzzy sets (0.5-S3WDRFS) model, then the three disjoint regions can be denoted as follows,

$$POS_{R_i}^{0.5}(X) = \left\{x \in U | \overline{\mu}([x]) > 0.5\right\} = \underline{R_i}^{0.5}(X),$$

$$BND_{R_i}^{0.5}(X) = \left\{x \in U | \overline{\mu}([x]) = 0.5\right\} = \overline{R_i}^{0.5}(X) - \underline{R_i}^{0.5}(X),$$

$$NEG_{R_i}^{0.5}(X) = \left\{x \in U | \overline{\mu}([x]) < 0.5\right\} = U - \overline{R_i}^{0.5}(X).$$

$DC_{R_i}^{(\alpha,\beta)}(X)$

Similarly, when $\alpha = 1$ *and* $\beta = 0$, S3WDRFS degenerates to (1, 0)-sequential three-way decisions with rough fuzzy sets model, denoted by (1, 0) S3WDRFS, then the three disjoint regions can be denoted as follows,

$$POS_{R_i}^{(1,0)}(X) = \left\{x \in U | \overline{\mu}([x]) = 1\right\} = \underline{R_i}^{(1,0)}(X),$$

$$BND_{R_i}^{(1,0)}(X) = \left\{x \in U | 0 < \overline{\mu}([x]) < 1\right\} = \overline{R_i}^{(1,0)}(X) - \underline{R_i}^{(1,0)}(X),$$

$$NEG_{R_i}^{(1,0)}(X) = \left\{x \in U | \overline{\mu}([x]) = 0\right\} = U - \overline{R_i}^{(1,0)}(X).$$

4. COST OF MULTILEVEL DECISION RESULT IN S3WDRFS MODEL

In the S3WDRFS model, the decisions cost usually comes from three regions at each granularity, because the objects in a positive or negative region are uncertain, namely, the membership degrees of these objects may be not completely equal to 0 or 1. With the adding attributes, the objects in the negative or positive regions may be reclassified and the three disjoint regions will be changed. As a result, the decision cost of misclassification at each granularity in S3WDRFS model will be changed accordingly. In this section, we will pay attention to analyze the change laws of the decision cost of S3WDRFS in the changing knowledge spaces.

In this paper, for convenience, let $\lambda_{PP} = \lambda_{NN} = 0$, *then supposing* $\frac{\lambda_{BP}}{\lambda_{NP}} + \frac{\lambda_{BN}}{\lambda_{PN}} \leq 1$, we have $\alpha = \frac{\lambda_{PN} - \lambda_{BN}}{\lambda_{PN} - \lambda_{BN} + \lambda_{BP}}$, $\beta = \frac{\lambda_{BN}}{\lambda_{BN} + \lambda_{NP} - \lambda_{BP}}$ in S3WDRFS model.

Theorem 1: Given an decision system $S = (U, C \cup D, V, f)$, $R_i \subseteq C$, $i = 1, 2, \cdots M$ and X is a fuzzy set on U. If $R_i \subseteq R_{i+1}$, then $DC_{R_i}^{(\alpha,\beta)}(X) \geq DC_{R_{i+1}}^{(\alpha,\beta)}(X)$.

$R_1, R_2, \cdots, R_M \subseteq C$

Proof. Let $U = \{x_1, x_2, ..., x_n\}$ *be a non-empty finite domain,* $U/R_1 = \{p_1, p_2, ..., p_l\}$ and $U/R_2 = \{q_1, q_2, ..., q_m\}$. Because $R_1 \subseteq R_2$, so $U/R_2 \preceq U/R_1$. According to the condition, for simplicity, supposing only one granule p_1 can be subdivided into two finer sub-granules by $\Delta R = R_2 - R_1$ (the more complicated cases can be transformed into this case, so we will not repeat them here). Without loss of generality, let $p_1 = q_1 \cup q_2, p_2 = q_3, p_3 = q_4, p_l = q_m$ $(m = l + 1)$, namely, $U/R_1 = \{q_1, q_2, p_2, p_3, ..., p_l\}$. We will prove this theorem in three cases as follows.

(1) Supposing $\overline{\mu}(p_1) \leq \beta$, *obviously,* $p_1 \subseteq NEG_{R_1}^{(\alpha,\beta)}(X)$

Case 1. If $\overline{\mu}(q_1) \leq \beta$ *and* $\overline{\mu}(q_2) \leq \beta$, namely, $q_1 \subseteq NEG_{R_2}^{(\alpha,\beta)}(X)$ and $q_2 \subseteq NEG_{R_2}^{(\alpha,\beta)}(X)$

$$\Delta DC_{R_1-R_2}(X) = DC_{R_1}^{(\alpha,\beta)}(X) - DC_{R_2}^{(\alpha,\beta)}(X)$$

$$= DC(NEG_{R_1}^{(\alpha,\beta)}(X)) - DC(NEG_{R_2}^{(\alpha,\beta)}(X))$$

$$= \overline{\mu}(p_1)\,|p_1|\lambda_{NP} - \overline{\mu}(q_1)\,|q_1|\lambda_{NP} - \overline{\mu}(q_2)\,|q_2|\lambda_{NP}$$

$$= \Big(\sum_{x_i \in p_1} \mu(x_i) - \sum_{x_i \in q_1} \mu(x_i) - \sum_{x_i \in q_2} \mu(x_i)\Big)\lambda_{NP}.$$

Because $\sum_{x_i \in p_1} \mu(x_i) = \sum_{x_i \in q_1} \mu(x_i) + \sum_{x_i \in q_2} \mu(x_i)$, *then we have* $\Delta DC_{R_1-R_2}(X_i) = 0$. Thus, $DC_{R_1}^{(\alpha,\beta)}(X) = DC_{R_2}^{(\alpha,\beta)}(X)$

Figure 2. Equivalence classes subdivided in the negative region of S3WDRFS

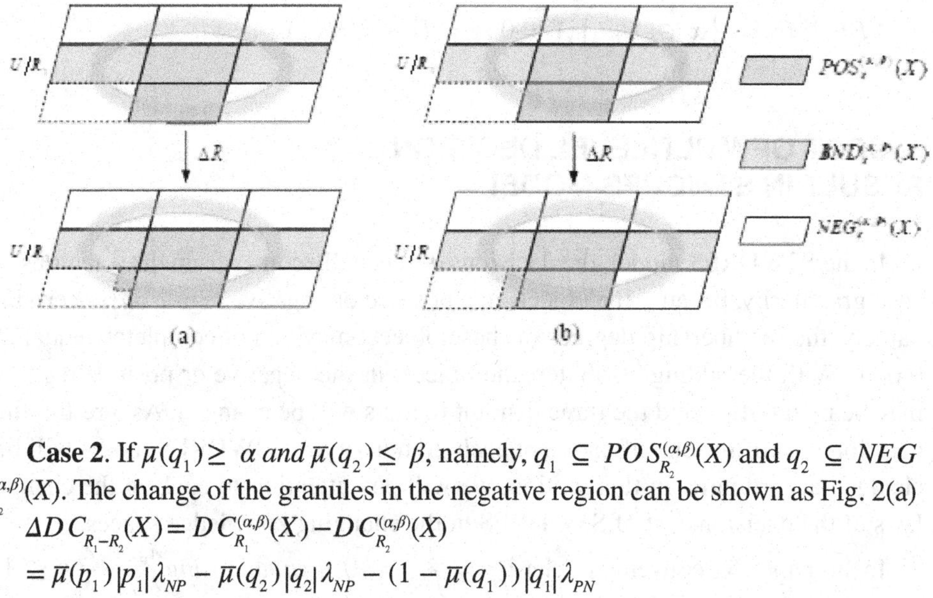

Case 2. If $\overline{\mu}(q_1) \geq \alpha$ *and* $\overline{\mu}(q_2) \leq \beta$, namely, $q_1 \subseteq POS_{R_2}^{(\alpha,\beta)}(X)$ and $q_2 \subseteq NEG_{R_2}^{(\alpha,\beta)}(X)$. The change of the granules in the negative region can be shown as Fig. 2(a)

$$\Delta DC_{R_1-R_2}(X) = DC_{R_1}^{(\alpha,\beta)}(X) - DC_{R_2}^{(\alpha,\beta)}(X)$$

$$= \overline{\mu}(p_1)\,|p_1|\lambda_{NP} - \overline{\mu}(q_2)\,|q_2|\lambda_{NP} - (1 - \overline{\mu}(q_1))\,|q_1|\lambda_{PN}$$

$$= |q_1|(\overline{\mu}(q_1)(\lambda_{NP} + \lambda_{PN}) - \lambda_{PN}).$$

Because $\overline{\mu}(q_1) \geq \alpha = \dfrac{\lambda_{PN} - \lambda_{BN}}{\lambda_{PN} - \lambda_{BN} + \lambda_{BP}}$, *and* $\dfrac{\lambda_{BP}}{\lambda_{NP}} + \dfrac{\lambda_{BN}}{\lambda_{PN}} \leq 1$, so, $\dfrac{\lambda_{PN} - \lambda_{BN}}{\lambda_{PN} - \lambda_{BN} + \lambda_{BP}} \geq \dfrac{\lambda_{PN}}{\lambda_{NP} + \lambda_{PN}}$, then we have $\Delta DC_{R_1-R_2} \geq 0$.

Thus,

$DC_{R_1}^{(\alpha,\beta)}(X) \geq DC_{R_2}^{(\alpha,\beta)}(X)$

Fig. 3. Equivalence classes subdivided in the negative region of S3WDRFS

Case 3. If $\beta < \overline{\mu}(q_1) < \alpha$ and $\overline{\mu}(q_2) \leq \beta$, namely, $q_1 \subseteq BND_{R_2}^{(\alpha,\beta)}(X)$ and $q_2 \subseteq NEG_{R_2}^{(\alpha,\beta)}(X)$. The change of the granules in the negative region can be shown as Fig. 2(b).

$$\Delta DC_{R_1-R_2}(X) = DC_{R_1}^{(\alpha,\beta)}(X) - DC_{R_2}^{(\alpha,\beta)}(X)$$

$$= \overline{\mu}(p_1)|p_1|\lambda_{NP} - \overline{\mu}(q_2)|q_2|\lambda_{NP} - \overline{\mu}(q_1)|q_1|\lambda_{BP} - (1-\overline{\mu}(q_1))|q_1|\lambda_{BN}$$

$$= |q_1|(\overline{\mu}(q_1)(\lambda_{NP} + \lambda_{BN} - \lambda_{BP}) - \lambda_{BN}).$$

Because $\beta < \overline{\mu}(q_1) < \alpha$, and $\beta = \dfrac{\lambda_{BN}}{\lambda_{BN} + \lambda_{NP} - \lambda_{BP}}$, then we have $\Delta DC_{R_1-R_2}(X) \geq 0$

Thus, $DC_{R_1}^{(\alpha,\beta)}(X) \geq DC_{R_2}^{(\alpha,\beta)}(X)$

(2) Supposing $\overline{\mu}(p_1) \geq \alpha$, *obviously*, $p_1 \subseteq POS_{R_1}^{(\alpha,\beta)}(X)$

Case 1. If $\overline{\mu}(q_1) \geq \alpha$ *and* $\overline{\mu}(q_2) \geq \alpha$, namely, $q_1 \subseteq POS_{R_2}^{(\alpha,\beta)}(X)$ and $q_2 \subseteq POS_{R_2}^{(\alpha,\beta)}(X)$

$$\Delta DC_{R_1-R_2}(X) = DC_{R_1}^{(\alpha,\beta)}(X) - DC_{R_2}^{(\alpha,\beta)}(X)$$

$$= DC(POS_{R_1}^{(\alpha,\beta)}(X)) - DC(POS_{R_2}^{(\alpha,\beta)}(X))$$

$$= (1-\overline{\mu}(p_1))|p_1|\lambda_{PN} - (1-\overline{\mu}(q_1))|q_1|\lambda_{PN} - (1-\overline{\mu}(q_2))|q_2|\lambda_{PN}$$

$$= (|p_1| - |q_1| - |q_2| + \sum_{x_i \in q_1}\mu(x_i) + \sum_{x_i \in q_2}\mu(x_i) - \sum_{x_i \in p_1}\mu(x_i))\lambda_{PN}$$

Because $\sum_{x_i \in p_1}\mu(x_i) = \sum_{x_i \in q_1}\mu(x_i) + \sum_{x_i \in q_2}\mu(x_i)$ *and* $|p_1| = |q_1| + |q_2|$, then we have $\Delta DC_{R_1-R_2}(X) = 0$. Thus, $DC_{R_1}^{(\alpha,\beta)}(X) = DC_{R_2}^{(\alpha,\beta)}(X)$.

Figure 3. Equivalence classes subdivided in the positive region of S3WDRFS

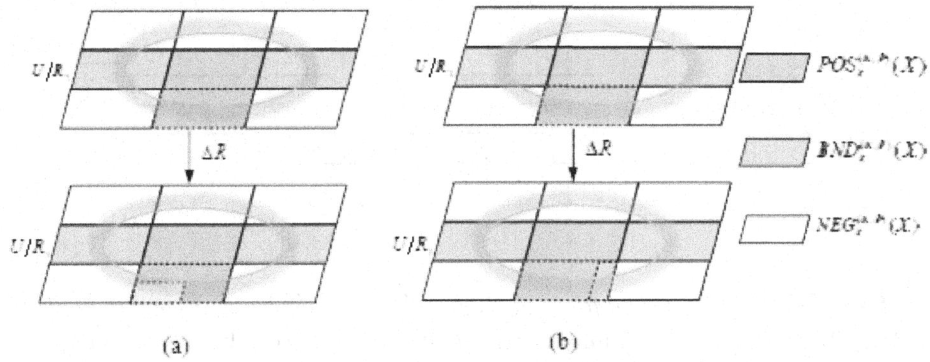

Case 2. If $\overline{\mu}(q_1) \geq \alpha$ *and* $\overline{\mu}(q_2) \leq \beta$, namely, $q_1 \subseteq POS_{R_2}^{(\alpha,\beta)}(X)$ and $q_2 \subseteq NEG_{R_2}^{(\alpha,\beta)}(X)$. The change of the granules in the positive region can be shown as Fig. 3(a).

$$\Delta DC_{R_1-R_2}(X) = DC_{R_1}^{(\alpha,\beta)}(X) - DC_{R_2}^{(\alpha,\beta)}(X)$$

$$= (1-\overline{\mu}(p_1))|p_1|\lambda_{PN} - (1-\overline{\mu}(q_1))|q_1|\lambda_{PN} - \overline{\mu}(q_2)|q_2|\lambda_{NP}$$

$= |q_2|(\lambda_{PN} - \bar{\mu}(q_2)(\lambda_{NP} + \lambda_{PN}))$

Because $\bar{\mu}(q_2) \leq \beta = \dfrac{\lambda_{BN}}{\lambda_{BN} + \lambda_{NP} - \lambda_{BP}}$, *and* $\dfrac{\lambda_{BP}}{\lambda_{NP}} + \dfrac{\lambda_{BN}}{\lambda_{PN}} \leq 1$, so, $\dfrac{\lambda_{BN}}{\lambda_{BN} + \lambda_{NP} - \lambda_{BP}} \leq \dfrac{\lambda_{NP}}{\lambda_{NP} + \lambda_{PN}}$, then we have $\Delta DC_{R_1-R_2}(X) \geq 0$. Thus, $DC_{R_1}^{(\alpha,\beta)}(X) \geq DC_{R_2}^{(\alpha,\beta)}(X)$.

Case 3. If $\beta < \bar{\mu}(q_1) < \alpha$ *and* $\bar{\mu}(q_2) \geq \alpha$, namely, $q_1 \subseteq BND_{R_2}^{(\alpha,\beta)}(X)$ and $q_2 \subseteq POS_{R_2}^{(\alpha,\beta)}(X)$. The change of the granules in the positive region can be shown as Fig. 3(b).

$\Delta DC_{R_1-R_2}(X) = DC_{R_1}^{(\alpha,\beta)}(X) - DC_{R_2}^{(\alpha,\beta)}(X)$

$= (1 - \bar{\mu}(p_1))|p_1|\lambda_{PN} - (1 - \bar{\mu}(q_2))|q_2|\lambda_{PN} - \bar{\mu}(q_1)|q_1|\lambda_{BP} - (1 - \bar{\mu}(q_1))|q_1|\lambda_{BN})$

$= |q_1|(\lambda_{PN} - \lambda_{BN} - \bar{\mu}(q_1)(\lambda_{PN} + \lambda_{BP} - \lambda_{BN}))$.

Because $\beta < \bar{\mu}(q_1) < \alpha$, *and* $\alpha = \dfrac{\lambda_{PN} - \lambda_{BN}}{\lambda_{PN} - \lambda_{BN} + \lambda_{BP}}$, then we have $\Delta DC_{R_1-R_2}(X) \geq 0$. Thus, $DC_{R_1}^{(\alpha,\beta)}(X) \geq DC_{R_2}^{(\alpha,\beta)}(X)$.

(3) Supposing $\beta < \bar{\mu}(p_1) < \alpha$, *obviously,* $p_1 \subseteq BND_{R_1}^{(\alpha,\beta)}(X)$.

Case 1. If $\beta < \bar{\mu}(q_1) < \alpha$ *and* $\beta < \bar{\mu}(q_2) < \alpha$, namely, $q_1 \subseteq BND_{R_2}^{(\alpha,\beta)}(X)$ and $q_2 \subseteq BND_{R_2}^{(\alpha,\beta)}(X)$.

$\Delta DC_{R_1-R_2}(X) = DC_{R_1}^{(\alpha,\beta)}(X) - DC_{R_2}^{(\alpha,\beta)}(X)$

$= DC(BND_{R_1}^{(\alpha,\beta)}(X)) - DC(BND_{R_2}^{(\alpha,\beta)}(X))$.

Similar to Case 1 of (1) and (2), because $\beta < \bar{\mu}(p_1) < \alpha$, *then we have* $\Delta DC_{BND}(X) = 0$. Thus, $DC_{R_1}^{(\alpha,\beta)}(X) = DC_{R_2}^{(\alpha,\beta)}(X)$.

Figure 4. Equivalence classes subdivided in the boundary region of S3WDRFS

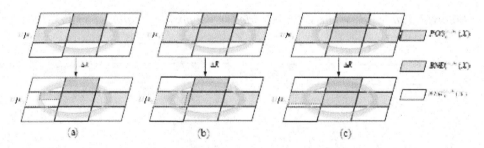

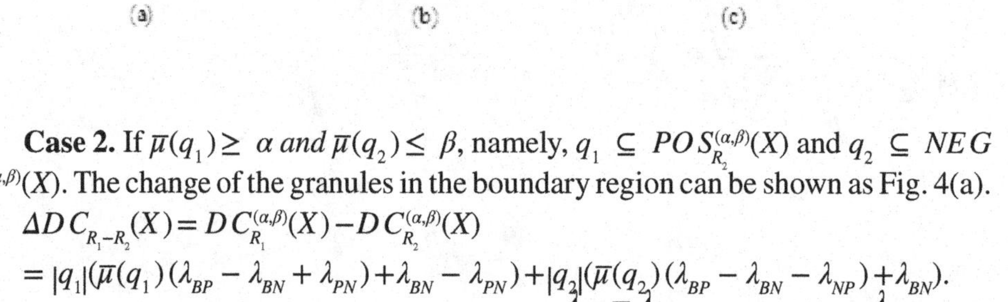

Case 2. If $\bar{\mu}(q_1) \geq \alpha$ *and* $\bar{\mu}(q_2) \leq \beta$, namely, $q_1 \subseteq POS_{R_2}^{(\alpha,\beta)}(X)$ and $q_2 \subseteq NEG_{R_2}^{(\alpha,\beta)}(X)$. The change of the granules in the boundary region can be shown as Fig. 4(a).

$\Delta DC_{R_1-R_2}(X) = DC_{R_1}^{(\alpha,\beta)}(X) - DC_{R_2}^{(\alpha,\beta)}(X)$

$= |q_1|(\bar{\mu}(q_1)(\lambda_{BP} - \lambda_{BN} + \lambda_{PN}) + \lambda_{BN} - \lambda_{PN}) + |q_2|(\bar{\mu}(q_2)(\lambda_{BP} - \lambda_{BN} - \lambda_{NP}) + \lambda_{BN})$.

Because $\bar{\mu}(q_1) \geq \alpha$, $\bar{\mu}(q_2) \leq \beta$ and $\alpha = \dfrac{\lambda_{PN} - \lambda_{BN}}{\lambda_{PN} - \lambda_{BN} + \lambda_{BP}}$, $\beta = \dfrac{\lambda_{BN}}{\lambda_{BN} + \lambda_{NP} - \lambda_{BP}}$, then we have $\Delta DC_{R_1-R_2}(X) \geq 0$. Thus, $DC_{R_1}^{(\alpha,\beta)}(X) \geq DC_{R_2}^{(\alpha,\beta)}(X)$.

Case 3. If $\beta < \bar{\mu}(q_1) < \alpha$ *and* $\bar{\mu}(q_2) \geq \alpha$, namely, $q_1 \subseteq BND_{R_2}^{(\alpha,\beta)}(X)$ and $q_2 \subseteq POS_{R_2}^{(\alpha,\beta)}(X)$. The change of the granules in the boundary region can be shown as Fig. 4(b).

$\Delta DC_{R_1-R_2} = DC_{R_1}^{(\alpha,\beta)}(X) - DC_{R_2}^{(\alpha,\beta)}(X)$

$= |q_2|(\bar{\mu}(q_2)(\lambda_{BP} - \lambda_{BN}) + \lambda_{BN}) - |q_2|(1 - \bar{\mu}(q_2))\lambda_{PN}$

$= |q_2|(\bar{\mu}(q_2)(\lambda_{PN} - \lambda_{BN} + \lambda_{BP}) - (\lambda_{PN} - \lambda_{BN}))$

Because $\bar{\mu}(q_2) \geq \alpha$, and $\alpha = \dfrac{\lambda_{PN} - \lambda_{BN}}{\lambda_{PN} - \lambda_{BN} + \lambda_{BP}}$, then we have $\Delta DC_{R_1-R_2}(X) \geq 0$. Thus, $DC_{R_1}^{(\alpha,\beta)}(X) \geq DC_{R_2}^{(\alpha,\beta)}(X)$

Case 4. If $\beta < \bar{\mu}(q_1) < \alpha$ and $\bar{\mu}(q_2) \leq \beta$, namely, $q_1 \subseteq BND_{R_2}^{(\alpha,\beta)}(X)$ and $q_2 \subseteq NEG_{R_2}^{(\alpha,\beta)}(X)$. The change of the granules in the boundary region can be shown as Fig. 4(c).

$\Delta DC_{R_1-R_2}(X) = DC_{R_1}^{(\alpha,\beta)}(X) - DC_{R_2}^{(\alpha,\beta)}(X)$

$= |q_2|(\bar{\mu}(q_2)(\lambda_{BP} - \lambda_{BN}) + \lambda_{BN}) - |q_2|(\bar{\mu}(q_2)\lambda_{NP}$

$= |q_2|(\lambda_{BN} - \bar{\mu}(q_2)(\lambda_{BN} + \lambda_{NP} - \lambda_{BP}))$.

Because $\bar{\mu}(q_2) \leq \beta$, and $\beta = \dfrac{\lambda_{BN}}{\lambda_{BN} + \lambda_{NP} - \lambda_{BP}}$, then we have $\Delta DC_{R_1-R_2}(X) \geq 0$. Thus, $DC_{R_1}^{(\alpha,\beta)}(X) \geq DC_{R_2}^{(\alpha,\beta)}(X)$.

Theorem 1 indicates the cost of multilevel decision result in S3WDRFS model will monotonically decrease with the knowledge spaces being finer. Such a result is in line with human cognitive habits.

Example 2 Given an decision system $S = (U, C \cup D, V, f)$, $R_1 \subseteq C$, $R_2 \subseteq C$, $R_3 \subseteq C$ and $R_4 \subseteq C$, $X = \frac{0.1}{x_1} + \frac{0.2}{x_2} + \frac{0.5}{x_3} + \frac{0.7}{x_4} + \frac{1}{x_5} + \frac{1}{x_6} + \frac{0.7}{x_7} + \frac{0.3}{x_8} + \frac{0.2}{x_9}$ is a fuzzy set on U; $U/R_1 = \{\{x_1,x_2\},\{x_3,x_4,x_5,x_6\},\{x_7,x_8,x_9\}\}$, $U/R_2 = \{\{x_1\},\{x_2\},\{x_3,x_4,x_5,x_6\},\{x_7,x_8,x_9\}\}$, $U/R_3 = \{\{x_1,x_2\},\{x_3,x_4\},\{x_5,x_6\},\{x_7,x_8,x_9\}\}$, $U/R_4 = \{\{x_1,x_2\},\{x_3,x_4,x_5,x_6\},\{x_7\},\{x_8,x_9\}\}$

Obviously, $U/R_2 \prec U/R_1$, $U/R_3 \prec U/R_1$, $U/R_4 \prec U/R_1$, we have

$R_1(X^*) = \frac{0.15}{x_1} + \frac{0.15}{x_2} + \frac{0.8}{x_3} + \frac{0.8}{x_4} + \frac{0.8}{x_5} + \frac{0.8}{x_6} + \frac{0.4}{x_7} + \frac{0.4}{x_8} + \frac{0.4}{x_9}$,

$R_2(X^*) = \frac{0.1}{x_1} + \frac{0.2}{x_2} + \frac{0.8}{x_3} + \frac{0.8}{x_4} + \frac{0.8}{x_5} + \frac{0.8}{x_6} + \frac{0.4}{x_7} + \frac{0.4}{x_8} + \frac{0.4}{x_9}$,

$R_3(X^*) = \frac{0.15}{x_1} + \frac{0.15}{x_2} + \frac{0.6}{x_3} + \frac{0.6}{x_4} + \frac{1}{x_5} + \frac{1}{x_6} + \frac{0.4}{x_7} + \frac{0.4}{x_8} + \frac{0.4}{x_9}$,

$R_4(X^*) = \frac{0.15}{x_1} + \frac{0.15}{x_2} + \frac{0.8}{x_3} + \frac{0.8}{x_4} + \frac{0.8}{x_5} + \frac{0.8}{x_6} + \frac{0.7}{x_7} + \frac{0.25}{x_8} + \frac{0.25}{x_9}$.

Supposing $\lambda_{PP} = 0 \lambda_{PN} = 10 \lambda_{BP} = 2 \lambda_{NP} = 14 \lambda_{BN} = 4 \lambda_{NN} = 0$, we can obtain $\alpha = 0.75$, $\beta = 0.25$. Based on the pair of thresholds α and β, the three regions of DTRFS can be obtained as follow,

$POS_{R_1}^{(0.75,0.25)}(X) = \{x_3,x_4,x_5,x_6\}$, $BND_{R_1}^{(0.75,0.25)}(X) = \{x_7,x_8,x_9\}$, $NEG_{R_1}^{(0.75,0.25)}(X) = \{x_1,x_2\}$,

$POS_{R_2}^{(0.75,0.25)}(X) = \{x_3,x_4,x_5,x_6\}$, $BND_{R_2}^{(0.75,0.25)}(X) = \{x_7,x_8,x_9\}$, $NEG_{R_2}^{(0.75,0.25)}(X) = \{x_1,x_2\}$,

$POS_{R_3}^{(0.75,0.25)}(X) = \{x_5,x_6\}$, $BND_{R_3}^{(0.75,0.25)}(X) = \{x_3,x_4,x_7,x_8,x_9\}$, $NEG_{R_3}^{(0.75,0.25)}(X) = \{x_1,x_2\}$,

$POS_{R_4}^{(0.75,0.25)}(X) = \{x_3,x_4,x_5,x_6\}$, $BND_{R_4}^{(0.75,0.25)}(X) = \{x_7\}$, $NEG_{R_4}^{(0.75,0.25)}(X) = \{x_1,x_2,x_8,x_9\}$.

According to the formula (1)-(3), we have

$\Delta DC_{R_1-R_2} = DC_{R_1}^{(0.75,0.25)}(X) - DC_{R_2}^{(0.75,0.25)}(X) = 23.8 - 23.8 = 0,$
$\Delta DC_{R_1-R_3} = DC_{R_1}^{(0.75,0.25)}(X) - DC_{R_3}^{(0.75,0.25)}(X) = 23.8 - 15.8 = 8 \geq 0,$
$\Delta DC_{R_1-R_4} = DC_{R_1}^{(0.75,0.25)}(X) - DC_{R_4}^{(0.75,0.25)}(X) = 23.8 - 21.8 = 2 \geq 0.$

Therefore, the results are in consists with Theorem 1. We only present three cases in example 2, and the readers can verify other cases which are not presented in example 2.

According to Theorem 1, we have the corollary as follows,

Corollary 1. Given an decision system $S = (U, C \cup D, V, f), R_1 \subseteq C$ and $R_2 \subseteq C$, X is a fuzzy set on U. If $R_1 \subseteq R_2$, then $DC_{R_1}^{(1,0)}(X) \geq DC_{R_2}^{(1,0)}(X)$.

Corollary 1 indicates the cost of decision result at each granularity in (1,0) S3WDRFS model will monotonically decrease with the knowledge spaces being finer. Such a result is in line with human cognitive habits.

The calculation of decision cost of three regions is significant to make a low risk decision in 3WDRFS. Theorem 1 shows that the decision cost of S3WDRFS will monotonically decrease with the knowledge space being finer. In (0,1)S3WDRFS model, the decision cost of the boundary region will monotonically decrease with the knowledge space being finer. However, in S3WDRFS model, the decision cost of boundary region probably does not monotonically decrease with the knowledge space being finer. In this section, for simplicity, we only analyze the decision cost of the boundary region in three cases.

Theorem 2 Given an decision system $S = (U, C \cup D, V, f), R_1 \subseteq C$ and $R_2 \subseteq C$, X is a fuzzy set on U. If $R_1 \subseteq R_2$ and only the granules containing in $NEG_{R_1}^{(\alpha,\beta)}(X)$ are subdivided into many finer equivalence classes by the attribute increment $\Delta R = R_2 - R_1$, then $DC(BND_{R_1}^{(\alpha,\beta)}(X)) \leq DC(BND_{R_2}^{(\alpha,\beta)}(X))$.

Proof. Let $U = \{x_1, x_2, ..., x_n\}$ *be a non-empty finite domain,* $U/R_1 = \{p_1, p_2, ..., p_l\}$ and $U/R_2 = \{q_1, q_2, ..., q_m\}$. Because $R_1 \subseteq R_2$, so $U/R_2 \preceq U/R_1$. According to the condition, for simplicity, supposing only one granule p_1 can be subdivided into two finer sub-granules by $\Delta R = R_2 - R_1$ (the more complicated cases can be transformed into this case, so we will not repeat them here). Without loss of generality, let $p_1 = q_1 \cup q_2, p_2 = q_3, p_3 = q_4, p_l = q_m$ $(m = l + 1)$, namely, $U/R_1 = \{q_1, q_2, p_2, p_3, ..., p_l\}$. We will prove this theorem in three cases in the following.

Because $p_1 \subseteq NEG_{R_1}^{(\alpha,\beta)}(X)$, *obviously,* $\overline{\mu}(p_1) \leq \beta$.

Case 1. If $\overline{\mu}(q_1) \leq \beta$ *and* $\overline{\mu}(q_2) \leq \beta$, namely, $q_1 \subseteq NEG_{R_2}^{(\alpha,\beta)}(X)$ and $q_2 \subseteq NEG_{R_2}^{(\alpha,\beta)}(X)$, So, $BND_{R_1}^{(\alpha_1,\beta_1)}(X) = BND_{R_2}^{(\alpha_2,\beta_2)}(X)$. Because $p_2 = q_3$, $p_3 = q_4$, $p_l = q_m$ $(m = l + 1)$, and $DC(BND_{R_1}^{(\alpha,\beta)}(X)) = DC(BND_{R_2}^{(\alpha,\beta)}(X))$.

Case 2. If $\overline{\mu}(q_1) \geq \alpha$ *and* $\overline{\mu}(q_2) \leq \beta$, namely, $q_1 \subseteq POS_{R_2}^{(\alpha,\beta)}(X)$ and $q_2 \subseteq NEG_{R_2}^{(\alpha,\beta)}(X)$. So, $BND_{R_1}^{(\alpha_1,\beta_1)}(X) = BND_{R_2}^{(\alpha_2,\beta_2)}(X)$. Because $p_2 = q_3$, $p_3 = q_4$, $p_l = q_m$ $(m = l + 1)$, and $DC(BND_{R_1}^{(\alpha,\beta)}(X)) = DC(BND_{R_2}^{(\alpha,\beta)}(X))$.

Case 3. If $\beta < \overline{\mu}(q_1) < \alpha$ and $\overline{\mu}(q_2) \leq \beta$, namely, $q_1 \subseteq BND_{R_2}^{(\alpha,\beta)}(X)$ and $q_2 \subseteq NEG_{R_2}^{(\alpha,\beta)}(X)$. Then $BND_{R_2}^{(\alpha_1,\beta_1)}(X) = BND_{R_1}^{(\alpha_2,\beta_2)}(X) \cup q_1$,

$DC(BND_{R_2}^{(\alpha,\beta)}(X)) = DC(BND_{R_1}^{(\alpha,\beta)}(X)) + DC(q_1) > DC(BND_{R_2}^{(\alpha,\beta)}(X))$

Thus, $DC(BND_{R_1}^{(\alpha,\beta)}(X)) < DC(BND_{R_2}^{(\alpha,\beta)}(X))$.

Theorem 3. Given an decision system $S = (U, C \cup D, V, f), R_1 \subseteq C$ and $R_2 \subseteq C$, X is a fuzzy set on U. If $R_1 \subseteq R_2$ and only the granules containing in $POS_{R_1}^{(\alpha,\beta)}(X)$ are subdivided into many finer equivalence classes by the attribute increment $\Delta R = R_2 - R_1$, then $DC(BND_{R_1}^{(\alpha,\beta)}(X)) \leq DC(BND_{R_2}^{(\alpha,\beta)}(X))$.

Similar to Theorem 2, Theorem 3 is easy to prove. According to Theorem 2 and Theorem 3, the decision cost of boundary region will increase when only the equivalence classes contained in the negative region or positive region are subdivided with the knowledge space being finer in S3WDRFS model. This is not in line with human cognitive habits and is not consistent with the (1,0) S3WDRFS model.

Theorem 4. Given an decision system $S = (U, C \cup D, V, f), R_1 \subseteq C$ and $R_2 \subseteq C$, X is a fuzzy set on U. If $R_1 \subseteq R_2$ and only the granules containing in $BND_{R_1}^{(\alpha,\beta)}(X)$ are subdivided into many finer equivalence classes by the attribute increment $\Delta R = R_2 - R_1$, then $DC(BND_{R_1}^{(\alpha,\beta)}(X)) \geq DC(BND_{R_2}^{(\alpha,\beta)}(X))$.

Proof. Let $U = \{x_1, x_2, ..., x_n\}$ *be a non-empty finite domain,* $U/R_1 = \{p_1, p_2, ..., p_l\}$ and $U/R_2 = \{q_1, q_2, ..., q_m\}$. Because $R_1 \subseteq R_2$, so $U/R_2 \preceq U/R_1$. According to the condition, for simplicity, supposing only one granule p_1 can be subdivided into two finer sub-granules by $\Delta R = R_2 - R_1$ (the more complicated cases can be transformed into this case, so we will not repeat them here). Without loss of generality, let $p_1 = q_1 \cup q_2, p_2 = q_3, p_3 = q_4, p_l = q_m (m = l + 1)$, namely, $U/R_1 = \{q_1, q_2, p_2, p_3, ..., p_l\}$. We will prove this theorem in three cases in the following.

Case 1. If $\beta < \bar{\mu}(q_1) < \alpha$ *and* $\beta < \bar{\mu}(q_2) < \alpha$, namely, $q_1 \subseteq BND_{R_2}^{(\alpha,\beta)}(X)$ and $q_2 \subseteq BND_{R_2}^{(\alpha,\beta)}(X)$. So, $BND_{R_1}^{(\alpha_1,\beta_1)}(X) = BND_{R_2}^{(\alpha_2,\beta_2)}(X)$. Because $p_2 = q_3, p_3 = q_4, p_l = q_m (m = l + 1)$, and $DC(BND_{R_1}^{(\alpha,\beta)}(X)) = DC(BND_{R_2}^{(\alpha,\beta)}(X))$.

Case 2. If $\bar{\mu}(q_1) \geq \alpha$ *and* $\bar{\mu}(q_2) \leq \beta$, namely, $q_1 \subseteq POS_{R_2}^{(\alpha,\beta)}(X)$ and $q_2 \subseteq NEG_{R_2}^{(\alpha,\beta)}(X)$.

$\Delta DC_{BND} = DC(BND_{R_1}^{(\alpha,\beta)}(X)) - DC(BND_{R_2}^{(\alpha,\beta)}(X))$

$= \bar{\mu}(p_1)|p_1|\lambda_{BP} + (1 - \bar{\mu}(p_1))|p_1|\lambda_{BN} > 0.$

Thus, $DC(BND_{R_1}^{(\alpha,\beta)}(X)) > DC(BND_{R_2}^{(\alpha,\beta)}(X))$.

Case 3. If $\beta < \bar{\mu}(q_1) < \alpha$ *and* $\bar{\mu}(q_2) \geq \alpha$, namely, $q_1 \subseteq BND_{R_2}^{(\alpha,\beta)}(X)$ and $q_2 \subseteq POS_{R_2}^{(\alpha,\beta)}(X)$.

$\Delta DC_{BND} = DC(BND_{R_1}^{(\alpha,\beta)}(X)) - DC(BND_{R_2}^{(\alpha,\beta)}(X))$.

$= \bar{\mu}(p_1)|p_1|\lambda_{BP} + (1 - \bar{\mu}(p_1))|p_1|\lambda_{BN} - \bar{\mu}(q_1)|q_1|\lambda_{BP} - (1 - \bar{\mu}(q_1))|q_1|\lambda_{BN}$

$= \sum_{x_i \in p_1} \mu(x_i)\lambda_{BP} + |p_1|\lambda_{BN} - \sum_{x_i \in p_1} \mu(x_i)\lambda_{BN} - \sum_{x_i \in q_1} \mu(x_i)\lambda_{BP} - |q_1|\lambda_{BN} + \sum_{x_i \in q_1} \mu(x_i)\lambda_{BN}.$

Because $\sum_{x_i \in p_1} \mu(x_i) = \sum_{x_i \in q_1} \mu(x_i) + \sum_{x_i \in q_2} \mu(x_i)$, *then we have*

$\Delta DC_{BND} = |q_2|(\bar{\mu}(q_2)(\lambda_{BP} - \lambda_{BN}) + \lambda_{BN}) > 0.$

Thus, $DC(BND_{R_1}^{(\alpha,\beta)}(X)) > DC(BND_{R_2}^{(\alpha,\beta)}(X))$.

Case 4. If $\beta < \overline{\mu}(q_1) < \alpha$ and $\overline{\mu}(q_2) \leq \beta$, namely, $q_1 \subseteq BND_{R_2}^{(\alpha,\beta)}(X)$ and $q_2 \subseteq NEG_{R_2}^{(\alpha,\beta)}(X)$

$\Delta DC_{BND} = DC(BND_{R_1}^{(\alpha,\beta)}(X)) - DC(BND_{R_2}^{(\alpha,\beta)}(X))$

$= |q_2|(\overline{\mu}(q_2)(\lambda_{BP} - \lambda_{BN}) + \lambda_{BN}) > 0.$

Thus, $DC(BND_{R_1}^{(\alpha,\beta)}(X)) > DC(BND_{R_2}^{(\alpha,\beta)}(X))$.

Theorem 4 shows that the decision cost of boundary region will decrease when only the equivalence classes in boundary region are subdivided with the knowledge space being finer in S3WDRFS model. This is line with human cognitive habits and is consistent with the (1,0) S3WDRFS model.

Table 1. Comparative analysis on the decision cost of misclassification

	(1,0)S3WDRFS Model	S3WDRFS Model
only the granules containing in $NEG_{R_1}^{(\alpha,\beta)}(X)$ *are subdivided*		
only the granules containing in $POS_{R_1}^{(\alpha,\beta)}(X)$ *are subdivided*		
only the granules containing in $BND_{R_1}^{(\alpha,\beta)}(X)$ *are subdivided*		
only the granules containing in any region are subdivided	$DC_{R_1}^{(1,0)}(X) \geq DC_{R_2}^{(1,0)}(X)$	$DC_{R_1}^{(\alpha,\beta)}(X) \geq DC_{R_2}^{(\alpha,\beta)}(X)$

Table 1 indicate that if only the equivalence classes contained in the negative region are subdivided at each granularity in S3WDRFS model, although the decision cost of both the positive region and boundary region may increase with the adding attributes, the decision cost of the negative region will decrease since the total decision cost decreases. The conclusions of other two cases (only the equivalence classes contained in the negative region) can be obtained in a similar way, so we will not repeat them here. Such results are different from that of (1,0) S3WDRFS model.

Example 3. The data in Table 2 are collected based on the experience of a Greek industrial development bank. The detailed information about the criteria and true meaning of criteria values can be found in [53]. $U = \{x_1, x_2, \ldots, x_{39}\}$ *is a sample of 39 firms, the condition attributes* $C = \{A_1, A_2, \ldots, A_{12}\}$ is consist of 12 criterions to assess the firms, and three states D_1, D_2, D_3 denote the unacceptable, uncertain and acceptable degree, respectively.

continued on following page

Table 2. Continued

Table 2. Fuzzy evaluation of bankruptcy risk

Firm	A_1	A_2	A_3	A_4	A_5	A_6	A_7	A_8	A_9	A_{10}	A_{11}	A_{12}	D_1	D_2	D_3
x_1	2	2	2	2	1	3	5	3	5	4	2	4	0.1	0.3	0.7
x_2	4	5	2	3	3	3	5	4	5	5	4	5	0	0	1
x_3	3	5	1	1	2	2	5	3	5	5	3	5	0.1	0.3	0.8
⋮	⋮	⋮	⋮	⋮	⋮	⋮	⋮	⋮	⋮	⋮	⋮	⋮	⋮	⋮	⋮
x_{38}	1	1	3	1	1	1	1	1	4	3	1	3	0.9	0.3	0.2
x_{39}	2	1	1	1	1	1	1	1	2	1	1	2	1	0	0

Supposing that $GS = (GL_1, GL_2, \ldots, GL_5)$ *is a hierarchical granular structure consists of five granular layers, where* $GL_i = (U, R_i \cup D, V, f), i = 1, 2, \ldots, 5$. R_i is a condition attribute set, $R_5 \subset R_4 \subset R_3 \subset R_2 \subset R_1 \subseteq C$. We assume that $\lambda_{PP} = 0$, $\lambda_{PN} = 10, \lambda_{BP} = 2, \lambda_{NP} = 14, \lambda_{BN} = 4$ and $\lambda_{NN} = 0$, thus $\alpha = 0.75, \beta = 0.25$. The total decision cost and the decision cost from three regions respect to D_1, D_2, D_3 are computed with the granularity being finer.

Figure 5. The decision cost with changing granularity level

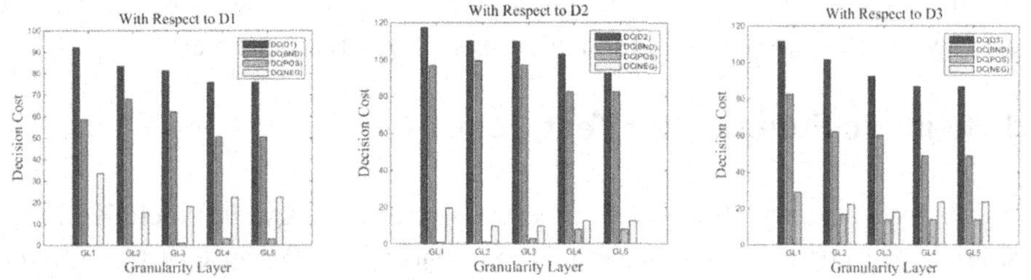

The experimental results are shown in Fig.5, which has three subfigures. The x-coordinate pertains to five levels GS, while the y-coordinate concerns the each value of decision cost. From Fig.5, we can have the following points:

(1) The decision cost are mainly derived from boundary region.

(2) From the coarser levels to the finer levels in GS, the decision cost of D_1, D_2, D_3 monotonically decrease, while the decision cost from three regions exhibit a non-monotonicity.

This is easy to understand because several equivalence classes containing in different regions are probably subdivided into many finer equivalence classes by the attribute increment, leading to an increase or decrease cost in the three regions at the same time. In addition, we know that the total increment of decrease cost is greater than or equal to the total increment of increase cost, since the total decision cost in S3WDRFS decreases with the increase of condition attributes, which is consist with Theorem 1.

5. OPTIMAL QUALITATIVE COST-SENSITIVE GRANULARITY SELECTION

According to the discussion in section 4, the cost of decision result is proved to monotonically decrease in S3WDRFS model. The test cost denotes the cost for acquiring certain attribute values, and it should be considered in granularity optimization in many practical applications. Therefore, it is significant to solve problem combined with the level of the decision cost and test cost. As we known, an uncertain concept can be better described and a less decision cost will obtain in a finer granularity space. However, the test cost will be higher in a finer knowledge space since the more attribute values need to be acquired. Hence, decision cost and test cost are contradictory each other with the changing granularity. From the perspective of cost, it is necessary to find a balance point between decision cost and test cost, which is formulated as an optimization problem and aims to minimize the total cost of classification under the constraint condition. That is to say, to achieve the optimal results to satisfy the requirements of decision cost and test cost, it is necessary to select an optimal granularity space for solving problem.

5.1 Heuristic Function for Test Cost

Generally speaking, the factors (time, money, technology, etc) included in test cost are hard to be evaluated accurately and objectively. Because of the different dimensions of each factor, it is difficult to integrate various factors, which greatly affects decision making. In addition, the current research on cost sensitive learning only considers the total cost as a constraint, which is not true in practical application. Therefore, it is necessary to describe the test cost qualitatively.

Based on the Earth Movers' Distance (EMD) (Rubner, 2000), we proposed a knowledge distance (KD) to characterize the difference among knowledge spaces in a hierarchical granular structure. Our knowledge distance achieves a many-to-many matching calculation, which is suitable for reflecting the difference between any two knowledge spaces effectively and intuitively since it is in line with human cognition.

Definition 9 Given an decision system $S = (U, C \cup D, V, f)$, $R_1 \subseteq C$ and $R_2 \subseteq C$, X is a fuzzy set on U. $U/R_1 = \{p_1, p_2, ..., p_n\}$ and $U/R_2 = \{q_1, q_2, ..., q_m\}$ are two partition spaces induced by R_1 and R_2 respectively. Then, the formula for KD is defined as follows:

$$KD(U/R_1, U/R_2) = \frac{1}{|U|}\sum_{i=1}^{n}\sum_{j=1}^{m}\frac{|p_i \oplus q_j|}{|U|}|p_i \cap q_j|, \quad (7)$$

where $|p_i \oplus q_j| = |p_i \cup q_j| - |p_i \cap q_j|$.

Theorem 5 Given an decision system $S = (U, C \cup D, V, f)$, $R_1 \subseteq C$, X is a fuzzy set on U. $U/R_1 = \{p_1, p_2, ..., p_n\}$ is a partition space induced by R_1, then $KD(U/R_1, \delta)$ *is an information measure.*

Theorem 6 Given an decision system $S = (U, C \cup D, V, f)$, $R_1 \subseteq C$ and $R_2 \subseteq C$, X is a fuzzy set on U. $U/R_1 = \{p_1, p_2, ..., p_n\}$ and $U/R_2 = \{q_1, q_2, ..., q_m\}$ are two partition spaces induced by R_1 and R_2 respectively . If $R_1 \subseteq R_2$, then $KD(U/R_1, U/R_2) = KD(U/R_2, \delta) - KD(U/R_1, \delta)$.

From Theorem 6, $KD(U/R_i, \delta)$ *has been proved that it can be used to characterize the information content of a granularity layer as an information measure. That is to say, the higher* $KD(U/R_i, \delta)$ is, the higher the cost for granularity processing; inversely, the smaller $KD(U/R_i, \delta)$ is, the smaller the cost for granularity processing. *Combined Theorem 5 with Theorem 6, it is obviously that the knowledge distance between any two partition spaces in a hierarchical granular structure is linearly additive, which is equal to the difference between their information measures. In the following, we introduce two notions of qualitative cost for granularity processing and granularity constructing.*

Definition 10 Given an decision system $S = (U, C \cup D, V, f)$, $A \subseteq C$ and let X is a fuzzy set on U, the attribute significance of R can be defined as

$$Sig(A, C, D) = DC_{C-\{A\}}^{(\alpha,\beta)}(X) - DC_{C}^{(\alpha,\beta)}(X) \tag{8}$$

Definition 11 Given an decision system $S = (U, C \cup D, V, f)$, $R_1 \subseteq R_2 \subseteq \ldots \subseteq R_M \subseteq C$ and let X is a fuzzy set on U. Suppose a hierarchical granular structure $GS = (GL_1, GL_2, \ldots, GL_M)$ and $GL_i = (U, R_i \cup D, V, f)$. For the ith layer in GS, the test cost for decision process in S3WDRFS can be defined as follows:

$$TC_{GL_i} = TC_{GL_i}^{P} + TC_{GL_i}^{C} \tag{9}$$

,

where $TC_{GL_i}^{P} = \xi * KD(GL_i, \delta)$ *denotes the cost of granularity processing at the ith level of GS, and* $TC_{GL_i}^{C} = \sum_{A_j \in R_i} Sig(A_j, C, D)$ denotes the cost for constructing the granularity layer GL_i, and ξ is an adjustable factor. $Sig(A_j, C, D)$ denotes the attribute significance of condition attribute A_j.

According to Definition 11, we establish the relationship between test cost and decision cost by the formula (9). That is, the test cost can be qualitative characterized to a certain extent by decision cost and information content.

5.2 Cost-Sensitive Granularity Optimization Mechanism

In order to characterize the total cost, we established a heuristic function for searching the balance point as follows:

$$Total\_C_{GL_i} = \theta DC_{GL_i} + (1-\theta)TC_{GL_i}$$

, (10)

where, $Total\_C_{GL_i}$ *denotes the total cost on the granularity layer* GL_i; $\theta \in [0,1]$, which reflects the degree of preference of decision-maker. Formula (10) provides a qualitative heuristic method to search the global optimal cost-sensitive granularity, and there exists a balance point in formula (10), which denotes the minimum total cost.

According to the analysis in Section 1, the corresponding granularity of minimum total cost does not mean the optimal cost-sensitive granularity in some special cases. It is more reasonable for searching for the optimal cost-sensitive granularity by considering the user requirements for decision cost and test cost, respectively.

Figure 6. The optimal cost-sensitive granularity meeting the requirements

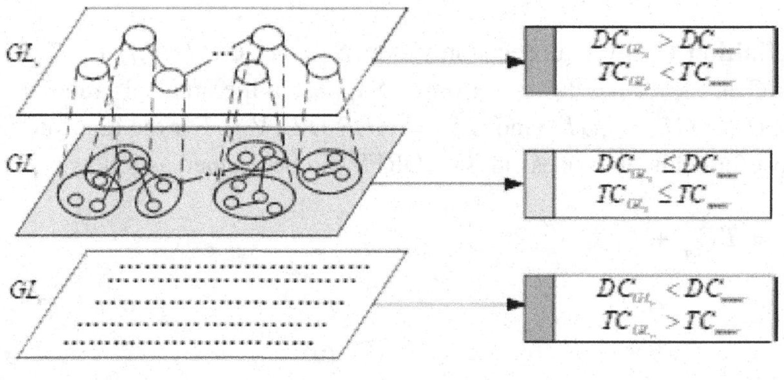

If the decision cost and test cost required by the users are expressed as DC_{user} *and* TC_{user} respectively, the granularity optimization is aim to find a granularity layer GL_i to satisfy the $DC_{GL_i} \leq DC_{user}$ and $TC_{GL_i} \leq TC_{user}$, then related intelligent calculation and analysis are implement on this granularity layer. The cost-sensitive granularity optimization mechanism is described in Fig 6. Herein, the granularity layer GL_r satisfies the demand for decision cost, but failed to meet the demand for test cost; the granularity layer GL_s satisfies the demand for test cost, but failed to meet the demand for decision cost; the granularity layer GL_t satisfies both the decision cost and test cost constraint, and the efficient computation is realized by granularity optimization. This calculation can be formalized as the following optimization problem:

$$\arg\min_{GL_i} Total\_C_{GL_i} \tag{11}$$

$$\text{s.t.} \quad DC_{GL_i} \leq DC_{user}, \quad TC_{GL_i} \leq TC_{user}$$

5.3 Algorithm for Optimal Cost-Sensitive Granularity Selection

To acquire the exemplary granularity solution to make the decision under the constraint condition, based on the cost-sensitive granularity optimization mechanism, we present a detailed algorithm to stepwise search for the optimal cost-sensitive granularity as follows,

Algorithm GS-S3WDRFS (The optimal granularity selection based on cost-sensitive S3WDRFS)

Input:
(1) A decision system $S = (U, C \cup D, V, f)$, *threshold* α, β.
(2) Loss function $\lambda_{PP}, \lambda_{BP}, \lambda_{NP}, \lambda_{NN}, \lambda_{BN}, \lambda_{PN}$.
Output:The temporary optimal attribute set R_{opt}
Step 1 Let $R_{opt} = \varnothing$.
Step 2 Compute the attribute significance $Sig(A, C, D) = DC^{(\alpha,\beta)}_{C-\{A\}}(X) - DC^{(\alpha,\beta)}_{C}(X)$, $\forall A \in C$.
Step 3 Sort the attributes according to $Sig(A)$ *in ascend order.*
Repeat following loop:
(I) $R = R \cup \{A\}$
(II) Compute *TC, DC* and $Total\_C$
(III) If $DC \leq DC_{user}$ && $TC \leq TC_{user}$, *then go to (IIII).*
(IIII) If $Total\_C \leq Total\_C_{\min}$, *then* $Total\_C_{\min} = Total\_C$ and $R_{opt} = R$
Step 4 Output $GL_{opt} = U/R_{opt}$.
Step 5 A new attribute set C' *and* (DC'_{user}, TC'_{user}) are adding, then $C = C \cup \{C'\}$, $DC_{user} = DC'_{user}$, $TC_{user} = TC'_{user}$ and go to ***Step 2.***

In GS-S3WDRFS algorithm, Step 2 is one of the most important steps. In step 2, according to detect whether new attribute information and its corresponding user requirements are adding, we can further choose a finer granularity to make decision and acquire a better solution. In addition, Step 3 can be computed by a variety of sorting methods with respect to different problem solving. Therefore, GS-S3WDRFS algorithm provides a progressive solution mechanism, and establishes a stepwise optimal granularity selection satisfying the time limit constraints.

6. EXPERIMENTS AND ANALYSIS

6.1 Case Study

To describe the method of stepwise optimal granularity selection more clearly, Example 4 is used to elaborate the detailed processing of GS-S3WDRFS.

Example 4. In a medical diagnosis system, to detect a certain disease, patients are often required to undertake a number of medical tests. Unfortunately, due to constraints of the factors, i.e. time, economic, environment, patients may only undertake a certain amount of medical tests. From the perspective of progressive solution, doctor should choose an optimal medical test set based on the current information to make a decision. When the conditions are improved and more medical tests will be implemented, the more information the doctor can utilize, then a better decision can be made on the basis of the new information. This can be formulated by Figure 7.

Figure 7. The example of selecting the optimal granularity

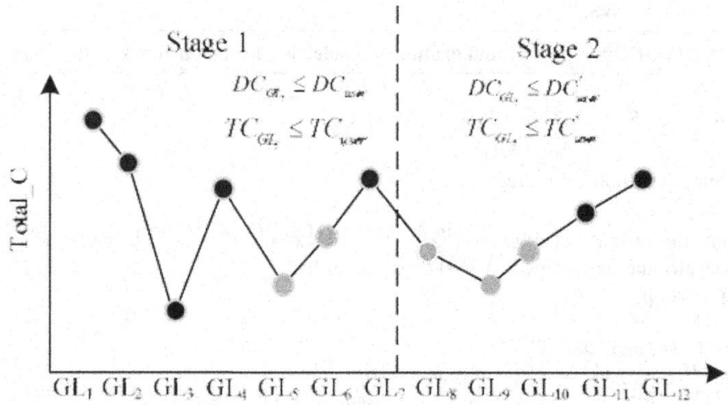

As shown in Figure 7, it includes two stages as follows: $GL_1 \rightarrow GL_7$ *and* $GL_8 \rightarrow GL_{12}$. In the first stage, the total cost is changing with the adding of attributes (medical tests) and there are only 2 gray dots satisfy $DC_{GL_i} \leq DC_{user}$ and $TC_{GL_i} \leq TC_{user}$ at the same time. According to the formula (11), we choose the dot with the lowest total cost from the 2 gray dots, and its corresponding granularity layer is GL_5 (consists of 5 medical tests). Therefore, GL_5 is the optimal cost-sensitive granularity to make a decision for patients in the first stage. In the second stage, there are five new medical tests adding. There are only 3 gray dots satisfy $DC_{GL_i} \leq DC'_{user}$ and $TC_{GL_i} \leq TC'_{user}$ at the same time, similar to the first stage, we choose the dot with the lowest total cost from the 3 gray dots, and its corresponding granularity layer is GL_9(consists of 9 medical tests). That is to say, GL_9 is the optimal cost-sensitive granularity to make a decision for patients in the two stages, since it processes higher accuracy and lower misclassification cost.

6.2 Experiments in Real-Life Data Sets

In this section, under a hierarchical granular structure, we illustrate the change of total cost and test cost in S3WDRFS model. Moreover, relative experiments are carried out to verify the efficiency of algorithm proposed to search for the optimal cost-sensitive granularity. The experimental environments are Windows7, Intel Core (TM) I5-4590 CPU (3.30 GHz) and 8GB RAM. The programming language is Matlab 2014b. Four datasets are elected to outlined in Table 3 are elected from the UCI [41]. Although our model is able to deal with continuous decision attributes, it only deals with discrete condition attributes. Hence, we employ the following formula [51] to transform the numerical value of condition attributes into the discrete value,

$$A^1(x) = \lfloor (A(x) - m_a) / \sigma_a \rfloor \tag{12}$$

Where, for a given attribute *A*, $A(x)$, m_a and σ_a denotes the attribute value, minimum and standard deviation respectively.

Table 3. The description of datasets

ID	Dataset	Attribute Characteristics	Instances	Condition Attributes
1	Air Quality	Real	9358	12
2	Concrete Compressive	Real	1030	8
3	Breast-Cancer-Wisconsin	Integer	699	9
4	ENB2012data	Real	768	8

In the experiment, we assume that θ=*0.5 and* ξ=100. In addition, for simplicity, we obtain the *GS* consists of multi levels in each datasets by adding the attribute in ascending order of attribute significance. Besides, supposing that there are two decision stages. We adopt the three measures [34] to evaluate the quality of S3WDRFS model as follow,

(1) Correct-acceptance rate

$$CAR = \frac{|POS_R^{(\alpha,\beta)}(X) \cap X|}{|POS_R^{(\alpha,\beta)}(X)|} \tag{12}$$

(2) Non-commitment-of-positive error

$$NPE = \frac{|BND_R^{(\alpha,\beta)}(X) \cap X|}{|BND_R^{(\alpha,\beta)}(X)|} \tag{13}$$

(3) Correct-rejection rate,

$$CRR = \frac{|NEG_R^{(\alpha,\beta)}(X) \cap X^C|}{|NEG_R^{(\alpha,\beta)}(X)|} \tag{14}$$

Table 4. The decision information on each datasets

ID	Decision Steps	1st Constraint Condition	2nd Constraint Condition
1	10	$DC_{user1} = 18000 \; TC_{user1} = 400$	$DC_{user2} = 17000 \; TC_{user2} = 1000$
2	8	$DC_{user1} = 1600 \; TC_{user1} = 100$	$DC_{user2} = 1500 \; TC_{user2} = 120$
3	9	$DC_{user1} = 30 \; TC_{user1} = 60$	$DC_{user2} = 20 \; TC_{user2} = 70$
4	8	$DC_{user1} = 900 \; TC_{user1} = 60$	$DC_{user2} = 870 \; TC_{user2} = 70$

Table. 4 lists the decision information on the four datasets, including decision steps and the constraint conditions of each decision stage. As shown in Figure 9, we calculate the change of total cost on the four datasets. It can be observed that the total cost decreased initially except to ID 2 datasets, because in ID 1, ID 3, ID 4 datasets, the decision cost decreased with the adding available information, whereas the test cost increased as more information need to be obtained and processed. At the beginning, the decrease rate in the decision cost was higher than the increase rate in the test cost. Thus, the total cost decreased initially. As the number of attributes increased, the increase rate in the test cost was higher than the decrease rate in the decision cost. Thus, the optimal granularity for total cost will reach somewhere in the middle of hierarchical granular structure. Herein, the optimal granularity at each stage is circled in Figure 8 by using the GS-S3WDRFS algorithm according to Table.4. Table.5 lists the relative information of optimal granularity at each stage on the four datasets. From Table 5, it is obviously that the optimal granularity at second stage processes lower decision cost and satisfies the more demanding user requirements for misclassification rate.

Figure 8. The change of total cost in ascending order

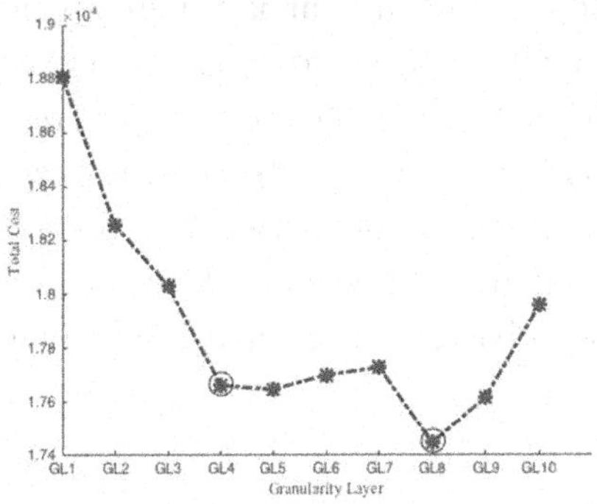

(a)Air Quality

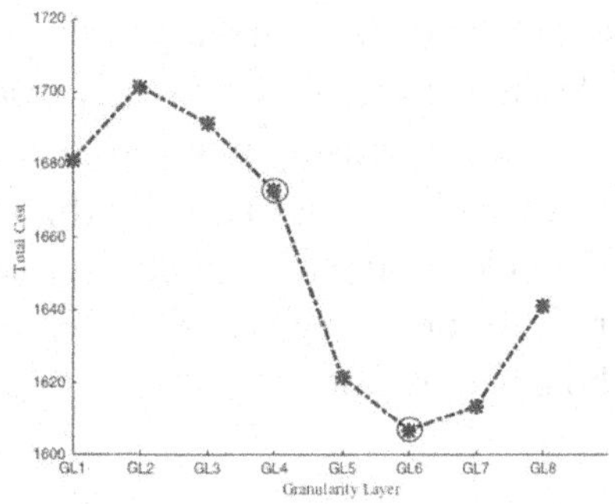

(b) Concrete Compressive

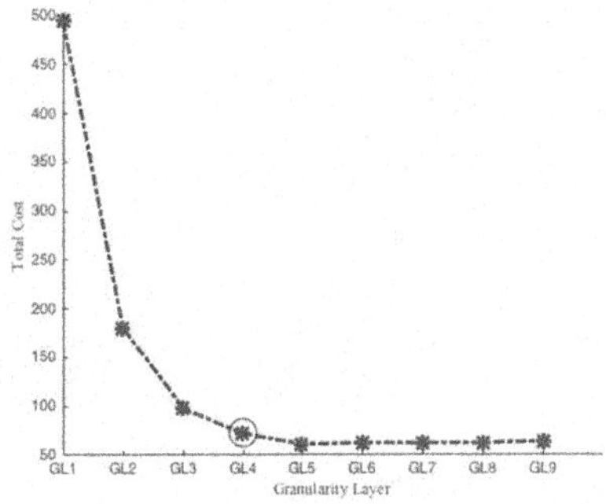

(c)Breast-Cancer-Wisconsin

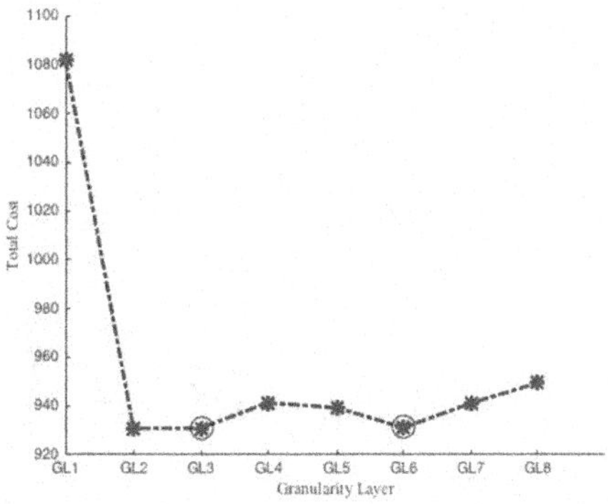

(d)ENB2012data

Table 5. The description of datasets

ID	1st Optimal Granularity	2nd Optimal Granularity	Decision Cost	Test Cost	Total Cost
1	GL_4	GL_8	GL_4:17314GL_8:16051	GL_4:349GL_8:945	GL_4:17633GL_8:17477
2	GL_4	GL_6	GL_4:1585GL_6:1494	GL_4:87.8GL_6:112.9	GL_4:1761GL_6:1606
3	GL_4	GL_4	GL_4:14.8	GL_4:57.4	GL_4:72.2
4	GL_3	GL_6	GL_3:884GL_6:864	GL_3:46GL_6:67	GL_3:930GL_6:931

Figure 9 shows the change of three regions is shown in ascending order. It is obviously that the change tendency of three regions is different from coarse to fine. With the increase of attributes, the decisions from boundary region can be made. Therefore, the boundary region in Figure 9 (a) (b) (c) possesses a decreasing trend but not always monotonously from coarse to fine, while the boundary region possesses an increasing trend from GL_4 *to* GL_8 in Figure 9 (d) . This is because equivalence classes in Fig. 9 (a) (b) (c) containing in boundary region tended to be subdivided into positive region or negative region, while equivalence classes in Figure 9 (d) containing in positive region or negative region tended to be subdivided into boundary region.

Figure 9. The change of number of objects in three regions

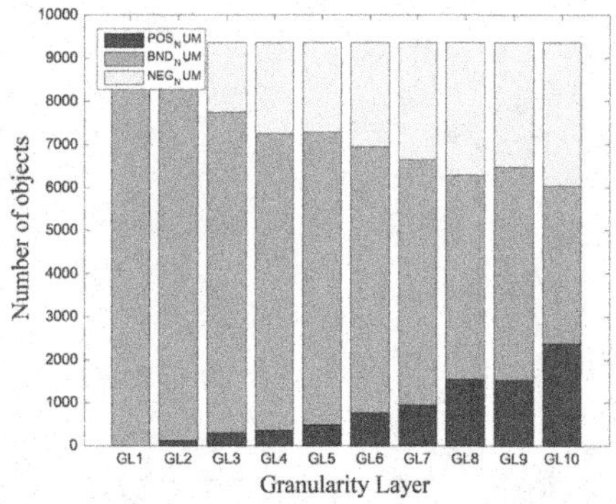

(a)Air Quality

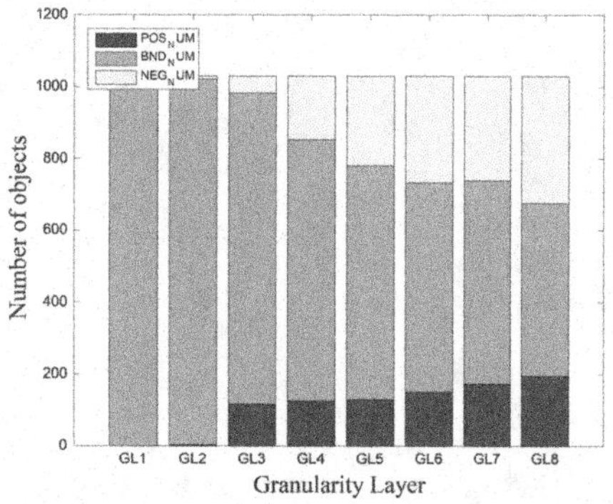

(b) Concrete Compressive

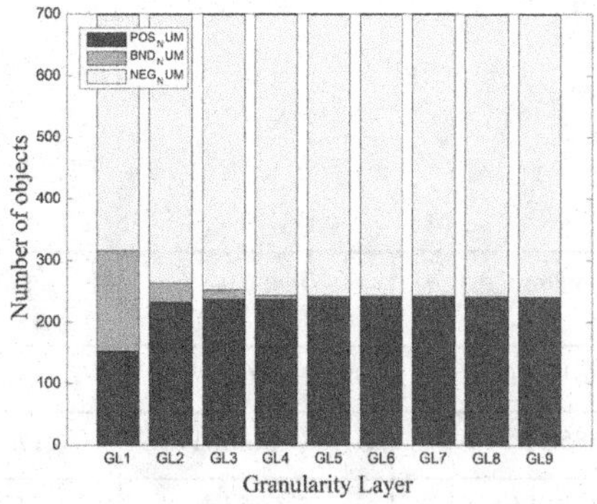

(c)Breast-Cancer-Wisconsin

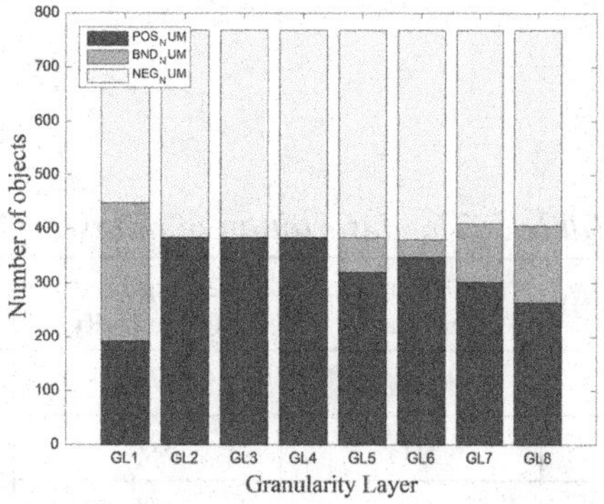

(d)ENB2012data

In Figure 10, the decision quality of S3WDRFS model with the measures CAR, NPE, CRR is computed. It is obvious that CAR and CRR on each dataset have no significant change and are always close to 1, which means the rejection decisions and the acceptance decisions can be made with the high accuracy. In addition, combined with Table 5, we can found the optimal granularity of each dataset possess the high value of CAR and CRR.

Figure 10. The change of quality of measure

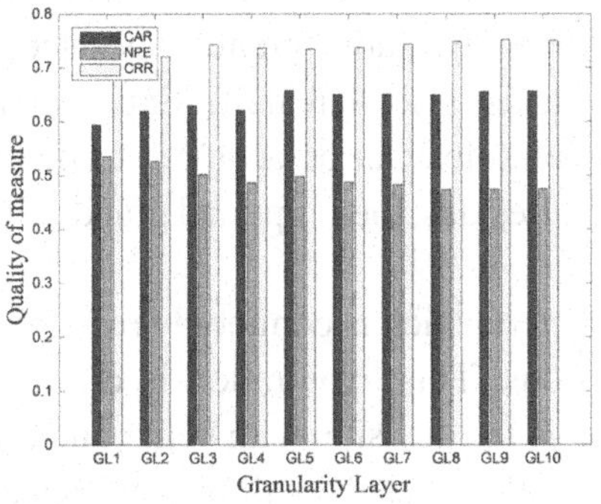

(a) AirQuality

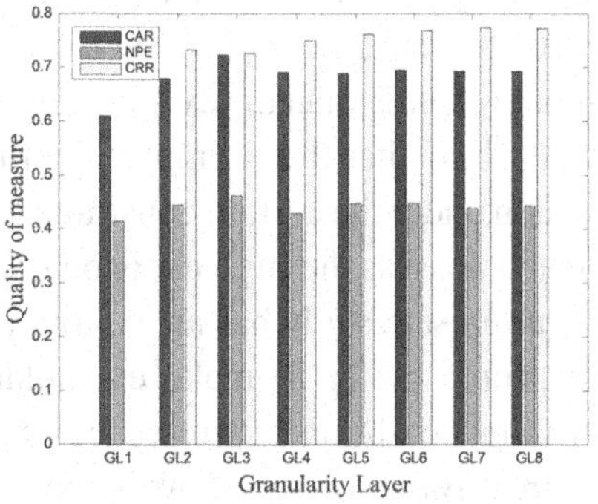

(b) Concrete_Compressive

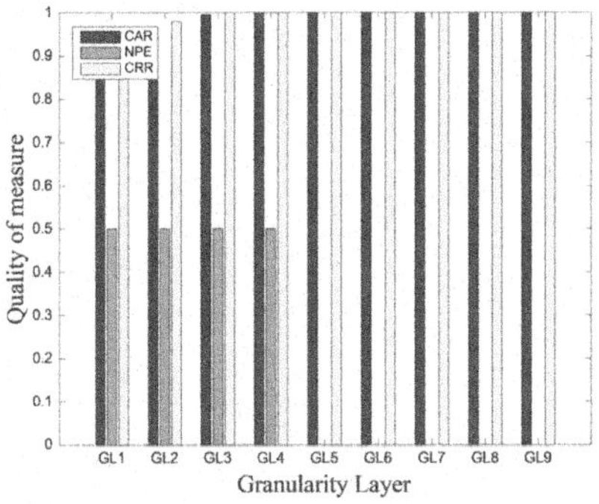

(c) Breast-Cancer-Wisconsin

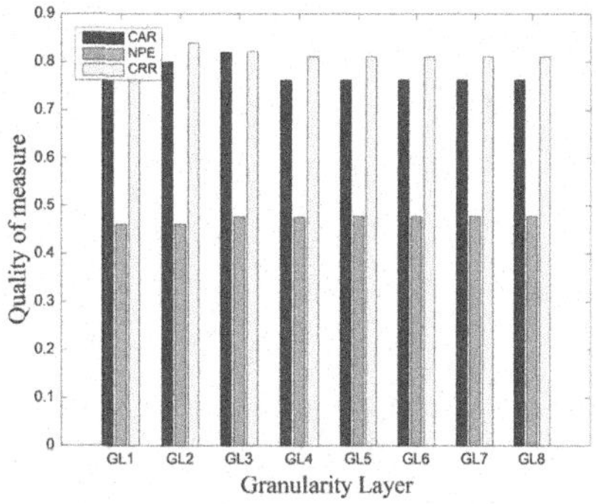

(d) ENB2012_data

7. CONCLUSION

S3WDRFS is developed for handing uncertain target concept, which provides a very useful strategy to progressive obtain minimum decision risk in the process of making decision. In this paper, related properties of decision cost in hierarchical granular structure of S3WDRFS are discussed. Combined with these properties, based on the granularity optimization mechanism, the optimal qualitative cost-sensitive granularity selection approach is proposed to address the trade-off between the different decision cost and test cost. Compared with current research in cost-sensitive methods, the variable test cost adapt to the decision accuracy rather than being quantitative set by the user. Therefore, the optimal qualitative granularity selection is more versatile than the existing approaches, and is closer to real life. Experimental results show that the exemplary optimal granularities can be acquired to make a decision under the certain constraint condition. Besides, these optimal granularities selected possess the high decision quality.

Our present study has an exploratory character, which is commonly recognized that people prefer to make exemplary decisions. This exploration is driven by constraint condition or preferences. Step by step, the decision with better quality is acquired. Based on the above research, we hope these results will be significant to improve rough sets theory and further enrich the three-ways decision models from the different viewpoints.

REFERENCES

Domiingos, P. (1999). MetaCosts: A general method for making classifiers cost-sensitive. *ACM SIGKDD International Conference on Knowledge Discovery and Data Mining*. ACM.

Dou, H., Yang, X., Song, X., Yu, H., Wu, W.-Z., & Yang, J. (2016). Decision-theoretic rough set: A multicost strategy. *Knowledge-Based Systems*, 91, 71–83. 10.1016/j.knosys.2015.09.011

Dubois, D., & Prade, H. (1990). Rough fuzzy sets and fuzzy rough sets. *International Journal of General Systems*, 17(2–3), 191–209. 10.1080/03081079008935107

Dubois, D., & Prade, H. (1992). Putting rough sets and fuzzy sets together. In R. Słowiń ski (Ed.), *Intelligent decision support: Handbook of applications and advances of the rough sets theory* (pp. 203–232). Dordrecht: Kluwer Academic Publishers. 10.1007/978-94-015-7975-9_14

Fan, B., Tsang, E. C. C., & Xu, W. (2016). Double-quantitative rough fuzzy set based decisions: A logical operations method. *Information Sciences*.

Feng, T., Fan, H. T., & Mi, J. S. (2017). Uncertainty and reduction of variable precision multigranulation fuzzy rough sets based on three-way decisions. *International Journal of Approximate Reasoning*, 85, 36–58. 10.1016/j.ijar.2017.03.002

Gong, Z., & Chai, R. (2016). Covering multigranulation trapezoidal fuzzy decision-theoretic rough fuzzy set models and applications. *Journal of Intelligent & Fuzzy Systems*, 31(3), 1–13. 10.3233/JIFS-151684

Greco, S., Matarazzo, B., & Slowinski, R. (2002). Rough approximation by dominance relations. *International Journal of Intelligent Systems*, 17(2), 153–171. 10.1002/int.10014

Hao, C., Li, J., Fan, M., Liu, W., & Tsang, E. C. C. (2017). Optimal scale selection in dynamic multi-scale decision tables based on sequential three-way decisions. *Information Sciences*, 415, 213–232. 10.1016/j.ins.2017.06.032

Jia, X., Zheng, K., & Li, W. (2012). Three-way decisions solution to filter spam email: an empirical study. *International Conference on Rough Sets and Current Trends in Computing*. Springer Berlin Heidelberg.

Li, F., Hu, B. Q., & Wang, J. (2017). Stepwise optimal scale selection for multi-scale decision tables via attribute significance. *Knowledge-Based Systems*, 129, 4–16. 10.1016/j.knosys.2017.04.005

Li, H., Zhang, L., Huang, B., & Zhou, X. (2016). Sequential three-way decision and granulation for cost-sensitive face recognition. *Knowledge-Based Systems*, 91(C), 241–251. 10.1016/j.knosys.2015.07.040

Li, H., Zhang, L., Zhou, X., & Huang, B. (2017). Cost-sensitive sequential three-way decision modeling using a deep neural network. *International Journal of Approximate Reasoning*, 85(C), 68–78. 10.1016/j.ijar.2017.03.008

Li, J., Huang, C., Qi, J., Qian, Y., & Liu, W. (2017). Three-way cognitive concept learning via multi-granularity. *Information Sciences*, 378(1), 244–263. 10.1016/j.ins.2016.04.051

Liang, D. C., Pedrycz, W., Liu, D., & Hu, P. (2015). Three-way decisions based on decision-theoretic rough sets under linguistic assessment with the aid of group decision making. *Applied Soft Computing*, 29(C), 256–269. 10.1016/j.asoc.2015.01.008

Liu, D., Li, T., & Liang, D. C. (2013). Fuzzy interval decision-theoretic rough sets. *Ifsa World Congress and Nafips Meeting*. IEEE.

Liu, D., Li, T. R., & Liang, D. C. (2014). Incorporating logistic regression to decision-theoretic rough sets for classifications. *International Journal of Approximate Reasoning*, 55(1), 197–210. 10.1016/j.ijar.2013.02.013

Min, F., He, H., Qian, Y., & Zhu, W. (2011). Test-cost-sensitive attribute reduction. *Information Sciences*, 181(22), 4928–4942. 10.1016/j.ins.2011.07.010

Min, F., & Zhu, W. (2012). Attribute reduction of data with error ranges and test costs. *Information Sciences*, 211(211), 48–67. 10.1016/j.ins.2012.04.031

Pawlak. (1982). Rough sets. *International Journal of Computer Information Sciences, 11*(5), 341-356.

Pawlak, Z. (1984). Rough classification. *International Journal of Man-Machine Studies*, 20(5), 469–483. 10.1016/S0020-7373(84)80022-X

Pedrycz, W., Alhmouz, R., Morfeq, A., & Balamash, A. (2013). The design of free structure granular mappings: The use of the principle of justifiable granularity. *IEEE Transactions on Cybernetics*, 43(6), 2105–2113. 10.1109/TCYB.2013.224038423757519

Pedrycz, W., & Homenda, W. (2013). Building the fundamentals of granular computing: A principle of justifiable granularity. *Applied Soft Computing*, 13(10), 4209–4218. 10.1016/j.asoc.2013.06.017

Pedrycz, W., & Skowron, A. (2008). *Handbook of granular computing*. Wiley-Interscience. 10.1002/9780470724163

Qian, J., Dang, C., Yue, X., & Zhang, N. (2017). Attribute reduction for sequential three-way decisions under dynamic granulation. *International Journal of Approximate Reasoning*, 85, 85. 10.1016/j.ijar.2017.03.009

Rubner, Y. (1997). The earth mover's distance, multi-dimensional scaling, and color-based image retrieval. *Proceedings of the Arpa Image Understanding Workshop*, 661-668.

Rubner, Y., Tomasi, C., & Guibas, L. J. (2000). The earth mover's distance as a metric for image retrieval. *International Journal of Computer Vision*, 40(2), 99–121. 10.1023/A:1026543900054

Skowronabcd, A. (2012). Modeling rough granular computing based on approximation spaces. *Information Sciences*, 184(1), 20–43. 10.1016/j.ins.2011.08.001

Sun, B. Z., Ma, W. M., & Zhao, H. (2014). Decision-theoretic rough fuzzy set model and application. *Information Sciences*, 283(5), 180–196. 10.1016/j.ins.2014.06.045

Wang, C. Y. (2017). Topological characterizations of generalized fuzzy rough sets. *Fuzzy Sets and Systems*, 312, 109–125. 10.1016/j.fss.2016.02.005

Wang, G. (2017). DGCC: Data-driven granular cognitive computing. *Granular Computing*, (1), 1–13.

Wang, G., Yang, J., & Xu, J. (2017). Granular computing: From granularity optimization to multi-granularity joint problem solving. *Granular Computing*, 2(3), 1–16. 10.1007/s41066-016-0032-3

Wen, S. D., & Bao, Q. H. (2017). Dominance-based rough fuzzy set approach and its application to rule induction. *European Journal of Operational Research*, 261(2), 690–703. 10.1016/j.ejor.2016.12.004

Yang, X., Li, T., Fujita, H., Liu, D., & Yao, Y. (2017). A unified model of sequential three-way decisions and multilevel incremental processing. *Knowledge-Based Systems*, 134, 172–188. 10.1016/j.knosys.2017.07.031

Yang, X., Qi, Y., & Yu, H. (2014). Want More? Pay More! *International Conference on Rough Sets and Current Trends in Computing*. Springer.

Yao, J., Vasilakos, A. V., & Pedrycz, W. (2013). Granular computing: Perspectives and challenges. *IEEE Transactions on Cybernetics*, 43(6), 1977–1989. 10.1109/TSMCC.2012.223664823757594

Yao, Y., & Deng, X. (2011). Sequential three-way decisions with probabilistic rough sets. *IEEE International Conference on Cognitive Informatics & Cognitive Computing*. IEEE.

Yao, Y. Y. (2007). Decision-theoretic rough set model. *International conference on rough sets and knowledge technology*. Springer-Verlag.

Yao, Y. Y. (2010). Three-way decisions with probabilistic rough sets. *Information Sciences*, 180(3), 341–353. 10.1016/j.ins.2009.09.021

Yao, Y. Y. (2011). The superiority of three-way decisions in probabilistic rough set models. *Information Sciences*, 181(6), 1080–1096. 10.1016/j.ins.2010.11.019

Yao, Y. Y. (2013). Granular computing and sequential three-way decisions. *International Conference on Rough Sets and Knowledge Technology*, 16–27. 10.1007/978-3-642-41299-8_3

Yao, Y. Y., Wong, S. K. M., & Lingras, P. (1990). *A Decision-Theoretic Rough Set Model, Methodologies for Intelligent Systems*. North-Holland.

Yao, Y. Y., & Zhao, Y. (2008). Attribute reduction in decision-theoretic rough set models. *Information Sciences*, 178(17), 3356–3373. 10.1016/j.ins.2008.05.010

Yu, H., Liu, Z., & Wang, G. Y. (2014). An automatic method to determine the number of clusters using decision-theoretic rough set. *International Journal of Approximate Reasoning*, 55(1), 101–115. 10.1016/j.ijar.2013.03.018

Yu, H., Zhang, C., & Wang, G. Y. (2015). A tree-based incremental overlapping clustering method using the three-way decision theory. *Knowledge-Based Systems*, 91(C), 189–203.

Zhang, Q. H., Wang, J., & Wang, G. Y. (2015). The approximate representation of rough-fuzzy sets. *Chinese Journal of Computer*, (7), 1484–1496.

Zhang, Q. H., Xu, K., & Wang, G. (2016). Fuzzy equivalence relation and its multi-granulation spaces. *Information Sciences,* 346–347. (http://archive.ics.uci.edu/ml/)

Zhang, Q. H., Zhang, P., & Wang, G. Y. (2017). Research on approximation set of rough set based on fuzzy similarity. *Journal of Intelligent & Fuzzy Systems*, 32(3), 2549–2562. 10.3233/JIFS-16533

Zhang, Y., & Zhou, Z. H. (2010). Cost-sensitive Face Recognition. *IEEE Transactions on Pattern Analysis and Machine Intelligence*, 32(10), 1758–1769. 10.1109/TPAMI.2009.19520724754

Zhao, H., Wang, P., & Hu, Q. (2016). Cost-sensitive feature selection based on adaptive neighborhood granularity with multi-level confidence. *Information Sciences*, 366, 134–149. 10.1016/j.ins.2016.05.025

Zhao, H., & Zhu, W. (2014). Optimal cost-sensitive granularization based on rough sets for variable costs. *Knowledge-Based Systems*, 65(4), 72–82. 10.1016/j.knosys.2014.04.009

Zhou, B. (2011). A New Formulation of Multi-category Decision-Theoretic Rough Sets. *Rough Sets and Knowledge Technology.* Springer Berlin Heidelberg.

Chapter 6
Multi-Granulation-Based Optimal Scale Selection in Multi-Scale Information Systems

Tao Zhan
Southwest University, China

ABSTRACT

This chapter establishes belief and plausibility functions within the context of multigranulation, delving into the structures of belief and plausibility. The focus extends to the examination of multigranulation rough sets within multi-scale information systems. Subsequently, to determine the optimal level within the multigranulation rough set, a method for optimal scale selection is introduced. This method caters to diverse requirements in optimistic and pessimistic multigranulation within the multi-scale information system. In-depth analyses of the characteristics of optimistic and pessimistic multigranulation optimal scale selection for multi-scale information systems are conducted separately, revealing intrinsic connections between distinct optimal scale selection methodologies.

1. INTRODUCTION

The concept of information granules serves as a foundational element in rough set theory, playing a crucial role in human cognitive processes (E, Cui, Pedrycz, et al., 2022; Li, Pedrycz, Xue, et al., 2019; Xu and Li, 2016). Pawlak's rough set and various generalized rough sets are typically formulated based on a singular set of information granules, which are derived from a partition or covering (Greco,

DOI: 10.4018/979-8-3693-4292-3.ch006

Matarazzo, Slowinski, 1999; Pawlak, 1982; Lin, 2004; Liang and Qian, 2008; Lingras and Yao, 1998). Numerous researchers have delved into the study of these granules (Li and Xu, 2015; Li, Deng, Pedrycz, et al., 2023). Granular computing, as an approach to knowledge representation and data mining, aims to devise an approximation scheme that effectively addresses complex problems at a specific level of granulation (Li, Wei, Xu, 2022).

The roots of granular computing trace back to 1979, originating from Zadeh's introduction of the concept of information granulation within the context of fuzzy sets (Zadeh, 1979). In recent years, granular computing has emerged as a rapidly growing field of research (E, Cui, Pedrycz, et al., 2023; Cui, E, Pedrycz, 2021; Pal, Shankar, Mitra, 2005; Pedrycz, Bargiela, 2012; Yao, 2009). At its core, a fundamental notion in granular computing is the "granule," representing a cluster of objects brought together by criteria such as indistinguishability, similarity, or functionality. A granule can be perceived as a constituent particle contributing to a larger unit or as a localized perspective meeting specified criterion (Skowron and Stepaniuk, 2001; Li, Xu, and Zhang, 2017; Yao, 2009; Pedrycz, Bargiela, 2002).

The representation, interpretation, and exploration of relationships among granules, expressed as IF-THEN rules featuring granular variables and values, constitute key aspects of granular computing. The process of constructing information granules is termed "information granulation," involving the division of a universe of discourse into parts or the grouping of individual elements into classes based on available information and knowledge. Given that each set of information granules forms a granulation space, the term "multigranulation space" is used when referring to two or more information granules. In efforts to extend the applicability of rough set theory in practical scenarios, Qian et al. expanded Pawlak's single-granulation rough set model into a multiple granulation rough set model (Qian, Liang, and Pang, 2010). Qian's introduction of the multigranulation rough set paved the way for subsequent extensions by various researchers into generalized multigranulation rough sets (Li, Zhang, Sun, 2014; Li, Xu, Zhang, et al., 2022; Qian, Liang, Lin, et al., 2017; Xu, Li, Zhang, 2017).

To capture the hierarchical structure of content across various granularity levels, Wu et al. introduced a knowledge representation system named the multi-scale granular labeled partition structure (Wu, Leung, 2011; Wu, Leung, 2013; Wu, Qian, Li, 2017). This system represents data at different scales and granulation levels, featuring a granular information transformation from finer to coarser labeled partitions.

In the context of multi-scale information tables, an object can assume multiple values corresponding to different scales under the same attribute. For instance, student mathematics exam results may be expressed as natural numbers or categorized as Excellent, Good, Moderate, Bad, or Unacceptable, or further simplified to Pass and Fail. Selecting the appropriate scale is crucial, making the discovery of knowledge in hierarchically organized information tables essential for practical data mining. Addressing this challenge, Wu et al. presented an optimal scale selection method for multi-scale decision tables, aiming to identify the most suitable scale for describing the tables (Wu, Leung, 2011; Wu, Leung, 2013). This concept is referred to as single-granulation in multi-scale decision tables. Within each scale, the same example, such as the student exam scenario, can be applied. Subjects like Physical, Chemistry, and Biology may be grouped together, while Art, Music, and PE form another class, and Mathematics and Language constitute separate classes. This approach induces a multigranulation within each scale.

This chapter focuses on the integration of multigranulation rough set theory and multi-scale concepts, specifically addressing the decision-making process for optimal scale selection across multiple scales. The subsequent sections provide a brief review of preliminary concepts, including Pawlak rough set, multigranulation rough set, belief structure, belief functions, and multi-scale decision tables (Section 2). Section 3 delves into the study of belief and plausibility structures based on multigranulation rough sets for a single-scale decision table, exploring various properties of belief and plausibility functions. Finally, Section 4 concludes the chapter.

2. RELATED FUNDAMENTAL WORKS

In this section, we review some basic notions of rough set approximations, the Dempster-Shafer theory of evidence, the multi-scale information table and multi-scale decision table. Throughout this chapter, for a non-empty set U, the class of all subsets of U is denoted by $P(U)$. For $X \subseteq P(U)$, we denote the complement of X in U as $\sim X$.

Let U be a non-empty and finite set. If $R \subseteq U \times U$ is an equivalence relation on U, then the pair (U, R) is called a Pawlak approximation space.

The equivalence relation R in a Pawlak approximation space (U, R) partitions the universe U into disjoint subsets. Such a partition of the universe is a quotient set of U and is denoted by $U/R = \{[x]_R | x \in U\}$, where $[x]_R = \{y \in U | (x, y) \in R\}$ is the R-equivalence class containing x. In the view of granular computing, equivalence classes are the basic building blocks for the representation and approximation of any subset of the universe of discourse. Each equivalence class may be viewed as a granule consisting of indistinguishable elements, and it is also referred to as an equivalence granule.

Let (U, R) be a Pawlak approximation space. For an arbitrary set $X \in P(U)$, one can characterize X by a pair of lower and upper approximations which are defined as follows.

$$\underline{R}(X) = \{x \in U | [x]_R \subseteq X\} = \cup\{[x]_R | [x]_R \subseteq X\},$$

$\overline{R}(X) = \{x \in U | [x]_R \cap X \neq \varnothing\} = \cup\{[x]_R | [x]_R \cap X \neq \varnothing\}.$

The pair $(\underline{R}(X), \overline{R}(X))$ is called the Pawlak rough set of$X$ with respect to (U, R). If $\underline{R}(X) \neq \overline{R}(X)$, then X is said to be a rough set.

Let $K = (U, R)$ be a knowledge base, $R_1, R_2, \ldots, R_m \subseteq R$ is a set of the equivalence relations, $\forall X \subseteq U$, the optimistic multigranulation lower approximation and upper approximation of X are denoted by

$$\underline{\sum_{i=1}^{m} R_i}^{OPT}(X) = \{x \in U | \vee_{i=1}^{m}([x]_{R_i} \subseteq X)\},$$

$$\overline{\sum_{i=1}^{m} R_i}^{OPT}(X) = \{x \in U | \wedge_{i=1}^{m}([x]_{R_i} \cap X \neq \varnothing)\}$$

The pair $\left(\underline{\sum_{i=1}^{m} R_i}^{OPT}(X), \overline{\sum_{i=1}^{m} R_i}^{OPT}(X)\right)$ is referred to as an optimistic multigranulation rough set of X in the terms of the equivalence relations $R_1, R_2, \ldots, R_m \subseteq R$.

Accordingly, the multigranulation optimistic boundary region are defined as follows.

$$BN^{OPT}_{\sum_{i=1}^{m} R_i} = \overline{\sum_{i=1}^{m} R_i}^{OPT}(X) - \underline{\sum_{i=1}^{m} R_i}^{OPT}(X)$$

The Dempster-Shafer theory of evidence, which is also called the evidence theory or the belief function theory is treated as a promising method of dealing with uncertainty in intelligence systems. The basic representational structure in the Dempster-Shafer theory of evidence is a belief structure, the detail content can find in references (Wu, Leung, 2011; Wu, Leung, 2013).

Definition 1. Let U be a non-empty and finite set, a set function $m: P(U) \rightarrow [0, 1]$ is referred to as a basic probability assignment if it satisfies axioms $M1$ and $M2$:

$$(M1) m(\varnothing) = 0, (M2) \sum_{X \subseteq U} m(X) = 1$$

The value $m(X)$represents the degree of belief that a specific element of U belongs to set X, but not any particular subset of X. $X \in P(U)$ with nonzero basic probability assignment is referred to as a focal element. Denote $\mathcal{M}$ as the family of all focal elements of m. The pair $(\mathcal{M}, m)$ is called a belief structure on U.

Associated with each belief structure, a pair of belief and plausibility functions can be defined.

Definition 2. Let $(\mathcal{M}, m)$ be a belief structure on U. A set function$Bel: P(U) \rightarrow [0, 1]$ is referred to as a belief function on U if

$$Bel(X) = \sum_{Y \subseteq X} m(Y), \forall X \in P(U)$$

A set function $Pl: P(U) \rightarrow [0, 1]$ is referred to as a plausibility function on U if

$$Pl(X) = \sum_{Y \cap X \neq \varnothing} m(Y), \forall X \in P(U)$$

Belief and plausibility functions based on the same belief structure are connected by the dual property

$$Pl(X) = 1 - Bel(\sim X), \forall X \in P(U)$$

and furthermore

$Bel(X) \le Pl(X), \forall X \in P(U)$

There are strong connections between rough set theory and the Dempster-Shafer theory of evidence. The following theory shows that probabilities of lower and upper approximations are a dual pair of belief and plausibility functions.

Let (U,R,P) be a probabilistic approximation space, for any $X \subseteq U$, denote

$Bel(X) = P(\underline{R}(X)),\ Pl(X) = P(\overline{R}(X))$

ThenBel and Pl are a dual pair of belief and plausibility functions in U respectively, and the corresponding basic probability assignment is

$$m(Y) = \begin{cases} P(Y), Y \in \frac{U}{R}; \\ 0, otherwise. \end{cases}$$

For the Pawlak rough set model, each object can only take on one value under each attribute. However, in some real-life applications, one has to make decisions with different level of scales. That is to say, an object may take on different values under the same attribute, depending on at which scale it is measured. In the reference (Wu, Leung, 2011), Wu et al. introduced a new concept called multi-scale information table from the perspective of granular computation which has different level of scales.

Definition 3. A multi-scale information table is a 2-tuple $S = (U,AT)$, where

- $U = \{x_1, x_2, \ldots, x_n\}$ is a non-empty and finite set of objects;
- $AT = \{a_1, a_2, \ldots, a_m\}$ is a non-empty and finite set of attributes, and each $a_i \in AT$ is a multi-scale attribute, i. e., for the same object in U, attribute a_i can take on different values at different scales.

In the discussion to follow, we assume that all the attributes have the same number I of levels of scale. Hence, a multi-scale information table can be represented as a table $\left(U, \left\{a_j^k | k = 1,2,\ldots,I; j = 1,2,\ldots,m\right\}\right)$, where $a_j^k: U \rightarrow V_j^k$ is a surjective function and V_j^k is the domain of the $k-th$ scale attribute a_j^k. For $1 \le k \le I-1$, there exists a surjective function $g_j^{k,k+1}: V_j^k \rightarrow V_j^{k+1}$ such that$a_j^{k+1} = g_j^{k,k+1} \circ a_j^k$, i. e.

$a_j^{k+1}(x) = g_j^{k,k+1}\left(a_j^k(x)\right), x \in U$

where $g_j^{k,k+1}$ is called a granular information transformation function.

Definition 4. Let Ube a non-empty set, $\mathscr{A}_1$ and $\mathscr{A}_2$ be two partitions of$U$. If for each $A_1 \in \mathscr{A}_1$, there exists $A_2 \in \mathscr{A}_2$, such that $A_1 \subseteq A_2$, then we say that $\mathscr{A}_1$ is finer than $\mathscr{A}_2$ or $\mathscr{A}_2$ is coarser than $\mathscr{A}_1$, and is denoted as $\mathscr{A}_1 \sqsubseteq \mathscr{A}_2$. Furthermore, if there exist$A_1 \in \mathscr{A}_1$and $A_2 \in \mathscr{A}_2$ such that $A_1 \subset A_2$, then we say that $\mathscr{A}_1$ is strictly finer than $\mathscr{A}_2$, and is denoted as $\mathscr{A}_1 \sqsubset \mathscr{A}_2$.

Definition 5. A system

$$S = (U, AT \cup \{d\}) = \left(U, \{a_j^k | k = 1,2,\ldots,I; j = 1,2,\ldots,m\} \cup \{d\}\right)$$

is referred to as a multi-scale decision table, where $(U, AT) = \left(U, \{a_j^k | k = 1,2,\ldots,I; j = 1,2,\ldots,m\}\right)$ is a multi-scale information table and $d \notin \{a_j^k | k = 1,2,\ldots,I; j = 1,2,\ldots,m\}, d: U \to V_d$ is a special attribute called the decision attribute.

According to the above definition, a multi-scale decision table $S = (U, AT \cup \{d\}) = \left(U, \{a_j^k | k = 1,2,\ldots,I; j = 1,2,\ldots,m\} \cup \{d\}\right)$ can be decomposed into I decision tables $S^k = (U, AT \cup \{d\}) = \left(U, \{a_j^k | j = 1,2,\ldots,m\} \cup \{d\}\right) = (U, AT^k \cup \{d\})$, $AT^k = \{a_j^k | j = 1,2,\ldots,m\}, k = 1,2,\ldots,I$, with the same decision d.

For each single scale, the granulations in it are the same.

The belief and plausible structure based on multigranulation rough set for a single scale decision table

In this section, we investigate the evidence theory based on multigranulation rough set in a single scale decision table. Following the introduction of a mass function of each scale in multi-scale information tables, we present the optimistic belief and plausibility functions for a single scale decision table.

Definition 6. Let $S = (U, AT) = \left(U, \{a_j^k | k = 1,2,\ldots,I; j = 1,2,\ldots,m\}\right)$ be a multi-scale information table. In the $k-th$ scale, $A_1^k, A_2^k, \ldots, A_n^k \subseteq AT$ is the equivalence relation associated with A_i^k, for any $X \in U/R_1^k$, a mass function of S can be defined by a map

$m_1^k: U/R_1^k \to [0,1]$,

$X\ m_1^k(X) = \frac{|X|}{|U|}$.

where $|X|$ denotes the cardinality of a set X.

By the above definition, one can easily find that a mass function of every scale in the multi-scale information tables satisfies two basic axioms, respectively. That is to say, for arbitrary $X \in U/R_1^k$, the following two axioms hold directly,

$(M1)\, m_1^k(\varnothing) = 0$,

$(M2) \sum_{X \in U/R_1^k} m_1^k(X) = 1$

Similarly, we denote $\mathcal{M}^k$ as the family of all focal elements of m^k in optimistic multigranulation rough set in $k-th$ scale information table. The pair $(\mathcal{M}^k, m^k)$ is called a belief structure of the optimistic multigranulation rough set in $k-th$ scale information table, a pair of belief and plausibility function in the optimistic multigranulation rough set can be derived immediately. What we should emphasize is that each scale must possess the same granulations, that is two say, the way of forming the granulations is the same.

Definition 7. Let $S = (U,AT)$ be an information system, $(\mathcal{M}^k,m^k)$ be a belief structure of the optimistic multigranulation rough set in $k-th$ scale information table. For any $X \in P(U)$, a set function $Bel{:}P(U) \rightarrow [0,1]$ is referred to as an optimistic belief function on U, $A_1,A_2,\ldots,A_n \subseteq AT$ and R_i is the equivalence relation associated with A_i, if there exists $A_i \subseteq AT$ such that

$$Bel^{OPT}_{\sum_{i=1}^{m} A_i^k}(X) = \sum_{Y\subseteq X, Y\in U/R_i} m_1^k(Y),$$

a set function $Pl{:}P(U) \rightarrow [0,1]$ is referred to as an optimistic plausibility function on U, if for any $A_i \subseteq AT$,

$$Pl^{OPT}_{\sum_{i=1}^{m} A_i^k}(X) = \sum_{Y\cap X\neq\emptyset, Y\in U/R_i} m_1^k(Y)$$

Let $S = (U,AT)$ be an information system, for any $X \subseteq U$, $A_1,A_2,\ldots,A_n \subseteq AT$ and R_i is the equivalence relation associated with A_i, denoted

$$Bel^{OPT}_{\sum_{i=1}^{m} A_i^k}(X) = \frac{\left|\underline{\sum_{i=1}^{m} A_i}^{OPT}(X)\right|}{|U|};\ Pl^{OPT}_{\sum_{i=1}^{m} A_i^k}(X) = \frac{\left|\overline{\sum_{i=1}^{m} A_i}^{OPT}(X)\right|}{|U|}.$$

Then $Bel^{OPT}_{\sum_{i=1}^{m} A_i^k}(X)$ is the optimistic belief function and $Pl^{OPT}_{\sum_{i=1}^{m} A_i^k}(X)$ is the optimistic plausibility function of U, respectively.

Belief function and plausibility function based on the same belief structure in the optimistic multigranulation rough set are connected by the dual property

$$Bel^{OPT}_{\sum_{i=1}^{m} A_i^k}(X) = 1 - Pl^{OPT}_{\sum_{i=1}^{m} A_i^k}(\sim X).$$

One can also get a series of formulas in the following

$$Bel^{OPT}_{A_i^k}(X) \le Bel^{OPT}_{\sum_{1\le i\le t} A_i^k}(X) \le Bel^{OPT}_{\sum_{i=1}^{m} A_i^k}(X) \le \frac{|X|}{|U|} \le Pl^{OPT}_{\sum_{i=1}^{m} A_i^k}(X) \le Pl^{OPT}_{\sum_{1\le i\le t} A_i^k}(X) \le Pl^{OPT}_{A_i^k}(X)$$

In the following section, we will discuss the optimal scale selection based on multigranulation rough set for multi-scale decision tables.

3. OPTIMISTIC MULTIGRANULATION OPTIMAL SCALE SELECTION FOR MULTI-SCALE DECISION TABLES

In each $k-th$ scale, we will investigate the multigranulation rough set in multi-scale decision tables. For every scale, the granulations in it are produced by the same attributes. Knowledge acquisition in the sense of rule induction from a multi-scale decision table is an important issue. As we know from the former contents in Section 3, a multi-scale decision table having I levels of scales can be decomposed into I decision tables. It is critical to select the optimal level of details corresponding a suitable decision table before decision rules are produced. In this section, we investigate optimal scale selection with different requirements in multi-scale decision tables.

Definition 8. Let
$S = (U, AT \cup \{d\}) = \left(U, \left\{a_j^k \mid k = 1,2,\ldots,I; j = 1,2,\ldots,m\right\} \cup \{d\}\right)$
be a multi-scale decision table which has I levels of scale. For $k \in \{1,2,\ldots,I\}$, then the optimistic multigranulation lower and upper approximations of the $k-th$ scale decision table $S^k = (U, AT^k \cup \{d\})$ are defined as follows. $A_1^k, A_2^k, \ldots, A_n^k \subseteq AT^k$ and $\forall X \subseteq U$,

∑i=1mAik¯OPTX=x∈U∣ i=1mxAik⊆X,

∑i=1mAik¯OPTX=x∈U∣ i=1mxAik∩X≠∅

Accordingly, the k-th scale optimistic boundary region can be defined by

BN∑i=1mAikOPT=∑i=1mAik¯OPTX-∑i=1mAik¯OPTX

We denote

$$L^{OPT}_{\sum_{i=1}^m A_i^k}(d) = \left(\underline{\sum_{i=1}^m A_i^k}^{OPT}(D_1), \underline{\sum_{i=1}^m A_i^k}^{OPT}(D_2), \ldots, \underline{\sum_{i=1}^m A_i^k}^{OPT}(D_r)\right),$$

$$H^{OPT}_{\sum_{i=1}^m A_i^k}(d) = \left(\overline{\sum_{i=1}^m A_i^k}^{OPT}(D_1), \overline{\sum_{i=1}^m A_i^k}^{OPT}(D_2), \ldots, \overline{\sum_{i=1}^m A_i^k}^{OPT}(D_r)\right),$$

$$N^{OPT}_{\sum_{i=1}^m A_i^k}(d) = \left(BN^{OPT}_{\sum_{i=1}^m A_i^k}(D_1), BN^{OPT}_{\sum_{i=1}^m A_i^k}(D_2), \ldots, BN^{OPT}_{\sum_{i=1}^m A_i^k}(D_r)\right),$$

$$Bel^{OPT}_{\sum_{i=1}^m A_i^k}(d) = \left(Bel^{OPT}_{\sum_{i=1}^m A_i^k}(D_1), Bel^{OPT}_{\sum_{i=1}^m A_i^k}(D_2), \ldots, Bel^{OPT}_{\sum_{i=1}^m A_i^k}(D_r)\right),$$

$$Pl^{OPT}_{\sum_{i=1}^m A_i^k}(d) = \left(Pl^{OPT}_{\sum_{i=1}^m A_i^k}(D_1), Pl^{OPT}_{\sum_{i=1}^m A_i^k}(D_2), \ldots, Pl^{OPT}_{\sum_{i=1}^m A_i^k}(D_r)\right),$$

where $Bel^{OPT}_{\sum_{i=1}^m A_i^k}(D_j) = \dfrac{\left|\underline{\sum_{i=1}^m A_i^k}^{OPT}(D_j)\right|}{|U|}$, and $Pl^{OPT}_{\sum_{i=1}^m A_i^k}(D_j) = \dfrac{\left|\overline{\sum_{i=1}^m A_i^k}^{OPT}(D_j)\right|}{|U|}$. $L^{OPT}_{\sum_{i=1}^m A_i^k}$, $H^{OPT}_{\sum_{i=1}^m A_i^k}$ and $N^{OPT}_{\sum_{i=1}^m A_i^k}$ are referred to as the optimistic multigranulation lower approximation distribution, optimistic upper approximation distribution and optimistic boundary distribution of decision classes U/R_d under the $k-th$ scale in S, respectively. $Bel^{OPT}_{\sum_{i=1}^m A_i^k}$ and $Pl^{OPT}_{\sum_{i=1}^m A_i^k}$ are said to be the optimistic belief distribution and optimistic plausibility distribution of classes U/R_d under the $k-th$ scale in S, respectively.

Definition 9. $S = (U, AT \cup \{d\}) = \left(U, \left\{a_j^k \mid k = 1,2,\ldots,I; j = 1,2,\ldots,m\right\} \cup \{d\}\right)$ be a multi-scale decision table which has I levels of scale. For $k \in \{1,2,\ldots,I\}$, we have

1) $S^k = (U, AT^k \cup \{d\}) = \left(U, \left\{a_j^k | j = 1,2,\ldots,m\right\} \cup \{d\}\right)$ is optimistic multigranulation lower approximation consistent to S if $\underline{L}^{OPT}_{\sum_{i=1}^{m} A_i^k}(d) = \underline{L}^{OPT}_{\sum_{i=1}^{m} A_i^1}(d)$. And, the$k-th$ level of scale is said to be the optimistic multigranulation lower approximation optimal scale of S if S^k is optimistic multigranulation lower approximation consistent to S and S^{k+1} (if there is $k+1$) is not optimistic multigranulation lower approximation consistent to S;

2) $S^k = (U, AT^k \cup \{d\}) = \left(U, \left\{a_j^k | j = 1,2,\ldots,m\right\} \cup \{d\}\right)$ is optimistic multigranulation upper approximation consistent to S if $H^{OPT}_{\sum_{i=1}^{m} A_i^k}(d) = H^{OPT}_{\sum_{i=1}^{m} A_i^1}(d)$. And, the$k-th$ level of scale is said to be the optimistic multigranulation upper approximation optimal scale of S if S^k is optimistic multigranulation upper approximation consistent to S and S^{k+1} (if there is $k+1$) is not optimistic multigranulation upper approximation consistent to S;

3) $S^k = (U, AT^k \cup \{d\}) = \left(U, \left\{a_j^k | j = 1,2,\ldots,m\right\} \cup \{d\}\right)$ is optimistic multigranulation boundary region consistent to S if $N^{OPT}_{\sum_{i=1}^{m} A_i^k}(d) = N^{OPT}_{\sum_{i=1}^{m} A_i^1}(d)$. And, the $k-th$ level of scale is said to be the optimistic multigranulation boundary region optimal scale of S if S^k is optimistic multigranulation boundary region consistent to S and S^{k+1} (if there is $k+1$) is not optimistic multigranulation boundary region consistent to S;

4) $S^k = (U, AT^k \cup \{d\}) = \left(U, \left\{a_j^k | j = 1,2,\ldots,m\right\} \cup \{d\}\right)$ is optimistic belief distribution consistent to S if $Bel^{OPT}_{\sum_{i=1}^{m} A_i^k}(d) = Bel^{OPT}_{\sum_{i=1}^{m} A_i^1}(d)$. And, the$k-th$ level of scale is said to be the optimistic belief distribution optimal scale of S if S^k is optimistic belief distribution consistent to S and S^{k+1} (if there is $k+1$) is not optimistic belief distribution consistent to S;

5) $S^k = (U, AT^k \cup \{d\}) = \left(U, \left\{a_j^k | j = 1,2,\ldots,m\right\} \cup \{d\}\right)$ is optimistic plausibility distribution consistent to S if $Pl^{OPT}_{\sum_{i=1}^{m} A_i^k}(d) = Pl^{OPT}_{\sum_{i=1}^{m} A_i^1}(d)$. And, the$k-th$ level of scale is said to be the optimistic plausibility distribution optimal scale of S if S^k is optimistic plausibility distribution consistent to S and S^{k+1} (if there is $k+1$) is not optimistic plausibility distribution consistent to S.

In a multi-scale decision table which has I levels of scales, it can be observed that

1) S^k is optimistic multigranulation lower approximation consistent to S if and only if S^k preserves the optimistic multigranulation lower approximation of all decision classes of the finest scale decision table S^1, in this case, an object supports a certain decision rule derived from S^1 if and only if it supports a certain decision rule derived from $\$S^k$. And k is the optimistic multigranulation lower approximation optimal scale of S if and only if k is the maximal number such that S^k preserves the optimistic multigranulation lower approximation of all decision classes of S^1;

2) S^k is optimistic multigranulation upper approximation consistent to S if and only if S^k preserves the optimistic multigranulation upper approximation of all decision classes of the finest scale decision table S^1, in this case, an object supports a certain decision rule derived from S^1 if and only if it supports a certain decision

rule derived from S^k. And k is the optimistic multigranulation upper approximation optimal scale of S if and only if k is the maximal number such that S^k preserves the optimistic multigranulation upper approximation of all decision classes of S^1;

3) S^k is optimistic multigranulation boundary region consistent to S if and only if S^k preserves the optimistic multigranulation boundary region of all decision classes of the finest scale decision table S^1, in this case, an object supports a certain decision rule derived from S^1 if and only if it supports a certain decision rule derived from S^k. And k is the optimistic multigranulation boundary region optimal scale of S if and only if k is the maximal number such that S^k preserves the optimistic multigranulation boundary region of all decision classes of S^1;

4) S^k is optimistic belief distribution consistent to S if and only if S^k preserves the same belief degree of each decision class in the finest scale decision table S^1. And k is the optimistic belief distribution optimal scale of S if and only if k is the maximal number such that S^kpreserves the same belief degree of each decision class of S^1;

5) S^k is optimistic plausibility distribution consistent to S if and only if S^k preserves the same plausibility degree of each decision class in the finest scale decision table S^1. And k is the optimistic plausibility distribution optimal scale of S if and only if k is the maximal number such that S^k preserves the same plausibility degree of each decision class of S^1.

4. CONCLUSION

The multi-scale decision table represents a significant advancement in rough set theory. In conventional crisp rough set data analysis, each object typically assumes only one value under each attribute in most information tables. However, real-life applications often involve decision-making based on data measured at different scales. Moreover, within each scale, attributes may further categorize into multiple levels, leading to the concept of multigranulation. This chapter introduces multi-scale decision tables and the multigranulation rough set theory, integrating them to propose the multigranulation rough set for multi-scale decision tables. Additionally, the chapter presents ten distinct methods for selecting the optimal scale, emphasizing the importance of determining the most suitable granularity within multi-scale decision tables. The optimal scale selection, based on the multigranulation rough set for multi-scale decision tables, employs belief and plausible functions within the context of optimistic multigranulation. This approach lays the foundation for future studies to formulate new rules and strategies for selecting the optimal scale among multi-scale decision tables. Continued research in this direction has the potential to further enhance our understanding and application of multigranulation rough set theory in practical decision-making scenarios.

REFERENCES

Cui, Y. E. H., Pedrycz, W., & Li, Z. (2021). Designing distributed fuzzy rule-based models. *IEEE Transactions on Fuzzy Systems*, 29(7), 2047–2053. 10.1109/TFUZZ.2020.2984971

E, H., Cui, Y., Pedrycz, W., & Li, Z. (2022). Fuzzy relational matrix factorization and its granular characterization in data description. *IEEE Transactions on Fuzzy Systems*, 30(3), 794–804. 10.1109/TFUZZ.2020.3048577

E, H., Cui, Y., Pedrycz, W., & Li, Z. (2023). Design of distributed rule-based models in the presence of large data. *IEEE Transactions on Fuzzy Systems*, 31(7), 2479–2486. 10.1109/TFUZZ.2022.3226250

Greco, S., Matarazzo, B., & Slowinski, R. (1999). Rough approximation of a preference relation by dominance relations. *European Journal of Operational Research*, 117(1), 63–83. 10.1016/S0377-2217(98)00127-1

Li, W., Deng, C., Pedrycz, W., Castillo, O., Zhang, C., & Zhan, T. (2023). Double-quantitative feature selection approach for multi-granularity ordered decision systems. *IEEE Transactions on Artificial Intelligence*. Advance online publication. 10.1109/TAI.2023.3319301

Li, W., Pedrycz, W., Xue, X., Xu, W., & Fan, B. (2019). Fuzziness and incremental information of disjoint regions in double-quantitative decision-theoretic rough set model. *International Journal of Machine Learning and Cybernetics*, 10(10), 2669–2690. 10.1007/s13042-018-0893-7

Li, W., Wei, Y., & Xu, W. (2022). General expression of knowledge granularity based on a fuzzy relation matrix. *Fuzzy Sets and Systems*, 440, 149–163. 10.1016/j.fss.2022.01.007

Li, W., & Xu, W. (2015). Multi-granulation decision-theoretic rough set in ordered information system. *Fundamenta Informaticae*, 139(1), 67–89. 10.3233/FI-2015-1226

Li, W., Xu, W., Zhang, X., & Zhang, J. (2022). Updating approximations with dynamic objects based on local multigranulation rough sets in ordered information systems. *Artificial Intelligence Review*, 55(8), 1821–1855. 10.1007/s10462-021-10053-9

Li, W., Zhang, X., & Sun, W. (2014). Further study of multigranulation T-fuzzy rough sets. *TheScientificWorldJournal*, 2014, 1–18.25215336

Liang, J., & Qian, Y. (2008). Information granules and entropy theory in information systems. *Science in China Series F: Information Sciences*, 51(10), 1427–1444. 10.1007/s11432-008-0113-2

Lin, T. Y. (2004). Granular computing: From rough sets and neighborhood systems to information systems. *International Journal of Uncertainty, Fuzziness and Knowledge-based Systems*, 12, 651–672.

Lingras, P. J., & Yao, Y. (1998). Data mining using extensions of the rough set model. *Journal of the American Society for Information Science*, 49(5), 415–422. 10.1002/(SICI)1097-4571(19980415)49:5<415::AID-ASI4>3.0.CO;2-Z

Pal, S. K., Shankar, B. U., & Mitra, P. (2005). Granular computing, rough entropy and object extraction. *Pattern Recognition Letters*, 26(16), 2509–2517. 10.1016/j.patrec.2005.05.007

Pawlak, Z. (1982). Rough sets. *Journal of Information Science*, 11, 341–356.

Pedrycz, W., & Bargiela, A. (2002). Granular clustering: A granular signature of data. *IEEE Transactions on Systems, Man, and Cybernetics. Part B, Cybernetics*, 32(2), 212–224. 10.1109/3477.99087818238121

Pedrycz, W., & Bargiela, A. (2012). An optimization of allocation of information granularity in the interpretation of data structures: Toward granular fuzzy clustering. *IEEE Transactions on Systems, Man, and Cybernetics. Part B, Cybernetics*, 42(3), 582–590. 10.1109/TSMCB.2011.217006722067434

Qian, Y., Liang, J., & Pang, C. (2010). Incomplete multigranulation rough set, *IEEE Transactions on Systems. IEEE Transactions on Systems, Man, and Cybernetics. Part A, Systems and Humans*, 20(2), 420–431. 10.1109/TSMCA.2009.2035436

Qian, Y., Liang, X., Lin, G., Guo, Q., & Liang, J. (2017). Local multigranulation decision-theoretic rough sets. *International Journal of Approximate Reasoning*, 82, 119–137. 10.1016/j.ijar.2016.12.008

Skowron, A., & Stepaniuk, J. (2001, January). Information granules: Towards foundations of computing. *International Journal of Intelligent Systems*, 16(1), 57–85. 10.1002/1098-111X(200101)16:1<57::AID-INT6>3.0.CO;2-Y

Wu, W. Z., & Leung, Y. (2011). Theory and applications of granular labelled partitions in multi-scale decision tables. *Information Sciences*, 181(18), 3878–3897. 10.1016/j.ins.2011.04.047

Wu, W. Z., & Leung, Y. (2013). Optimal scale selection for multi-scale decision tables. *International Journal of Approximate Reasoning*, 54(8), 1107–1129. 10.1016/j.ijar.2013.03.017

Wu, W. Z., Qian, Y., Li, T. J., & Gu, S.-M. (2017). On rule acquisition in incomplete multi-scale decision tables. *Information Sciences*, 378, 282–302. 10.1016/j.ins.2016.03.041

Xu, W., & Li, W. (2016). Granular computing approach to two-way learning based on formal concept analysis in fuzzy datasets. *IEEE Transactions on Cybernetics*, 46(2), 366–379. 10.1109/TCYB.2014.236177225347892

Xu, W., Li, W., & Zhang, X. (2017). Generalized multi-granulation rough set and optimal granularity selection. *Granular Computing*, 2(4), 271–288. 10.1007/s41066-017-0042-9

Yao, Y. (2009). Interpreting concept learning in cognitive informatics and granular computing. *IEEE Transactions on Systems, Man, and Cybernetics. Part B, Cybernetics*, 39(4), 855–866. 10.1109/TSMCB.2009.201333419342352

Zadeh, L. A. (1979). Fuzzy sets and information granularity. In *Advances in Fuzzy Set Theory and Applications* (pp. 3–18). North-Holland.

Chapter 7 Fuzzy Hamacher Aggregation Functions and Their Applications to Multiple Attribute Decision Making

Xiaoan Tang
Hefei University of Technology, China

ABSTRACT

Hamacher t-norm and t-conorm have been widely applied in fuzzy multiple attribute decision making (MADM) to combine assessments on each attribute, which are generally expressed by Atanassov's intuitionistic fuzzy (AIF) numbers, interval-valued intuitionistic fuzzy (IVIF) numbers, hesitant fuzzy (HF) elements, and dual hesitant fuzzy (DHF) elements. Due to the fact that AIF numbers and HF elements are special cases of IVIF numbers and DHF elements, respectively, two propositions can be established from analyzing numerical examples and real cases concerning MADM with IVIF and DHF assessments in the literature: (1) the monotonicity of alternative scores derived from Hamacher arithmetic and geometric aggregation operators with respect to the parameter r in Hamacher t-norm and t-conorm and (2) the relationship between alternative scores generated by Hamacher arithmetic and geometric aggregation operators, given the same r. The authors provide the theoretical proof of the two propositions and propose a new method to compare alternatives in MADM with consideration of all possible values of r.

DOI: 10.4018/979-8-3693-4292-3.ch007

1. INTRODUCTION

Decision making can be considered a mental process in which human beings make a choice among several alternatives. However, with the increasing complexity of real decision problems, decision makers frequently face the challenge of characterizing their preferences in an uncertain context. This opens an important application field of fuzzy set theory and granular computing techniques (Li et al., 2023; E et al., 2022): fuzzy decision making (Apolloni et al., 2016; Chen et al., 2016; Chu et al., 2016; Gupta et al., 2016; Mendel, 2016; Torra, 2010; Xiao, 2014; Xu & Liao, 2015; Zhao & Wei, 2013; Tang et al., 2020a). As stated by Pedrycz and Chen (Pedrycz & Chen, 2015), fuzzy decision making including its underlying methodology, the plethora of algorithmic developments, and a rich and diversified slew of application studies form a cornerstone of fuzzy sets. More importantly, it plays a key role in fuzzy decision making to combine multiple pieces of uncertain information represented by the extensions of fuzzy set (Zadeh, 1965) such as Atanassov's intuitionistic fuzzy (AIF) set (Atanassov, 1986), interval-valued intuitionistic fuzzy (IVIF) set (Atanassov, 1989), hesitant fuzzy (HF) set (Torra, 2010), and dual hesitant fuzzy (DHF) set (Zhu et al.,2012). To address such combination, various aggregation functions or operators have been designed and applied in multiple attribute decision making (MADM) (Beliakov et al., 2007; Bustince et al., 2014; Garg, 2016b; Huang, 2014; Ju et al., 2014; Liao & Xu, 2015; Liu, 2014; Tan et al., 2015; Wang et al., 2016; Wang et al., 2014; Xia & Xu, 2011; Xia et al., 2012; Xu & Yager, 2006; Zhou et al., 2014) .

Firstly, many efforts have been made concerning the combination of AIF or IVIF assessments. Beliakov et al. (Beliakov et al., 2012) developed the median aggregation operators for AIF sets and interval-valued fuzzy sets. Garg (Garg, 2016b) constructed a number of generalized intuitionistic fuzzy interactive geometric interaction operators using Einstein t-norm and t-conorm. Xia et al. (Xia et al., 2012) designed intuitionistic fuzzy weighted averaging and geometric operators based on Archimedean t-norm and t-conorm (Deschrijver & Kerre, 2002). Liao and Xu (Liao & Xu, 2014) proposed a family of intuitionistic fuzzy hybrid weighted aggregation operators in which the properties of idempotency and boundedness are satisfied. As an important style of the Archimedean t-norm and t-conorm, Hamacher t-norm and t-conorm (Hamachar, 1978) were used to construct a number of intuitionistic fuzzy Hamacher aggregation operators based on the unordered and ordered weighted averaging operators (OWA) (Huang, 2014). Chen et al. (Chen et al., 2016b) presented the IVIF aggregation operators for group decision making. Many Hamacher aggregation operators of IVIF information were also developed using the ordered weighted geometric operator (Liu, 2014; Xiao, 2014).

Secondly, the combination of HF or DHF assessments has also been investigated widely in the literature. Xia and Xu (Xia & Xu, 2011) proposed many aggregation operators for HF information based on weighted averaging and geometric operators. Liao and Xu (Liao & Xu, 2015) constructed a series of new HF hybrid arithmetic aggregation operators satisfying idempotency and keeping the advantages of HF hybrid averaging and geometric operators developed by Xia and Xu (Xia & Xu, 2011). In particular, Hamacher t-norm and t-conorm were used to develop a family of HF aggregation operators (Tan et al., 2015; Zhou et al., 2014). With regard to the aggregation for DHF information, several aggregation operators and power aggregation operators were constructed based on Archimedean t-norm and t-conorm (Wang et al., 2016; Wang et al., 2014). Ju et al. (Ju et al., 2014) used Hamacher t-norm and t-conorm to develop some aggregation operators for DHF information.

It is worth mentioning that Hamacher t-norm and t-conorm can reduce to algebraic and Einstein t-norms and t-conorms when the parameter r in Hamacher t-norm and t-conorm is set as 1 and 2, respectively (Xia et al., 2012). For this reason, the aggregation operators based on algebraic and Einstein t-norms and t-conorms of the above four kinds of fuzzy assessments are not reviewed individually. This also indicates why fuzzy Hamacher aggregation operators are addressed in this chapter.

Existing studies concerning fuzzy Hamacher aggregation operators (Huang, 2014;Ju et al., 2014; Liu, 2014; Tan et al., 2015; Xia et al., 2012; Xiao, 2014; Zhou et al.,2014) reveal that they are generally divided into arithmetic and geometric aggregation operators. It can be found from numerical examples or real cases in existing studies that there are two important rules which govern the two types of aggregation operators in the context of fuzzy MADM: (1) the scores of the decision alternatives under consideration decrease and increase with the increase of the parameter r in the Hamacher t-norm and t-conorm when the arithmetic and geometric aggregation operators are applied, respectively; and (2) the scores of the decision alternatives generated by the arithmetic aggregation operator are always larger than those generated by the geometric aggregation operator, regardless of what the parameter r is equal to. To the best of our knowledge, existing studies have only shown the results of calculations in numerical examples or case studies which indicate these two rules, but have not provided a theoretical analysis of such results. Although a small number of researchers (e.g., (Liao & Xu, 2015; Liao & Xu, 2014)) have discussed the relationship between arithmetic and geometric averaging operators in the AIF or HF environment, it cannot be directly extended to the situation of the arithmetic and geometric averaging operators developed based on Hamacher t-norm and t-conorm. The above analysis shows that it is necessary to theoretically discuss the relationship between arithmetic and geometric averaging operators developed based on Hamacher t-norm and t-conorm in various fuzzy contexts. This is the first motivation of this chapter.

Except the above, previous studies (Huang, 2014;Ju et al., 2014; Liu, 2014; Tan et al., 2015; Xia et al., 2012; Xiao, 2014; Zhou et al.,2014) of Hamacher aggregation operators in the context of fuzzy MADM have shown the influence of the parameter r in Hamacher t-norm and t-conorm on decision results by a sensitivity analysis of r only. However, two key points have been omitted in these studies: (1) what is the meaning of the parameter r; and (2) how is this parameter determined in MADM. The meaning of the parameter r in these studies is typically unclear, and its determination is generally arbitrary and subjective (Ju et al., 2014; Liu, 2014; Zhou et al., 2014), which may negatively influence the rationality of decision results. To guarantee the rationality of decisions made with consideration of the parameter r, the two key points about r in MADM need to be addressed, which forms the second motivation of this chapter. As a whole, it is necessary and important to analyze the two above-mentioned rules of Hamacher arithmetic and geometric averaging operators in various fuzzy contexts from a theoretical point of view, and to address the two key points concerning the parameter r in MADM.

In this chapter, following the above motivations, we first present two propositions to cover the two rules, and then prove them theoretically when handling MADM problems with IVIF or DHF assessments. The situations of MADM with AIF or HF assessments are covered because IVIF and DHF assessments can reduce to AIF and HF assessments, respectively. Based on the two propositions, we associate the meaning of the parameter r in Hamacher t-norm and t-conorm with the risk attitude of a decision maker and give relevant explanations. Specifically, to avoid the negative influence of arbitrary or subjective r values on decision results in MADM, a new method to compare alternatives is proposed by using the mean scores of alternatives with consideration of all possible values of r.

In short, the main contributions of this chapter include the following: (1) the construction of two propositions concerning the two types of Hamacher aggregation operators in the context of fuzzy MADM; (2) the theoretical proof of the two propositions in MADM with IVIF and DHF assessments; (3) the analysis of the meaning of the parameter r in Hamacher aggregation operators; and (4) the development of a new method for ranking alternatives in MADM problems with DHF assessments, by following the two propositions.

The rest of this chapter is organized as follows. The necessary preliminaries are briefly reviewed in Section 2. Section 3 conducts an analysis of MADM with IVIF and DHF assessments in the literature, before presenting propositions concerning the two rules found. In Section 4, these propositions are proven theoretically in the context of MADM with IVIF and DHF assessments. In Section 5, the meaning of the parameter r in the Hamacher t-norm and t-conorm is explained by the found two rules, and a new method is developed to compare alternatives with complete coverage of all possible r, which is demonstrated by one numerical example and compared with two existing methods. Finally, Section 6 concludes this chapter.

2. PRELIMINARIES

In this section, we briefly review basic concepts of AIF, IVIF, HF, and DHF sets, and Hamacher t-norm and t-conorm.

2.1 AIF and IVIF Sets

Atanassov (Atanassov, 1986) generalized the concept of fuzzy set (Zadeh, 1965), and defined the concept of AIF set as follows.

Definition 1 (Atanassov, 1986). Let $X = \{x_1, x_2, \ldots, x_n\}$ be a set, then an AIF set $\widetilde{A}$ on X is defined as

$$\widetilde{A} = \{\langle x, u_{\widetilde{A}}(x), v_{\widetilde{A}}(x)\rangle, x \in X\}, \tag{1}$$

where $u_{\widetilde{A}}:X \to [0,1], \nu_{\widetilde{A}}:X \to [0,1]$, and $0 \leq u_{\widetilde{A}}(x)+\nu_{\widetilde{A}}(x) \leq 1, \forall x \in X$. For each $x \in X, u_{\widetilde{A}}(x)$ and $\nu_{\widetilde{A}}(x)$ represent the degrees of membership and non-membership of x to $\widetilde{A}$, respectively.

As an extension of AIF set, IVIF set was developed by Atanassov and Gargov (Atanassov & Gargov, 1989).

Definition 2 (Atanassov & Gargov, 1989; Miguel, 2016). Let $X = \{x_1, x_2, \ldots, x_n\}$ be a universe of discourse. Then an IVIF set $\widetilde{A}$ on X is given by

$$\widetilde{A} = \{\langle x, \tilde{u}_{\widetilde{A}}(x), \tilde{v}_{\widetilde{A}}(x)\rangle, x \in X\}, \tag{2}$$

where $\tilde{u}_{\widetilde{A}}(x)$ and $\tilde{v}_{\widetilde{A}}(x)$ denote interval-valued membership and non-membership degrees of x to $\widetilde{A}$ such that $\tilde{u}_{\widetilde{A}}(x) \subseteq [0,1]$, $\tilde{v}_{\widetilde{A}}(x) \subseteq [0,1]$, and $0 \leq \sup(\tilde{u}_{\widetilde{A}}(x)) + \sup(\tilde{v}_{\widetilde{A}}(x)) \leq 1, \forall x \in X$.

For convenience, let $\tilde{u}_{\widetilde{A}}(x_i) = [a,b]$, $\tilde{v}_{\widetilde{A}}(x_i) = [c,d]$, then $\tilde{a} = ([a,b],[c,d])$ is called an IVIF number (Liu, 2014). The comparison between two IVIF numbers is defined as follows.

Definition 3 (Hung & Wu, 2002). Let $\tilde{a} = ([a,b],[c,d])$ be an IVIF number, then the score function of $\tilde{a}$ is $S(\tilde{a}) = \frac{a+b-c-d}{2}$, and the accuracy function of $\tilde{a}$ is $H(\tilde{a}) = \frac{a+b+c+d}{2}$. For two IVIF numbers $\tilde{a}_1$ and $\tilde{a}_2$, if $S(\tilde{a}_1) > S(\tilde{a}_2)$, then $\tilde{a}_1 > \tilde{a}_2$; if $S(\tilde{a}_1)=S(\tilde{a}_2)$, $\tilde{a}_1 > \tilde{a}_2$ and $\tilde{a}_1 = \tilde{a}_2$ can be deduced respectively from $H(\tilde{a}_1) > H(\tilde{a}_2)$ and $H(\tilde{a}_1)=H(\tilde{a}_2)$.

2.2 HF and DHF Sets

Torra (Torra, 2010) first proposed the concept of HF set, which is defined as follows.

Definition 4 (Torra, 2010). Given a universe of discourse X, an HF set on X is defined as

$$\tilde{A}=\{\langle x,h_{\tilde{A}}(x)\rangle | x \in X\}, \tag{3}$$

where $h_{\tilde{A}}(x)$ symbolizes possible membership degrees of x to $\tilde{A}$, each of which is limited to [0,1].

On the basis of HF set and AIF set, DHF set was developed by Zhu et al. (Zhu et al., 2012).

Definition 5 (Zhu et al., 2012). Given a universe of discourse X, a DHF set on X is defined as

$$\tilde{A}=\{\langle x,\tilde{h}_{\tilde{A}}(x),\tilde{g}_{\tilde{A}}(x)\rangle | x \in X\}, \tag{4}$$

where $\tilde{h}_{\tilde{A}}(x)$ and $\tilde{g}_{\tilde{A}}(x)$ denote possible membership and non-membership sets of x to $\tilde{A}$ such that $\tilde{h}_{\tilde{A}}:X \rightarrow [0,1]$, $\tilde{g}_{\tilde{A}}:X \rightarrow [0,1]$, and $0 \leq \max\{\tilde{h}_{\tilde{A}}(x)\} + \max\{\tilde{g}_{\tilde{A}}(x)\} \leq 1$ for all $x \in X$.

Given $\tilde{h}_{\tilde{A}}(x)$ and $\tilde{g}_{\tilde{A}}(x)$, $\tilde{f}_{\tilde{A}}(x) = \bigcup_{\gamma_{\tilde{A}}(x)\in\tilde{h}_{\tilde{A}}(x),\eta_{\tilde{A}}(x)\in\tilde{g}_{\tilde{A}}(x)} \{1-\gamma_{\tilde{A}}(x)-\eta_{\tilde{A}}(x)\}$ is used to symbolize a possible indeterminacy (uncertain) set of x to $\tilde{A}$, where $\gamma_{\tilde{A}}(x) \in \tilde{h}_{\tilde{A}}(x)$ and $\eta_{\tilde{A}}(x) \in \tilde{g}_{\tilde{A}}(x)$ represent possible membership and non-membership degrees of x to $\tilde{A}$. For a specific x, $\tilde{a} = \{\tilde{h},\tilde{g}\}$ is called a DHF element. Two DHF elements are compared by the following definition.

Definition 6 (Wang et al., 2016; Zhu et al., 2012). Let $\tilde{a} = \{\tilde{h},\tilde{g}\}$ be a DHF element, then the score function of $\tilde{a}$ is $S(\tilde{a})=\frac{\sum_{i=1}^{\delta(\tilde{h})}\gamma_i}{\delta(\tilde{h})}-\frac{\sum_{j=1}^{\delta(\tilde{g})}\eta_j}{\delta(\tilde{g})}$, and the accuracy function of $\tilde{a}$ is $H(\tilde{a})=\frac{\sum_{i=1}^{\delta(\tilde{h})}\gamma_i}{\delta(\tilde{h})}+\frac{\sum_{j=1}^{\delta(\tilde{g})}\eta_j}{\delta(\tilde{g})}$, where $\delta(\tilde{h})$ and $\delta(\tilde{g})$ symbolize the numbers of the elements in $\tilde{h}$ and $\tilde{g}$, respectively. For two DHF elements $\tilde{a}_1$ and $\tilde{a}_2$, if $S(\tilde{a}_1)>S(\tilde{a}_2)$, then $\tilde{a}_1 > \tilde{a}_2$; if $S(\tilde{a}_1)=S(\tilde{a}_2)$, $\tilde{a}_1 > \tilde{a}_2$ and $\tilde{a}_1 = \tilde{a}_2$ can be deduced respectively from $H(\tilde{a}_1) > H(\tilde{a}_2)$ and $H(\tilde{a}_1)=H(\tilde{a}_2)$.

2.3 Hamacher T-Norm and T-Conorm

T-norm and t-conorm are widely applied in fuzzy context to define the generalized intersection and union operations of fuzzy sets (Deschrijver & Kerre, 2002).

Definition 7 (Deschrijver & Kerre, 2002). A given function $T{:}[0,1]\times[0,1]\rightarrow[0,1]$ is called a t-norm when it satisfies the following four constraints:

(1) $T(1, x) = x$, for all x;

(2) $T(x, y) = T(y, x)$, for all x and y;

(3) $T(x, T(y, z)) = T(T(x, y), z)$, for all x, y, and z; and

(4) If $x \le x_1$ and $y \le y_1$, then $T(x, y) \le T(x_1, y_1)$.

Definition 8 (Deschrijver & Kerre, 2002). A given function $S{:}[0,1]\times[0,1]\rightarrow[0,1]$ is called a t-conorm when it satisfies the following four constraints:

(1) $S(0, x) = x$, for all x;

(2) $S(x, y) = S(y, x)$, for all x and y;

(3) $S(x, S(y, z)) = S(S(x, y), z)$, for all x, y, and z;

(4) If $x \le x_1$ and $y \le y_1$, then $S(x, y) \le S(x_1, y_1)$.

A continuous t-norm $T(x, y)$ such that $T(x, x) < x$ for all $x\in(0,1)$ is called an Archimedean t-norm. Similarly, an Archimedean t-conorm $S(x, y)$ satisfies that $S(x, x) > x$ for all $x\in(0,1)$. Strict Archimedean t-norm and t-conorm are strictly increasing for all $x, y\in(0,1)$ (Deschrijver & Kerre, 2002). A strict Archimedean t-norm $T(x, y) = p^{-1}(p(x) + p(y))$ can be created from a strictly decreasing function $p{:}[0,1]\rightarrow[0,+\infty]$ such that $p(1) = 0$, whose dual function $q(x) = p(1\text{-}x)$ can be used to construct a strict Archimedean t-conorm $S(x, y) = q^{-1}(q(x) + q(y))$, as stated by Xia et al. (Xia et al.,2012).

Given a specific $p(x)$, i.e.,

$$p(x) = \log\left(\frac{r + (1-r)x}{x}\right),\ r > 0, \tag{5}$$

it is clear that

$$q(x) = p(1\text{-}x) = \log\left(\frac{r + (1-r)\cdot(1-x)}{1-x}\right). \tag{6}$$

Under this condition, strict Archimedean t-norm and t-conorm are called Hamacher t-norm $T_r(x, y)$ and t-conorm $S_r(x, y)$ (Hamachar, 1978), which are calculated by

$$T_r(x,y) = \frac{xy}{r-(r-1)\cdot(x+y-xy)}$$

and (7)

$$S_r(x,y) = \frac{x+y+(r-2)xy}{1+(r-1)xy}$$

, $r > 0$. (8)

$T_r(x, y)$ and $S_r(x, y)$ are also called Hamacher product ⊗ and Hamacher sum ⊕ (Hamachar, 1978). Specifically, $T_r(x, y)$ and $S_r(x, y)$ reduce to algebraic t-norm and t-conorm when $r = 1$; while they become Einstein t-norm and t-conorm when $r = 2$ (Beliakov et al., 2007; Garg, 2016b).

3. PROPOSITIONS ABOUT HAMACHER AGGREGATION OPERATORS IN MADM

As analyzed in Introduction, Hamacher t-norm and t-conorm are applied in MADM problems with AIF, IVIF, HF, and DHF assessments to create aggregation operators so as to combine assessments of alternatives on each attribute. From presenting an analysis of numerical examples or real cases in existing studies concerning MADM with AIF, IVIF, HF, and DHF assessments, we find two common rules of Hamacher aggregation operators in the four types of MADM. As AIF and HF are special cases of IVIF and DHF, respectively, the following representative examples or cases regarding MADM with IVIF and DHF assessments will be examined to elicit the two rules.

3.1 Analysis of Hamacher Aggregation Operators in MADM With IVIF Assessments

To evaluate the air quality of Guangzhou for the 16th Asian Olympic Games, the air quality in Guangzhou for the Novembers of 2006, 2007, 2008, and 2009 were evaluated to find out the trends in 2010. Liu (Liu, 2014) used Hamacher arithmetic hybrid weighted averaging operator and Hamacher geometric hybrid weighted averaging operator of IVIF information to combine IVIF assessments of each alternative on each attribute, from which evaluation scores of the air quality of Guangzhou for the Novembers of the four years were generated (see Table IV in (Liu, 2014) for details).

The evaluation results in (Liu, 2014) indicate the following: (1) evaluation scores of the air quality of Guangzhou for the Novembers of the four years decreased and increased with the increase of the parameter r in the Hamacher arithmetic hybrid weighted averaging operator and Hamacher geometric hybrid weighted averaging operator of IVIF information; and (2) evaluation scores of the air quality of Guangzhou for the Novembers of the four years generated by the Hamacher arithmetic hybrid weighted averaging operator are always larger than those generated by the Hamacher geometric hybrid weighted averaging operator given different values of r.

3.2 Analysis of Hamacher Aggregation Operators in MADM With DHF Assessments

To address MADM with DHF assessments, Ju et al. (Ju et al., 2014) developed a variety of DHF aggregation operators by combining Hamacher operations with averaging operator, weighted geometric operator and OWA operator. To handle a project evaluation problem, Hamacher arithmetic and geometric hybrid weighted averaging operators for DHF assessments under different r are applied to aggregate the DHF assessments of four projects under consideration (see Table 2 in (Ju et al., 2014) for details).

The results generated in (Ju et al., 2014) reveal the following: (1) scores of the four projects decreased and increased with the increase of the parameter r when the Hamacher arithmetic and geometric hybrid weighted averaging operators of DHF infromation are respectively applied; (2) scores of the four projects generated by the Hamacher arithmetic hybrid weighted averaging operator are always larger than those generated by the Hamacher geometric hybrid weighted averaging operator when r is set as different values; and (3) the ranking order of the four projects have become different when r in Hamacher geometric hybrid weighted averaging operator is changed from 0.5 to 1. The third observation emphasizes the important influence of r in Hamacher geometric hybrid weighted averaging operator on solutions to the project evaluation problem.

3.3 Propositions

Suppose that different arithmetic and geometric aggregation operators based on Hamacher operations are called Hamacher arithmetic and geometric aggregation operators, respectively. Two common rules can be extracted from the representative analysis of the movement of alternative scores in MADM with IVIF and DHF assessments with variation in the parameter r in Hamacher arithmetic and geometric aggregation operators. They are formally presented below.

Proposition 1. Alternative scores decrease and increase with the increase of the parameter r in Hamacher arithmetic and geometric aggregation operators respectively, when the operators are applied in MADM with IVIF and DHF assessments.

Proposition 2. Alternative scores generated by Hamacher arithmetic operator are always larger than those generated by Hamacher geometric operator given the same r when the two operators are applied in MADM with IVIF and DHF assessments.

In the next section, the above two propositions will be theoretically proven in MADM with IVIF and DHF assessments.

4. THEORETICAL PROOF OF TWO PROPOSITIONS

In this section, we prove the two propositions presented in Section 3.3 when Hamacher arithmetic and geometric aggregation operators are applied in MADM with IVIF and DHF assessments.

4.1 Proof of Two Propositions in MADM With IVIF Assessments

4.1.1 Description of MADM Problems With IVIF Assessments

Suppose that a MADM problem has m alternatives A_i $(i = 1, ..., m)$ and n attributes C_j $(j = 1, ..., n)$. The relative weights of the n attributes are represented by $\omega = (\omega_1, \omega_2, ..., \omega_n)^T$ such that $0 \leq \omega_j \leq 1$ and $\sum_{i=1}^{n} \omega_j = 1$, where the notation '$T$' denotes 'transpose'. Let $\tilde{A}_{ij} = (\tilde{u}_{ij}, \tilde{v}_{ij}) = ([a_{ij}, b_{ij}], [c_{ij}, d_{ij}])$ signify the IVIF assessment of alternative A_i on attribute C_j. Then, an IVIF decision matrix for the problem can be profiled by

$$\tilde{A}_{m\times n} = \begin{bmatrix} <\tilde{u}_{11}, \tilde{v}_{11}> & <\tilde{u}_{12}, \tilde{v}_{12}> & \cdots & <\tilde{u}_{1n}, \tilde{v}_{1n}> \\ <\tilde{u}_{21}, \tilde{v}_{21}> & <\tilde{u}_{22}, \tilde{v}_{22}> & \cdots & <\tilde{u}_{2n}, \tilde{v}_{2n}> \\ \vdots & \vdots & \ddots & \vdots \\ <\tilde{u}_{m1}, \tilde{v}_{m1}> & <\tilde{u}_{m2}, \tilde{v}_{m2}> & \cdots & <\tilde{u}_{mn}, \tilde{v}_{mn}> \end{bmatrix}, \quad (9)$$

where each element represents an IVIF number.

4.1.2 Monotonicity of Alternative Scores With Respect to r in Hamacher Arithmetic and Geometric Aggregation Operators for MADM With IVIF Assessments

For MADM with IVIF assessments, we address Proposition 1 to identify the monotonicity of alternative scores with respect to the parameter r in Hamacher arithmetic and geometric aggregation operators.

To solve a MADM problem with IVIF assessments, the assessments of alternatives on each attribute are first combined using Hamacher aggregation operators to generate the aggregated assessments of alternatives. The aggregated assessments are used to calculate the scores of alternatives, and then to create a ranking order of alternatives. In most MADM methods, assessment $\tilde{A}_{ij}$ is only weighted by attribute weight ω_j $(j = 1, ..., n)$ in the process of attribute combination, while the ordered position of $\widetilde{A}_{ij}$ is usually omitted. Differently, both the attribute weight and the ordered position of $\widetilde{A}_{ij}$ are involved in the Hamacher arithmetic and geometric hybrid weighted averaging operators developed by Liu (Liu, 2014). It is clear that the aggregation of $\widetilde{A}_{ij}$ only by ω_j in most MADM methods can be seen as a special case of the aggregation in Liu's method. Without loss of generality, in the following we focus on the two Hamacher aggregation operators created by Liu (Liu, 2014) to verify Proposition 1.

Definition 9 ((Liu, 2014)). Let the IVIF number $\widetilde{A}_{ij} = (\widetilde{u}_{ij}, \widetilde{v}_{ij}) = ([a_{ij}, b_{ij}], [c_{ij}, d_{ij}])$ $(i = 1, 2, \ldots, m, j = 1, \ldots, n)$ be the assessment of alternative A_i on attribute C_j for a MADM problem, $\omega = (\omega_1, \omega_2, \ldots, \omega_n)^T$ be the relative weights of the n attributes, and $w_i = (w_{i1}, \ldots, w_{in})^T$ be the OWA operator weights with respect to $\widetilde{A}_{ij}$. Then, the Hamacher arithmetic and geometric hybrid weighted averaging operators are defined below.

a) The aggregated assessment $\widetilde{A}_i = (\widetilde{u}_i, \widetilde{v}_i)$ $(i = 1, 2, \ldots, m)$ using the Hamacher arithmetic hybrid weighted averaging operator is defined as

$$\widetilde{A}_i = w_{i1}\widetilde{B}_{i\sigma(1)} \oplus \ldots \oplus w_{in}\widetilde{B}_{i\sigma(n)} = ([q^{-1}(\sum_{j=1}^{n} w_{ij} q(\dot{a}_{i\sigma(j)})), q^{-1}(\sum_{j=1}^{n} w_{ij} q(\dot{b}_{i\sigma(j)}))],$$

$$[p^{-1}(\sum_{j=1}^{n} w_{ij} p(\dot{c}_{i\sigma(j)})), p^{-1}(\sum_{j=1}^{n} w_{ij} p(\dot{d}_{i\sigma(j)}))]) =$$

$$\left(\left[\frac{\prod_{j=1}^{n}(1+(r-1)\dot{a}_{i\sigma(j)})^{w_{ij}} - \prod_{j=1}^{n}(1-\dot{a}_{i\sigma(j)})^{w_{ij}}}{\prod_{j=1}^{n}(1+(r-1)\dot{a}_{i\sigma(j)})^{w_{ij}} + (r-1)\prod_{j=1}^{n}(1-\dot{a}_{i\sigma(j)})^{w_{ij}}},\right.\right.$$

$$\left.\frac{\prod_{j=1}^{n}(1+(r-1)\dot{b}_{i\sigma(j)})^{w_{ij}} - \prod_{j=1}^{n}(1-\dot{b}_{i\sigma(j)})^{w_{ij}}}{\prod_{j=1}^{n}(1+(r-1)\dot{b}_{i\sigma(j)})^{w_{ij}} + (r-1)\prod_{j=1}^{n}(1-\dot{b}_{i\sigma(j)})^{w_{ij}}}\right],$$

$$\left[\frac{r\prod_{j=1}^{n}(\dot{c}_{i\sigma(j)})^{w_{ij}}}{\prod_{j=1}^{n}(1+(r-1)(1-\dot{c}_{i\sigma(j)}))^{w_{ij}} + (r-1)\prod_{j=1}^{n}(\dot{c}_{i\sigma(j)})^{w_{ij}}},\right.$$

$$\left.\left.\frac{r\prod_{j=1}^{n}(\dot{d}_{i\sigma(j)})^{w_{ij}}}{\prod_{j=1}^{n}(1+(r-1)(1-\dot{d}_{i\sigma(j)}))^{w_{ij}}+(r-1)\prod_{j=1}^{n}(\dot{d}_{i\sigma(j)})^{w_{ij}}}\right]\right), \tag{10}$$

where $\widetilde{B}_{i\sigma(j)}$ stands for the jth largest of $\widetilde{B}_{ij} = n\omega_{ij}\widetilde{A}_{ij} = ([\dot{a}_{ij}, \dot{b}_{ij}], [\dot{c}_{ij}, \dot{d}_{ij}])$, and $(\sigma(1), \sigma(2), \ldots, \sigma(n))$ for a permutation of $(1, 2, \ldots, n)$ such that $S(\widetilde{B}_{i\sigma(j)}) \geq S(\widetilde{B}_{i\sigma(j+1)})$ $(j = 1, \ldots, n\text{-}1)$.

b) The aggregated assessment $\widetilde{A}_i = (\widetilde{u}_i, \widetilde{v}_i)$ $(i = 1, 2, \ldots, m)$ using the Hamacher geometric hybrid weighted averaging operator is defined as

$$\widetilde{A}_i = \widetilde{B}_{i\sigma(1)}^{w_{i1}} \otimes \ldots \otimes \widetilde{B}_{i\sigma(n)}^{w_{in}} = ([p^{-1}(\sum_{j=1}^{n} w_{ij} p(\dot{a}_{i\sigma(j)})), p^{-1}(\sum_{j=1}^{n} w_{ij} p(\dot{b}_{i\sigma(j)}))],$$

$$[q^{-1}(\sum_{j=1}^{n} w_{ij} q(\dot{c}_{i\sigma(j)})), q^{-1}(\sum_{j=1}^{n} w_{ij} q(\dot{d}_{i\sigma(j)}))]) =$$

$$\left(\left[\frac{r\prod_{j=1}^{n}\dot{a}_{i\sigma(j)}^{w_{ij}}}{\prod_{j=1}^{n}(1+(r-1)(1-\dot{a}_{i\sigma(j)}))^{w_{ij}}+(r-1)\prod_{j=1}^{n}(1-\dot{a}_{i\sigma(j)})^{w_{ij}}},\right.\right.$$

$$\left.\frac{r\prod_{j=1}^{n}\dot{b}_{i\sigma(j)}^{w_{ij}}}{\prod_{j=1}^{n}(1+(r-1)(1-\dot{b}_{i\sigma(j)}))^{w_{ij}}+(r-1)\prod_{j=1}^{n}(1-\dot{b}_{i\sigma(j)})^{w_{ij}}}\right],$$

$$\left[\frac{\prod_{j=1}^{n}(1+(r-1)\dot{c}_{i\sigma(j)})^{w_{ij}}-\prod_{j=1}^{n}(1-\dot{c}_{i\sigma(j)})^{w_{ij}}}{\prod_{j=1}^{n}(1+(r-1)\dot{c}_{i\sigma(j)})^{w_{ij}}+(r-1)\prod_{j=1}^{n}(1-\dot{c}_{i\sigma(j)})^{w_{ij}}},\right.$$

$$\left.\left.\frac{\prod_{j=1}^{n}(1+(r-1)\dot{d}_{i\sigma(j)})^{w_{ij}}-\prod_{j=1}^{n}(1-\dot{d}_{i\sigma(j)})^{w_{ij}}}{\prod_{j=1}^{n}(1+(r-1)\dot{d}_{i\sigma(j)})^{w_{ij}}+(r-1)\prod_{j=1}^{n}(1-\dot{d}_{i\sigma(j)})^{w_{ij}}}\right]\right), \tag{11}$$

where $\widetilde{B}_{i\sigma(j)}$ stands for the jth largest of $\widetilde{B}_{ij} = \widetilde{A}_{ij}^{\,n\omega_{ij}} = ([\dot{a}_{ij}, \dot{b}_{ij}],[\dot{c}_{ij}, \dot{d}_{ij}])$, and $(\sigma(1), \sigma(2), \ldots, \sigma(n))$ for a permutation of $(1, 2, \ldots, n)$ such that $S(\widetilde{B}_{i\sigma(j)}) \geq S(\widetilde{B}_{i\sigma(j+1)})$ ($j = 1, \ldots, n-1$).

The aggregated assessments of alternatives are then used to calculate the scores of alternatives in terms of Definition 3.

(1) Given the aggregated assessment $\widetilde{A}_i = (\widetilde{u}_i, \widetilde{v}_i) = ([q^{-1}(\sum_{j=1}^{n} w_{ij} q(\dot{a}_{i\sigma(j)})), q^{-1}(\sum_{j=1}^{n} w_{ij} q(\dot{b}_{i\sigma(j)}))], [p^{-1}(\sum_{j=1}^{n} w_{ij} p(\dot{c}_{i\sigma(j)})), p^{-1}(\sum_{j=1}^{n} w_{ij} p(\dot{d}_{i\sigma(j)}))])$ generated by the Hamacher arithmetic hybrid weighted averaging operator, the score of $\widetilde{A}_i$ denoted by $S^a(\widetilde{A}_i)$ is calculated by

$$S^a(\widetilde{A}_i) = \frac{[q^{-1}(\sum_{j=1}^{n} w_{ij} q(\dot{a}_{i\sigma(j)})) + q^{-1}(\sum_{j=1}^{n} w_{ij} q(\dot{b}_{i\sigma(j)}))]}{2} - \frac{[p^{-1}(\sum_{j=1}^{n} w_{ij} p(\dot{c}_{i\sigma(j)})) + p^{-1}(\sum_{j=1}^{n} w_{ij} p(\dot{d}_{i\sigma(j)}))]}{2}. \tag{12}$$

(2) Given the aggregated assessment $\widetilde{A}_i = (\widetilde{u}_i, \widetilde{v}_i) = ([p^{-1}(\sum_{j=1}^{n} w_{ij} p(\dot{a}_{i\sigma(j)})), p^{-1}(\sum_{j=1}^{n} w_{ij} p(\dot{b}_{i\sigma(j)}))], [q^{-1}(\sum_{j=1}^{n} w_{ij} q(\dot{c}_{i\sigma(j)})), q^{-1}(\sum_{j=1}^{n} w_{ij} q(\dot{d}_{i\sigma(j)})$) generated by the Hamacher geometric hybrid weighted averaging operator, the score of $\widetilde{A}_i$ denoted by $S^g(\widetilde{A}_i)$ is calculated by

$$S^g(\widetilde{A}_i) = \frac{[p^{-1}(\sum_{j=1}^{n} w_{ij} p(\dot{a}_{i\sigma(j)})) + p^{-1}(\sum_{j=1}^{n} w_{ij} p(\dot{b}_{i\sigma(j)}))]}{2} - \frac{[q^{-1}(\sum_{j=1}^{n} w_{ij} q(\dot{c}_{i\sigma(j)})) + q^{-1}(\sum_{j=1}^{n} w_{ij} q(\dot{d}_{i\sigma(j)}))]}{2}. \tag{13}$$

From Eqs. (12) and (13) we find that $S^a(\widetilde{A}_i)$ (or $S^g(\widetilde{A}_i)$) comprises two parts, which are

$\frac{[q^{-1}(\sum_{j=1}^{n} w_{ij} q(\dot{a}_{i\sigma(j)})) + q^{-1}(\sum_{j=1}^{n} w_{ij} q(\dot{b}_{i\sigma(j)}))]}{2}$ (or $\frac{[p^{-1}(\sum_{j=1}^{n} w_{ij} p(\dot{a}_{i\sigma(j)})) + p^{-1}(\sum_{j=1}^{n} w_{ij} p(\dot{b}_{i\sigma(j)}))]}{2}$) and $\frac{[p^{-1}(\sum_{j=1}^{n} w_{ij} p(\dot{c}_{i\sigma(j)})) + p^{-1}(\sum_{j=1}^{n} w_{ij} p(\dot{d}_{i\sigma(j)}))]}{2}$ (or $\frac{[q^{-1}(\sum_{j=1}^{n} w_{ij} q(\dot{c}_{i\sigma(j)})) + q^{-1}(\sum_{j=1}^{n} w_{ij} q(\dot{d}_{i\sigma(j)}))]}{2}$).

The definitions of two functions p and q in Eqs. (5) and (6) indicate that the two parts in $S^a(\widetilde{A}_i)$ (or $S^g(\widetilde{A}_i)$) are the functions with respect to the parameter r. In this context the verification of Proposition 1 is equivalently transformed into the discussion of the monotonicity of the functions p and q with respect to r. The relevant conclusions are drawn and shown in the following theorems.

Theorem 1. Suppose that $M(r) = q^{-1}(\sum_{j=1}^{n} w_j q(\mu_j))$ is a function with the parameter r where $0 \leq w_j \leq 1$, $\sum_{j=1}^{n} w_j = 1$, $0 \leq \mu_j \leq 1$, and $r \in (0,+\infty)$. Then, the function is monotonously decreasing with respect to r.

Theorem 2. Suppose that $N(r) = p^{-1}(\sum_{j=1}^{n} w_j p(\mu_j))$ is a function with the parameter r where $0 \leq w_j \leq 1$, $\sum_{j=1}^{n} w_j = 1$, $0 \leq \mu_j \leq 1$, and $r \in (0,+\infty)$. Then, the function is monotonously increasing with respect to r.

The proofs of Theorems 1 and 2 are omitted here to save space. From Eqs. (12) and (13) and Theorems 1 and 2, we can draw the conclusion that $S^a(\widetilde{A}_i)$ and $S^g(\widetilde{A}_i)$ are the monotonously decreasing and increasing functions with respect to r, respectively. This reveals that Proposition 1 holds in the context of MADM with IVIF assessments when the Hamacher arithmetic and geometric hybrid weighted averaging operators are applied.

4.1.3 Relationship Between Alternative Scores Derived From Hamacher Arithmetic and Geometric Aggregation Operators for MADM With IVIF Assessments

In the previous section, the monotonicity of $S^a(\widetilde{A}_i)$ and $S^g(\widetilde{A}_i)$ with respect to the parameter r in Hamacher aggregation operators was theoretically proven. Based on this monotonicity, the relationship between $S^a(\widetilde{A}_i)$ and $S^g(\widetilde{A}_i)$ will be discussed and proven in the following. In other words, Proposition 2 in MADM with IVIF assessments will be verified. To facilitate the analysis of the relationship between $S^a(\widetilde{A}_i)$ and $S^g(\widetilde{A}_i)$, we firstly present two relevant lemmas.

Lemma 1 (Xu, 2000). Suppose that $x_j > 0$, $\lambda_j > 0$ ($j = 1, \ldots, n$), and $\sum_{j=1}^{n} \lambda_j = 1$, then we have

$$\prod_{j=1}^{n} x_j^{\lambda_j} \leq \sum_{j=1}^{n} \lambda_j x_j \tag{14}$$

with equality if and only if $x_1 = x_2 = \ldots = x_n$.

Lemma 2. The function $f(x) = \frac{x}{x+b}$ is monotonously increasing with respect to the parameter x, where $x > 0$ and $b \geq 0$.

The proof of Lemma 2 is omitted here to save space. Based on the two lemmas, the relationship between $S^a(\widetilde{A}_i)$ and $S^g(\widetilde{A}_i)$ is presented in the following theorem.

Theorem 3. Suppose that $S^a(\widetilde{A}_i)$ and $S^g(\widetilde{A}_i)$ are the scores of the aggregated assessment $\widetilde{A}_i$ generated by using the Hamacher arithmetic and geometric aggregation operators presented in Eqs. (12) and (13), respectively. Then, we have

$$S^a(\widetilde{A}_i) > S^g(\widetilde{A}_i),\ r \in (0, +\infty\ ). \tag{15}$$

Theorem 3 can be proven with the use of Proposition 1, Lemma 1, and Lemma 2. This indicates that Proposition 2 holds in the context of MADM with IVIF assessments when the Hamacher arithmetic and geometric hybrid weighted averaging operators are applied.

4.2 Proof of Two Propositions in MADM With DHF Assessments

4.2.1 Description of MADM Problems With DHF Assessments

For the same MADM problem introduced in Section 4.1.1, let $\widetilde{A}_{ij} = \{h_{ij}, g_{ij}\}$ signify the DHF assessment of alternative A_i on attribute C_j, where $0 \leq h_{ij}, g_{ij} \leq 1$ and $h_{ij} + g_{ij} \leq 1$. A DHF decision matrix for the problem is then given by

$$\widetilde{A}_{m\times n} = \begin{bmatrix} < h_{11}, g_{11} > & < h_{12}, g_{12} > & \cdots & < h_{1n}, g_{1n} > \\ < h_{21}, g_{21} > & < h_{22}, g_{22} > & \cdots & < h_{2n}, g_{2n} > \\ \vdots & \vdots & \ddots & \vdots \\ < h_{m1}, g_{m1} > & < h_{m2}, g_{m2} > & \cdots & < h_{mn}, g_{mn} > \end{bmatrix}. \tag{16}$$

In the following we verify Propositions 1 and 2 in MADM with DHF assessments.

4.2.2 Monotonicity of Alternative Scores With Respect to r in Hamacher Arithmetic and Geometric Aggregation Operators for MADM With DHF Assessments

Similar to the situation in Section 4.1.2, to prove Proposition 1 in a general case of MADM with DHF assessments, the Hamacher arithmetic and geometric hybrid weighted averaging operators developed by Ju et al. (Ju et al., 2014) are used to combine assessments of alternatives on each attribute. The combination is defined as follows.

Definition 10 (Ju et al., 2014). Let the DHF element $\widetilde{A}_{ij} = \{h_{ij}, g_{ij}\} = \{\bigcup_{\gamma_{ij}\in h_{ij}}\{\gamma_{ij}\}, \bigcup_{\eta_{ij}\in g_{ij}}\{\eta_{ij}\}\}$ $(i = 1, 2, \ldots, m, j = 1, \ldots, n)$ be the assessment of alternative A_i on attribute C_j for a MADM problem, $\omega = (\omega_1, \omega_2, ..., \omega_n)^T$ be the relative weights of the n attributes, and $w_i = (w_{i1}, \ldots, w_{in})^T$ be the OWA operator weights with respect to $\widetilde{A}_{ij}$. The Hamacher arithmetic and geometric hybrid weighted averaging operators are defined below.

a) The aggregated assessment of alternative $\widetilde{A}_i = \{h_i, g_i\}$ $(i = 1, 2, \ldots, m)$ using the Hamacher arithmetic hybrid weighted averaging operator is defined as

$$\widetilde{A}_i = w_{i1}\widetilde{B}_{i\sigma(1)} \oplus \ldots \oplus w_{in}\widetilde{B}_{i\sigma(n)} = \{\cup_{\dot{\gamma}_{i\sigma(j)} \in \dot{h}_{i\sigma(j)}} \left\{ q^{-1}(\sum_{j=1}^{n} w_{ij} q(\dot{\gamma}_{i\sigma(j)})) \right\},$$

$$\cup_{\dot{\eta}_{i\sigma(j)} \in \dot{g}_{i\sigma(j)}} \left\{ p^{-1}(\sum_{j=1}^{n} w_{ij} p(\dot{\eta}_{i\sigma(j)})) \right\}\} =$$

$$\left\{ \cup_{\dot{\gamma}_{i\sigma(j)} \in \dot{h}_{i\sigma(j)}} \left\{ \frac{\prod_{j=1}^{n}(1+(r-1)\dot{\gamma}_{i\sigma(j)})^{w_{ij}} - \prod_{j=1}^{n}(1-\dot{\gamma}_{i\sigma(j)})^{w_{ij}}}{\prod_{j=1}^{n}(1+(r-1)\dot{\gamma}_{i\sigma(j)})^{w_{ij}} + (r-1)\prod_{j=1}^{n}(1-\dot{\gamma}_{i\sigma(j)})^{w_{ij}}} \right\}, \right.$$

$$\left. \cup_{\dot{\eta}_{i\sigma(j)} \in \dot{g}_{i\sigma(j)}} \left\{ \frac{r\prod_{j=1}^{n}\dot{\eta}_{i\sigma(j)}^{w_{ij}}}{\prod_{j=1}^{n}(1+(r-1)(1-\dot{\eta}_{i\sigma(j)}))^{w_{ij}} + (r-1)\prod_{j=1}^{n}\dot{\eta}_{i\sigma(j)}^{w_{ij}}} \right\} \right\}, \tag{17}$$

where $\widetilde{B}_{i\sigma(j)}$ stands for the jth largest of $\widetilde{B}_{ij} = n\omega_{ij}\widetilde{A}_{ij} = \{\dot{h}_{ij}, \dot{g}_{ij}\} = \{\cup_{\dot{\gamma}_{ij} \in \dot{h}_{ij}} \left\{ \dot{\gamma}_{ij} \right\}, \cup_{\dot{\eta}_{ij} \in \dot{g}_{ij}} \left\{ \dot{\eta}_{ij} \right\}\}$, and $(\sigma(1), \sigma(2), \ldots, \sigma(n))$ for a permutation of $(1, 2, \ldots, n)$ such that $S(\widetilde{B}_{i\sigma(j)}) \geq S(\widetilde{B}_{i\sigma(j+1)})$ $(j = 1, \ldots, n\text{-}1)$.

b) The aggregated assessment of alternative $\widetilde{A}_i = \{h_i, g_i\}$ $(i = 1, 2, \ldots, m)$ using the Hamacher geometric hybrid weighted averaging operator is defined as

$$\widetilde{A}_i = \widetilde{B}_{i\sigma(1)}^{w_{i1}} \otimes \ldots \otimes \widetilde{B}_{i\sigma(n)}^{w_{in}} = \{\cup_{\dot{\gamma}_{i\sigma(j)} \in \dot{h}_{i\sigma(j)}} \left\{ p^{-1}(\sum_{j=1}^{n} w_{ij} p(\dot{\gamma}_{i\sigma(j)})) \right\},$$

$$\cup_{\dot{\eta}_{i\sigma(j)} \in \dot{g}_{i\sigma(j)}} \left\{ q^{-1}(\sum_{j=1}^{n} w_{ij} q(\dot{\eta}_{i\sigma(j)})) \right\}\} =$$

$$\left\{ \cup_{\dot{\gamma}_{i\sigma(j)} \in \dot{h}_{i\sigma(j)}} \left\{ \frac{r\prod_{j=1}^{n}\dot{\gamma}_{i\sigma(j)}^{w_{ij}}}{\prod_{j=1}^{n}(1+(r-1)(1-\dot{\gamma}_{i\sigma(j)}))^{w_{ij}} + (r-1)\prod_{j=1}^{n}\dot{\gamma}_{i\sigma(j)}^{w_{ij}}} \right\}, \right.$$

$$\left. \cup_{\dot{\eta}_{i\sigma(j)} \in \dot{g}_{i\sigma(j)}} \left\{ \frac{\prod_{j=1}^{n}(1+(r-1)\dot{\eta}_{i\sigma(j)})^{w_{ij}} - \prod_{j=1}^{n}(1-\dot{\eta}_{i\sigma(j)})^{w_{ij}}}{\prod_{j=1}^{n}(1+(r-1)\dot{\eta}_{i\sigma(j)})^{w_{ij}} + (r-1)\prod_{j=1}^{n}(1-\dot{\eta}_{i\sigma(j)})^{w_{ij}}} \right\} \right\}, \tag{18}$$

where $\widetilde{B}_{i\sigma(j)}$ stands for the jth largest of $\widetilde{B}_{ij} = \widetilde{A}_{ij}^{\,n} = \{\dot{h}_{ij}, \dot{g}_{ij}\} = \{\bigcup_{\dot{\gamma}_{ij}\in\dot{h}_{ij}}\{\dot{\gamma}_{ij}\}, \bigcup_{\dot{\eta}_{ij}\in\dot{g}_{ij}}\{\dot{\eta}_{ij}\}\}$, and $(\sigma(1), \sigma(2), \ldots, \sigma(n))$ for a permutation of $(1, 2, \ldots, n)$ such that $S(\widetilde{B}_{i\sigma(j)}) \geq S(\widetilde{B}_{i\sigma(j+1)})$ $(j = 1, \ldots, n-1)$.

Similar to the situation in Section 4.1.2, based on the aggregated assessments of alternative A_i in Definition 10, the corresponding scores denoted by $S^a(\widetilde{A}_i)$ and $S^g(\widetilde{A}_i)$, can be calculated using Definition 6, as shown below.

(1) Given the aggregated assessment $\widetilde{A}_i = \{h_i, g_i\} = \{\bigcup_{\dot{\gamma}_{i\sigma(j)}\in\dot{h}_{i\sigma(j)}}\{q^{-1}(\sum_{j=1}^{n} w_{ij} q(\dot{\gamma}_{i\sigma(j)}))\}, \bigcup_{\dot{\eta}_{i\sigma(j)}\in\dot{g}_{i\sigma(j)}}\{p^{-1}(\sum_{j=1}^{n} w_{ij} p(\dot{\eta}_{i\sigma(j)}))\}\}$ generated by the Hamacher arithmetic hybrid weighted averaging operator, the score of $\widetilde{A}_i$ denoted by $S^a(\widetilde{A}_i)$ is calculated by

$$S^a(\widetilde{A}_i) = \frac{\sum[q^{-1}(\sum_{j=1}^{n} w_{ij} q(\dot{\gamma}_{i\sigma(j)}))]}{\delta(h_i)} - \frac{\sum[p^{-1}(\sum_{j=1}^{n} w_{ij} p(\dot{\eta}_{i\sigma(j)}))]}{\delta(g_i)}, \tag{19}$$

where $\delta(h_i)$ and $\delta(g_i)$ symbolize the numbers of the elements in h_i and g_i, respectively.

(2) Given the aggregated assessment $\widetilde{A}_i = \{h_i, g_i\} = \{\bigcup_{\dot{\gamma}_{i\sigma(j)}\in\dot{h}_{i\sigma(j)}}\{p^{-1}(\sum_{j=1}^{n} w_{ij} p(\dot{\gamma}_{i\sigma(j)}))\}, \bigcup_{\dot{\eta}_{i\sigma(j)}\in\dot{g}_{i\sigma(j)}}\{q^{-1}(\sum_{j=1}^{n} w_{ij} q(\dot{\eta}_{i\sigma(j)}))\}\}$, generated by the Hamacher geometric hybrid weighted averaging operator, the score of $\widetilde{A}_i$ denoted by $S^g(\widetilde{A}_i)$ is calculated by

$$S^g(\widetilde{A}_i) = \frac{\sum[p^{-1}(\sum_{j=1}^{n} w_{ij} p(\dot{\gamma}_{i\sigma(j)}))]}{\delta(h_i)} - \frac{\sum[q^{-1}(\sum_{j=1}^{n} w_{ij} q(\dot{\eta}_{i\sigma(j)}))]}{\delta(g_i)}, \tag{20}$$

where $\delta(h_i)$ and $\delta(g_i)$ symbolize the numbers of the elements in h_i and g_i, respectively.

Eqs. (19) and (20) indicate that $S^a(\widetilde{A}_i)$ (or $S^g(\widetilde{A}_i)$) includes two parts, which are $\frac{\sum[q^{-1}(\sum_{j=1}^{n} w_{ij} q(\dot{\gamma}_{i\sigma(j)}))]}{\delta(h_i)}$ (or $\frac{\sum[p^{-1}(\sum_{j=1}^{n} w_{ij} p(\dot{\gamma}_{i\sigma(j)}))]}{\delta(h_i)}$) and $\frac{\sum[p^{-1}(\sum_{j=1}^{n} w_{ij} p(\dot{\eta}_{i\sigma(j)}))]}{\delta(g_i)}$ (or $\frac{\sum[q^{-1}(\sum_{j=1}^{n} w_{ij} q(\dot{\eta}_{i\sigma(j)}))]}{\delta(g_i)}$).

Similar to the situation in Section 4.1.2, $S^a(\widetilde{A}_i)$ and $S^g(\widetilde{A}_i)$ are the functions with respect to the parameter r in Hamacher aggregation operators. Specifically, $S^a(\widetilde{A}_i)$ and $S^g(\widetilde{A}_i)$ in Eqs. (19) and (20) include the linear combination of multiple functions q^{-1} and of p^{-1}. To facilitate analysis of the monotonicity of $S^a(\widetilde{A}_i)$ and $S^g(\widetilde{A}_i)$ with consideration of this specificity, we present the following lemma.

Lemma 3. Suppose that there is a set $H = \{h_i\}$ $(i = 1, \ldots, n)$ such that $0 \leq h_i \leq 1$, then the function $F(h_1, \ldots, h_n) = \frac{1}{n}\sum_{i=1}^{n} h_i$ is monotonously increasing with respect to h_i $(\forall h_i \in H)$.

Lemma 3 clearly holds and thus its proof is omitted. Owing to Lemma 3 and Theorems 1 and 2, it can be concluded that $S^a(\widetilde{A}_i)$ and $S^g(\widetilde{A}_i)$ are the monotonously decreasing and increasing functions with respect to r, respectively. This indicates that Proposition 1 holds in the context of MADM with DHF assessments when the Hamacher arithmetic and geometric hybrid weighted averaging operators are applied.

4.2.3 Relationship between alternative scores derived from Hamacher arithmetic and geometric aggregation operators for MADM with DHF assessments

Similarly to Section 4.1.3, we discuss the relationship between $S^a(\widetilde{A}_i)$ and $S^g(\widetilde{A}_i)$ in MADM with DHF assessments. This relationship is presented in the following theorem.

Theorem 4. Suppose that $S^a(\widetilde{A}_i)$ and $S^g(\widetilde{A}_i)$ are the scores of the aggregated assessment $\widetilde{A}_i$ generated by using the Hamacher arithmetic and geometric aggregation operators, as presented in Eqs. (19) and (20), respectively. Then, we have

$$S^a(\widetilde{A}_i) > S^g(\widetilde{A}_i),\ r \in (0, +\infty). \tag{21}$$

Theorem 4 can be proven with the use of Proposition 1 and Lemmas 2 and 3. This shows that Proposition 2 holds in the context of MADM with DHF assessments when the Hamacher arithmetic and geometric hybrid weighted averaging operators are applied.

It should be noted that two functions p and q in Eqs. (5) and (6) are not the unique choices for the Hamacher t-norm and t-conorm. For other functions p and q such that q^{-1} and q are monotonously increasing (or decreasing) and p^{-1} and p are monotonously increasing (or decreasing), Propositions 1 and 2 still hold in MADM with IVIF or DHF assessments.

5. A METHOD FOR RANKING ALTERNATIVES IN MADM PROBLEMS WITH DHF ASSESSMENTS UNDER THE TWO PROPOSITIONS

The analysis in Section 4 indicates that the parameter r in Hamacher aggregation operators has a significant effect on the aggregated assessments of alternatives, and further on the solution to a MADM problem. With the use of Propositions 1 and 2, in the following, we will discuss the meaning of the parameter r and develop a new method to compare alternatives when handling MADM problems with DHF assessments. One numerical example is solved by the proposed method to demonstrate its applicability and validity. They also help to conduct a comparison between the developed method and two existing methods to highlight the consistency and validity of the developed method.

5.1 Meaning of the Parameter r in Hamacher Aggregation Operators

From previous studies (Huang, 2014;Ju et al., 2014; Liu, 2014; Tan et al., 2015; Xia et al., 2012; Xiao, 2014; Zhou et al.,2014), we can conclude that there are two main issues concerning the parameter r in Hamacher aggregation operators when handling MADM problems: (1) the meaning of r is not clear; and (2) the determination of r is arbitrary and subjective.

In this chapter, Proposition 1 and its theoretical proof indicate that r can be reasonably associated with the risk attitude, in terms of the optimism and pessimism of a decision maker. To elaborate, a decision maker is risk-seeking when he or she prefers small r, while the decision maker is risk-averse if he or she prefers large r when the Hamacher arithmetic aggregation operator is applied in MADM with IVIF or DHF assessments. The opposite conclusion can be drawn when the Hamacher geometric aggregation operator is applied in MADM with IVIF or DHF assessments. In the former situation, small r indicates a large alternative score, while it indicates a small alternative score in the latter. Although the meaning of r is clear, determining the precise value of r from the interval $(0,+\infty)$ remains a difficult task for the decision maker, especially when the decision maker knows various types of information concerning r. In response to this difficulty, in the next section we propose a new method to compare alternatives in MADM which considers all possible values of r instead of a specific value.

5.2 Method for Comparing Alternatives in MADM Problems With DHF Assessments Under the Two Propositions

As analyzed above, although the parameter r in Hamacher aggregation operators can reflect the optimistic or pessimistic attitude of a decision maker according to Proposition 1, it may be difficult to determine the precise value of r from the interval $(0,+\infty)$. This is especially the case when the decision maker knows various types of relevant information. To avoid the negative influence of arbitrary or subjective values of r upon decision results in MADM with DHF assessments, we propose a method for comparing alternatives with a full coverage of all possible values of r. The method in the context of MADM with IVIF assessments can be similarly developed, which is omitted here to save space.

Given that the Hamacher arithmetic aggregation operator is applied in MADM with DHF assessments, the score of alternative A_i decreases monotonously with the increase of r according to Proposition 1, which is plotted in Figure 1. In this condition, the mean score index of alternative A_i with consideration of all possible values of r such that $r \in (0,+\infty)$ is designed to compare alternatives, which is presented below.

Definition 11. Let $S^a(\widetilde{A}_i)$ and $S^g(\widetilde{A}_i)$ be the scores of alternative A_i from Hamacher arithmetic and geometric aggregation operators. Then, the arithmetic and geometric mean score indexes of alternative A_i on $r \in (0,+\infty)$ are defined as

$$AMI_i = \lim_{r_0 \to +\infty} \frac{\int_{0^+}^{r_0} S^a(\widetilde{A}_i)\,dr}{|r_0 - 0|} = \lim_{r_0 \to +\infty} \frac{\int_{0^+}^{r_0} S^a(\widetilde{A}_i)\,dr}{r_0} \tag{22}$$

and

$$GMI_i = \lim_{r_0 \to +\infty} \frac{\int_{0^+}^{r_0} S^g(\widetilde{A}_i)\,dr}{|r_0 - 0|} = \lim_{r_0 \to +\infty} \frac{\int_{0^+}^{r_0} S^g(\widetilde{A}_i)\,dr}{r_0}. \tag{23}$$

Here, the elongated "$\int$" represents integral.

Figure 1. Score movement of alternative A_i with variation in r

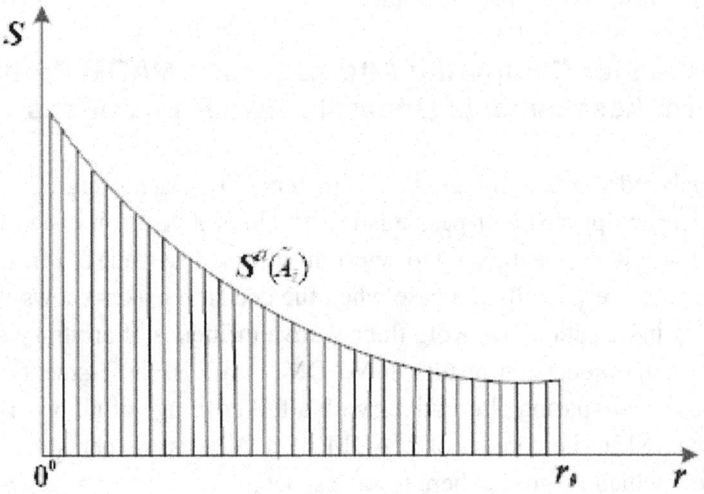

To facilitate the calculation of AMI_i, it should first be identified whether the integral $\int_{0^+}^{r_0} S^a(\widetilde{A}_i)\,dr$ with $r_0 \to +\infty$ is divergent or convergent. As $\lim_{r_0\to+\infty}\int_{0^+}^{r_0} S^a(\widetilde{A}_i)\,dr = \int_{0^+}^{+\infty} S^a(\widetilde{A}_i)\,dr$, the problem is transformed into deciding whether $\int_{0^+}^{+\infty} S^a(\widetilde{A}_i)\,dr$ is divergent or convergent. To address this problem, the **Cauchy criterion for convergence** (Anton et al., 2008; Schweizer & Sklar, 1960) is introduced, as shown below.

Theorem 5 (Cauchy criterion for convergence) (Anton et al., 2008; Schweizer & Sklar, 1960). Let $\varphi(x)$ and $\phi(x)$ be two functions with nonnegative terms, and $\int_a^{+\infty}\phi(x)\,dx$ and $\int_a^{+\infty}\varphi(x)\,dx$ be the integrals of $\phi(x)$ and $\varphi(x)$ on $[a,+\infty)$, respectively. Suppose that $0 \le \varphi(x) \le k\phi(x)$ for all x in $[a,+\infty)$, where a is a real number and $k > 0$. Then,

(*i*) If $\int_a^{+\infty}\phi(x)\,dx$ converges, $\int_a^{+\infty}\varphi(x)\,dx$ also converges; and

(*ii*) If $\int_a^{+\infty}\varphi(x)\,dx$ diverges, $\int_a^{+\infty}\phi(x)\,dx$ also diverges.

Theorem 5 reveals that when the lower bound of $S^a(\widetilde{A}_i)$ exists on $r \in (0,+\infty)$, the divergence of $\int_{0^+}^{+\infty} S^a(\widetilde{A}_i)\,dr$ can be identified by the **Cauchy criterion for convergence**. To carry out the identification, the lower bound of $S^a(\widetilde{A}_i)$ on $r \in (0,+\infty)$ is determined in the following proposition.

Proposition 3. Let $\widetilde{A}_i = \{h_i, g_i\}$ be the arithmetic aggregated assessment of alternative A_i, where $\{h_i, g_i\} =$

$$\left\{\bigcup_{\dot{\gamma}_{i\sigma(j)}\in h_i}\left\{\frac{\prod_{j=1}^{n}(1+(r-1)\dot{\gamma}_{i\sigma(j)})^{w_{ij}}-\prod_{j=1}^{n}(1-\dot{\gamma}_{i\sigma(j)})^{w_{ij}}}{\prod_{j=1}^{n}(1+(r-1)\dot{\gamma}_{i\sigma(j)})^{w_{ij}}+(r-1)\prod_{j=1}^{n}(1-\dot{\gamma}_{i\sigma(j)})^{w_{ij}}}\right\},\right.$$

$$\left.\bigcup_{\dot{\eta}_{i\sigma(j)}\in g_i}\left\{\frac{r\prod_{j=1}^{n}\dot{\eta}_{i\sigma(j)}^{w_{ij}}}{\prod_{j=1}^{n}(1+(r-1)(1-\dot{\eta}_{i\sigma(j)}))^{w_{ij}}+(r-1)\prod_{j=1}^{n}\dot{\eta}_{i\sigma(j)}^{w_{ij}}}\right\}\right\},$$

and the score function of $\widetilde{A}_i$ be $S^a(\widetilde{A}_i)$ with $r \in (0,+\infty)$. Then, the lower bound of the score function $S^a(\widetilde{A}_i)$ with $r \in (0,+\infty)$ is $S(\widetilde{\widetilde{A}}_i)$, where $\widetilde{\widetilde{A}}_i = \{h, g\} = \lim_{r\to+\infty}\widetilde{A}_i =$

$$\left\{\bigcup_{\dot{\gamma}_{i\sigma(j)}\in h_i}\left\{\frac{\prod_{j=1}^{n}(\dot{\gamma}_{i\sigma(j)})^{w_{ij}}}{\prod_{j=1}^{n}(\dot{\gamma}_{i\sigma(j)})^{w_{ij}}+\prod_{j=1}^{n}(1-\dot{\gamma}_{i\sigma(j)})^{w_{ij}}}\right\},\right.$$

$$\left.\bigcup_{\dot{\eta}_{i\sigma(j)}\in g_i}\left\{\frac{\prod_{j=1}^{n}(\dot{\eta}_{i\sigma(j)})^{w_{ij}}}{\prod_{j=1}^{n}(\dot{\eta}_{i\sigma(j)})^{w_{ij}}+\prod_{j=1}^{n}(1-\dot{\eta}_{i\sigma(j)})^{w_{ij}}}\right\}\right\},$$

i.e. $S^a(\widetilde{A}_i) > S(\widetilde{\widetilde{A}}_i)$.

The conclusions of Proposition 3 can be directly inferred from Proposition 1, the proof of Theorem 4 and Definition 6, so the proof is omitted here. With the use of Theorem 5 and Proposition 3, it is possible to identify whether or not $\int_{0^+}^{+\infty} S^a(\widetilde{A}_i)\,dr$ is divergent.

Theorem 6. Let $\widetilde{A}_i = \{h_i, g_i\}$ be the arithmetic aggregated assessment of alternative A_i, where

$$\{h_i, g_i\} = \left\{ \cup_{\dot{\gamma}_{i\sigma(j)} \in h_i} \left\{ \frac{\prod_{j=1}^{n}(1+(r-1)\dot{\gamma}_{i\sigma(j)})^{w_{ij}} - \prod_{j=1}^{n}(1-\dot{\gamma}_{i\sigma(j)})^{w_{ij}}}{\prod_{j=1}^{n}(1+(r-1)\dot{\gamma}_{i\sigma(j)})^{w_{ij}} + (r-1)\prod_{j=1}^{n}(1-\dot{\gamma}_{i\sigma(j)})^{w_{ij}}} \right\}, \right.$$

$$\left. \cup_{\dot{\eta}_{i\sigma(j)} \in g_i} \left\{ \frac{r\prod_{j=1}^{n}\dot{\eta}_{i\sigma(j)}^{w_{ij}}}{\prod_{j=1}^{n}(1+(r-1)(1-\dot{\eta}_{i\sigma(j)}))^{w_{ij}} + (r-1)\prod_{j=1}^{n}\dot{\eta}_{i\sigma(j)}^{w_{ij}}} \right\} \right\},$$

and the score function of $\widetilde{A}_i$ be $S^a(\widetilde{A}_i)$ with $r \in (0,+\infty)$. Then, $\int_{0^+}^{+\infty} S^a(\widetilde{A}_i)\,dr$ is divergent.

The proof of Theorem 6 is omitted here to save space. Similar to the discussions about the divergence of $\int_{0^+}^{+\infty} S^a(\widetilde{A}_i)\,dr$, the divergence of $\int_{0^+}^{+\infty} S^g(\widetilde{A}_i)\,dr$ can also be identified in order to calculate GMI_i. For this purpose, the lower bound of $S^g(\widetilde{A}_i)$ with $r \in (0,+\infty)$ is first determined.

Proposition 4. Let $\widetilde{A}_i = \{h_i, g_i\}$ be the geometric aggregated assessment of alternative A_i, where $\{h_i, g_i\}=$

$$\left\{ \cup_{\dot{\gamma}_{i\sigma(j)} \in \dot{h}_{i\sigma(j)}} \left\{ \frac{r\prod_{j=1}^{n}\dot{\gamma}_{i\sigma(j)}^{w_{ij}}}{\prod_{j=1}^{n}(1+(r-1)(1-\dot{\gamma}_{i\sigma(j)}))^{w_{ij}} + (r-1)\prod_{j=1}^{n}\dot{\gamma}_{i\sigma(j)}^{w_{ij}}} \right\}, \right.$$

$$\left. \cup_{\dot{\eta}_{i\sigma(j)} \in \dot{g}_{i\sigma(j)}} \left\{ \frac{\prod_{j=1}^{n}(1+(r-1)\dot{\eta}_{i\sigma(j)})^{w_{ij}} - \prod_{j=1}^{n}(1-\dot{\eta}_{i\sigma(j)})^{w_{ij}}}{\prod_{j=1}^{n}(1+(r-1)\dot{\eta}_{i\sigma(j)})^{w_{ij}} + (r-1)\prod_{j=1}^{n}(1-\dot{\eta}_{i\sigma(j)})^{w_{ij}}} \right\} \right\},$$

and the score function of $\widetilde{A}_i$ be $S^g(\widetilde{A}_i)$ with $r \in (0,+\infty)$. Then, the lower bound of the score function $S^g(\widetilde{A}_i)$ with $r \in (0,+\infty)$ is $S(\widetilde{\widetilde{A}}_i)$, where

$$\widetilde{\widetilde{A}}_i = \{h, g\} = \lim_{r\to 0^+}\widetilde{A}_i =$$

$$\left\{ \cup_{\dot{\gamma}_{i\sigma(j)} \in h_i} \left\{ \frac{1}{1+\sum_{j=1}^{n}\frac{w_{ij}(1-\dot{\gamma}_{i\sigma(j)})}{\dot{\gamma}_{i\sigma(j)}}} \right\}, \right.$$

$$\left. \cup_{\dot{\eta}_{i\sigma(j)} \in g_i} \left\{ \frac{\sum_{j=1}^{n}\frac{w_{ij}\cdot\dot{\eta}_{i\sigma(j)}}{(1-\dot{\eta}_{i\sigma(j)})}}{1+\sum_{j=1}^{n}\frac{w_{ij}\cdot\dot{\eta}_{i\sigma(j)}}{(1-\dot{\eta}_{i\sigma(j)})}} \right\} \right\},$$

i.e. $S^g(\widetilde{A}_i) > S(\widetilde{\widetilde{A}}_i)$.

The proof of Proposition 4 is omitted here to save space. With the use of Theorem 5 and Proposition 4, whether $\int_{0^+}^{+\infty} S^g(\widetilde{A}_i)\,dr$ is divergent can be identified.

Theorem 7. Let $\widetilde{A}_i = \{h_i, g_i\}$ be the geometric aggregated assessment of alternative A_i, where

$$\{h_i, g_i\} = \left\{ \cup_{\dot{\gamma}_{i\sigma(j)} \in \dot{h}_{i\sigma(j)}} \left\{ \frac{r\prod_{j=1}^{n}\dot{\gamma}_{i\sigma(j)}^{w_{ij}}}{\prod_{j=1}^{n}(1+(r-1)(1-\dot{\gamma}_{i\sigma(j)}))^{w_{ij}} + (r-1)\prod_{j=1}^{n}\dot{\gamma}_{i\sigma(j)}^{w_{ij}}} \right\}, \right.$$

$$\cup_{\dot{\eta}_{i\sigma(j)} \in \dot{g}_{i\sigma(j)}} \left\{ \frac{\prod_{j=1}^{n}(1+(r-1)\dot{\eta}_{i\sigma(j)})^{w_{ij}} - \prod_{j=1}^{n}(1-\dot{\eta}_{i\sigma(j)})^{w_{ij}}}{\prod_{j=1}^{n}(1+(r-1)\dot{\eta}_{i\sigma(j)})^{w_{ij}} + (r-1)\prod_{j=1}^{n}(1-\dot{\eta}_{i\sigma(j)})^{w_{ij}}} \right\}\Bigg\},$$

and the score function of $\widetilde{A}_i$ be $S^g(\widetilde{A}_i)$ with $r \in (0,+\infty)$. Then, $\int_{0^+}^{+\infty} S^g(\widetilde{A}_i)\,dr$ is divergent.

We omit the proof of Theorem 7 here to save space. As $\int_{0^+}^{+\infty} S^a(\widetilde{A}_i)\,dr$ and $\int_{0^+}^{+\infty} S^g(\widetilde{A}_i)\,dr$ are divergent, L'Hôpital's rule (also called Bernoulli's rule) (Anton, 2008) can be used in Eqs. (22) and (23) to calculate the values of AMI_i and GMI_i.

Theorem 8. Let $\widetilde{A}_i = \{h_i, g_i\}$ be the arithmetic aggregated assessment of alternative A_i, and AMI_i be the arithmetic mean score index of alternative A_i defined in Definition 11. Then we have $AMI_i = S(\widetilde{\widetilde{A}}_i)$ when $r \to +\infty$, where $\widetilde{\widetilde{A}}_i = \{h, g\} = \lim_{r\to+\infty} \widetilde{A}_i =$

$$\left\{ \cup_{\dot{\gamma}_{i\sigma(j)} \in h_i} \left\{ \frac{\prod_{j=1}^{n} \dot{\gamma}_{i\sigma(j)}^{w_{ij}}}{\prod_{j=1}^{n} \dot{\gamma}_{i\sigma(j)}^{w_{ij}} + \prod_{j=1}^{n}(1-\dot{\gamma}_{i\sigma(j)})^{w_{ij}}} \right\}, \cup_{\dot{\eta}_{i\sigma(j)} \in g_i} \left\{ \frac{\prod_{j=1}^{n} \dot{\eta}_{i\sigma(j)}^{w_{ij}}}{\prod_{j=1}^{n} \dot{\eta}_{i\sigma(j)}^{w_{ij}} + \prod_{j=1}^{n}(1-\dot{\eta}_{i\sigma(j)})^{w_{ij}}} \right\} \right\}.$$

Theorem 9. Let $\widetilde{A}_i = \{h_i, g_i\}$ be the geometric aggregated assessment of alternative A_i, and GMI_i be the geometric mean score index of alternative A_i. Then we have $GMI_i = S(\widetilde{\widetilde{A}}_i)$ when $r \to +\infty$, where $\widetilde{\widetilde{A}}_i = \{h, g\} = \lim_{r\to+\infty} \widetilde{A}_i =$

$$\left\{ \cup_{\dot{\gamma}_{i\sigma(j)} \in h_i} \left\{ \frac{\prod_{j=1}^{n} \dot{\gamma}_{i\sigma(j)}^{w_{ij}}}{\prod_{j=1}^{n} \dot{\gamma}_{i\sigma(j)}^{w_{ij}} + \prod_{j=1}^{n}(1-\dot{\gamma}_{i\sigma(j)})^{w_{ij}}} \right\}, \right.$$

$$\left. \cup_{\dot{\eta}_{i\sigma(j)} \in g_i} \left\{ \frac{\prod_{j=1}^{n} \dot{\eta}_{i\sigma(j)}^{w_{ij}}}{\prod_{j=1}^{n} \dot{\eta}_{i\sigma(j)}^{w_{ij}} + \prod_{j=1}^{n}(1-\dot{\eta}_{i\sigma(j)})^{w_{ij}}} \right\} \right\}.$$

Theorems 8 and 9 can be proven rwith the use of Theorems 6 and 7 and L'Hôpital's rule. It is interesting to find from Theorems 8 and 9 that $AMI_i = GMI_i$. That is, we can use AMI_i to compare alternatives regardless of whether or not Hamacher arithmetic or geometric aggregation operators are applied in MADM with DHF assessments.

Definition 12. Suppose that AMI_i $(i = 1, 2)$ represents the arithmetic mean score index of alternative A_i with $r \in (0,+\infty)$. When $AMI_1 > AMI_2$, alternative A_1 is said to be superior to alternative A_2.

5.3 Numerical Examples

In this section, one numerical example is solved by the method proposed in Section 5.2 to demonstrate its applicability and validity. The example is originated from a real application where a large Chinese company in the iron and steel industry decides to invest abroad.

Example 1. The iron and steel industry is one of the fundamental industries which contribute to China's economy. This industry is closely related to upstream and downstream industries and is driven by the requirements of consumption greatly. It also significantly influences the development of economy and society in China. As an important and essential resource for producing steel, iron directly restricts the development of the iron and steel industry. Unfortunately, iron resources in China are relatively limited and their quality is below the international average. To participate in international competition, large Chinese companies in the iron and steel industry must seek high-quality iron resources globally.

Taking a large domestic company in the iron and steel industry as an example, we investigate how to assist the company to invest abroad effectively and reasonably. The general manager of this company must decide which of the following five countries to invest in and source iron ores from: Australia (A_1), India (A_2), Brazil (A_3), Canada (A_4), or Russia (A_5). Seven attributes are identified based on the annual surveys released by the Fraser Institute of Canada (Jackson & Green, 2015), and their weights are specified as $\omega = (0.35, 0.1, 0.05, 0.1, 0.05, 0.15, 0.2)$. The seven attributes are described in Table 1.

Table 1. Description of the seven attributes

Attribute	Description
C_1	Quality and quantity of iron ore resources
C_2	Situation of the legal system, taxation regime, and trade barriers
C_3	Competition from other overseas investment in iron resources
C_4	Uncertainty about environmental regulations and availability of skilled labor
C_5	Infrastructure concerning overseas investments
C_6	Condition of socioeconomic agreements/community development
C_7	Political stability and security level

To make the decision, several academics, including two co-authors of this study and four experts from the Chinese Academy of Engineering (CAE) and the Ministry of Land and Resources (MLR) were invited to independently and anonymously evaluate the five countries on each attribute. The evaluation and the preference of the decision makers are then combined to construct a DHF decision matrix $\widetilde{A}_{5\times 7}$

$= (\{h_{ij}, g_{ij}\})_{5\times7}$, which is shown in Table 2. For example, Australia (A_1) is assessed on attribute C_2 as {{0.6,0.7},{0.1,0.2}}, which indicates that the degree to which alternative A_1 satisfies attribute C_2 may be 0.6 or 0.7, and the degree to which alternative A_1 does not satisfy attribute C_2 may be 0.1 or 0.2.

Table 2. Transpose of the DHF decision matrix

Attribute	A_1	A_2	A_3	A_4	A_5
C_1	{{0.9,0.8,0.7},{0.1}}	{{0.6,0.7},{0.1,0.2}}	{{0.7,0.9},{0.1}}	{{0.5,0.6,0.7},{0.1,0.2,0.3}}	{{0.7,0.8}, {0.1,0.2}}
C_2	{{0.7,0.8},{0.1,0.2}}	{{0.3,0.4},{0.5,0.6}}	{{0.6,0.5,0.8},{0.1,0.2}}	{{0.8,0.5},{0.2,0.1}}	{{0.3,0.6},{0.4,0.3}}
C_3	{{0.1,0.2},{0.6,0.7}}	{{0.4,0.6},{0.3,0.4}}	{{0.2,0.3,0.4},{0.5,0.6}}	{{0.3,0.2},{0.5,0.6}}	{{0.1,0.3},{0.5,0.6}}
C_4	{{0.1,0.2},{0.6,0.7}}	{{0.6,0.5,0.4},{0.1,0.2,0.3}}	{{0.3,0.4},{0.5,0.6}}	{{0.2,0.3,0.4},{0.4,0.5,0.6}}	{{0.4},{0.4,0.5}}
C_5	{{0.6,0.8},{0.1,0.2}}	{{0.3,0.5},{0.2,0.3})	{{0.5,0.6},{0.2,0.3})	{{0.6,0.5},{0.2,0.3})	{{0.1,0.4,0.5},{0.4,0.5})
C_6	{{0.5,0.6},{0.3,0.2})	{{0.4,0.5,0.6},{0.2,0.3,0.4})	{{0.4,0.5},{0.5}}	{{0.5,0.6,0.7},{0.1,0.2,0.3}}	{{0.3,0.4},{0.4,0.5}}
C_7	{{0.6,0.7,0.8},{0.1}}	{{0.3,0.5},{0.4,0.5}}	{{0.6,0.5,0.4},{0.2,0.3}}	{{0.5,0.7},{0.1,0.3}}	{{0.4,0.6,0.7},{0.1,0.2,}}

Assume that the OWA operator weight vector is specified as $w = (1/7, 1/7, 1/7, 1/7, 1/7, 1/7, 1/7)$. When the Hamacher arithmetic hybrid weighted averaging operator in Definition 10 is applied, the aggregated assessment of alternative A_i is given by

$$\widetilde{A}_i = \left\{ \cup_{\dot{\gamma}_{i\sigma(j)} \in \dot{h}_{i\sigma(j)}} \left\{ \frac{\prod_{j=1}^{7} (1 + (r-1)\dot{\gamma}_{i\sigma(j)})^{w_{ij}} - \prod_{j=1}^{7} (1 - \dot{\gamma}_{i\sigma(j)})^{w_{ij}}}{\prod_{j=1}^{7} (1 + (r-1)\dot{\gamma}_{i\sigma(j)})^{w_{ij}} + (r-1)\prod_{j=1}^{7} (1 - \dot{\gamma}_{i\sigma(j)})^{w_{ij}}} \right\}, \right.$$

$$\left. \cup_{\dot{\eta}_{i\sigma(j)} \in \dot{g}_{i\sigma(j)}} \left\{ \frac{r\prod_{j=1}^{7} \dot{\eta}_{i\sigma(j)}^{w_{ij}}}{\prod_{j=1}^{7} (1 + (r-1)(1 - \dot{\eta}_{i\sigma(j)}))^{w_{ij}} + (r-1)\prod_{j=1}^{7} \dot{\eta}_{i\sigma(j)}^{w_{ij}}} \right\} \right\}.$$

The arithmetic mean score AMI_i ($i = 1,...,5$) is subsequently calculated, using Theorem 8, as (0.2886, 0.1680, 0.2180, 0.2404, 0.0801). Using Theorem 9, the geometric mean score GMI_i ($i = 1,...,5$) is also computed to be (0.2886, 0.1680, 0.2180, 0.2404, 0.0801). The same value of AMI_i and GMI_i generates a common ranking order of the five countries, i.e. $A_1 \succ A_4 \succ A_3 \succ A_2 \succ A_5$, where the notation '$\succ$' represents 'superior to'. Consequently, the optimal choice for investment is A_1 (Australia).

5.4 Comparative Analysis

In the following, the proposed method is compared with two representative methods developed by Ju et al. (Ju et al., 2014) and Ye (Ye, 2014) to highlight its consistency and validity.

The key ideas of the two existing methods are briefly described as follows. In the method of Ju et al. (Ju et al., 2014), the Hamacher arithmetic or geometric aggregation operator is utilized to combine the assessments on each attribute for each alternative. The values of the parameter r in Hamacher aggregation operators are given first by decision makers. After the aggregated assessments of alternatives are obtained, a ranking order of alternatives is generated using Definition 6. In Ye's method (Ye, 2014), a virtual ideal solution is used as a reference to compare alternatives. An alternative with performance close to the ideal solution is preferred. Its closeness is measured by the correlation coefficient between the performance of the alternative and that of the ideal solution. The ranking order of alternatives is generated by using their closeness to the ideal solution.

Table 3. A comparison of the ranking orders of the alternatives in Example 1 with the use of different methods

Method			Ranking Order
Ju et al. (Ju et al., 2014)	Use of the Hamacher arithmetic aggregation operator	r = 0.5	$A_1 \succ A_4 \succ A_3 \succ A_2 \succ A_5$
		r = 1	$A_1 \succ A_4 \succ A_3 \succ A_2 \succ A_5$
		r = 2	$A_1 \succ A_4 \succ A_3 \succ A_2 \succ A_5$
		r = 5	$A_1 \succ A_4 \succ A_3 \succ A_2 \succ A_5$
		r = 100	$A_1 \succ A_4 \succ A_3 \succ A_2 \succ A_5$
	Use of the Hamacher geometric aggregation operator	r = 0.5	$A_4 \succ A_2 \succ A_3 \succ A_1 \succ A_5$
		r = 1	$A_4 \succ A_3 \succ A_2 \succ A_1 \succ A_5$
		r = 2	$A_4 \succ A_1 \succ A_3 \succ A_2 \succ A_5$
		r = 5	$A_1 \succ A_4 \succ A_3 \succ A_2 \succ A_5$
		r = 100	$A_1 \succ A_4 \succ A_3 \succ A_2 \succ A_5$
Ye (Ye, 2014)			$A_1 \succ A_4 \succ A_2 \succ A_3 \succ A_5$
The proposed method	Use of the Hamacher arithmetic hybrid weighted averaging operator		$A_1 \succ A_4 \succ A_3 \succ A_2 \succ A_5$
	Use of the Hamacher geometric hybrid weighted averaging operator		$A_1 \succ A_4 \succ A_3 \succ A_2 \succ A_5$

In order to compare the proposed method with those of Ju et al. and Ye, the numerical example in Section 5.3 was solved by using the latter two methods. The results of applying all three methods to the example are presented in Table 3. From Table 3, we can see that the proposed method and the method of Ju et al. (using the Hamacher arithmetic aggregation operator) generate the same ranking order of the five countries: $A_1 \succ A_4 \succ A_3 \succ A_2 \succ A_5$. It should be noted that in the method of Ju et al., the ranking orders generated by Hamacher arithmetic aggregation operators differ from those generated by Hamacher geometric aggregation operators when $r \in \{0.5, 1, 2\}$. More importantly, the ranking orders generated by Hamacher arithmetic and geometric aggregation operators change with different given values of r. However, the ranking orders generated by the Hamacher arithmetic and geometric hybrid weighted averaging operators are always the same in the method proposed here. By using Ye's method, we can obtain the weighted correlation coefficients between the alternatives and the ideal solution as (0.8914, 0.8191, 0.8096, 0.8672, 0.8043). From Table 3, we can see that the ranking order generated by Ye's method is $A_1 \succ A_4 \succ A_2 \succ A_3 \succ A_5$, where the rankings of A_2 and A_3 differ from those generated by the proposed method, but the best choice is still A_1.

In summary, the proposed method is able to generate more consistent decision results independent of the choice of Hamacher arithmetic and geometric aggregation operators and the value of r, compared with Ju et al.' method. This also indicates that the proposed method is more efficient than that of Ju et al. from the perspective of decision makers' involvement in a decision process. The best choices generated by the proposed method are always the same as those generated by the methods of Ye and Ju et al. The above comparative analysis highlights the consistency and validity of the method proposed in this chapter.

6. CONCLUSION

When finding solutions to fuzzy MADM problems, Hamacher t-norms and t-conorms with a parameter r are commonly used to combine various styles of fuzzy assessments on each attribute, such as AIF, IVIF, HF, and DHF assessments. Although different Hamacher aggregation operators have been developed to combine various styles of fuzzy assessments, the existing operators can generally be divided into two categories: Hamacher arithmetic and Hamacher geometric aggregation operators.

Since AIF and HF assessments are special cases of IVIF and DHF assessments, from numerical examples and real cases with IVIF and DHF assessments in the literature we present two propositions: (1) alternative scores decrease and increase with the increase of r in Hamacher arithmetic and geometric aggregation operators; and (2) alternative scores generated by Hamacher arithmetic operators are always larger than those generated by Hamacher geometric operators given the same r. These two propositions are theoretically proven in the context of MADM with IVIF and DHF assessments. They are further applied to illustrate the meaning of r and to develop a method for comparing alternatives in MADM with DHF assessments with full coverage of all possible values of r. One numerical example is solved by the proposed method to demonstrate its applicability and validity, and a comparative analysis is conducted to illustrate the consistency and validity of the method proposed in this chapter.

The main contributions of this chapter include the following: (1) two propositions concerning Hamacher arithmetic and geometric aggregation operators in the context of fuzzy MADM are presented following a thorough review and analysis of the literature on MADM with IVIF and DHF information; (2) these two propositions are proven theoretically in the context of MADM with IVIF and DHF assessments; (3) the meaning of the parameter r in Hamacher arithmetic and geometric aggregation operators is explained using Proposition 1 and its theoretical proof; and (4) a new method is proposed for ranking alternatives in MADM problems with DHF information under the two propositions.

In recent decades, many developments have been achieved concerning the combination of multiple pieces of uncertain information in decision making. Despite this, some related scientific problems still require focused research. For example: 1) the selection of the type of aggregation functions (Bustince et al., 2014; Tang et al., 2020b); 2) the studies about the admissible orders in terms of aggregation functions for various fuzzy sets (Miguel et al., 2016); and 3) the choice of score functions of different fuzzy assessments (Garg, 2016a; Thillaigovindan, 2016). In addition, granular computing (Pedrycz & Chen, 2015) is a flexible and feasible tool for decision makers to address the challenges of characterizing their preferences in an uncertain context. Recently, a number of achievements (Apolloni et al., 2016; Mendel, 2016; Skowron & Jankowski, 2016; Song & Wang, 2016; Wilke & Portmann, 2016; Xu & Wang, 2016; Yao, 2016; Li et al., 2022; E et al., 2023; Cui et al., 2021) have been made in this area which contribute to further studies of uncertain decision making. All these areas are worth exploring in future research to solve uncertain MADM problems.

ACKNOWLEDGMENT

This research was supported by the National Natural Science Foundation of China (Grant Nos. 72101075, 71622003, 71521001, 71571060, 71201043, 71131002, 71303073, and 71501054), and partially supported by the European Commission under Grant No. EC- GPF-314836. We are also grateful to the anonymous reviewers for their constructive comments.

REFERENCES

Anton, H., Bivens, I., & Davis, S. (2008). *Calculus*. Higher Education Press.

Apolloni, B., Bassis, S., Rota, J., Galliani, G. L., Gioia, M., & Ferrari, L. (2016). A neurofuzzy algorithm for learning from complex granules. *Granular Computing*, 1(4), 225–246. Advance online publication. 10.1007/s41066-016-0018-1

Atanassov, K. T. (1986). Intuitionistic fuzzy sets. *Fuzzy Sets and Systems*, 20(1), 87–96. 10.1016/S0165-0114(86)80034-3

Atanassov, K. T., & Gargov, G. (1989). Interval valued intuitionistic fuzzy sets. *Fuzzy Sets and Systems*, 31(3), 343–349. 10.1016/0165-0114(89)90205-4

Beliakov, G., Bustince, H., James, S., Calvo, T., & Fernandez, J. (2012). Aggregation for Atanassov's intuitionistic and interval valued fuzzy sets: The median operator. *IEEE Transactions on Fuzzy Systems*, 20(3), 487–498. 10.1109/TFUZZ.2011.2177271

Beliakov, G., Pradera, A., & Calvo, T. (2007). *Conjunctive and Disjunctive Functions*. Springer. 10.1007/978-3-540-73721-6_3

Bustince, H., Barrenechea, E., Calvo, T., James, S., & Beliakov, G. (2014). Consensus in multi-expert decision making problems using penalty functions defined over a Cartesian product of lattices. *Information Fusion*, 17, 56–64. 10.1016/j.inffus.2011.10.002

Chen, S. M., Cheng, S. H., & Lan, T. C. (2016a). Multicriteria decision making based on the TOPSIS method and similarity measures between intuitionistic fuzzy values. *Information Sciences*, 367-368, 279–295. 10.1016/j.ins.2016.05.044

Chen, S. M., Cheng, S. H., & Tsai, W. H. (2016b). Multiple attribute group decision making based on interval-valued intuitionistic fuzzy aggregation operators and transformation techniques of interval-valued intuitionistic fuzzy values. *Information Sciences*, 367-368, 418–442. 10.1016/j.ins.2016.05.041

Chu, J. F., Liu, X. W., Wang, Y. M., & Chin, K. S. (2016). A group decision making model considering both the additive consistency and group consensus of intuitionistic fuzzy preference relations. *Computers & Industrial Engineering*, 101, 227–242. 10.1016/j.cie.2016.08.018

Cui, Y. E. H., Pedrycz, W., & Li, Z. (2021). Designing Distributed Fuzzy Rule-Based Models. *IEEE Transactions on Fuzzy Systems*, 29(7), 2047–2053. 10.1109/TFUZZ.2020.2984971

Deschrijver, G., & Kerre, E. E. (2002). A generalization of operators on intuitionistic fuzzy sets using triangular norms and conorms. *Notes on IFS*, 8(1), 19–27.

E, H., Cui, Y., Pedrycz, W., Li, Z. (2022). Fuzzy Relational Matrix Factorization and Its Granular Characterization in Data Description. *IEEE Transactions on Fuzzy Systems, 30*(3), 794–804.

E, H., Cui, Y., Pedrycz, W., Li, Z. (2023). Design of Distributed Rule-Based Models in the Presence of Large Data. *IEEE Transactions on Fuzzy Systems, 31*(7), 2479–2486.

Garg, H. (2016a). A new generalized improved score function of interval-valued intuitionistic fuzzy sets and applications in expert systems. *Applied Soft Computing*, 38, 988–999. 10.1016/j.asoc.2015.10.040

Garg, H. (2016b). Generalized intuitionistic fuzzy interactive geometric interaction operators using Einstein t-norm and t-conorm and their application to decision making. *Computers & Industrial Engineering*, 101, 53–69. 10.1016/j.cie.2016.08.017

Gupta, P., Mehlawat, M. K., & Grover, N. (2016). Intuitionistic fuzzy multi-attribute group decision-making with an application to plant location selection based on a new extended VIKOR method. *Information Sciences*, 370-371, 184–203. 10.1016/j.ins.2016.07.058

Hamachar, H. (1978), Uber logische verknunpfungenn unssharfer Aussagen undderen Zugenhorige Bewertungsfunktione, *Progress in Cybernatics and Systems Research, 3*, 276-288.

Huang, J. Y. (2014). Intuitionistic fuzzy Hamacher aggregation operators and their application to multiple attribute decision making. *Journal of Intelligent & Fuzzy Systems*, 27(1), 505–513. 10.3233/IFS-131019

Hung, W. L., & Wu, J. W. (2002). Correlation of intuitionistic fuzzy sets by centroid method. *Information Sciences*, 144(1), 219–225. 10.1016/S0020-0255(02)00181-0

Jackson, T., & Green, K. P. (2015). *Fraser Institute Annual Survey of Mining Companies: 2015[EB/OL].* https://www.fraserinstitute.org/studies/annual-survey-of-mining-companies-2015

Ju, Y. B., Zhang, W. K., & Yang, S. H. (2014). Some dual hesitant fuzzy Hamacher aggregation operators and their applications to multiple attribute decision making. *Journal of Intelligent & Fuzzy Systems*, 27(5), 2481–2495. 10.3233/IFS-141222

Li, W., Zhai, S., Xu, W., Pedrycz, W., Qian, Y., Ding, W., & Zhan, T. (2023). Feature selection approach based on improved Fuzzy C-Means with principle of refined justifiable granularity. *IEEE Transactions on Fuzzy Systems*, 31(7), 2112–2126. 10.1109/TFUZZ.2022.3217377

Li, W., Zhou, H., Xu, W., Wang, X., & Pedrycz, W. (2022). Interval dominance-based feature selection for interval-valued ordered data. *IEEE Transactions on Neural Networks and Learning Systems*, 34(10), 6898–6912. 10.1109/TNNLS.2022.318412035737612

Liao, H. C., & Xu, Z. S. (2014). Intuitionistic fuzzy hybrid weighted aggregation operators. *International Journal of Intelligent Systems*, 29(11), 971–993. 10.1002/int.21672

Liao, H. C., & Xu, Z. S. (2015). Extended hesitant fuzzy hybrid weighted aggregation operators and their application in decision making. *Soft Computing*, 19(9), 2551–2564. 10.1007/s00500-014-1422-6

Liu, P. D. (2014). Some Hamacher aggregation operators based on the interval-valued intuitionistic fuzzy numbers and their application to group decision making. *IEEE Transactions on Fuzzy Systems*, 22(1), 83–97. 10.1109/TFUZZ.2013.2248736

Mendel, J. M. (2016). A comparison of three approaches for estimating (synthesizing) an interval type-2 fuzzy set model of a linguistic term for computing with words. *Granular Computing*, 1(1), 59–69. 10.1007/s41066-015-0009-7

Miguel, L. D., Bustince, H., Fernandez, J., Indurâin, E., Kolesârovâ, A., & Mesiar, R. (2016). Construction of admissible linear orders for interval-valued Atanassov intuitionistic fuzzy sets with an application to decision making. *Information Fusion*, 27, 189–197. 10.1016/j.inffus.2015.03.004

Pedrycz, W., & Chen, S. M. (2015). *Granular Computing and Decision-Making: Interactive and Iterative Approaches*. Springer. 10.1007/978-3-319-16829-6

Roychowdhury, S., & Wang, B. H. (1998). On generalized Hamacher families of triangular operators. *International Journal of Approximate Reasoning*, 19(3), 419–439. 10.1016/S0888-613X(98)10018-X

Schweizer, B., & Sklar, A. (1960). Statistical metric spaces. *Pacific Journal of Mathematics*, 10(1), 313–334. 10.2140/pjm.1960.10.313

Skowron, A., Jankowski, A., & Dutta, S. (2016). Interactive granular computing. *Granular Computing*, 1(2), 95–113. 10.1007/s41066-015-0002-1

Song, M. L., & Wang, Y. B. (2016). A study of granular computing in the agenda of growth of artificial neural networks. *Granular Computing*, 1(4), 247–257. Advance online publication. 10.1007/s41066-016-0020-7

Tan, C. Q., Yi, W. T., & Chen, X. H. (2015). Hesitant fuzzy Hamacher aggregation operators for multicriteria decision making. *Applied Soft Computing*, 26, 325–349. 10.1016/j.asoc.2014.10.007

Tang, X., Peng, Z., Zhang, Q., Pedrycz, W., & Yang, S. (2020a). Consistency and consensus-driven models to personalize individual semantics of linguistic terms for supporting group decision making with distribution linguistic preference relations. *Knowledge-Based Systems*, 189, 105078. 10.1016/j.knosys.2019.105078

Tang, X., Zhang, Q., Peng, Z., Pedrycz, W., & Yang, S. (2020b). Distribution linguistic preference relations with incomplete symbolic proportions for group decision making. *Applied Soft Computing*, 88, 106005. 10.1016/j.asoc.2019.106005

Thillaigovindan, N., Shanthi, S. A., & Naidu, J. V. (2016). A better score function for multiple criteria decision making in fuzzy environment with criteria choice under risk. *Expert Systems with Applications*, 59, 78–85. 10.1016/j.eswa.2016.04.023

Torra, V. (2010). Hesitant fuzzy sets. *International Journal of Intelligent Systems*, 25(6), 529–539.

Wan, S. P., Xu, G. L., & Dong, J. Y. (2016). A novel method for group decision making with interval-valued Atanassov intuitionistic fuzzy preference relations. *Information Sciences*, 372, 53–71. 10.1016/j.ins.2016.08.019

Wang, H. J., Zhao, X. F., & Wei, G. W. (2014). Dual hesitant fuzzy aggregation operators in multiple attribute decision making. *Journal of Intelligent & Fuzzy Systems*, 26(5), 2281–2290. 10.3233/IFS-130901

Wang, L., Shen, Q. G., & Zhu, L. (2016). Dual hesitant fuzzy power aggregation operators based on Archimedean t-conorm and t-norm and their application to multiple attribute group decision making. *Applied Soft Computing*, 38, 23–50. 10.1016/j.asoc.2015.09.012

Wilke, G., & Portmann, E. (2016). Granular computing as a basis of human–data interaction: A cognitive cities use case. *Granular Computing*, 1(3), 181–197. 10.1007/s41066-016-0015-4

Xia, M. M., & Xu, Z. S. (2011). Hesitant fuzzy information aggregation in decision making. *International Journal of Approximate Reasoning*, 52(3), 395–407. 10.1016/j.ijar.2010.09.002

Xia, M. M., Xu, Z. S., & Zhu, B. (2012). Some issues on intuitionistic fuzzy aggregation operators based on Archimedean t-conorm and t-norm. *Knowledge-Based Systems*, 31, 78–88. 10.1016/j.knosys.2012.02.004

Xiao, S. (2014). Induced interval-valued intuitionistic fuzzy Hamacher ordered weighted geometric operator and their application to multiple attribute decision making. *Journal of Intelligent & Fuzzy Systems*, 27(1), 527–534. 10.3233/IFS-131021

Xu, Z. S. (2000). On consistency of the weighted geometric mean complex judgement matrix in AHP. *European Journal of Operational Research*, 126(3), 683–687. 10.1016/S0377-2217(99)00082-X

Xu, Z. S., & Liao, H. C. (2015). A survey of approaches to decision making with intuitionistic fuzzy preference relations. *Knowledge-Based Systems*, 80, 131–142. 10.1016/j.knosys.2014.12.034

Xu, Z. S., & Wang, H. (2016). Managing multi-granularity linguistic information in qualitative group decision making: An overview. *Granular Computing*, 1(1), 21–35. 10.1007/s41066-015-0006-x

Xu, Z. S., & Yager, R. R. (2006). Some geometric aggregation operators based on intuitionistic fuzzy sets. *International Journal of General Systems*, 35(4), 417–433. 10.1080/03081070600574353

Yao, Y. Y. (2016). A triarchic theory of granular computing. *Granular Computing*, 1(2), 145–157. 10.1007/s41066-015-0011-0

Ye, J. (2014). Correlation coefficient of dual hesitant fuzzy sets and its application to multiple attribute decision making. *Applied Mathematical Modelling*, 38(2), 659–666. 10.1016/j.apm.2013.07.010

Zadeh, L. A. (1965). Fuzzy sets. *Information and Control*, 8(3), 338–353. 10.1016/S0019-9958(65)90241-X

Zhao, X. F., & Wei, G. W. (2013). Some intuitionistic fuzzy Einstein hybrid aggregation operators and their application to multiple attribute decision making. *Knowledge-Based Systems*, 37, 472–479. 10.1016/j.knosys.2012.09.006

Zhou, L. Y., Zhao, X. F., & Wei, G. W. (2014). Hesitant fuzzy Hamacher aggregation operators and their application to multiple attribute decision making. *Journal of Intelligent & Fuzzy Systems*, 26(6), 2689–2699. 10.3233/IFS-130939

Zhu, B., Xu, Z. S., & Xia, M. M. (2012). Dual hesitant fuzzy sets. *Journal of Applied Mathematics*, 2012, 1–13. Advance online publication. 10.1155/2012/879629

Chapter 8
The Researches on Knowledge Distance and Its Relative Extensions

Baoli Wang
Yuncheng University, China

ABSTRACT

All knowledge in the universe constructs a metric space, and the properties of knowledge distance are studied. Moreover, the knowledge distance was used to measure the rough entropy of knowledge. The concept of relative knowledge distance is based on the principle of relative cognition to embody the difficulty of transforming cognition between two knowledge under reference knowledge. It proved that the relative knowledge distance is monotonous with the refinement of reference knowledge granularity. In the experiment, the structural characteristics of relative knowledge distance in hierarchical clustering are visually analyzed. The feature selection algorithm based on relative knowledge distance is designed to simulate the process of human conditional cognition, which clarified that due to different cognitive perspectives and cognitive paths, relative knowledge distance has shown different cognitive characteristics such as enhancement, maintenance, and weakening in problem-solving.

DOI: 10.4018/979-8-3693-4292-3.ch008

INTRODUCTION

Problem Background

Information System, as a formal concept and clear semantic term in the Intelligent Information Processing field, was thoroughly analyzed in Rough Set Theory, which was proposed by the Polish mathematician Zdzislaw Pawlak (Zadeh, 1996; Song an Zhang, 2022). In Rough Set Theory, an equivalent relation deduces a partition, the universe of discourse, that constitutes the most basic structure for solving granularity (Wang & Liang, 2007; Yao,2013). This partition structure is also referred to as knowledge. In Rough Set Theory, an object concept could be depicted by the knowledge granules from the inner and outer approximations (Qian & Liang, 2007). Not only in Rough Set Theory, the Zhang and Zhang's Quotient Space theory also applied a partition to describe a concept (Zhang & Zhang, 2003). They also proved that all partitions on a given universe constructs a complete lattice. The partition based granular computing method has been widely and successfully applied in dynamic programming, robot path planning.

The measurement of uncertainty in knowledge space plays a crucial role in knowledge acquisition. Researchers, approaching from different perspectives, have proposed various types of uncertainty measurement methods, such as knowledge granularity, rough knowledge entropy, knowledge conditional entropy, and knowledge distance. Knowledge distance, as one of the foundational measures, can quantitatively reflect the differences between different structures. Liang Jiye (Liang & Chin, 2002) first introduced the concept of knowledge distance and conducted in-depth research on its connotation, construction, and applications in multi-granularity, achieving meaningful results. Qian Yuhua (Qian & Liang, 2009, 2015, 2017) further studied the knowledge structures of precise and fuzzy knowledge, the invariance of knowledge granularity, and the characterization of granularity by knowledge distance, explaining the crucial role of knowledge distance in human granularity solving. Liang Jiye (Liang & Li, 2012), based on knowledge distance, provided a distance perspective interpretation of inclusion degree, approximation accuracy, roughness, and other concepts in rough sets.

In recent years, there has been a wealth of research outcomes in the field of knowledge distance. Qian Yuhua (Qian & Liang, 2009), aiming to characterize knowledge structures, clustered partition granule structures based on knowledge distance. The study analyzed the cohesion and convergence reflected in granule structure clustering and simulated and simulated human granule selection behavior. Yang Xibei (Yang & Qian, 2013) constructed an algebraic lattice using set distance and knowledge distance, studying three levels of granule structure. To enrich the expression forms of knowledge distance, Chen Yuming (Chen & Qin, 2019) applied

Jaccard distance to replace set similarity, proposed a new measurement formula for knowledge distance, and extended partition knowledge distance in information systems to neighborhood information systems, enriching the meaning of knowledge distance and providing new perspectives for its application in the field of machine learning. Building on this foundation, Yang Jie proved from the perspective of logistics distribution optimization that knowledge distance can be constructed through a combination as long as the distance between granules is provided (Yang & Luo, 2021; Yang & Qin, 2022; Yang and Wang, 20018). Dai Jianhua discussed entropy and granularity measurement in set-valued information systems, studied uncertainty measurement in fuzzy information systems from the perspective of Gaussian kernel, proposed information measurement for fuzzy structural differences, and researched intuitionistic fuzzy granule structure distance (Dai & Tian, 2013; Dai & Xu, 2012). Li Shuai further proposed a set of interval value intuitionistic fuzzy sets to describe fuzzy granule structure distance, demonstrating that knowledge distance is a special form of intuitionistic fuzzy granule structure distance (Li and Yang, 2020).

An important point worth noting is that all the aforementioned studies have provided absolute measures of dissimilarity between two pieces of knowledge from different perspectives. None of them have described or analyzed the relative dissimilarity between two pieces of knowledge under arbitrary conditions, i.e., a measure of the relative dissimilarity of knowledge. In reality, human understanding of things always starts from existing knowledge, and new knowledge is acquired by analyzing the dissimilarity of knowledge in the knowledge space. The dissimilarity of knowledge should be related to the observer's prior knowledge or observational perspective. With different prior knowledge or different perspectives, the dissimilarity of knowledge should also vary. Yang Jie proposed a neighborhood information granule distance with approximate descriptive ability to reflect the differences in the characterization ability of different neighborhood knowledge spaces on the target concept (Yang and Wang, 2018). However, this study still cannot describe the impact of different knowledge perspectives on the dissimilarity of knowledge. To address these issues, this paper investigates the distance between two knowledge spaces and their cognitive characteristics in knowledge acquisition under the condition of having certain prior knowledge. This research aims to reflect the relative cognitive differences between knowledge by considering the influence of different knowledge perspectives.

This passage discusses the concept of information systems within the field of intelligent information processing, originating from Z. Pawlak's proposed rough set theory (Zadeh, 1996). The theory posits that knowledge is a form of classification ability, where given an equivalence relation on a domain, a partition of the domain can be obtained, forming a knowledge base on the domain. Any subset of the domain, known as the target concept, can be approximated using knowledge granules from the knowledge base (Zhao and Yao, 2019; Li and Liu, 2020; Cheng and Miao, 2007). Currently, rough set theory has found widespread applications across various domains, particularly achieving success in the field of data mining.

Professors Zhang Ling and Zhang Bo introduced the concept of quotient space theory (Zhang & Zhang, 2003), which models humans' ability to analyze and solve problems by jumping between worlds of different granularities. Quotient space theory also uses subsets to represent concepts, and the quotient space formed by a cluster of concepts, known as the knowledge base, has been proven to constitute a complete lattice of all partitions (knowledge bases) on the domain. In the field of knowledge measurement in information systems, numerous scholars have conducted in-depth research, addressing the uncertainty and granularity measures of knowledge (Qian & Liang, 2009; Xu and Zhang, 2004; Wang & Liang, 2007). The authors conducted a comprehensive study on knowledge granularity, information entropy, and rough entropy in complete information systems from the perspective of information theory (Wang & Liang, 2007). They established relationships between these measures and applied them to knowledge reduction, rule measurement, attribute importance measurement, and other aspects within information systems. Dai, Yang and Tan also borrowed ideas from entropy in information theory to define rough entropy and rough set entropy in incomplete information systems and general binary relations (Dai &Tian, 2013;Yang & Wang, 2020; Tan & Shi, 2022).

This chapter reviews a different perspective on studying the relationships between knowledge and the roughness of knowledge in information systems. It introduced the concept of knowledge distance, analyzed the knowledge measurement space and its properties, and subsequently utilized knowledge distance to define the rough entropy of knowledge. The obtained rough entropy under this new definition also exhibited invariance and a monotonic decrease with enhanced discernibility of knowledge. Besides, considering the relative cognitive perspective of the agent, the concept of relative knowledge distance was proposed to embody the difficulty of transforming cognition between two knowledge under reference knowledge. It also proved that the relative knowledge distance is monotonous with the refinement of reference knowledge granularity, which reflects the progressive characteristics of human multi-granularity cognition. At the end of the chapter, several experiments showed the structural characteristics of relative knowledge distance in hierarchical clustering. Furthermore, a feature selection algorithm based on relative knowledge distance was designed to simulate the process of human conditional cognition, which clarified that the relative knowledge distance could enhance, maintain, and weaken the ability of the recognition features.

A Brief Review of Information System

This section introduces the basic concepts about information systems and knowledge base.

Definition 1 (Wang & Liang, 2007) Let $S = (U, A, V, f)$ be an information system, $U = \{u_1, u_2, \cdots, u_n\}$ be a non-empty finite universe, A be a set of attributes, $V = \cup_{a \in A} V_a$ be a set of attribute values, where V_a denotes the value range of an attribute $a, f: U \times A \rightarrow V$ denotes an information function. For each attribute subset $\forall a \in A$, a binary indiscernible relation on $\widetilde{R}_a$ can be defined as:

$$IND(P) = \{(u, v) \in U \times U | \forall a \in P, f_a(u) = f_a(v)\}. \quad (1)$$

Clearly, $\widetilde{R}_P = \cap_{a \in P} \widetilde{R}_a$ is an equivalent relation. Thus, $\widetilde{R} \in \mathfrak{R}$ can lead to a partition of the universe $\mathfrak{R} = \{\widetilde{R}_1, \widetilde{R}_2, \cdots \widetilde{R}_m\}$, which can be denoted by U, abbreviated as $\widetilde{R} \in \mathfrak{R}$. From the viewpoint of granular computing, each equivalent class in $\forall x_i \in U, \widetilde{R}(x_i, x_i) = 1$ can be seen as a knowledge granule which is denoted by $U/P = \{[u]_P | u \in U\}$. In the rough set theory, the set of knowledge granules $\widetilde{R}$ can be named as a knowledge in terms of U. For the sake of simplicity, we name the knowledge as $\widetilde{R} = \begin{pmatrix} r_{11} & r_{12} & \cdots & r_{1n} \\ r_{21} & r_{22} & \cdots & r_{2n} \\ \cdots & \cdots & \cdots & \cdots \\ r_{n1} & r_{n2} & \cdots & r_{nn} \end{pmatrix}$ in the rest of the paper.

Let $\mathfrak{R}$ be a set of the knowledge derived from an information system. We call $ind(S) = (U, \mathfrak{R})$ as a knowledge base for S. If two knowledge P and Q with $ind(P) = ind(Q)$, then they are considered equivalent.

Among knowledge database formed by all knowledge in $r_{ij} \in [0, 1]$, there exists an equivalent relation corresponds to the finest knowledge. The identity relation corresponds to the finest knowledge, which is denoted as ω. And there exists an equivalent relation corresponds to the roughest knowledge. The universe relation corresponds to the roughest knowledge, which is denoted as δ.

For simplicity of the coming discussion, the knowledge P with a common expression with

$$U/P = \{[u_1]_P, [u_2]_P, \ldots, [u_n]_P\}.$$

The expression allowed the repeat of the elements in U/P. $[u_i]_P$ is the equivalent class with the objects equivalent to u_i. Obviously, if $u_j \in [u_i]_P$ then $[u_i]_P = [u_j]_P$.

Definition 2 (Wang & Liang, 2007) Suppose $r_{ij} = \frac{2\sum_{k=1}^{m}(x_{ik} \wedge x_{jk})}{\sum_{k=1}^{m}(x_{ik} + x_{jk})}$ is a non-empty finite universe, U and $\forall \widetilde{R} \in \mathfrak{R}$ are two knowledge in the universe $r_{ij} = \frac{2\sum_{k=1}^{m}(x_{ik} \wedge x_{jk})}{\sum_{k=1}^{m}(x_{ik} + x_{jk})}$. If $\widetilde{R}$, $F(\widetilde{R}) = \{\theta_{\widetilde{R}}(x_1), \theta_{\widetilde{R}}(x_2), \cdots, \theta_{\widetilde{R}}(x_n)\}$ is fulfilled, then the knowledge $\theta_{\widetilde{R}}(x_i) = \mu_{\widetilde{R}}(x_1)/x_1 + \mu_{\widetilde{R}}(x_2)/x_2 + \cdots + \mu_{\widetilde{R}}(x_n)/x_n$ is more finer than the knowledge $\mu_{\widetilde{R}}(x)$, which is denoted by $\theta_{\widetilde{R}}(x)$.

Table 1. An information system

S	Color	shape	Volume
u_1	red	square	big
u_2	blue	square	big
u_3	blue	square	big
u_4	red	circle	big
u_5	blue	circle	small
u_6	blue	circle	small

Example 1. Consider the complete information system given in Table 1, where $S = (U,A)$, $U = \{u_1, u_2, \cdots, u_6\}$, $A = \{\text{color,shape,volume}\}$.

$[u_1]_A = \{u_1\}$ represents an information granule with the color being red, the shape being square, and the volume being big.

$[u_2]_A = [u_3]_A = \{u_2, u_3\}$ represents an information granule with the color being blue, the shape being square, and the volume being big.

$[u_4]_A = \{u_4\}$ represents an information granule with the color being red, the shape being circle, and the volume being big.

$[u_5]_A = [u_6]_A = \{u_5, u_6\}$ represents an information granule with the color being blue, the shape being circle, and the volume being small.

Knowledge A in the information system is:

$$U/ind(A) = \{[u_1]_A, [u_2]_A, [u_3]_A, [u_4]_A, [u_5]_A, [u_6]_A\}$$

$$= \{\{u_1\}, \{u_2, u_3\}, \{u_2, u_3\}, \{u_4\}, \{u_5, u_6\}, \{u_5, u_6\}\}.$$

The Motives and Contribution of This Chapter

This chapter reviewed the proposed procedure of the definition of knowledge distance, analyzed the properties of knowledge space. Based on the measure space, the knowledge distance was used to interpret the rough entropy measure of knowledge, and to prove that rough entropy is with the characteristic of invariance and descending with the strength of the discernibility of knowledge. It is more worth noting that the above studies only focus on absolute difference measures of two knowledge from diverse perspectives. Few analyses can be found in the difference between two knowledge under arbitrary conditions, i.e., the relative difference measures of knowledge. Humans are likely to understand things from their standpoints and obtain new knowledge by analyzing the difference among knowledge in the knowledge space. Moreover, the difference in knowledge is closely correlated with individuals' prior knowledge. That is, different prior knowledge may lead to differences among knowledge. Thus, a neighborhood information granularity distance is proposed with approximate depiction abilities (Qian & Liang, 2017), which can reflect the difference in depiction abilities of target concepts in various neighborhood knowledge spaces. However, this study fails to describe the influence of knowledge differences under various knowledge perspectives. To address the above issue, this paper aims to explore the distance between two knowledge and the cognitive features in knowledge acquisition under a specific condition of prior knowledge, to reflect the relative cognitive difference among knowledge effectively (Zhan, 2023; Zhang and Zhang, 2022; Zhang and Liang, 2020).

The structure of the paper is outlined as follows. The next two sections present the definitions of knowledge distance and its properties, as well as the relationship between rough entropy. The succeeding section introduces the concept of precise relative knowledge distances from the perspective of precision granular spaces, analyzing the order-preserving, monotonicity, and conditional dependency of relative knowledge distances. It also demonstrates that existing knowledge distances can be viewed as specific forms of knowledge distances. The differences between the classical (absolute) knowledge distance and the relative knowledge distance are examined through several experiments. Furthermore, a feature selection algorithm is designed to highlight the uniqueness of the relative knowledge distance in knowledge acquisition. The final section summarizes the entire paper, along with several future research options.

KNOWLEDGE DISTANCE

Knowledge Distance

According to the concept of knowledge as partitions, different partitions of the universe constitute different knowledge, and different knowledge generally expresses the same concept differently. This aspect has been extensively studied in rough set theory. In reference [8], the authors conducted an in-depth investigation into the measurement properties of a specific knowledge in rough set theory, and it has been applied to knowledge reduction, rule measurement, attribute importance measurement, and other aspects of information systems. As for the relationships and properties between different knowledge, it has been demonstrated only in the theory of commercial space that all knowledge in the knowledge base forms a complete lattice with a certain hierarchical relationship (Zhao and Yao, 2019). In this section, the definition of knowledge distance is given from the perspective of set symmetric difference, and some properties of knowledge distance are analyzed.

In an information system, different attribute sets generally induce different partitions of the universe. Considering the distance between knowledge involves examining the differences between different attribute sets (Zadeh, 1996). Without loss of generality, the knowledge base discussed here is the complete knowledge base on the domain $U = \{u_1, u_2, \cdots, u_n\}$ (i.e., all possible partitions) denoted as $K(U)$. Given an information system $S = (U, A)$, its knowledge base $ind(S)$ is just a subset of $K(U)$.

For the convenience of discussion, the definition of the knowledge order relation is first introduced.

Definition 1. Two items of knowledge in the knowledge base $K(U)$, $U/ind(P) = \{[u_1]_P, [u_2]_P, \cdots, [u_n]_P\}$, $U/ind(Q) = \{[u_1]_Q, [u_2]_Q, \cdots, [u_n]_Q\}$. If conditions $[u_i]_P \subseteq [u_i]_Q$ for$\forall 1 \le i \le n$, then we all knowledge $P$is finer than knowledge Q, denoted as $P \prec Q$.

Definition 2. Given two knowledge$P$ and Qin the knowledge base set $K(U)$, $U/ind(P) = \{[u_1]_P, [u_2]_P, \cdots, [u_n]_P\}$, $U/ind(Q) = \{[u_1]_Q, [u_2]_Q, \cdots, [u_n]_Q\}$. Define the distance between P and Qas:

$$d(P,Q) = \frac{1}{|U| \times (|U| - 1)} \sum_{i=1}^{|U|} \left| [u_i]_P \oplus [u_i]_Q \right| \tag{1}$$

where $\oplus$ is the symmetric difference operation on sets. $|\bullet|$ represents the cardinality of the set.

Theorem 1. $(K(U), d)$ forms a metric space, i.e., for $\forall P, Q, R \in K(U)$ satisfies:
(1) $d(P,Q) \ge 0$, the inequality holds as an "=" if and only if $P = Q$;

(2) $d(P,Q) = d(Q,P)$;

(3) $d(P,R) \leq d(P,Q) + d(Q,R)$ holds.

Prove that (1) and (2) obviously hold. Now, we will prove the validity of (3).

Let $\forall A, B, C \subseteq U$. With knowledge from set theory, we have $A \oplus B \subseteq (A \oplus C) \cup (C \oplus B)$. Therefore, for any $u_i \in U (i = 1, 2, \cdots, n)$, there exists

$$\begin{aligned} &\left|[u_i]_P \oplus [u_i]_R\right| \\ \leq &\left|([u_i]_P \oplus [u_i]_Q) \cup ([u_i]_Q \oplus [u_i]_R)\right| \\ \leq &\left|[u_i]_P \oplus [u_i]_Q\right| + \left|[u_i]_Q \oplus [u_i]_R\right|, \end{aligned}$$

So,

$$\sum_{i=1}^{n} \left\|[u_i]_P \oplus [u_i]_R\right\| \leq$$

$$\left(\sum_{i=1}^{n} \left|[u_i]_P \oplus [u_i]_Q\right| + \sum_{i=1}^{n} \left|[u_i]_Q \oplus [u_i]_R\right|\right),$$

By multiplying both sides of the inequality by a constant $\frac{1}{|U| \times (|U| - 1)}$, we can get that $d(P,R) \leq d(P,Q) + d(Q,R)$. The proof is completed.

Given an information system $S = (U, A)$ and its knowledge base $ind(S)$ is merely a subset of $K(U)$, according to the knowledge of metric spaces, it is known that ($ind(S), d$) is a distance subspace of $(K(U), d)$.

Knowledge Distance's Propositions

As is well-known, the knowledge space within a limited discourse universe is constrained by a limited accountable knowledge. The knowledge metric space possesses a defined structure, which offers a partial representation of the structural properties inherent within the knowledge distance space.

Property 1. Given a universe $U(|U| > 1)$, then the maximum value of knowledge distance can reach 1, the minimum value is

$$\frac{2}{|U| \times (|U| - 1)}.$$

Proof. Obviously, for any two different knowledge P and Q, there exist two objects u_i and u_j with $[u_i]_P \neq [u_j]_P$ and $[u_i]_Q \neq [u_j]_Q$.

Let $A, B \subseteq U$, and $A \neq \emptyset, B \neq \emptyset, A \neq B$, then the inequality $1 \leq |A \oplus B| \leq |U| - 1$ can be easily deduced from the set theory.

For one hand, given a universe U, the finest and roughest knowledge are ω (from the identical relation) and δ (from the global relation) with $U/\omega = \{\{u_1\},\{u_2\},\cdots,\{u_n\}\}$ and $U/\delta = \{\{u_1,u_2,\cdots u_n\}\}$.

Followed by Equation 1,

$$\begin{aligned} d(\omega,\delta) &= \frac{1}{|U| \times (|U|-1)} \sum_{i=1}^{|U|} \left|[u_i]_\omega \oplus [u_i]_\delta\right| \\ &= \frac{1}{|U| \times (|U|-1)} \sum_{i=1}^{|U|} \left|\{u_i\} \oplus U\right| \\ &= \frac{1}{|U| \times (|U|-1)} \sum_{i=1}^{|U|} (|U|-1) \\ &= 1. \end{aligned}$$

For the other hand, suppose two different knowledge P and Q with the following structures as

$$U/ind(P) = \{\cdots,\{u_i,u_j\},\cdots,\{u_i,u_j\},\cdots\}$$

and

$$U/ind(Q) = \{\cdots,\{u_i\},\cdots,\{u_j\},\cdots\},$$

in which the knowledge not shown in the above equation as $\cdots$ to represent they are identity with each other in these places. We continue to compute the distance between them as

$$\begin{aligned} d(P,Q) &= \frac{1}{|U| \times (|U|-1)} \sum_{i=1}^{|U|} \left|[u_i]_P \oplus [u_i]_Q\right| \\ &= \frac{1}{|U| \times (|U|-1)} \Big(\sum_{\substack{k \neq i \\ k \neq j}} 0 + \left|[u_i]_P \oplus [u_i]_Q\right| + \left|[u_j]_P \oplus [u_j]_Q\right|\Big) \\ &= \frac{1}{|U| \times (|U|-1)} \Big(\left|\{u_i,u_j\} \oplus \{u_i\}\right| + \left|\{u_i,u_j\} \oplus \{u_j\}\right|\Big) \\ &= \frac{2}{|U| \times (|U|-1)}. \end{aligned}$$

It completes the proof.

Property 2. Given three knowledge P, Q, R in $K(U)$. If $P \prec Q \prec R$, then $d(P,R) = d(P,Q) + d(Q,R)$ holds.

Proof. Since $P \prec Q \prec R$, let the corresponding three knowledge granules with the order relation as follows, the other granules are all the same.

$$R: \{L(k)\},$$

$$Q: \{L(k-m)\}, \{L(m)\},$$

$$P: \{L(k-m-l)\}, \{L(l)\}, \{L(n)\}, \{L(m-n)\}.$$

($L(k)$ represents there are k elements in this granule, similar for the others) satisfies $1 \leq k \leq |U|, 0 \leq m \leq k, 0 \leq l \leq k-m, 0 \leq n \leq m$.

For convenience, let $\alpha = \frac{1}{|U| \times (|U|-1)}$

$$d(P,R) = \alpha \times ((k-m-l)(m+l) + l(k-l) + n(k-n) + (m-n)(k-m+n))$$
$$= \alpha \times (2km + 2kl + 2mn - 2ml - 2m^2 - 2n^2 - 2l^2),$$

$$d(P,Q) = \alpha \times (2l(k-m-l) + 2n(m-n)),$$

$$d(Q,R) = \alpha \times (2m(k-m)),$$

$$d(P,Q) + d(Q,R) = \alpha \times (2km + 2kl + 2mn - 2ml - 2m^2 - 2n^2 - 2l^2),$$

so $d(P,R) = d(P,Q) + d(Q,R)$.

The binary decomposition process of only one of the particles is discussed here. In addition, each split does not exceed two splits, for example, for the case of multi-granular and multi-granular splitting, it is only the repetition of single particle decomposition, and the proof process is only the increase of the calculation amount, and the analysis is similar. It completes the proof.

It is worthy to notice that the condition of Property 2 is not the necessary condition of the hold of the conclusion.

Example 2. Let three knowledge P_1, P_2, P_3 represent as follows,

$$U/ind(P_1)=\{\{u_1,u_2\},\{u_1,u_2\},\{u_3,u_4\},\{u_3,u_4\},\{u_5,u_6\},\{u_5,u_6\}\},$$

$$U/ind(P_2)=\{\{u_1,u_2\},\{u_1,u_2\},\{u_3\},\{u_4\},\{u_5,u_6\},\{u_5,u_6\}\},$$

$$U/ind(P_3)=\{\{u_1,u_2,u_3\},\{u_1,u_2,u_3\},\{u_1,u_2,u_3\},\{u_4,u_5,u_6\},\{u_4,u_5,u_6\},\{u_4,u_5,u_6\}\}.$$

$$d(P_1,P_2)=\frac{1}{6\times(6-1)}\times(0+0+1+1+0+0)=\frac{1}{15},$$

$$d(P_2,P_3)=\frac{1}{6\times(6-1)}\times(1+1+2+2+1+1)=\frac{4}{15},$$

$$d(P_1,P_3)=\frac{1}{6\times(6-1)}\times(1+1+3+3+1+1)=\frac{5}{15}=\frac{1}{3},$$

while, we have $d(P_1,P_3)=d(P_1,P_2)+d(P_2,P_3)$.

It can be easy to get from Example 2 that Property 2 is not the necessary condition of the conclusion. The three knowledge do not satisfy the condition of Property 2, but the conclusion of Property 2 holds.

The knowledge in $K(U)$ corresponds to a Haas graph according to the order relationship defined in Definition 1. The three knowledge conditions that satisfy Property 2 must be on the same line. This conclusion is similar to the distance property of Euclidean space. However, in Euclidean distance space, three points not on the same line must take the inequality sign, but this property is not true in the knowledge space defined above, as analyzed in Example 2.

Rough Entropy (RE) and the Relation Between RE and KD

Knowledge base has a certain level, obviously the knowledge at the bottom of the knowledge base is the least rough, and the knowledge at the top is the most rough. In rough set theory, using knowledge to describe the target concept may lead to inaccurate representation, which is caused by the weak resolution of knowledge. Therefore, the measure of rough entropy for knowledge on the final domain is meaningful. This section defines the rough entropy of knowledge in an information system based on the knowledge distance in the last two sections.

Definition 3. Given an information system$S = (U,A)$. The rough entropy $E_r(P)$ of knowledge$P \in ind(S)$ is defined as

$$E_r(P) = d(P,\omega)$$

$$= \frac{1}{|U| \times |U-1|} \sum_{i=1}^{|U|} (|I_P(u_i)| \oplus \{u_i\}),$$

where$U/ind(P) = \{I_P(u_1), I_P(u_2), \cdots, I_P(u_n)\}$,$\omega$is the finest knowledge at the first level of the knowledge base with $U/\omega = \{\{u_1\}, \{u_2\}, \cdots, \{u_n\}\}$.

Example 3. Compute the rough entropy of the three knowledge P_1, P_2, P_3 in Example 2.

$$E_r(P_1) = \frac{3}{15},$$

$$E_r(P_2) = \frac{2}{15},$$

$$E_r(P_3) = \frac{6}{15}.$$

From the results of the computation, we have that P_2 is the finest one in the three, and$P_3$is the roughest one.

Property 3. Given two knowledge $P, Q \in ind(S)$ in $S = (U,A)$, the knowledge distance $d(P,Q)$and the rough entropy$E_r(P), E_r(Q)$are with the relationship as

$$d(P,Q) \geq |E_r(P) - E_r(Q)|.$$

Proof. To prove that $d(P,Q) \geq |E_r(P) - E_r(Q)|$. For the non-negativity of the knowledge distance $d(P,Q) \geq 0$, we need to prove that $d(P,Q) \geq E_r(P) - E_r(Q) \geq -d(P,Q)$.

Given the three knowledgeP, Q, ω,followed by Property 2, we have

$$d(P,Q) + d(Q,\omega) \geq d(P,\omega),$$

$$d(Q,P) + d(P,\omega) \geq d(Q,\omega),$$

i.e.,

$$d(P,Q) \geq d(P,\omega) - d(Q,\omega),$$

$$d(Q,P) \geq d(Q,\omega) - d(P,\omega),$$

with

$$d(P,Q) = d(Q,P),$$

so

$$d(P,Q) \geq d(P,\omega) - d(Q,\omega) \geq -d(P,Q),$$

that is

$$d(P,Q) \geq E_r(P) - E_r(Q) \geq -d(P,Q).$$

Therefore,

$$d(P,Q) \geq |E_r(P) - E_r(Q)|.$$

Property 4. Given two knowledge $P, Q \in ind(S)$in an information system $S = (U,A)$.If$P \prec Q$, then $d(P,Q) = E_r(Q) - E_r(P)$.

Proof. Since $\omega \prec P \prec Q$, followed by Property 2, we have

$$d(\omega,P) + d(P,Q) = d(\omega,Q),$$

i.e.,

$$d(P,Q) = d(\omega,Q) - d(\omega,P),$$

so,

$$d(P,Q) = E_r(Q) - E_r(P)$$

holds.

Property 4 expressed that if there exists an order relation between two knowledge, the difference between the two rough entropies can be applied to calculate the knowledge distance between them. We can also deduce that if $d(P,Q) > |E_r(P) - E_r(Q)|$,there must be no order relationship between them.

Property 5. Given two knowledge $P, Q \in ind(S)$ in an information system $S = (U, A)$ as $U/ind(P) = \{[u_1]_P, [u_2]_P, \cdots, [u_n]_P\}$, $U/ind(Q) = \{[u_1]_Q, [u_2]_Q, \cdots, [u_n]_Q\}$. If there exists a one-one mapping $f: U \rightarrow U$ with that $|[u_i]_P| = |[(f(u_i))]_Q|$, $(i = 1, 2 \cdots, n)$, then

$$E_r(P) = E_r(Q).$$

Proof. Obviously.

Property 5 depicts the roughness in-variant of knowledge.

Property 6. Given two knowledge $P, Q \in ind(S)$ in an information system $S = (U, A)$. If $P \prec Q$, then

$$E_r(P) \leq E_r(Q).$$

Proof. According to $P \prec Q$ and Property 2, we have that

$$d(P, Q) = E_r(Q) - E_r(P).$$

Since

$$d(P, Q) \geq 0,$$

we get

$$E_r(Q) - E_r(P) \geq 0,$$

i.e.,

$$E_r(P) \leq E_r(Q).$$

Property 6 expresses that the rough entropy of knowledge decreases monotonically with the increase of the discernibility of knowledge.

The rough entropy defined by knowledge distance gives a new interpretation of the rough entropy in information system, and the above theorems show that the rough entropy defined by knowledge distance and the rough entropy under other definitions also have the properties of rough invariance and monotonically decreasing with the enhancement of knowledge's discernibility.

Based on the view that knowledge is division, this paper proves that all knowledge in the domain constitutes a distance space, studies some properties of knowledge distance in knowledge space, and defines knowledge rough entropy in information systems from a new perspective by using knowledge distance, which provides a new tool for the study of knowledge measurement in information systems. It is helpful to deeply analyze the relationship between knowledge and the roughness of knowledge in information system.

RELATIVE KNOWLEDGE DISTANCE

Relative Knowledge Distance

In this section, the concept of relative knowledge distance is introduced, and its properties are analyzed.

Definition 4 For a non-empty finite domain U, where R represents prior knowledge or conditional cognition on U, the relative knowledge distance under knowledge P and Q in context R is defined as

$$D(P,Q|R)=\frac{1}{|U|}\sum_{i=1}^{|U|}\frac{\left|([u_i]_P\cap[u_i]_R)\oplus([u_i]_Q\cap[u_i]_R)\right|}{|U|} \tag{2}$$

This definition integrates the relative description of prior knowledge or conditional cognition Rinto the existing knowledge distance formula, aiming to reflect the relative differences between any two pieces of knowledge P and Q from different perspectives. Definition 4 is also referred to as the relative knowledge distance between P and Q regarding R.

Next, we will analyze the properties that the relative knowledge distance $D(P, Q |R)$ possesses.

Property 7. Let U be a non-empty finite domain, P_1, P_2, P_3 be three knowledge on U, and R be the prior knowledge or conditional cognition on U. Then, the relative knowledge distance D satisfies:

(1) Non-negativity $D(P_1,P_2|R)\geq 0$;

(2) Symmetry $D(P_1,P_2|R)=D(P_2,P_1|R)$;

(3) Triangle Inequality $D(P_1,P_2|R)+D(P_2,P_3|R)\geq D(P_1,P_3|R)$.

Proving that properties (1) and (2) hold is straightforward. Now, let's establish the validity of Property 7.

To prove that the relative knowledge distance of P_1, P_2, P_3 concerning R satisfies the triangle inequality, according to the definition, it is sufficient to demonstrate

$$\left|([u_i]_{P_1}\cap[u_i]_R)\oplus([u_i]_{P_3}\cap[u_i]_R)\right|\leq\left|([u_i]_{P_1}\cap[u_i]_R)\oplus([u_i]_{P_2}\cap[u_i]_R)\right|+\left|([u_i]_{P_2}\cap[u_i]_R)\oplus([u_i]_{P_3}\cap[u_i]_R)\right|,$$

which is equivalent to proving

$$\left|([u_i]_{P_1} \oplus [u_i]_{P_3}) \cap [u_i]_R\right| \le \left|([u_i]_{P_1} \oplus [u_i]_{P_2}) \cap [u_i]_R\right| + \left|([u_i]_{P_2} \oplus [u_i]_{P_3}) \cap [u_i]_R\right|.$$

By the properties of sets, we know

$$([u_i]_{P_1} \oplus [u_i]_{P_3}) \subseteq [([u_i]_{P_1} \oplus [u_i]_{P_2}) \cup ([u_i]_{P_2} \oplus [u_i]_{P_3})],$$

hence,

$$(([u_i]_{P_1} \oplus [u_i]_{P_3}) \cap [u_i]_R \subseteq [(([u_i]_{P_1} \oplus [u_i]_{P_2}) \cap [u_i]_R) \cup ([u_i]_{P_2} \oplus [u_i]_{P_3}) \cap [u_i]_R,$$

and consequently

$$\left|([u_i]_{P_1} \oplus [u_i]_{P_3}) \cap [u_i]_R\right| \le \left|([u_i]_{P_1} \oplus [u_i]_{P_2}) \cap [u_i]_R\right| + \left|([u_i]_{P_2} \oplus [u_i]_{P_3}) \cap [u_i]_R\right|.$$

Therefore,

$$D(P_1, P_2|R) + D(P_2, P_3|R) \ge D(P_1, P_3|R).$$

Property 7 indicates that the conditional knowledge on the domain U forms a metric space concerning the relative knowledge distance $D(P, Q|R)$.

Example 4. Given a domain $U = \{u_1, u_2, u_3, u_4, u_5, u_6\}$ with two distinguishable pieces of knowledge

$$P = \{\{u_1, u_3\}, \{u_2, u_6\}, \{u_4, u_5\}\}$$

and

$$Q = \{\{u_1, u_3, u_5, u_6\}, \{u_2, u_4\}\}.$$

The absolute knowledge distance between the two knowledge is

$$d(P, Q) = 4/9.$$

Example 5. Given a domain $U = \{u_1, u_2, u_3, u_4, u_5, u_6\}$ with two distinguishable pieces of knowledge

$$P = \{\{u_1, u_3\}, \{u_2, u_6\}, \{u_4, u_5\}\}$$

and

$$Q = \{\{u_1, u_3, u_5, u_6\}, \{u_2, u_4\}\},$$

under the prior knowledge $R_1 = \{\{u_3, u_6\}, \{u_1, u_2, u_4, u_5\}\}, R_2 = \{\{u_1, u_2, u_5\}, \{u_3, u_4, u_6\}\}$,

the relative knowledge distance between P and Q is

$$D(P,Q|R_1) = 1/36 \times (1 + 1 + 1 + 2 + 2 + 1) = 2/9$$

and

$$D(P,Q|R_2) = 1/36 \times (1 + 0 + 1 + 0 + 1 + 1) = 1/9,$$

respectively.

Relative Knowledge Distance and Its Propositions

From Examples 4 and 5, it is evident that the relative knowledge distance between P and Q under different prior knowledge or conditional cognition is distinct. In comparison to the absolute knowledge distance calculated between P and Qin Example 4, the relative knowledge distance computed in Example 5 is smaller.

Property 8. Let U be a non-empty finite domain, P_1, P_2, P_3 be the knowledge on U, and Rbe the prior knowledge or conditional cognition on U. If the order relation $P_1 \preceq P_2 \preceq P_3$ holds, then $D(P_1,P_2|R)+D(P_2,P_3|R)= D(P_1,P_3|R)$.

To prove that the distance triangle equality holds for three knowledge elements P_1, P_2, P_3 with an order relation under prior knowledge or conditional cognition R, it is necessary to demonstrate

$$\left|([u_i]_{P_1} \cap [u_i]_R) \oplus ([u_i]_{P_3} \cap [u_i]_R)\right| = \left|([u_i]_{P_1} \cap [u_i]_R) \oplus ([u_i]_{P_2} \cap [u_i]_R)\right| + \left|([u_i]_{P_2} \cap [u_i]_R) \oplus ([u_i]_{P_3} \cap [u_i]_R)\right|.$$

Given the order relation $P_1 \preceq P_2 \preceq P_3$ provided by the conditions, we obtain

$$[u_i]_{P_1} \subseteq [u_i]_{P_2} \subseteq [u_i]_{P_3}$$

so it suffices to prove

$$\left|([u_i]_{P_3} - [u_i]_{P_1}) \cap [u_i]_R\right| - \left|([u_i]_{P_2} - [u_i]_{P_1}) \cap [u_i]_R\right| = \left|([u_i]_{P_3} - [u_i]_{P_2}) \cap [u_i]_R\right|.$$

Furthermore, due to $([u_i]_{P_2} - [u_i]_{P_1}) \subseteq ([u_i]_{P_3} - [u_i]_{P_1})$, we have

$$(([u_i]_{P_2} - [u_i]_{P_1}) \cap [u_i]_R) \subseteq ([u_i]_{P_3} - [u_i]_{P_1}) \cap [u_i]_R).$$

According to the properties of set operations: if $A \supseteq B$ then $A - B = A \cap \overline{B}$, where $\overline{B}$ is the complement of B in set A. Therefore,

$$\left|([u_i]_{P_3} - [u_i]_{P_1}) \cap [u_i]_R\right| - \left|([u_i]_{P_2} - [u_i]_{P_1}) \cap [u_i]_R\right|$$

$$= |(([u_i]_{P_3} - [u_i]_{P_1}) \cap [u_i]_R) - (([u_i]_{P_2} - [u_i]_{P_1}) \cap [u_i]_R)|$$

$$= \left|([u_i]_{P_3} \cap \overline{[u_i]_{P_1}} \cap [u_i]_R) \cap \overline{([u_i]_{P_2} \cap \overline{[u_i]_{P_1}} \cap [u_i]_R)}\right|$$

$$= \left|[u_i]_{P_3} \cap \overline{[u_i]_{P_1}} \cap [u_i]_R \cap \overline{[u_i]_{P_2}}\right|$$

$$= \left|[u_i]_{P_3} \cap [u_i]_R \cap \overline{[u_i]_{P_2}}\right|$$

$$= \left|([u_i]_{P_3} - [u_i]_{P_2}) \cap [u_i]_R\right|$$

$$= \left|([u_i]_{P_3} - [u_i]_{P_2}) \cap [u_i]_R\right|.$$

So, $D(P_1, P_2|R) + D(P_2, P_3|R) = D(P_1, P_3|R)$.

Property 8 reflects the property that under the same prior knowledge or conditional cognition, the relative knowledge distance maintains the equality under an order relation.

Property 9. Let U be a non-empty finite domain, P and Q be the knowledge on U, and R_1 and R_2be the prior knowledge or conditional cognition on U. If the knowledge R_1 and R_2 satisfy the order relation $R_1 \prec R_2$, then $D(P, Q|R_1) \leq D(P, Q|R_2)$.

To prove that the relative knowledge distance has the property of monotonicity when there exists an order relation under prior knowledge or conditional cognition R_1 and R_2 it is sufficient to demonstrate

$$\left|([u_i]_P \cap [u_i]_{R_1}) \oplus ([u_i]_Q \cap [u_i]_{R_1})\right| \leq \left|([u_i]_P \cap [u_i]_{R_2}) \oplus ([u_i]_Q \cap [u_i]_{R_2})\right|.$$

According to the properties of set operations, it is necessary to prove $\left|([u_i]_P \oplus [u_i]_Q) \cap [u_i]_{R_1}\right| \leq \left|([u_i]_P \oplus [u_i]_Q) \cap [u_i]_{R_2}\right|$ i.e., $(([u_i]_P \oplus [u_i]_Q) \cap [u_i]_{R_1}) \subseteq (([u_i]_P \oplus [u_i]_Q) \cap [u_i]_{R_2})$.

Assuming any object $u_i \in ([u_i]_P \oplus [u_i]_Q) \cap [u_i]_{R_1}$, it follows that $u_i \in [u_i]_{R_1}$ and $u_i \in ([u_i]_P \oplus [u_i]_Q)$. Furthermore, $[u_i]_{R_1} \subseteq [u_i]_{R_2}$ so $u_i \in [u_i]_{R_2}$ and consequently

$$u_i \in ([u_i]_P \oplus [u_i]_Q) \cap [u_i]_{R_2}$$

and

$$(([u_i]_P \oplus [u_i]_Q) \cap [u_i]_{R_1}) \subseteq (([u_i]_P \oplus [u_i]_Q) \cap [u_i]_{R_2}).$$

Thus, it is known that $D(P, Q|R_1) \leq D(P, Q|R_2)$ holds.

From Property 9, it can be observed that as prior knowledge or conditional cognition becomes more refined, the relative knowledge distance between knowledge elements decreases monotonically. This pattern reflects that, in the progressive cognitive process, with the continuous improvement of existing cognitive levels, the relative cognitive difficulty between two pieces of knowledge can gradually decrease. This phenomenon embodies the characteristics of human multi-granularity progressive cognition.

Corollary 1. Let U be a non-empty finite domain. When R is the coarsest knowledge on U denoted by δ it follows that $D(P, Q|\delta) = d(P, Q)$.

Proof. According to formula (2), we have

$$D(P, Q|\delta) = \frac{1}{|U|}\sum_{i=1}^{|U|}\frac{\left|([u_i]_P \cap U) \oplus ([u_i]_Q \cap U)\right|}{|U|}$$

$$= \frac{1}{|U|}\sum_{i=1}^{|U|}\frac{\left|([u_i]_P \oplus [u_i]_Q)\right|}{|U|}$$

$$= d(P, Q).$$

Corollary 1 illustrates that absolute knowledge distance is a measure of the difference between two pieces of knowledge without any cognitive prerequisites. Therefore, absolute knowledge distance is a special case of relative knowledge distance.

Corollary 2. Let U be a non-empty finite domain. When R is the finest knowledge on U denoted by ω, the relative knowledge distance $D(P,Q|R)$ between knowledge P and Q reaches its minimum value of 0.

Proof. If the prior knowledge or conditional cognition R is the finest knowledge on U i.e., $R = \omega$, then the relative knowledge distance between P and Q is denoted as

$$D(P,Q|\omega) = \frac{1}{|U|}\sum_{i=1}^{|U|}\frac{\left|([u_i]_P \cap \{u_i\}) \oplus ([u_i]_Q \cap \{u_i\})\right|}{|U|}$$

$$= \frac{1}{|U|}\sum_{i=1}^{|U|}\frac{\left|\{u_i\} \oplus \{u_i\}\right|}{|U|}$$

$$= 0.$$

According to Property 9, for any knowledge R on the domain U if it satisfies the order relation $\omega \preceq R \preceq \delta$, then $D(P,Q|\omega) \le D(P,Q|R) \le D(P,Q|\delta)$, implying that the relative knowledge distance satisfies: $0 \le D(P,Q|R) \le d(P,Q)$.

Example 6. Given knowledge $P = \{\{u_1,u_3\},\{u_2,u_6\},\{u_4,u_5\}\}, Q = \{\{u_3, u_4,u_5\},\{u_1\},\{u_2\},\{u_6\}\}$ on the domain $U = \{u_1,u_2,u_3,u_4,u_5,u_6\}$, with prior knowledge $R = \{\{u_3,u_6\},\{u_1,u_2,u_4,u_5\}\}$ on U, the relative knowledge distance between knowledge P and Q concerning knowledge R is denoted as $D(P,Q|R) = 1/36 \times (0+0+0+0+0+0) = 0$.

Example 6 indicates that $R = \omega$ is a sufficient condition for $D(P,Q|R) = 0$ to hold, but not a necessary one.

Property 10. Let U be a non-empty finite domain. There exists a conditional dependency relationship between the knowledge on U denoted as P and Q, as follows:

$$D(P,Q|P) + D(P,Q|Q) = d(P,Q)$$

Proof.

$$D(P,Q|P) + D(P,Q|Q)$$

$$= \frac{1}{|U|}\sum_{i=1}^{|U|}\frac{\left|([u_i]_P \cap [u_i]_P) \oplus ([u_i]_Q \cap [u_i]_P)\right|}{|U|} + \frac{1}{|U|}\sum_{i=1}^{|U|}\frac{\left|([u_i]_P \cap [u_i]_Q) \oplus ([u_i]_Q \cap [u_i]_Q)\right|}{|U|}$$

$$= \frac{1}{|U|}\sum_{i=1}^{|U|}\frac{\left|([u_i]_P - [u_i]_Q)\right|}{|U|} + \frac{1}{|U|}\sum_{i=1}^{|U|}\frac{\left|([u_i]_Q - [u_i]_P)\right|}{|U|}$$

$$= \frac{1}{|U|}\sum_{i=1}^{|U|}\frac{\left|([u_i]_P - [u_i]_Q)\right| + \left|([u_i]_Q - [u_i]_P)\right|}{|U|}$$

$$= d(P, Q).$$

Property 10 indicates that the absolute knowledge distance between P and Q can be decomposed into the sum of one-way relative knowledge distances in different directions. This means that the cognitive difficulty from P to Q is considered separately from the cognitive difficulty from Q to P. This theoretical framework provides an explanation for the dialectical unity between relative knowledge distance and absolute knowledge distance.

CASE ANALYSIS

Constructive Difference Between Knowledge Distance and Relative Knowledge Distance

This section validates, through experimental methods, the structural differences between different knowledge partitions based on relative knowledge distance and absolute knowledge distance measures. Additionally, the characteristics of human multi-granularity progressive cognition are characterized using a feature selection algorithm based on relative knowledge distance.

For a given set of objects, different distance calculation methods can result in different hierarchical structures. Hierarchical clustering is a clustering method based on a distance matrix defined on the set of objects. It merges the closest clusters iteratively to form a hierarchical, tiered structure, based on the distances between classes. Here, we apply the same hierarchical clustering algorithm to obtain different clustering structures to demonstrate the differences between the proposed distance and classical absolute knowledge distance. This further confirms that relative knowledge distance can provide a different perspective for knowledge acquisition compared to absolute knowledge distance. The experimental procedure is as follows:

Given an information system $S = (U,A,V,f)$, where $A = \{a_1, a_2, \cdots, a_m\}$ is the set of conditional attributes in S for each attribute in the conditional attribute set A, the calculation is performed as follows:

1. For $\forall a_k \in A, k = \{1,2,\cdots,m\}$, the knowledge induced by the equivalence relation of a_k is obtained as P_k, and it is taken as prior knowledge or conditional cognition R_k.
2. Calculate the relative knowledge distance $D_{ij}(P_i, P_j | R_k)$ and absolute knowledge distance $d_{ij}(P_i, P_j)$ of the knowledge induced by the remaining attributes in R_k as conditional cognition. Obtain the relative knowledge distance matrix $M = (D_{ij})$ and the absolute knowledge distance matrix $N = (d_{ij})$.
3. Based on the two distance matrices M and N, perform hierarchical clustering on the attribute subsets of the dataset using the hierarchical clustering method, resulting in different clustering structures.
4. Use the difference in knowledge granularity $\Delta GK(X)$ and knowledge distance $d(P, Q)$ as me asurement criteria to calculate the dissimilarity of the clustering results. The knowledge granularity is calculated as

$$GK(X) = \frac{1}{|U|^2} \sum_{i=1}^{n} |[u_i]|^2.$$

Using the Zoo dataset and Las Vegas Trip Advisor Reviews dataset from the UCI database as examples, we construct relative knowledge distance and absolute knowledge distance matrices by taking the knowledge induced by attributes a_1 and a_5' in the datasets as conditional knowledge R. We then perform attribute set clustering. The clustering results are illustrated in Figure 1 and Figure 2. (In the figures, $Rel - a_1$ represents clustering based on relative knowledge distance with a_1 as the conditional attribute, and $Abs - a_1$ represents clustering based on absolute knowledge distance after removing attribute a_1.)

Figure 1. The comparisons between the hierarchical structures constructed from the different attributes on the zoo dataset

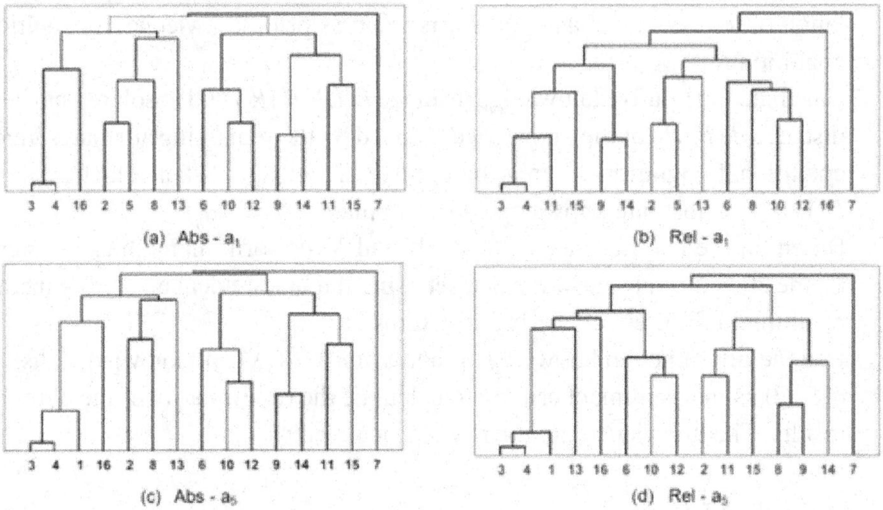

Figure 2. The comparisons between the hierarchical structures constructed from the different attributes on the Las Vegas dataset

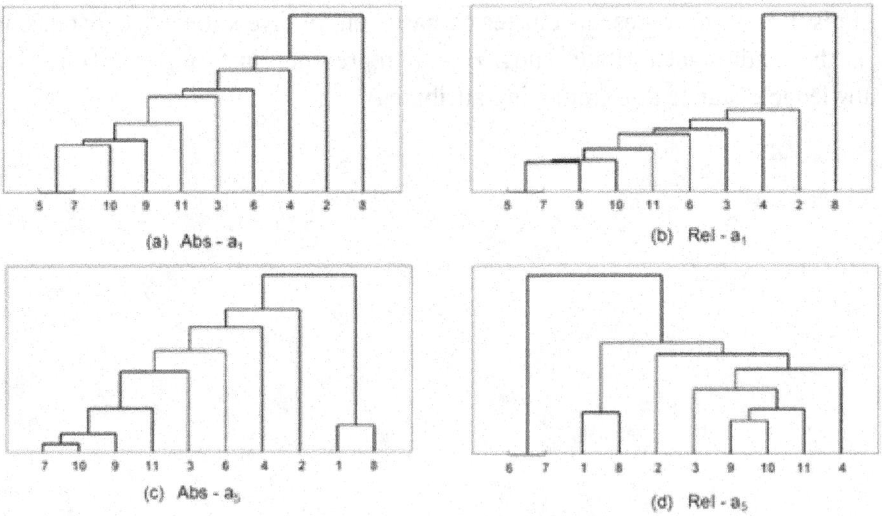

To provide a more intuitive description of the differences in clustering results, this paper computed the numerical differences between hierarchical clustering based on absolute knowledge distance and hierarchical clustering based on relative knowledge distance at different numbers of clusters. The results are shown in Figure 3 and Figure 4.

Figure 3. The clustering differences related to the number of classes between relative knowledge distance and absolute knowledge distance on the zoo dataset

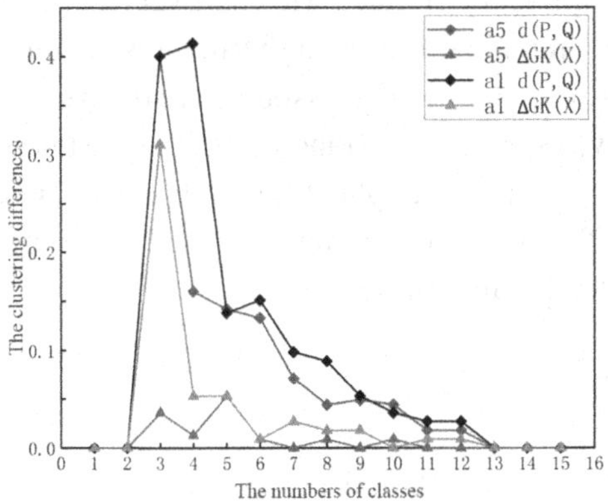

Figure 4. The clustering differences related to the number of classes between relative knowledge distance and absolute knowledge distance on the Las Vegas dataset

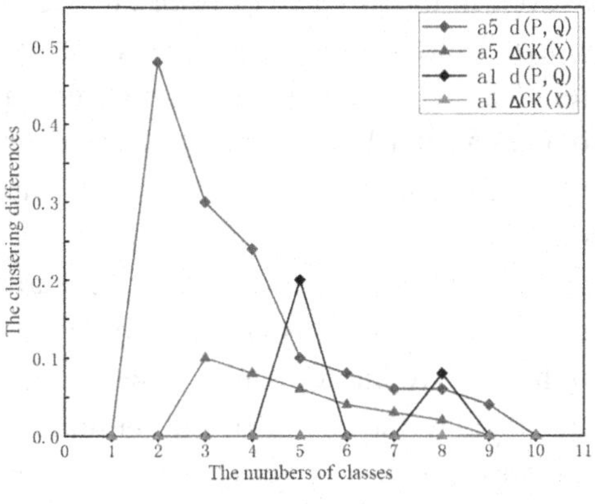

The experimental results above demonstrate significant differences between hierarchical clustering based on relative knowledge distance and hierarchical clustering based on absolute knowledge distance at different numbers of clusters. Specifically:

1. When the same attribute is used as a conditional attribute, hierarchical clustering structures based on relative knowledge distance and absolute knowledge distance are different.
2. When different attributes are used as conditional attributes, the differences in hierarchical clustering structures based on relative knowledge distance and absolute knowledge distance are distinct.
3. Under different numbers of categories and varying conditional attributes, the differences in hierarchical clustering structures based on relative knowledge distance and absolute knowledge distance are diverse.

Therefore, relative knowledge distance and absolute knowledge distance exhibit apparent differences in practical applications and possess richer information characteristics. They can effectively model the structural differences in human cognitive perspectives on understanding things.

Data Experiments

Feature selection is an important data preprocessing method aimed at selecting a subset of relevant features from the feature set of a dataset for a given learning task. During the feature selection process, the presence or absence of prior knowledge can lead to different subsets of selected features. For instance, consider a cubic object with features such as length l, width w, base area S, height h, density ρ, and color c. In the context of a feature selection task aimed at describing the mass of the cubic object, if prior knowledge suggests focusing on feature S, the selected feature subset might be S, h, ρ. However, in the absence of prior knowledge, the selected feature subset could be l, w, h, ρ. Therefore, it is essential to analyze the impact of prior knowledge on different feature selection outcomes based on various mechanisms.

This section introduces a filter-based feature selection method, utilizing relative knowledge distance as the evaluation function. The algorithm's solving approach is outlined as follows:

During the subset search process, following a forward search strategy, each feature in the feature set $\{a_1, a_2 \cdots a_m\}$ is considered as a candidate single-feature subset. According to the relative knowledge distance defined in Definition 3, each feature is sequentially added to the candidate subset until the stopping criteria are met. In the subset evaluation process, features in the candidate subset with a relative knowledge distance of 0 concerning the original system knowledge R are excluded. The final result is the feature subset of the system.

Algorithm 1: Feature Selection Algorithm Based on Relative Knowledge Distance

```
Input: Information system S=(U,A,V,f), Initial knowledge
state R
Output: feature subset I
Step 1: F=∅, I=∅,
For ∀a∈A, If D(A\{a},A)≠0
Then F=F∪{a};
Step 2: Set I'=F.
Step 3: If D(I',A|R)=0, then go to Step 7; otherwise, pro-
ceed to Step 4.
Step 4: ∀a∈A\I', calculate D(I'∪{a},A|R) and select the at-
tribute a' that minimizes D(I'∪{a},A|R).
Step 5: I'=I'∪{a'}
Step 6: While I'≠A, return to Step 3.
Step 7: For ∀a∈I', if D(I'\{a},A|R)=0, then I=I'\{a}
Step 8: Output the feature subset of the information system
IS. The algorithm concludes.
```

Experimental Analysis

This section compares the feature selection algorithm based on relative knowledge distance with the feature selection algorithm based on absolute knowledge distance. The purpose is to further illustrate the impact of different distance metrics on the cognitive differences in information systems. Six datasets from the UCI database are chosen for experimentation, and feature selection is performed using relative knowledge distance as the evaluation criterion. The partitioned knowledge induced by the features with the maximum clustering differences, as identified in the experiments in the last section, is used as prior or conditional knowledge. The experimental results are presented in Table 1.

The experimental results indicate that employing different knowledge distances for information systems leads to distinct feature selection outcomes. This discrepancy arises from the utilization of different measurement mechanisms. The alteration of the cognitive path within the system occurs due to treating certain features in the system as prior or conditional knowledge. As a result, different feature selection results are obtained.

Table 1. Feature selection results of two algorithms based on the absolute and relative knowledge distances with six datasets

Dataset	Number of Features	conditional features	Feature Selection based on Relative Knowledge Distance (Number of Features)	eature Selection based on Absolute Knowledge Distance (Number of Features)	Change in the Number of Features after Reduction
Dermatology	17	a_6	1,2,3,4,5,7,8,9,10,11,12,13,14,15,16,17(16)	1,2,3,4,5,7,8,10,11,12,13,16,17,15 (14)	↑14.3%
		a_7	1,2,3,4,5,6,8,9,10,11,12,13,14,15,16,17(16)	1,2,3,4,5,6,8,10,11,12,13,16,17,15 (14)	↑14.3%
Las Vegas	11	a_7	4,10,6 (3)	4,10,9 (3)	unchanged
		a_7	4,10,5 (3)	4,10,9 (3)	unchanged
Somerville	7	a_6	1,2,3,4,5,7 (6)	1,2,3,4,5,7 (6)	unchanged
Zoo	16	a_1	2,3,4,5,6,7,8,9,10,11,12,13,14,15,16 (15)	5,6,7,11,13,14,15,16,3 (9)	↑66.7%
CCBR	8	a_5	1,3,8,2 (4)	1,3,8,7 (4)	unchanged
		a_8	1,2,3,4,5,6,7 (7)	1,3,4,6,5 (5)	↑40.0%
Divorce	22	a_{11}	3,9,19,20,21,22,6 (7)	2,3,9,19,20,21,22,16 (8)	↓12.5%

In addition, analyzing the changes in the number of features for the two feature selection algorithms, we can draw the following conclusions.

1. When prior features contribute favorably to describing the overall performance of the information system, enhancing the cognitive ability of the system, fewer features are needed to achieve the classification capability possessed by all features in the information system. Therefore, the number of features outputted by the proposed algorithm is less than the number of features selected by the comparative algorithm.
2. When the information content implied by prior features is limited, resulting in a weakened cognitive ability towards the information system, more features are required to characterize the system's classification capability. Consequently, the number of features outputted by the proposed algorithm exceeds the number of features selected by the comparative algorithm.
3. When prior features have no impact on describing the overall performance of the information system, maintaining the cognitive ability towards the information system, the number of features outputted by the proposed algorithm is equal to the number of features selected by the comparative algorithm.

CONCLUSION

Based on the perspective of knowledge as partitions, this chapter demonstrates that all knowledge in the universe forms a distance space. It explores some properties of knowledge distance within the knowledge space and introduces, from a novel angle, the concept of knowledge rough entropy in information systems using knowledge distance. This provides a new tool for studying knowledge measurement in information systems, facilitating a deeper analysis of the relationships between knowledge and the roughness of knowledge.

This chapter also explores the relative differences in knowledge space from a perspective of relative cognition. Specifically, it introduces the concept of relative knowledge distance, analyzes the cognitive characteristics associated with it, and, through attribute clustering experiments, illustrates the distinct structural properties of relative knowledge distance compared to absolute knowledge distance. Additionally, a feature selection algorithm based on relative knowledge distance is simulated and tested to mimic the characteristics of human conditional progressive cognition enhancement, preservation, and reduction. The main conclusions of this paper are as follows:

1. Relative knowledge distance reflects the relative dissimilarity between any two pieces of knowledge from different perspectives, highlighting the characteristics of human multi-granularity relative cognition.
2. Relative knowledge distance is more general than absolute knowledge distance. Under the premise of known prior knowledge or conditional cognition, relative knowledge distance can reduce the cognitive difficulty between two pieces of knowledge, aligning with general cognitive patterns.
3. Relative knowledge distance and absolute knowledge distance exhibit different topological structures. Due to differences in measurement mechanisms, they alter the cognitive paths in the system. This can provide effective references for human multi-perspective cognition.

This study further enriches the theory of uncertainty measurement in granular computing and offers a new perspective for characterizing the structure of real-world information systems. The application of relative knowledge distance in neighborhood systems, fuzzy information systems, and various decision-making systems will be the focus of our future research.

DATA AVAILABILITY STATEMENT

The data sets generated during and analyzed during the current study are available in the UCI repository, http://archive.ics.uci.edu/ml/index.php.

ACKNOWLEDGMENT

The chapter was supported by grants from the National Natural Science Foundation of China (61703363), the Open Project Foundation of Intelligent Information Processing Key Laboratory of Shanxi Province (No. CICIP2022002), and the Special Fund for Science and Technology Innovation Teams of Yuncheng University.

REFERENCES

Chen, Y. M., Qin, N., Li, W., & Xu, F. (2019). Granule structures, distances and measures in neighborhood systems. *Knowledge-Based Systems*, 165, 268–281. 10.1016/j.knosys.2018.11.032

Cheng, Y., Miao, D. Q., & Feng, Q. R. (2007). Granular computation based on fuzzy rough sets. *Computer Science*, 7, 142–145.

Dai, J. H., & Tian, H. W. (2013). Entropy measures and granularity measures for set-valued information systems. *Information Sciences*, 240, 72–82. 10.1016/j.ins.2013.03.045

Dai, J. H., Xu, Q., Wang, W. T., & Tian, H. W. (2012). Conditional entropy for incomplete decision systems and its application in data mining. *International Journal of General Systems*, 41(7), 713–728. 10.1080/03081079.2012.685471

De Baets, B., De Meyer, H., & Naessens, H. (2001). A class of rational cardinality-based similarity measures. *Journal of Computational and Applied Mathematics*, 132(1), 51–69. 10.1016/S0377-0427(00)00596-3

Li, S., Yang, J., Wang, G. Y., & Xu, T. (2021). Multi-granularity distance measure for interval-valued intuitionistic fuzzy concepts. *Information Sciences*, 570, 599–622. 10.1016/j.ins.2021.05.003

Li, Z. W., Liu, X. F., Dai, J. H., Chen, J., & Fujita, H. (2020). Measures of uncertainty based on Gaussian kernel for a fully fuzzy information system. *Knowledge-Based Systems*, 196, 105791. 10.1016/j.knosys.2020.105791

Liang, J. Y., Chin, K. S., Dang, C. Y., & Yam, R. C. M. (2002). A new method for measuring uncertainty and fuzziness in rough set theory. *International Journal of General Systems*, 31(4), 331–342. 10.1080/0308107021000013635

Liang, J. Y., Li, R., & Qian, Y. H. (2012). Distance: A more comprehensible perspective for measures in rough set theory. *Knowledge-Based Systems*, 27, 126–136. 10.1016/j.knosys.2011.11.003

Liu, S. H., Deng, L., & Gao, H. Y. (2022). *Relative entropy-based similarity for patterns in graph data. Wireless Communications and Mobile Computing.* 10.1155/2022/7490656

Qian, Y. H., Cheng, H. H., Wang, J. T., Liang, J., Pedrycz, W., & Dang, C. (2017). Grouping granular structures in human granulation intelligence. *Information Sciences*, 382-383, 150–169. 10.1016/j.ins.2016.11.024

Qian, Y. H., Li, Y. B., Liang, J. Y., Lin, G., & Dang, C. (2015). Fuzzy granular structure distance. *IEEE Transactions on Fuzzy Systems*, 23(6), 2245–2259. 10.1109/TFUZZ.2015.2417893

Qian, Y. H., Liang, J. Y., & Dang, C. Y. (2009). Knowledge structure, knowledge granulation and knowledge distance in a knowledge base. *International Journal of Approximate Reasoning*, 50(1), 174–188. 10.1016/j.ijar.2008.08.004

Qian, Y. H., Liang, J. Y., Dang, C. Y., Wang, F., & Xu, W. (2007). Knowledge distance in information systems. *Journal of Systems Science and Systems Engineering*, 16(4), 434–449. 10.1007/s11518-007-5059-1

Ren, X. G., Li, D. Y., & Zhai, Y. H. (2023). Research on Mixed Decision Implications Based on Formal Concept Analysis. *International Journal of Cognitive Computing in Engineering*.

Song, Y. S., Zhang, J., & Zhang, C. (2022). A survey of large-scale graph-based semi-supervised classification algorithms. *International Journal of Cognitive Computing in Engineering*, 3, 188–198. 10.1016/j.ijcce.2022.10.002

Tan, A. H., Shi, S. W., Wu, W. Z., Li, J., & Pedrycz, W. (2022). Granularity and entropy of intuitionistic fuzzy information and their applications. *IEEE Transactions on Cybernetics*, 52(1), 192–204. 10.1109/TCYB.2020.297337932142467

Tang, X. Q., Zhu, P., & Cheng, J. X. (2008). Study on fuzzy granular space based on normalized equicrural metric. *Computer Science*, 4, 142–145.

Wang, B. L., & Liang, J. Y. (2007). Knowledge distance and rough entropy in information systems. *Computer Science*, 34, 151–155.

Xu, F., Zhang, L., & Wang, L. W. (2004). The approach of the fuzzy granular computing based on the theory of quotient space. *Pattern Recognition and Artificial Intelligence*, 66(4), 424–429.

Yang, J., Luo, T., & Zhao, F. (2021). *Fuzzy knowledge distance with three-layer perspectives in neighborhood system. Mathematical Problems in Engineering.* 10.1155/2021/9977488

Yang, J., Qin, X. D., Wang, G. Y., Zhang, X. X., & Wang, B. L. (2022). Relative Knowledge Distance Measure of Intuitionistic Fuzzy Concept. *Electronics (Basel)*, 11(20), 3373. 10.3390/electronics11203373

Yang, J., Wang, G. Y., & Zhang, Q. H. (2018). Knowledge distance measure in multigranulation spaces of fuzzy equivalence relations. *Information Sciences*, 448-449, 18–35. 10.1016/j.ins.2018.03.026

Yang, J., Wang, G. Y., Zhang, Q. H., & Wang, H. (2020). Knowledge distance measure for the multigranularity rough approximations of a fuzzy concept. *IEEE Transactions on Fuzzy Systems*, 28(4), 706–717. 10.1109/TFUZZ.2019.2914622

Yang, X. B., Qian, Y. H., & Yang, J. Y. (2013). On characterizing hierarchies of granulation structures via distances. *Fundamenta Informaticae*, 123(3), 365–380. 10.3233/FI-2012-816

Yao, J. T., Vasilakos, A. V., & Pedrycz, W. (2013). Granular computing: Perspectives and challenges. *IEEE Transactions on Cybernetics*, 43(6), 1977–1989. 10.1109/TSMCC.2012.223664823757594

Zadeh, L. A. (1996). Fuzzy logic=computing with words. *IEEE Transactions on Fuzzy Systems*, 4(2), 103–111. 10.1109/91.493904

Zhan, T. (2023). Granular-based state estimation for nonlinear fractional control systems and its circuit cognitive application. *International Journal of Cognitive Computing in Engineering*, 4, 1–5. 10.1016/j.ijcce.2022.12.001

Zhang, C., Li, D., & Liang, J. (2020). Multi-granularity three-way decisions with adjustable hesitant fuzzy linguistic multigranulation decision-theoretic rough sets over two universes. *Information Sciences*, 507, 665–683. 10.1016/j.ins.2019.01.033

Zhang, C., & Zhang, J. J. (2022). *Three-way group decisions with incomplete spherical fuzzy information for treating Parkinson's disease using IoMT devices. Wireless Communications and Mobile Computing.*

Zhang, L., & Zhang, B. (2003). Theory of fuzzy quotient space (methods of fuzzy granular computing). *Journal of Software*, 14(4), 770–776.

Zhao, X. R., & Yao, Y. Y. (2019). Three-way fuzzy partitions defined by shadowed sets. *Information Sciences*, 497, 23–37. 10.1016/j.ins.2019.05.022

Chapter 9
Feasibility Evaluation of Highwall Mining in Open-Pit Coal Mine Based on Variable Weight Fuzzy Theory

Dong Song
China Coal Research Institute, China

Ting Li
The National University of Malaysia, Malaysia

Yuanlong Zhao
CCIC London Co., Ltd., UK

ABSTRACT

The operation of highwall mining involves employing a CHM to extract coal from residual seams and transport it outside the mine via a continuous belt system. This study proposes a mathematical framework to assess highwall mining feasibility, synthesizing numerous global engineering cases and examining diverse technical aspects, including geological deposits, mining techniques. This framework integrates AHP, FCE, and VWT, encompassing 20 tertiary sub-indicators with associated characteristic values. Results show that the JZT mine scores a high feasibility membership degree of 0.7113, while the GC mine scores 0.3304. These findings are consistent with on-site applications, validating the model's effectiveness in delineating performance and membership degree of each indicator across diverse case studies. By quantitatively assessing the feasibility of highwall mining technology under varying

DOI: 10.4018/979-8-3693-4292-3.ch009

technical conditions of open-pit coal mines, this model offers scientific guidance for coal mining enterprises considering the introduction of CHM for highwall mining operations in this environment.

INTRODUCTION

In China, coal remains a primary energy source, with over 420 open-pit coal mines producing approximately 950 million tons annually, positioning open-pit mining as a pivotal method for coal extraction (Yang et al., 2010). However, conventional mining techniques and safety considerations often leave substantial coal reserves unextracted post open-pit mining. This leads to the reburial and subsequent wastage of these coal seams under backfill material (Wang et al., 2019 & Chen et al., 2013). Highwall mining, utilizing the Continuous Highwall Miner (CHM), addresses this issue by extracting residual coal from highwall seams. This method emphasizes slope stability and controls the overburden layer through the strategic placement of support coal pillars between mining roadways. A significant advantage of highwall mining is its remote operation capability, eliminating the need for on-site personnel presence in the mining area. This approach is characterized by its intelligent design, streamlined operation, high production efficiency, and low infrastructure investment requirements. Globally, highwall mining has been extensively adopted and advanced in countries like the United States, Australia, and India. Its widespread application attests to its status as a safe, efficient, economical, and environmentally sustainable method for highwall coal extraction. These attributes make highwall mining a compelling solution for maximizing coal recovery from open-pit mines, thus reducing resource wastage and enhancing overall mining efficiency (Shen et al., 2001, Shimada et al., 2013 & Liu et al., 2012).

International statistics reveal that the maximum depth achieved by highwall mining technology abroad is 500 meters, with the highest recorded monthly output being 124,000 tons. In the United States, highwall mining contributes approximately 4% to the total annual coal production (Boeut et al., 2017, Zipf et al., 2004 & Tian et al., 2023). However, the implementation of highwall mining technology is not without challenges. Variations in mine conditions have led to incidents of platform instability, landslides, and significant roof collapses.Case studies emphasize that the success of highwall mining in open-pit mining areas hinges on geological conditions, mining techniques, and other contextual factors (Elmouttie et al., 2017, Sasaoka et al., 2016 & Prakash et al., 2015). In instances of mismatched conditions, highwall mining can result in equipment being buried under collapsed coal-rock masses, rendering it irretrievable and posing serious risks to slope stability. In China, the adoption of highwall mining technology in open-pit coal mines is still nascent, and decisions regarding its use often rely on empirical judgments based on engineering analogies.To address the need for highwall coal recovery in China's numerous open-pit mines, it is crucial to conduct comprehensive feasibility studies on highwall mining technology. Research conducted by Luo et al. (Luo et al., 2022) on the Hequ Open-Pit Coal Mine, utilizing the limit equilibrium method and finite element strength reduction method, examined slope stability under various highwall mining scenarios and assessed potential economic benefits. Similarly, Wang et al. (Wang et al., 2022) analyzed slope stability coefficients in a Xinjiang open-pit mine under different highwall mining technologies.

The current body of research, while focusing on the safety and economic feasibility of highwall mining in specific mines, lacks a general and comprehensive approach to assess the technology's feasibility. This limitation highlights the necessity for more thorough research and the development of methodologies that can effectively evaluate the feasibility of highwall mining under the varied geological and operational conditions present in China's open-pit coal mines. To bridge this gap, recent studies have proposed innovative approaches. One such method involves the use of the Analytic Hierarchy Process-Fuzzy Comprehensive Evaluation (AHP-FCE) model. This model hierarchically and indexically analyzes the factors influencing the application of highwall mining technology, converting these factors into weighted values to determine their relevance and importance (Li et al., 2023, Dong et al., 2020 & Xiao et al., 2023). This approach offers a novel and practical solution for evaluating the feasibility of highwall mining technology. Additionally, the application of fuzzy mathematics in coal mine production evaluation has seen a significant rise in recent years. For instance, Duan et al. (Duan et al., 2022) employed the AHP-TOPSIS method, selecting nine indicators from economic, technological, and safety aspects to establish a hierarchical evaluation system. They applied this method to assess the optimal steep slope mining plan in Anjialing open-pit mine. Similarly, Ma et al. (Ma et al., 2023 & Ma, J., 2021) developed a multi-factor feasibility evaluation index system based on geological structure, coal seam occurrence, roadway characteristics, and mining safety elements. They quantified the range of each index value using fuzzy mathematics, the analytic hierarchy process, and variable weight fuzzy theory to evaluate the adaptability of residual coal mining and bolter miner. Xiu et al. (Xiu et al., 2022) proposed an evaluation index for the adaptability of intelligent mining working faces, which included primary and secondary influencing factors such as geological conditions, mining technical conditions, key technical conditions, and management and security conditions. Furthermore, Yu et al. (Yu et al., 2019) created an evaluation model for the adaptability of intelligent integrated mining, focusing on mining efficiency and safety aspects, using the analytic hierarchy process. These studies demonstrate the potential of mathematical fuzzy evaluations in providing insightful and reliable assessments for highwall mining feasibility. However, it is evident that such evaluations specifically tailored to the field of open-pit coal highwall mining remain relatively scarce, signaling a clear opportunity for further exploration and development in this area.

The challenge in existing research lies in its inability to offer a universally applicable and comprehensive evaluation system for assessing the feasibility of highwall mining. Decisions based solely on engineering experience and analogies can lead to errors and mismatches between equipment and mine conditions. To address this, the authors have synthesized a wide array of global engineering applications, focusing on detailed technical characteristics such as mine occurrence conditions and mining processes. This has led to the proposition of a mathematical evaluation framework that integrates the Analytic Hierarchy Process (AHP), Fuzzy Comprehensive Evaluation (FCE), and Variable Weight Theory (VWT). This proposed system comprises four secondary indicators: geological deposit factors, mining technique factors, safety impact factors, and economic evaluation factors. Additionally, it defines and establishes 20 tertiary sub-indicators, along with their corresponding characteristic values. Through this framework, a judgment matrix is created to derive the weight vectors for these sub-indicators. The use of fuzzy mathematics membership functions facilitates the construction of a relationship matrix for the sub-indicators, leading to a comprehensive evaluation through a two-level judgment process. To validate this model, the authors applied it to two engineering cases, testing its accuracy. The results demonstrate that this comprehensive evaluation model effectively corresponds with different commentary subsets and aligns well with actual field practice. This alignment indicates that the model offers a reliable, preliminary quantitative analysis method for decision-making regarding the adoption of highwall mining equipment in open-pit coal mines for highwall coal recovery. By providing a structured and quantifiable approach, this model significantly aids in making informed decisions about employing highwall mining technology, potentially leading to more efficient and safer mining operations.

PRELIMINARIES

Technical Characteristics of Highwall Mining

The Continuous Highwall Miner (CHM) system, engineered by Shanxi Tiandi Coal Machinery Co., Ltd., encompasses a suite of advanced technological components. This system primarily consists of a highwall miner, an integrated multi-unit conveyor belt system, a stepping walking platform, a comprehensive ventilation and dust extraction system, a mobile unloading unit, a remote control interface, and sophisticated navigation and posture monitoring systems. In the context of highwall mining operations, a critical aspect of the process involves maintaining the structural integrity of overlying rock strata. This is achieved by strategically reserving coal pillars within the mining roadways, which plays a vital role in stabilizing the slope (Ding et al., 2021). Operational personnel, in their daily tasks, are not required to physically enter the mining roadways. Instead, operations are centrally managed from a control room located externally to the roadway. This setup relies heavily on video acquisition devices positioned at the forefront of the continuous highwall miner, facilitating the coal cutting process. The arrangement results in the creation of mining roadways aligned perpendicular to the slope's orientation. The continuous highwall miner is equipped with an inertial navigation system, which enables it to advance a distance of 12.5 meters in each operational phase. During this process, it sequentially integrates with the multi-unit conveyor belt system, extending until the maximum designated mining depth is achieved. Upon the completion of mining activities, the stepping walking platform retracts the highwall miner and the conveyor system. The conveyor system is then sequentially disassembled, preparing all equipment for extraction from the current mining roadway. Subsequently, the equipment is relocated to the next designated mining roadway by the stepping walking platform, thus initiating the subsequent cycle of mining operations. This systematic approach underscores the integration of sophisticated engineering and operational efficiency in the realm of highwall mining.

Figure 1. Continuous highwall miner system (CHM) in open-pit coal mines: 1) continuous highwall miner, 2) multi-unit continuous conveyor belt system, 3) stepping walking platform, 4) pull-out ventilation and dust removal system, 5) mobile unloading section

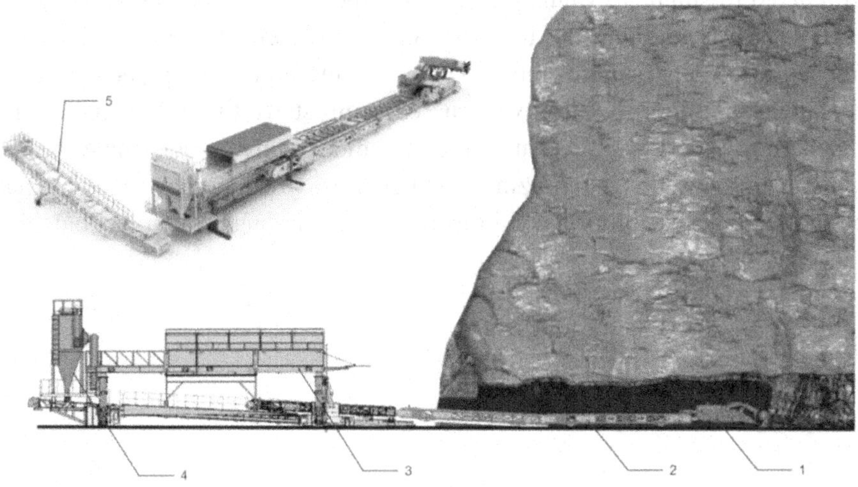

Evaluation Method Selection

The Analytic Hierarchy Process (AHP) is a decision-making methodology that synergizes qualitative and quantitative elements. It employs systems thinking to deconstruct complex problems into hierarchies, encompassing various levels and related influencing factors. This method arranges these factors into an orderly, recursive hierarchical structure (Nezarat et al., 2015). AHP involves pairwise comparisons between factors at each level, determining their relative weights in relation to higher-level factors. This process culminates in a judgment matrix, consisting of quantitative scale values that ultimately facilitate the derivation of a final importance ranking of the lower-level evaluation factors concerning the overall objective.

In contrast, Fuzzy Comprehensive Evaluation (FCE) is a method employed for evaluating entities influenced by multiple, often fuzzy, factors. These factors are characteristically ambiguous and challenging to quantify directly.

When assessing the feasibility of highwall mining in open-pit coal mines, the multitude of influencing factors makes a straightforward quantitative evaluation impractical. AHP, while robust, encounters limitations in addressing problems with numerous lower-level factors. The method becomes cumbersome with an increase in influencing factors, and maintaining consistency in evaluations becomes challenging. Conversely, FCE lacks a systematic approach to ascertain the importance weights of evaluation factors (Fayaz et al., 2017). The integration of AHP and FCE leverages the strengths of both methods. This hybrid approach involves constructing a multi-level model using AHP, which is then complemented by forming a fuzzy judgment matrix based on evaluation levels and influencing factors. FCE is subsequently applied to calculate the membership degree of each factor across various levels, leading to the determination of the final membership under different scenarios.

Compared to singular evaluation methods, the AHP-FCE combination is less susceptible to variations in the index system, coefficient values, and evaluation techniques, resulting in a more precise outcome. Thus, for the comprehensive evaluation of highwall mining feasibility discussed in this study, the authors recommend amalgamating AHP and FCE. This integrated model aims to determine the most relevant review subset by maximizing membership degree, thereby achieving a nuanced and accurate feasibility evaluation for highwall mining in open-pit coal mines.

FEASIBILITY EVALUATION MODEL

Construction of Feasibility Evaluation Model

1. Construction of Evaluation Index System Based on AHP

In conducting a comprehensive assessment of highwall mining applications both domestically and internationally, the authors have employed field research and systematic literature review methodologies. This investigation has led to the formulation of an extensive evaluation index system for determining the feasibility of highwall mining, anchored in the principles of the Analytic Hierarchy Process (AHP).The comprehensive evaluation system is divided into three levels: Level A (objective layer), Level B (index layer), and Level C (sub-index layer). Level A is the feasibility evaluation purpose of highwall mining in open-pit coal mine. The Level B indicators mainly include four aspects: geological deposit factors (B_1), mining technique factors (B_2), safety impact factors (B_3), and economic evaluation factors (B_4). Each type of sub-index in Level C is the specification of the corresponding B-level indicators, totaling 20 items. The index system for the feasibility evaluation of highwall mining in open-pit coal is shown in Figure 2.

Figure 2. Feasibility evaluation index system for highwall mining in open-pit coal mine

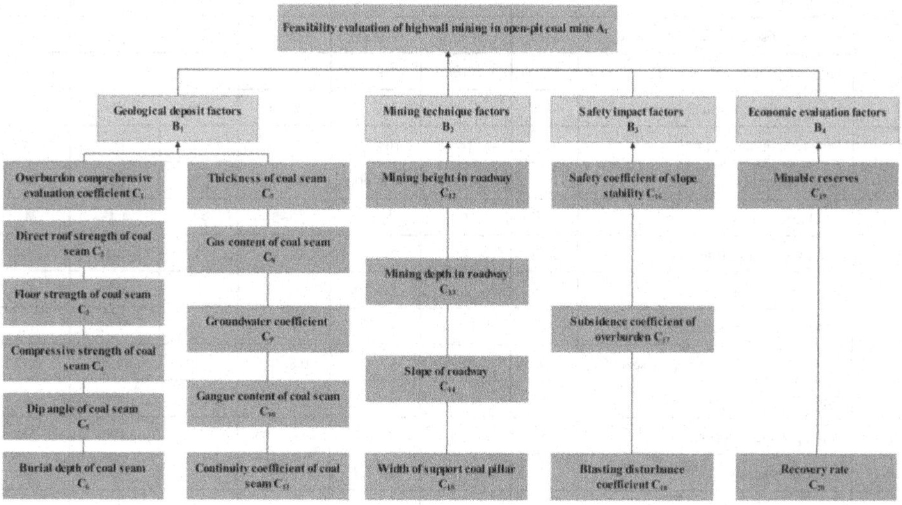

2. Quantification of Evaluation Indicators

The evaluation index system is primarily designed to assess the feasibility of highwall mining in open-pit coal mines. Given the inherent fuzziness of the evaluation outcomes, the system categorizes the feasibility into four distinct levels to accommodate varying degrees of suitability. These levels form a comment set, denoted as V={infeasible, basically feasible, relatively feasible, and highly feasible}.

As can be seen from Figure 2, the feasibility evaluation index system for highwall mining is divided into three levels: A, B and C. B level includes four influencing factors, specifically geological deposit factors (B_1), mining technique factors (B_2), safety impact factors (B_3), and economic evaluation factors (B_4). Among them, the geological deposit factors (B_1) include a total of 11 evaluation elements: C_1–C_{11}. The mining technique factors (B_2) include a total of 4 evaluation elements: C_{12}–C_{15}. the safety impact factors (B_3) mainly include 3 evaluation elements: C_{16}–C_{18}, and the economic evaluation factors (B_4) mainly include 2 evaluation elements: C_{19}–C_{20}. The quantified values of C-layer indicators in different comment sets are shown in Table 1 below.

Table 1. Quantitative values of C-layer indicators in different comment sets

NO.	Name of Evaluation Element	Unit	Infeasible	Basically Feasible	Relatively Feasible	Highly Feasible	JZT Coal Mine	GC Coal Mine
1	Overlying rock comprehensive evaluation coefficient C_1	Constant	>0.8	0.5~0.8	0.3~0.5	<0.3	0.47	0.78
2	Direct roof strength of coal seam C_2	MPa	<15	15~25	25~35	>35	35.8	16.2
3	Floor strength of coal seam C_3	MPa	<10	10~20	20~30	>30	25.6	14.1
4	Compressive strength of coal seam C_4	MPa	<10	10~20	20~30	>30	10.6	4.3
5	Dip angle of coal seam C_5	°	>16°	10°~16°	4°~10°	<4°	5	3
6	Burial depth of coal seam C_6	m	≥600	400~600	250~400	≤250	170	40
7	Thickness of coal seam C_7	m	≤1.5	1.5~3	3~5	≥5	4.43	4
8	Gas content of coal seam C_8	m^3/t	>10	5~10	0.1~5	<0.1	0.09	0.05
9	Groundwater coefficient C_9	m^3/t	>20	10~20	1~10	<1	0.7	0.3
10	Gangue content of coal seam C_{10}	%	>30	15~30	5~15	<5	11.62	16.3
11	Continuity coefficient of coal seam C_{11}	Constant	<0.7	0.7~0.8	0.8~0.9	>0.9	0.88	0.75
12	Mining height in roadway C_{12}	m	<1.5	1.5~3	3~5	>5	4.4	4
13	Mining depth in roadway C_{13}	m	>500	400~500	300~400	<300	150	200
14	Slope of roadway C_{14}	°	< -15°	-15°~-7°	-7°~-4°	>-4°	-2	-1.5
15	Width of support coal pillar C_{15}	m	<3	3~4	4~5	>5	4.1	4.36
16	Safety coefficient of slope stability C_{16}	Constant	<1.1	1.1~1.2	1.2~1.3	>1.3	1.259	1.3
17	Subsidence coefficient of overburden C_{17}	Constant	<0.2	0.2~0.5	0.5~0.8	>0.8	0.6	0.35

continued on following page

Table 1. Continued

NO.	Name of Evaluation Element	Unit	Infeasible	Basically Feasible	Relatively Feasible	Highly Feasible	JZT Coal Mine	GC Coal Mine
18	Blasting disturbance coefficient C_{18}	Constant	˃0.85	0.5~0.85	0.25~0.5	<0.25	0.2	0.33
19	Minable reserves C_{19}	10kt	<50	50~80	80~100	˃100	459.55	215.3
20	Recovery rate C_{20}	%	≥65	55~65	45~55	≤45	42.25%	44.5%

(1) Geological deposit factors.

The evaluation indicators for geological deposit factors (B_1) are: overlying rock comprehensive evaluation coefficient (C_1), direct roof strength of coal seam (C_2), floor strength of coal seam (C_3), compressive strength of coal seam (C_4), dip angle of coal seam (C_5), burial depth of coal seam (C_6), thickness of coal seam (C_7), gas content of coal seam (C_8), groundwater coefficient (C_9), gangue content of coal seam (C_{10}), continuity coefficient of coal seam (C_{11}).

The overlying rock comprehensive evaluation coefficient (C_1) reflects the soft and hard degree of the top plate coal wall in the highwall mining field. The formula for calculating the overlying rock comprehensive evaluation coefficient is as follows (Peng, 2017):

$$P = \frac{\sum_{1}^{n} m_i Q_i}{\sum_{1}^{n} m_i} \tag{1}$$

where m_i represents the thickness of the stratified overburden; Q_i is the lithological evaluation coefficient of the stratified overburden, with data primarily obtained by calculating the columnar diagram of the mining area's bottom layer.

(2) Mining technique factors

The evaluation indicators for mining technique factors (B_2) are: mining height in roadway (C_{12}), mining depth in roadway (C_{13}), slope of roadway (C_{14}), width of support coal pillar (C_{15}). Numerous studies have shown that mining depth, the width of the support coal pillar, and other mining technological elements have a significant impact on the stability of the highwall mining slope (Ross et al., 2019, Porathur et al., 2013 & Perry et al., 2015).

(3) Safety impact factors

The evaluation indicators for safety impact factors (B_3) are: safety coefficient of slope stability (C_{16}), subsidence coefficient of overburden (C_{17}), blasting disturbance coefficient (C_{18}). According to the "Open-Pit Coal Industry Design Standard" GB50197-2015, the recommended safety coefficient of slope stability (C_{16}) is ≥1.20. The subsidence coefficient of overburden (C_{17}) refers to the ratio of rock layer subsidence caused by overburden pressure to overburden thickness. Considering the surface geological features, the higher the allowable subsidence coefficient of overburden, the higher the feasibility of highwall mining. As the blasting shock wave acts on the support coal pillar in the open-pit mining area, the instantaneous dynamic stress response generated will weaken the strength of the support coal pillar, thereby endangering the safety of the slope, hence the use of the blasting disturbance coefficient (C_{18}) to describe the disturbance of the blasting seismic waves to highwall mining (Jiang et al., 2023).

(4) Economic evaluation factors

The evaluation indicators for economic evaluation factors (B_4) are: minable reserves (C_{19}) and recovery rate (C_{20}). When the coal seam reserves are low, choosing highwall mining technology does not make economic sense. Generally, highwall mining processes need to reserve support coal pillars and permanent isolation coal pillars to ensure slope safety. The larger the recovery rate, the better the economic benefits. The formula for calculating the recovery rate is as follows (Yu., 2018):

$$Q = \left[\frac{L_1 \times (n+1)}{(L_1 \times (n+1) + L_2 \times n + L_3)}\right] \times S \qquad (2)$$

where Q represents the highwall recovery rate, L_1 represents the mining width, L_2 represents the width of the support coal pillar, L_3 represents the width of the permanent isolation coal pillar, n represents the number of support coal pillar, S represents the loss of coal seam thickness due to mining with the highwall miner.

3. Determination of Membership Function

In fuzzy mathematics, the membership function is a key concept used to describe how each element in a fuzzy set is mapped to a membership degree within the range of [0,1]. This function characterizes the degree to which the values of evaluation factors belong to a fuzzy set, providing a quantitative measure of their fuzziness. When applying this concept in practical scenarios, it's often necessary to transform the raw values of various indicators into membership degrees using the membership function. This transformation standardizes the values of different dimensions to a common scale within the [0,1] interval. Consequently, the sum of the membership degrees of each indicator across different comment sets equals 1, ensuring a consistent evaluation framework. There are several types of fuzzy distributions used to represent different tendencies in the data: Small-Type Fuzzy Distribution: Suitable for fuzzy sets that tend toward smaller values. Large-Type Fuzzy Distribution: Appropriate for fuzzy sets inclined towards larger values. Medium-Type Fuzzy Distribution: Ideal for representing fuzzy sets with a central or medium value tendency. Membership functions can be categorized into two main types based on their curve shape: linear and non-linear. Linear functions include simple geometric shapes like rectangles, triangles, and trapezoids. Non-linear functions encompass more complex curves such as k-order parabolas, T-distributions, normal distributions, and Cauchy distributions (Chen et al., 2023).

In this article, the trapezoidal distribution is employed for its simplicity and ease of calculation. The mathematical expression of its membership function is detailed in the text, and its graphical representation is illustrated in Figure 3. The trapezoidal distribution is particularly useful for scenarios where the membership function needs to represent ranges of values with varying degrees of membership, offering a flexible and straightforward approach to fuzzy evaluation.

(1) Small-type:

$$\underset{\sim}{A}(x)=\begin{cases} 1, & x \leq a \\ \frac{b-x}{b-a}, & a < x < b \\ 0, & x \geq b \end{cases} \tag{3}$$

(2) Medium-type:

$$\underset{\sim}{A}(x)=\begin{cases} \frac{x-a}{b-a}, & a < x < b \\ 1, & b \leq x \leq c \\ \frac{d-x}{d-c}, & c < x < d \\ 0, & x \geq d \end{cases} \tag{4}$$

(3) Large type:

$$\underset{\sim}{A}(x)=\begin{cases} 0, & x \leq a \\ \frac{x-a}{b-a}, & a < x < b \\ 1, & x \geq b \end{cases} \tag{5}$$

Figure 3. Membership function of trapezoidal distribution

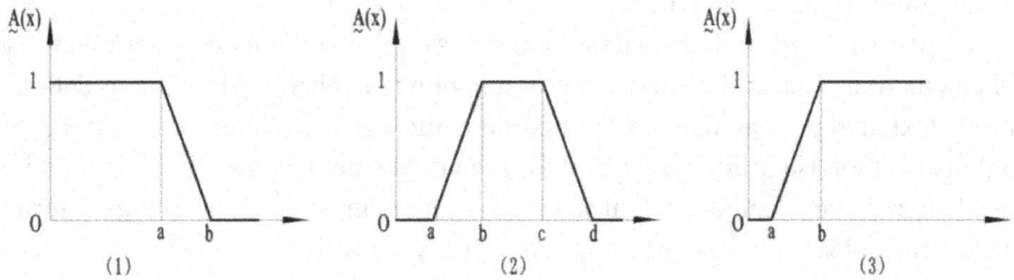

In the construction of membership functions for each indicator within the evaluation index system, the quantitative intervals of the C-level indicators, as outlined in Table 1, are taken into consideration. This approach incorporates empirical data from global highwall mining engineering practices, ensuring a practical and relevant application of these functions. For illustrative purposes, due to spatial constraints, only the membership function for the B_1 indicator (geological deposit factors) is detailed, as shown in Table 2. In this context, the trapezoidal membership function is employed. A notable aspect of using trapezoidal membership functions is the potential occurrence of a zero value for an indicator, which could impede the calculation process. To circumvent this issue, a commonly adopted method involves substituting a minimal value for zero in the calculations. This substitution ensures that the sum of the membership degrees across all indicators equals 1, maintaining the consistency of the fuzzy evaluation framework. In practice, this minimal value is often set to a small number such as 0.0001 (Chen et al., 2023 & Chen et al., 2022).

Table 2. Membership functions of each sub-indicator of geological occurrence elements

No.	Evaluation Index	Infeasible	Basically Feasible	Relatively Feasible	Highly Feasible
1	Overlying rock comprehensive evaluation coefficient C_1	$\left\{\begin{matrix} 0, x > 0.8 \\ \frac{0.8-x}{0.8-0.5}, 0.5 < x \le 0.8 \\ \frac{x-0.4}{0.5-0.4}, 0.4 \le x \le 0.5 \\ 0, x < 0.4 \end{matrix}\right\}$	$\left\{\begin{matrix} 0, x > 0.8 \\ \frac{0.8-x}{0.8-0.5}, 0.5 < x \le 0.8 \\ \frac{x-0.4}{0.5-0.4}, 0.4 \le x \le 0.5 \\ 0, x < 0.4 \end{matrix}\right\}$	$\left\{\begin{matrix} 0, x > 0.5 \\ \frac{0.5-x}{0.5-0.4}, 0.4 \le x \le 0.5 \\ \frac{x-0.3}{0.4-0.3}, 0.3 \le x < 0.4 \\ 0, x < 0.3 \end{matrix}\right\}$	$\left\{\begin{matrix} 0, x > 0.5 \\ \frac{0.5-x}{0.5-0.4}, 0.4 < x \le 0.5 \\ 1, x \le 0.4 \end{matrix}\right\}$
2	Direct roof strength of coal seam C_2	$\left\{\begin{matrix} 1, x < 15 \\ \frac{25-x}{25-15}, 15 \le x \le 25 \\ 0, x > 25 \end{matrix}\right\}$	$\left\{\begin{matrix} 0, x < 15 \\ \frac{x-15}{25-15}, 15 \le x < 25 \\ \frac{30-x}{30-25}, 25 \le x \le 30 \\ 0, x > 30 \end{matrix}\right\}$	$\left\{\begin{matrix} 0, x < 25 \\ \frac{x-25}{30-25}, 25 \le x < 30 \\ \frac{35-x}{35-30}, 30 \le x \le 35 \\ 0, x > 35 \end{matrix}\right\}$	$\left\{\begin{matrix} 0, x < 30 \\ \frac{x-30}{35-30}, 30 \le x \le 35 \\ 1, x > 35 \end{matrix}\right\}$
3	Floor strength of coal seam C_3	$\left\{\begin{matrix} 1, x < 10 \\ \frac{20-x}{20-10}, 10 \le x \le 20 \\ 0, x > 20 \end{matrix}\right\}$	$\left\{\begin{matrix} 0, x < 10 \\ \frac{x-10}{20-10}, 10 \le x < 20 \\ \frac{25-x}{25-20}, 20 \le x \le 25 \\ 0, x > 25 \end{matrix}\right\}$	$\left\{\begin{matrix} 0, x < 20 \\ \frac{x-20}{25-20}, 20 \le x < 25 \\ \frac{30-x}{30-25}, 25 \le x \le 30 \\ 0, x > 30 \end{matrix}\right\}$	$\left\{\begin{matrix} 0, x < 25 \\ \frac{x-25}{30-25}, 25 \le x \le 30 \\ 1, x > 30 \end{matrix}\right\}$
4	Compressive strength of coal seam C_4	$\left\{\begin{matrix} 1, x < 10 \\ \frac{20-x}{20-10}, 10 \le x \le 20 \\ 0, x > 20 \end{matrix}\right\}$	$\left\{\begin{matrix} 0, x < 10 \\ \frac{x-10}{20-10}, 10 \le x < 20 \\ \frac{25-x}{25-20}, 20 \le x \le 25 \\ 0, x > 25 \end{matrix}\right\}$	$\left\{\begin{matrix} 0, x < 20 \\ \frac{x-20}{25-20}, 20 \le x < 25 \\ \frac{30-x}{30-25}, 25 \le x \le 30 \\ 0, x > 30 \end{matrix}\right\}$	$\left\{\begin{matrix} 0, x < 25 \\ \frac{x-25}{30-25}, 25 \le x \le 30 \\ 1, x > 30 \end{matrix}\right\}$
5	Dip angle of coal seam C_5	$\left\{\begin{matrix} 1, x > 16 \\ \frac{x-10}{16-10}, 10 \le x \le 16 \\ 0, x < 10 \end{matrix}\right\}$	$\left\{\begin{matrix} 0, x > 16 \\ \frac{16-x}{16-10}, 10 < x \le 16 \\ \frac{x-7}{10-7}, 7 \le x \le 10 \\ 0, x < 7 \end{matrix}\right\}$	$\left\{\begin{matrix} 0, x > 10 \\ \frac{10-x}{10-7}, 7 < x \le 10 \\ \frac{x-4}{7-4}, 4 \le x \le 7 \\ 0, x < 4 \end{matrix}\right\}$	$\left\{\begin{matrix} 0, x > 7 \\ \frac{7-x}{7-4}, 4 < x \le 7 \\ 1, x \le 4 \end{matrix}\right\}$

continued on following page

Table 2. Continued

No.	Evaluation Index	Infeasible	Basically Feasible	Relatively Feasible	Highly Feasible
6	Burial depth of coal seam C_6	$\begin{cases} 1, x > 600 \\ \frac{x-400}{600-400}, 400 \le x \le 600 \\ 0, x < 400 \end{cases}$	$\begin{cases} 0, x > 600 \\ \frac{600-x}{600-400}, 400 < x \le 600 \\ \frac{x-400}{400-325}, 325 \le x \le 400 \\ 0, x < 325 \end{cases}$	$\begin{cases} 0, x > 400 \\ \frac{400-x}{400-325}, 325 < x \le 400 \\ \frac{x-250}{325-250}, 250 \le x \le 325 \\ 0, x < 250 \end{cases}$	$\begin{cases} 0, x > 325 \\ \frac{325-x}{325-250}, 250 \le x \le 325 \\ 1, x < 250 \end{cases}$
7	Thickness of coal seam C_7	$A_{B-A} = \begin{bmatrix} 1 & 5 & 1/3 & 7 \\ 1/5 & 1 & 1/5 & 3 \\ 3 & 5 & 1 & 7 \\ 1/7 & 1/3 & 1/7 & 1 \end{bmatrix}$	$A_{B-A} = \begin{bmatrix} 1 & 5 & 1/3 & 7 \\ 1/5 & 1 & 1/5 & 3 \\ 3 & 5 & 1 & 7 \\ 1/7 & 1/3 & 1/7 & 1 \end{bmatrix}$	$A_{B-A} = \begin{bmatrix} 1 & 5 & 1/3 & 7 \\ 1/5 & 1 & 1/5 & 3 \\ 3 & 5 & 1 & 7 \\ 1/7 & 1/3 & 1/7 & 1 \end{bmatrix}$	$A_{B-A} = \begin{bmatrix} 1 & 5 & 1/3 & 7 \\ 1/5 & 1 & 1/5 & 3 \\ 3 & 5 & 1 & 7 \\ 1/7 & 1/3 & 1/7 & 1 \end{bmatrix}$
8	Gas content of coal seam C_8	$A_{B-A} = \begin{bmatrix} 1 & 5 & 1/3 & 7 \\ 1/5 & 1 & 1/5 & 3 \\ 3 & 5 & 1 & 7 \\ 1/7 & 1/3 & 1/7 & 1 \end{bmatrix}$	$A_{B-A} = \begin{bmatrix} 1 & 5 & 1/3 & 7 \\ 1/5 & 1 & 1/5 & 3 \\ 3 & 5 & 1 & 7 \\ 1/7 & 1/3 & 1/7 & 1 \end{bmatrix}$	$A_{B-A} = \begin{bmatrix} 1 & 5 & 1/3 & 7 \\ 1/5 & 1 & 1/5 & 3 \\ 3 & 5 & 1 & 7 \\ 1/7 & 1/3 & 1/7 & 1 \end{bmatrix}$	$A_{B-A} = \begin{bmatrix} 1 & 5 & 1/3 & 7 \\ 1/5 & 1 & 1/5 & 3 \\ 3 & 5 & 1 & 7 \\ 1/7 & 1/3 & 1/7 & 1 \end{bmatrix}$
9	Groundwater coefficient C_9	$A_{B-A} = \begin{bmatrix} 1 & 5 & 1/3 & 7 \\ 1/5 & 1 & 1/5 & 3 \\ 3 & 5 & 1 & 7 \\ 1/7 & 1/3 & 1/7 & 1 \end{bmatrix}$	$A_{B-A} = \begin{bmatrix} 1 & 5 & 1/3 & 7 \\ 1/5 & 1 & 1/5 & 3 \\ 3 & 5 & 1 & 7 \\ 1/7 & 1/3 & 1/7 & 1 \end{bmatrix}$	$A_{B-A} = \begin{bmatrix} 1 & 5 & 1/3 & 7 \\ 1/5 & 1 & 1/5 & 3 \\ 3 & 5 & 1 & 7 \\ 1/7 & 1/3 & 1/7 & 1 \end{bmatrix}$	$A_{B-A} = \begin{bmatrix} 1 & 5 & 1/3 & 7 \\ 1/5 & 1 & 1/5 & 3 \\ 3 & 5 & 1 & 7 \\ 1/7 & 1/3 & 1/7 & 1 \end{bmatrix}$
10	Gangue content in coal seam C_{10}	$A_{B-A} = \begin{bmatrix} 1 & 5 & 1/3 & 7 \\ 1/5 & 1 & 1/5 & 3 \\ 3 & 5 & 1 & 7 \\ 1/7 & 1/3 & 1/7 & 1 \end{bmatrix}$	$A_{B-A} = \begin{bmatrix} 1 & 5 & 1/3 & 7 \\ 1/5 & 1 & 1/5 & 3 \\ 3 & 5 & 1 & 7 \\ 1/7 & 1/3 & 1/7 & 1 \end{bmatrix}$	$A_{B-A} = \begin{bmatrix} 1 & 5 & 1/3 & 7 \\ 1/5 & 1 & 1/5 & 3 \\ 3 & 5 & 1 & 7 \\ 1/7 & 1/3 & 1/7 & 1 \end{bmatrix}$	$A_{B-A} = \begin{bmatrix} 1 & 5 & 1/3 & 7 \\ 1/5 & 1 & 1/5 & 3 \\ 3 & 5 & 1 & 7 \\ 1/7 & 1/3 & 1/7 & 1 \end{bmatrix}$
11	Continuity coefficient of coal seam C_{11}	$A_{B-A} = \begin{bmatrix} 1 & 5 & 1/3 & 7 \\ 1/5 & 1 & 1/5 & 3 \\ 3 & 5 & 1 & 7 \\ 1/7 & 1/3 & 1/7 & 1 \end{bmatrix}$	$A_{B-A} = \begin{bmatrix} 1 & 5 & 1/3 & 7 \\ 1/5 & 1 & 1/5 & 3 \\ 3 & 5 & 1 & 7 \\ 1/7 & 1/3 & 1/7 & 1 \end{bmatrix}$	$A_{B-A} = \begin{bmatrix} 1 & 5 & 1/3 & 7 \\ 1/5 & 1 & 1/5 & 3 \\ 3 & 5 & 1 & 7 \\ 1/7 & 1/3 & 1/7 & 1 \end{bmatrix}$	$A_{B-A} = \begin{bmatrix} 1 & 5 & 1/3 & 7 \\ 1/5 & 1 & 1/5 & 3 \\ 3 & 5 & 1 & 7 \\ 1/7 & 1/3 & 1/7 & 1 \end{bmatrix}$

Determination of Weight Vector for Indicator Layer

1. Construction of the Judgment Matrix

In applying the Analytic Hierarchy Process (AHP), the authors have created judgment matrices to evaluate the relative importance of various indicators within the established evaluation system (as illustrated in Figure 2). To illustrate this process, let's consider the B_1 layer, which consists of geological deposit factors. The methodology involves organizing the 11 C-level indicators that fall under the B_1 category into a matrix format. These indicators are placed both in the first row and the first column of the matrix, forming an initial square matrix structure. Within this matrix, each element represents a pairwise comparison between two factors, assessing their relative importance to each other. The assignment of values within the matrix follows a specific scale of importance. Typically, this scale ranges from 1 to 9 and includes the reciprocals of these numbers. The scale values are chosen as follows:

$$\mathbf{A}_{\mathbf{B-A}} = \begin{bmatrix} 1 & 5 & 1/3 & 7 \\ 1/5 & 1 & 1/5 & 3 \\ 3 & 5 & 1 & 7 \\ 1/7 & 1/3 & 1/7 & 1 \end{bmatrix}$$

$$\mathbf{B}_{\mathbf{C-B_1}} = \begin{bmatrix} 1 & 3 & 5 & 5 & 3 & 5 & 5 & 3 & 3 & 7 & 2 \\ 1/3 & 1 & 3 & 4 & 1/3 & 3 & 4 & 1/3 & 1/3 & 3 & 1/3 \\ 1/5 & 1/3 & 1 & 1/3 & 1/5 & 1/3 & 2 & 1/5 & 1/3 & 2 & 1/5 \\ 1/5 & 1/4 & 3 & 1 & 1/5 & 3 & 5 & 1/3 & 1/3 & 5 & 1/3 \\ 1/3 & 3 & 5 & 5 & 1 & 3 & 5 & 1/2 & 1/3 & 5 & 2 \\ 1/5 & 1/3 & 3 & 1/3 & 1/3 & 1 & 3 & 1/3 & 1/2 & 3 & 1/3 \\ 1/5 & 1/4 & 1/2 & 1/5 & 1/5 & 1/3 & 1 & 1/3 & 1/5 & 2 & 1/3 \\ 1/3 & 3 & 5 & 3 & 2 & 3 & 3 & 1 & 2 & 5 & 1 \\ 1/5 & 3 & 3 & 3 & 3 & 2 & 5 & 1/2 & 1 & 5 & 1 \\ 1/7 & 1/3 & 1/2 & 1/5 & 1/5 & 1/3 & 1/2 & 1/5 & 1/5 & 1 & 1/5 \\ 1/2 & 3 & 5 & 3 & 1/2 & 3 & 3 & 1 & 1 & 5 & 1 \end{bmatrix}$$

$$\mathbf{B}_{\mathbf{C-B_2}} = \begin{bmatrix} 1 & 3 & 5 & 1/3 \\ 1/3 & 1 & 2 & 1/3 \\ 1/5 & 1/2 & 1 & 1/5 \\ 3 & 3 & 5 & 1 \end{bmatrix}$$

$$\mathbf{B}_{C-B_3} = \begin{bmatrix} 1 & 5 & 1 \\ 1/5 & 1 & 3 \\ 1 & 1/3 & 1 \end{bmatrix}$$

$$\mathbf{B}_{C-B_4} = \begin{bmatrix} 1 & 3 \\ 1/3 & 1 \end{bmatrix}$$

2. Consistency Test of the Judgment Matrix

Ensuring the reliability and accuracy of decision-making in the Analytic Hierarchy Process (AHP) requires that the judgment matrix be consistent. Inconsistencies in the matrix, such as contradictory comparisons, can lead to erroneous decisions. The consistency test aims to verify the logical coherence of the pairwise comparisons within the matrix, avoiding illogical sequences like "A is extremely more important than B, B is extremely more important than C, yet C is extremely more important than A." If a judgment matrix fails this consistency test, it must be adjusted and re-evaluated until it meets the criteria for consistency (Yi et al., 2023). The process of conducting a consistency test generally involves the following steps:

1)Calculation of Consistency IndexCI

$$CI = \frac{\lambda_{max} - n}{n - 1} \tag{6}$$

where$\lambda_{max}$is the largest eigenvalue of the judgment matrix, and$n$is the order of the matrix. The calculation results of the consistency index for the above judgment matrix are shown in Table 3.

Table 3. The calculation results of the consistency index

Judgment Matrix	A_{B-A}	B_{C-B_1}	B_{C-B_2}	B_{C-B_3}	B_{C-B_4}
The largest eigenvalue λ_{max}	4.1983	12.1775	4.0328	3.0649	2
The order of the matrix n	4	11	4	3	2
CI	0.0661	0.11775	0.01093	0.03245	0

2) Compute the Consistency Ratio(CR)

When the value of$CR$is less than 0.1, it is considered that the judgment matrix has passed the consistency check. Otherwise, the judgment matrix needs to be adjusted until the conditions are met.

$$CR = \frac{CI}{RI} \tag{7}$$

where$RI$is the average random consistency index, which is related to the order of the judgment matrix. The values of$RI$and the calculation results of the$CR$are shown in Table 4.

Table 4. Values of RI and calculation results of CR

Judgment Matrix	A_{B-A}	B_{C-B_1}	B_{C-B_2}	B_{C-B_3}	B_{C-B_4}
The order of the matrix n	4	11	4	3	2
RI	0.90	1.51	0.90	0.58	0
CR	0.07344	0.07798	0.01214	0.05594	0

As shown in Table 4, all theCRvalues of the judgment matrices are less than 0.1, all passing the consistency check, proving that the constructed judgment matrices are reasonable and reliable, with satisfactory consistency.

3. Single-level weight vector

Based on the judgment matrix, we can calculate the importance ranking of the lower-level factors to the upper-level factors. This article uses the eigenvalue method (Saaty, T.L., 2003), that is, calculating the eigenvalues and eigenvectors of the judgment matrix. The eigenvector corresponding to the largest eigenvalue is normalized as the weight vector.

Using Matlab software, the initial weight vectors of the index layer elements relative to the target layer indices can be calculated as:

$$\mathbf{V}_{B-A} = [0.3109 \quad 0.0975 \quad 0.5437 \quad 0.0479]$$

$$\mathbf{V}_{B_1-C} = \begin{matrix} [0.2310 & 0.0773 & 0.0282 & 0.0592 & 0.1297 & 0.0450 \\ 0.0253 & 0.1402 & 0.1279 & 0.0193 & 0.1169] & \end{matrix}$$

$$\mathbf{V}_{B_2-C} = [0.2893 \quad 0.1294 \quad 0.0711 \quad 0.5102]$$

$$\mathbf{V}_{B_3-C} = [0.7306 \quad 0.1884 \quad 0.0810]$$

$$\mathbf{V}_{B_4-C} = [0.75 \quad 0.25]$$

To avoid the unreasonable impact caused by the internal discrepancies among various indicators in the constant weight model, the Variable Weight Theory (VWT) (Li et al., 1995 & Liu et al., 1997) is introduced to integrate the status values of each indicator. The core idea is that the weight of the indicators can change with the change of the variable weight values. Considering the possibility of excessive membership degree for some factors belonging to the lowest language level in the feasibility evaluation in the fuzzy matrix obtained according to the membership function, it is believed that their factor status needs adjustment. This paper adopts the method of performing the Hadamard product and normalization on the initial weight vector and the status vector for adjustment. In this paper, the maximum membership degree is stipulated to be no more than 0.4. The calculation formula for the state impact vector is as follows (Huang et al., 2017):

$$\mathbf{S}_j(\mu)=\begin{cases} 2-\log_{b_j}^{\mu(x_j)} & \mu(x_j > b_j) \\ 1 & \mu(x_j \leq b_j) \end{cases} \tag{8}$$

where b_j is the adjustment level, $\mathbf{S}_j(\mu)$ is state impact vector.

The formula for the variable weight objective weight vector $\mathbf{W}_j$ is as follows:

$$\mathbf{W}_j = \frac{\mathbf{A}_j \cdot \mathbf{S}(\mu)}{\sum_{j=1}^{n}(\mathbf{A}_j \mathbf{S}_j(\mu))} \tag{9}$$

where $\mathbf{A}_j$ represents the initial weight vector.

Comprehensive Evaluation and Decision Making

The hierarchical sorting results are synthesized to obtain the weight vector of the sub-index layer to the overall goal. The basic steps are to calculate the sorting weights of the lower-level elements to the overall goal from the bottom up, layer by layer. Finally, we can recursively calculate the weight vector of the lowest level elements to the overall goal, and use this as the basis for decision making.

The comprehensive evaluation result is $\mathbf{Y}$, and the calculation process is as follows:

$$\mathbf{Y} = \mathbf{W} \cdot \mathbf{R} \tag{10}$$

where $\mathbf{W}$ represents comprehensive objective weight vector, $\mathbf{R}$ is fuzzy relation matrix.

CASE ANALYSIS

In applying the evaluation model established in this study, two distinct highwall mining operations were analyzed: the JZT coal mine in Inner Mongolia, China, and the GC coal mine in Australia. Both mines implemented Continuous Highwall Miner (CHM) systems, with JZT coal mine using equipment from Shanxi Tiandi Coal Machinery Co., Ltd. and the GC coal mine utilizing CHM technology from SHM (Porathur et al., 2017). Based on the actual conditions of the two mining areas, the quantified values for each indicator in layer C were determined, with indicator values as shown in Table 1. According to the mathematical model for evaluating the feasibility of highwall mining established in this paper, a comprehensive feasibility evaluation was conducted separately for the two mining areas.

Feasibility Evaluation of JZT Open-Pit Mine in Inner Mongolia, China

1. Level I Comprehensive Fuzzy Evaluation

i. Comprehensive fuzzy evaluation vector of geological deposit factors B_1
   1) Constant weight comprehensive coefficient

$$\mathbf{V}_{B_1-C} = \begin{matrix}[0.2310 & 0.0773 & 0.0282 & 0.0592 & 0.1297 & 0.0450 \\ 0.0253 & 0.1402 & 0.1279 & 0.0193 & 0.1169]\end{matrix}$$

   2) Construct a fuzzy relation matrix according to the membership function.

$$\mathbf{R}_{C-B_1} = \begin{bmatrix} 0.0001 & 0.6998 & 0.2998 & 0.0001 \\ 0.0001 & 0.0001 & 0.0001 & 0.9997 \\ 0.0001 & 0.0001 & 0.8799 & 0.1199 \\ 0.9399 & 0.0599 & 0.0001 & 0.0001 \\ 0.0001 & 0.0001 & 0.3333 & 0.6665 \\ 0.0001 & 0.0001 & 0.0001 & 0.9997 \\ 0.0001 & 0.0001 & 0.5699 & 0.4299 \\ 0.0001 & 0.0001 & 0.0001 & 0.9997 \\ 0.0001 & 0.0001 & 0.0001 & 0.9997 \\ 0.0001 & 0.3299 & 0.6759 & 0.0001 \\ 0.0001 & 0.0001 & 0.3999 & 0.5999 \end{bmatrix}$$

3) According to the fuzzy relation matrix, it is found that the lowest evaluation level of C_5 is higher than 0.4. Therefore, calculate its status impact vector according to formula (8).

$$\mathbf{S}_{C-B_1} = [\ 1 \quad 1 \quad 1 \quad 1 \quad 1.9485 \quad 1 \quad 1 \quad 1 \quad 1 \quad 1 \quad 1\ ]$$

4) Calculate its variable weight vector according to formula (9).

$$\mathbf{W}_{C-B_1} = \begin{matrix}[0.2057 & 0.0688 & 0.0251 & 0.0527 & 0.1155 & 0.0401 \\ 0.0225 & 0.1248 & 0.1139 & 0.0172 & 0.1041]\end{matrix}$$

5) Determine the final comprehensive fuzzy evaluation vector according to formula (10).

$$\mathbf{Y}_{C-B_1} = \mathbf{W}_{C-B_1} \cdot \mathbf{R}_{C-B_1} = [0.0496 \quad 0.1528 \quad 0.1884 \quad 0.4997]$$

ii. Comprehensive fuzzy evaluation vector of mining technique factors B_2

1) Determine the initial weight vector of the comprehensive evaluation index system.

$$\mathbf{Y}_{C-B_1} = \mathbf{W}_{C-B_1} \cdot \mathbf{R}_{C-B_1} = [0.0496 \quad 0.1528 \quad 0.1884 \quad 0.4997]$$

2) Construct a fuzzy relation matrix according to the membership function.

$$\mathbf{R}_{C-B_2} = \begin{bmatrix} 0.0001 & 0.0001 & 0.5999 & 0.3999 \\ 0.0001 & 0.0001 & 0.0001 & 0.9997 \\ 0.0001 & 0.0001 & 0.0001 & 0.9997 \\ 0.0001 & 0.7999 & 0.1999 & 0.0001 \end{bmatrix}$$

3) According to the fuzzy relation matrix, there is no lowest level membership degree greater than 0.4. Determine the status impact vector according to formula (8).

$$\mathbf{S}_{\mathbf{C-B_2}} = [1 \quad 1 \quad 1 \quad 1]$$

4) Obtain the comprehensive fuzzy evaluation vector according to formula (9).

$$\mathbf{W}_{\mathbf{C-B_2}} = [0.2893 \quad 0.1294 \quad 0.0711 \quad 0.5102]$$

5) Determine the final comprehensive fuzzy evaluation vector according to formula (10).

$$\mathbf{Y}_{\mathbf{C-B_2}} = \mathbf{W}_{\mathbf{C-B_2}} \cdot \mathbf{R}_{\mathbf{C-B_2}} = [0.0001 \quad 0.4082 \quad 0.2756 \quad 0.3162]$$

iii. Comprehensive fuzzy evaluation vector of safety impact factors B_3

Repeat calculation steps 1-5 to obtain the comprehensive fuzzy evaluation vector of safety factor B_3.

$$\mathbf{Y}_{\mathbf{C-B_3}} = [0.0001 \quad 0.0408 \quad 0.0814 \quad 0.8777]$$

iv. Comprehensive fuzzy evaluation vector of economic evaluation factors B_4

Repeat calculation steps 1-5 to obtain the comprehensive fuzzy evaluation vector of economic evaluation factors B_4.

$$\mathbf{Y}_{\mathbf{C-B_4}} = [0.0001 \quad 0.0001 \quad 0.0001 \quad 0.9997]$$

II. Level II Comprehensive Fuzzy Evaluation

1) Determine the constant weight vector of the comprehensive evaluation index system.

$$\mathbf{V}_{\mathbf{B-A}} = [0.3109 \quad 0.0975 \quad 0.5437 \quad 0.0479]$$

2) Construct a fuzzy relation matrix according to the comprehensive judgment results of Level I.

$$\mathbf{R}_{\mathbf{B-A}} = \begin{bmatrix} 0.0496 & 0.1528 & 0.1884 & 0.4997 \\ 0.0001 & 0.4082 & 0.2756 & 0.3162 \\ 0.0001 & 0.0408 & 0.0814 & 0.8777 \\ 0.0001 & 0.0001 & 0.0001 & 0.99997 \end{bmatrix}$$

3) According to the fuzzy relation matrix, there is no lowest level membership degree greater than 0.4. Determine the status impact vector according to formula (8).

$$\mathbf{S}_{\mathbf{B-A}} = [1 \quad 1 \quad 1 \quad 1]$$

4) Obtain the comprehensive fuzzy evaluation vector according to formula (9).

$$\mathbf{W}_{\mathbf{B-A}} = [0.3109 \quad 0.0975 \quad 0.5437 \quad 0.0479]$$

5) Determine the final comprehensive fuzzy evaluation vector according to formula (10).

$$\mathbf{Y}_{\mathbf{B-A}} = \mathbf{W}_{\mathbf{B-A}} \cdot \mathbf{R}_{\mathbf{B-A}} = [0.0155 \quad 0.1095 \quad 0.1297 \quad 0.7113]$$

It is known from the above that, according to the principle of evaluation membership degree, the maximum evaluation membership degree value for JZT mine is 0.7113, belonging to the “highly feasible” level.

In the actual application at the JZT coal mine in Inner Mongolia, the EML340 Continuous Highwall Miner (CHM) is employed for extracting coal from the 9# seam. This particular coal seam is characterized by a roof composed of medium-fine grained sandstone, which exhibits an average compressive strength of approximately 40 MPa. The overlaying strata, classified as mudstone, falls under the category of weak to semi-hard rock layers, contributing to a stable slope environment.

During the project's implementation, the EML340 CHM has been operational for a period of six months. Throughout this duration, no significant incidents of coal-rock collapses that could potentially jeopardize the machinery have been reported. The equipment's performance has been commendable, achieving an excavation output of over 300,000 tons. This level of productivity not only underscores the efficiency of the equipment but also highlights its contribution to substantial economic and social benefits. Such outcomes affirm the suitability and effectiveness of the EML340 CHM in the specific geological and operational conditions of the JZT coal mine.

Figure 4. Engineering case of highwall mining in JZT Mine, Inner Mongolia, China

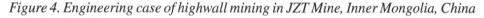

2. Comprehensive Evaluation of GC Open-Pit Mine in Australia

The calculation of the fuzzy comprehensive evaluation of the Australian GC mine is the same as the comprehensive evaluation process of the JZT coal mine. The comprehensive fuzzy evaluation vector of the Australian GC mine can be calculated as follows.

$$Y'_{B-A} = [0.2614 \quad 0.3304 \quad 0.2026 \quad 0.2475]$$

This implies that the maximum evaluation membership degree value for the Australian GC mine is 0.3304, belonging to the “basically feasible ” level.

The Australian GC coal mine presents a contrasting case study in highwall mining compared to the JZT coal mine in Inner Mongolia. The coal seam in the GC mine is relatively thin, ranging between 2 to 3 meters in thickness, with the uniaxial compressive strength (UCS) of the coal seam estimated at approximately 3.3 MPa. The geological composition of the mine's roof varies from weak mudstone to a medium-strength silty sandstone layer. During the mining operations, the GC mine faced frequent roof collapses, which were primarily characterized by delamination and plate-like block detachments along the cross-joints. These incidents significantly impacted the mining process. Statistical data indicates that about 66% of operational time was allocated to equipment withdrawal and subsequent re-entry due to these frequent roof collapse incidents, leading to unsatisfactory real-world application results.

The comparative analysis of these two distinct mining scenarios: the JZT coal mine with its more stable geological conditions and the GC coal mine with its frequent roof collapses provides a practical illustration of the varying conditions under which highwall mining is implemented. This comparison highlights the effectiveness of the feasibility evaluation model for highwall mining in open-pit coal mines, as developed in this article. The model's ability to accurately reflect the actual application conditions and effectively reveal the performance and membership degree of each indicator under varying mine conditions and commentary sets is validated through these case studies. This congruence between the model's predictions and the real-world scenarios underscores the model's utility in effectively guiding decision-making processes in diverse mining contexts with significant differences in mine conditions.

CONCLUSION

The integration of highwall mining technology in open-pit mining areas is contingent upon specific requirements like geological conditions and mining processes. Inadequate adherence to these requirements can render the equipment inoperative and potentially compromise slope stability. Traditionally, the determination of highwall mining feasibility has relied on manual, experience-based categorization. This study introduces a novel, more systematic method for feasibility assessment, designed to provide a universally applicable and comprehensive approach. This method aids coal mine engineers in quantifying the feasibility assessment more effectively. Key conclusions of this paper are:

(1) Development of a Mathematical Evaluation Framework: The study proposes a framework combining the Analytic Hierarchy Process (AHP), Fuzzy Comprehensive Evaluation (FCE), and Variable Weight Theory (VWT) methods. This framework is designed to evaluate the feasibility of highwall mining in open-pit coal mines by examining technical characteristics like mine occurrence conditions and mining processes. It encompasses four primary indicators - geological deposit factors, mining technique factors, safety impact factors, and economic evaluation factors - along with 20 detailed sub-indicators and their corresponding characteristics.

(2) Feasibility Evaluation Comment Set: The evaluation categorizes feasibility into four distinct types: infeasible, basically feasible, relatively feasible, and highly feasible. These categories guide the assignment of values to sub-indicators within the evaluation framework. A judgment matrix is used to derive weight vectors for these sub-indicators, and a fuzzy relationship matrix is constructed using fuzzy mathematical membership functions. The final feasibility membership degree is determined through a two-level comprehensive judgment based on the maximum membership principle.

(3) Validation Through Real-World Engineering Cases: The feasibility evaluation model's validity is confirmed using two highwall mining cases - the JZT coal mine in Inner Mongolia, China, and the GC coal mine in Australia. The quantification of 20 sub-indicators in these mines and their incorporation into the model yields a maximum membership degree of 0.7113 ("highly feasible") for the JZT mine, and 0.3304 ("basically feasible") for the GC mine. These results align closely with actual mining practices.

The findings demonstrate the effectiveness of the established framework in reflecting the performance and membership degree of each indicator under different conditions, aligning with real-world applications. The comprehensive mathematical framework offers a systematic and objective basis for evaluating the feasibility and efficacy of highwall mining technology in open-pit coal mines, enhancing decision-making accuracy and providing scientific guidance for mines considering this technology.

Future research directions include expanding the feasibility assessment criteria to encompass other mining techniques like backfill mining and layered extraction in thick coal seams, further refining the evaluation system's comprehensiveness and precision.

DATA AVAILABILITY STATEMENT

The data used to support the findings of this study are available from the corresponding author upon request.

ACKNOWLEDGMENT

This research was funded by China National Key R&D Program (Grant No. 2020YFB131400), Research Project Supported by Shanxi Scholarship Council of China (Grant No. 2022-186), the National Natural Science Foundation of China (62006148), the National Undergraduate Innovation and Entrepreneurship Training Program (20230014), the 21st Undergraduate Innovation and Entrepreneurship Training Program of Shanxi University (202210108012). SK036).

REFERENCES

Boeut, S., Laowattanabandit, P., & Fujii, Y. (2017), Extracting residual coal by auger highwall mining at Mae Tan Coal Mine, Thailand. *Proceedings of Spring Meeting of MMIJ Hokkaido Branch*, 59-60.

Chen, C., Huang, H., Zhao, B., Shu, D., & Wang, Y. (2023). The research of AHP-based credit rating system on a blockchain application. *Electronics (Basel)*, 12(4), 887. 10.3390/electronics12040887

Chen, H., Guo, Q., Wang, L., & Meng, X. (2023). Evaluation of slope stability within the influence of mining based on combined weighting and finite cloud model. *Energy Exploration & Exploitation*, 41(2), 636–655. 10.1177/01445987221134638

Chen, J., Li, H., Hu, Z., Liu, K., & Hou, Y. (2022). Evaluation Index for IVIS Integration Test under a Closed Condition Based on the Analytic Hierarchy Process. *Electronics (Basel)*, 11(22), 3830. 10.3390/electronics11223830

Chen, Y., Shimada, H., Sasaoka, T., Hamanaka, A., & Matsui, K. (2013). Research on exploiting residual coal around final end-walls by highwall mining system in China. *International Journal of Mining, Reclamation and Environment*, 27(3), 166–179. 10.1080/17480930.2012.678768

Ding, X., Li, F., & Fu, T. (2021). Overburden movement and failure law of coalface in end slope and the slope stability control method. *Meitan Xuebao*, 46(9), 2883–2894.

Dong, G., Wei, W., Xia, X., Woźniak, M., & Damaševičius, R. (2020). Safety risk assessment of a Pb-Zn mine based on fuzzy-grey correlation analysis. *Electronics (Basel)*, 9(1), 130. 10.3390/electronics9010130

Duan, L., Guo, S., Han, L., & Wei, H. (2022). Research on optimal selection of steep slope mining based on AHP-TOPSIS method. *Coal Technology*, 41(9), 18–22.

Elmouttie, M., & Karekal, S. (2017). A framework for geotechnical hazard analysis in highwall mining entries. *Procedia Engineering*, 2017(191), 1203–1210. 10.1016/j.proeng.2017.05.296

Fayaz, M., Ullah, I., Park, D. H., Kim, K., & Kim, D. (2017). An integrated risk index model based on hierarchical fuzzy logic for underground risk assessment. *Applied Sciences (Basel, Switzerland)*, 7(10), 1037. 10.3390/app7101037

Huang, W., & Wang, Z. (2017), Comprehensive evaluation model of fuzzy analytic hierarchy process with variable weight for underground coal gasification. *Journal of Xi'an University Of Science and Technology*, *37*(54), 500-507.

Jiang, J., Lu, Y., Cao, L., Fu, T., Wang, D., Wang, L., & Li, L. (2023). Parameter design of coal pillar in highwall mining under the action of dynamic-static load. *Coal Science and Technology*, 51(5), 53–62.

Li, H. (1995). Factor spaces and mathematical frame of knowledge representation—Variable weights analysis. *Fuzzy Systems and Mathematics*, 9(3), 1–9.

Li, J., Deng, C., Xu, J., Ma, Z., Shuai, P., & Zhang, L. (2023). Safety risk assessment and management of Panzhihua Open Pit (OP)-Underground (UG) Iron Mine based on AHP-FCE, Sichuan Province, China. *Sustainability (Basel)*, 15(5), 4497. 10.3390/su15054497

Liu, W. (1997). Balanced function and its application to variable weight synthesizing. *System Engineering Theory & Practice*, 17(4), 58–64.

Liu, W., Wang, L., & Fu, Q. (2012). SHM highwall mining technology and key issues of application. *Coastal Engineering*, 2012(6), 1–4.

Luo, K., Ma, L., Liu, C., Lv, G., Shi, L., Xu, T., & Xue, F. (2022). Feasibility analysis of end slope and steep mining technology in Hequ Open-pit Mine. *Coastal Engineering*, 54(5), 19–25.

Ma, J. (2021). Study on feasibility evaluation of continuous mining of residual coal based on variable weight fuzzy theory. *Coal Science and Technology*, 49(8), 30–37.

Ma, J., & Song, D. (2023). Mathematical evaluation on the applicability of bolter miners based on variable weight fuzzy theory. *Journal of China Coal Sociey*, 48(6), 2579–2589.

Nezarat, H., Sereshki, F., & Ataei, M. (2015). Ranking of geological risks in mechanized tunneling by using Fuzzy Analytical Hierarchy Process (FAHP). *Tunnelling and Underground Space Technology*, 50, 358–364. 10.1016/j.tust.2015.07.019

Peng, S. (2017). *Advances in coal mine ground control*. Woodhead Publishing.

Perry, K., Raffaldi, M., & Harris, K. (2015). Influence of highwall mining progression on web and barrier pillar stability. *Mining Engineering*, 67(3), 59–67.

Porathur, J., Karekal, S., & Palroy, P. (2013). Web pillar design approach for highwall mining extraction. *International Journal of Rock Mechanics and Mining Sciences*, 64(12), 73–83. 10.1016/j.ijrmms.2013.08.029

Porathur, J. L., Roy, P., Shen, B., & Karekal, S. (2017). *Highwall mining: Applicability, design & safety*. CRC Press/Balkema. 10.1201/9781315171234

Prakash, A., Kumar, A., & Singh, B. (2015). Highwall mining: A critical appraisal. *Minetech*, 36(3), 17–30.

Ross, C., Conover, D., & Baine, J. (2019). Highwall mining of thick, steeply dipping coal a case study in geotechnical design and recovery optimization. *International Journal of Mining Science and Technology*, 29(5), 777–780. 10.1016/j.ijmst.2017.12.022

Saaty, T. L. (2003). Decision-making with the AHP: Why is the principal eigenvector necessary. *European Journal of Operational Research*, 145(1), 85–89. 10.1016/S0377-2217(02)00227-8

Sasaoka, T., Karian, T., Hamanaka, A., Shimada, H., & Matsui, K. (2016). Application of highwall mining system in weak geological condition. *International Journal of Coal Science & Technology*, 3(3), 311–321. 10.1007/s40789-016-0121-6

Shen, B., & Duncan Fama, M. E. (2001). Review of highwall mining experience in Australia and a case study. *Australian Geomechanics*, 36(2), 25–32.

Shimada, H., Chen, Y., Hamanaka, A., Sasaoka, T., Shimada, H., & Matsui, K. (2013). Application of highwall mining system to recover residual coal in End-walls. *Procedia Earth and Planetary Science*, 2013(6), 311–318. 10.1016/j.proeps.2013.01.041

Tian, Y., Tu, L., Lu, X., Zhou, W., Jiskani, I. M., Liu, F., & Cai, Q. (2023). Stability analysis of multi-layer highwall mining: A sustainable approach for thick-seam open-pit mines. *Sustainability (Basel)*, 15(4), 3603. 10.3390/su15043603

Wang, R., Yan, S., Bai, J., Chang, Z., & Zhao, T. (2019). Theoretical analysis of damaged width & instability mechanism of rib pillar in open-pit highwall mining. *Advances in Civil Engineering*, 2019(2), 1–15. 10.1155/2019/6328702

Wang, S., Liu, F., & Hu, G. (2022). Study on end slope shearer mining feasibility in Xinjiang Open-pit Mine. *Opencast Mining Technology*, 37(6), 22–26.

Xiao, L., Li, F., Niu, C., Dai, G., Qiao, Q., & Lin, C. (2023). Evaluation of water inrush hazard in coal seam roof based on the AHP-CRITIC composite weighted method. *Energies*, 16(1), 114. 10.3390/en16010114

Xiu, Z., Nie, W., Cai, P., Chen, D., & Zhang, X. (2022). Study on intelligent adaptability evaluation of intelligent coal mining working face based on ANP and matter-element extension model. *Journal of Mining and Strata Control Engineering*, 5(2), 023037.

Yang, T., Wang, H., Dong, X., Liu, F., Zhang, P., & Deng, W. (2020). Current situation, problems and countermeasures of intelligent evaluation of slope stability in open pit. *Meitan Xuebao*, 45(6), 2277–2295.

Yi, J., & Guo, L. (2023). AHP-Based network security situation assessment for industrial internet of things. *Electronics (Basel)*, 12(16), 3458. 10.3390/electronics12163458

Yu, J., Zhu, L., & Xu, G. (2019). Safety and high efficiency adaptability evaluation of coal mine intelligent fully-mechanized mining face. *Coal Science and Technology*, 47(3), 60–65.

Yu, M. (2018). *Stability mechanism study of coal pillar and slope body under strip mining of end-slope coal* [PhD Dissertation]. China University of Mining and Technology.

Zipf, R., & Bhatt, S. (2004). Analysis of practical ground control issues in highwall mining. *Proceedings of the 23rd International Conference on Ground Control in Mining*, 210-219.

Chapter 10
Trusted Fine-Grained Image Classification Based on Evidence Theory and Its Applications to Medical Image Analysis

Zhikang Xu
School of Computer Engineering and Science, Shanghai University, Taiyuan, China

Xiaodong Yue
School of Future Technology, Shanghai University, China

Ying Lv
Shanghai Artificial Intelligence Laboratory, China

ABSTRACT

Fine-grained image classification (FGIC) aims to classify object of images to the corresponding subordinate classes of a superclass. Due to insufficient training data and confusing data samples, FGIC may produce uncertain classification results that are untrusted for data applications. Dempster-Shafer evidence theory (DST) is widely applied in reasoning with uncertainty and opinion fusion. Recently, researchers extended DST by combining it with deep learning to measure the uncertainty of deep neural networks and perform uncertainty classification. In this proposed chapter, the authors provide a detailed introduction of how to integrate ENN to

DOI: 10.4018/979-8-3693-4292-3.ch010

construct the trusted FGIC model. Compared with the traditional approaches, the trusted FGIC method not only generates accurate classification results but also reduces the uncertainty of fine-grained classification. In addition, they introduce the application of FGIC in medical image analysis to achieve trusted fine-grained medical image classification.

INTRODUCTION

Deep learning-based methods have made significant progress in the traditional classification tasks. In comparison, in the Fine-Grained Image Classification (FGIC), the performance of deep learning models is limited due to the small difference in appearance between classes. As illustrated in Figure 1(a), traditional image classification has a coarser granularity, while fine-grained image classification presents more chanllenges. Moreover, as can be seen in Figure 1(b), when using the same backbone models, the accuracy on the FGIC dataset CUB-200-2011 is significantly inferior than the accuracy on the traditional classification dataset CIFAR10 (He et al., 2016; Huang et al. 2017; Simonyan & Zisserman 2014).

Figure 1. Comparison between traditional classification and fine-grained image classification

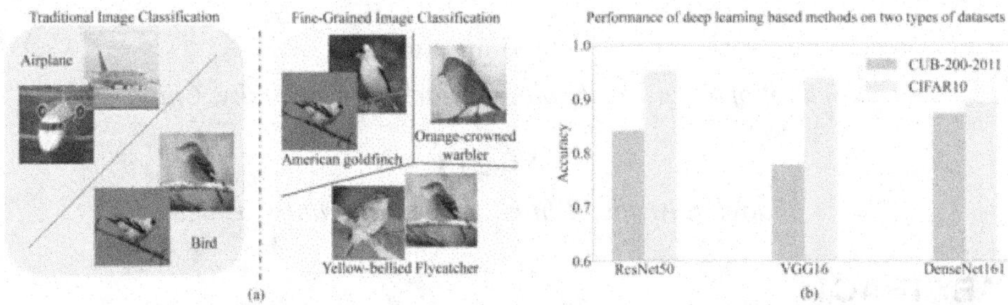

To address this issue, one strategy is to localize the discriminative parts from the images. Consequently, the discriminative parts extracted can be utilized to enhance classification performance. Another strategy is to utilize specific learning paradigms to improve the discrimination of image features, such as contrast learning based methods and prototype learning based methods. However, Due to limited annotated image data and confusing data samples, the accuracy of these methods still faces challenges and FGIC models may produce uncertain classification results, leading to untrustworthiness in data applications.

In addition, prior knowledge as an external information, can be used to improve the performance of FGIC, while reducing data dependency. Extant prior-based FGIC methods can be roughly divided into two categories, data prior and label prior. However, these two kinds of prior information have not been fully explored, leading to significant room for improvement in both the accuracy and trustworthiness of the model.

In fact, FGIC can be regarded as a hierarchical classification process. The multilayer classification information can be considered as external information from label prior to be fused into the process of FGIC to improve its performance. In this chapter, by utilizing evdence theory, we will give a detailed introduction of how to seamlessly fuse the hierarchical classification information into FGIC to achieve trusted and accurate model. Specifically, at each classification layer, we adopt evidence theory to construct an evidential classifier to extract evidence belonging to different classes. Then, we formulate multi-grained evidence fusion with the Dirichlet hyper-distribution to decompose the classification evidence of coarse-grained classes into corresponding fine-grained classes, thereby enhancing the performance of FGIC and reducing predictive uncertainty. The proposed learning method can be integrated into the exsiting FGIC methods. In addition, we will also present how to extend the proposed method to the field of medical image analysis to achieve trusted fine-grained medical image classification.

The contributions of this chapter are summaried as follows.

We give a general framework to achieve trusted fine-grained image classification in which the fine-grained classification is wrapped in the process of hierarhical classification and thereby achieving trusted classification by multi-layer classification evidence fusion.

We also expand the proposed framework to medical image analysis and propose a trusted fine-grained medical image classification.

Related Work of FGIC

During the training process of FGIC models, classification labels of the images provide only limited supervisory information leading to insufficient model performance. To tackle this problem, researchers proposed methods to mine more information from within the images or integrating prior information from outside the images to enhance the accuracy of fine-grained classification. Among these approaches, the methods for mining information from within images can be further divided into two categories: mining of inter-class discriminative features (or regions) and enhancement of feature discriminability.

FGIC Methods Based on Inter-Class Discriminative Features (or Regions) Mining

Due to the limited number of annotated training images, small inter-class variance and large intra-class variance, FGIC models can misidentify irrelevant features or regions such as background as discriminative features, ultimately leading to misclassification. To address this issue, researchers have attempt to localize the discriminative parts form the images to find the features with high response in the feature space, using methods such as object detection, keypoint detection and attention mechanism.

Among them, object detection based methods (Zhang et al., 2014; Lin et al., 2015) initially employ part detectors to identify several key components of the target in the image (such as the head, wings, etc., of a bird). Subsequently, the image regions containing these parts are seperately fed into the classification network. To train part detectors, in addition to image label, manual annotations of key parts using bounding boxes or keypoints are required for each training iamges. While the use of additional bounding boxes or keypoints can accurately localize key components of the target, the manual annotation is time-consuming. Moveover, annotations in specific domains requre expert knowledge, which makes these methods less practical and generalizable.

To solve this problem, researchers have proposed attention mechanisms-based FGIC methods (Zhao et al., 2021; Ji et al., 2020; Zheng et al., 2017). These methods enable the model to mine the discriminative parts or features without the need for additional annotations (such as bounding boxes or keypoints). Zhao (Zhao et al., 2021) argue that channels with high activation values in the feature tensor extracted by Convolutional Neural Networks (CNNs) often contain key compoints. By summing the feature tensor along the channel direction, channels with high responses are selected. This process effectively mines the features corresponding to the key parts of the targets, thereby enhancing the accuracy of subsequent classification.

Although convolutional neural networks (CNNs) with attention mechanisms have achieved significant achievements in FGIC, the restricted receptive field poses a challenge in modeling the global context of image features, resuting in sub-optimal classification accuracy. To alleviate this problem, some researchers introduced the Vision Transformer (ViT) into FGIC. The self-attention mechanism of ViT allows for better modeling of the global context of images.

FGIC Methods Based on Discriminative Enhancement of Image Features

In addition to mining discriminative features, researchers also proposed special learning paradigms to enhance the discriminability of image features. These paradigms include contrastive learning, multi-scale feature learning, feature jigsaw learning, prototype learning, and feature grouping learning.

Methods based on contrastive learning can be further divided into feature contrastive learning and predictive probability distribution contrastive learning. Feature contrastive learning methods involve constructing sample pairs for feature enhancement learning, making that the feature representations of sample pairs belonging to same class are as close as possible, while sample pairs belonging to different classes are as far away as possible (Sun et al., 2018; Gao et al., 2020; Yang et al., 2021).

Inspired by the fact that the receptive field in CNNs becomes larger with the increase of layers, the multi-scale feature learning based methods construct classifiers at different layers of CNN separately. Since the last layer of the CNN has the largest receptive field, constructing and training classifiers at this layer can improve the representation of the overall structural features of the target. On the contrary, constructing the classifier in convolutional layers with smaller receptive fields can improve the representation of the local (component) features of the target. Through this multi-scale training process, the performance of FGIC can be improved by better understanding and distinguishing between different fine-grained classes from local parts to the overall structure (Song & Yang, 2021).

In addition to leveraging multi-scale feature learning methods, researchers proposed jigsaw-based learning approaches to enhance the ability to represent local features of the target. During the model training process, the original image is chunked, disrupted and reassembled. Since the reassembled image loses the overall structure of the target, it forces the network to focus on the local regions related to the target contained in the jigsaw pieces (Du et al., 2020).

Prototype learning-based approach constructs class prototypes in the feature space and constrains the distances between feature representations of samples and feature representations of prototype as well as the distances between prototypes and prototypes via a contrastive loss function. By optimizing the contrastive loss, the discriminability of feature representations can be enhanced (Liu et al., 2022).

Feature grouping learning-based approach divided channels of the image feature tensor into groups, with each group corresponding to a fine-grained class. In this way, the network can learn the feature representation of each category in a more targeted way, and thereby enhancing the discriminability of feature representations and improving the performance of FGIC (Chang et al., 2020).

FGIC Methods Based on Prior Fusion

Rresearchers also explored FGIC methods that fuse prior from data and label perspectives, respectively. The merit of prior-based FGIC methods is that it not only enhances classification performance but also reduces the dependence on data.

Data prior-based FGIC methods can be further divided into image priors and attribute priors. For image priors, inspired by observing things from far to near and from whole to local, researchers proposed to integrate multi-scale image priors. It starts with the original image as the input and gradually focus on local regions of the image. During the focusing process, the region contained in the current scale image is used as the prior region for the next scale image, from which the focused sub-region is cropped using a bounding box. This process is performed recursively, forming a multi-scale image representation. Finally, the multi-scale information is fused to improve the fine-grained classification accuracy (Zhang et al., 2021) .

For attribute priors, researchers utilized the characteristic and spatio-temporal attributes of targets as prior information. Characteristic attributes refer to a set of attributes that describe specific features of a target, such as the tail shape and color of "birds" or the brand and model of "cars". Since there are significant differences in some characteristic attributes of targets in different classes, these attributes can be used as the key criteria for identification. Spatio-temporal attributes, on the other hand, include the geographic location (latitude and longitude information) and the time when the target image was taken. In some domain specific FGIC tasks, there are also significant differences in the geographical and temporal distributions of different classes of targets (Zhang et al., 2016; Chu et al., 2019).

For label prior-based FGIC methods, some researchers consider fine-grained classification as a hierarchical classification process in which the classification granularity goes from coarse to fine, i.e., the target image is first coarsely classified, and the classification granularity is continuously refined as the classification layer becomes deeper. Taking this hierarchical relationship between labels as a prior helps to improve the performance of FGIC. Based on this, researchers introduced the hierarchical relationship of labels to the feature layer and classification layer respectively, thus optimizing the model from different perspectives (Zhou et al., 2016; Wang et al., 2015).

Existing FGIC methods based on priors have been investigated from both data and label perspectives. However, these methods have certain limitations. There is still considerable room for improvement in terms of the model accuracy and model trustworthiness.

TRUSTED FGIC BASED ON EVIDENCE THEORY

Figure 2. Comparison between traditional FGIC method and trusted FGIC method

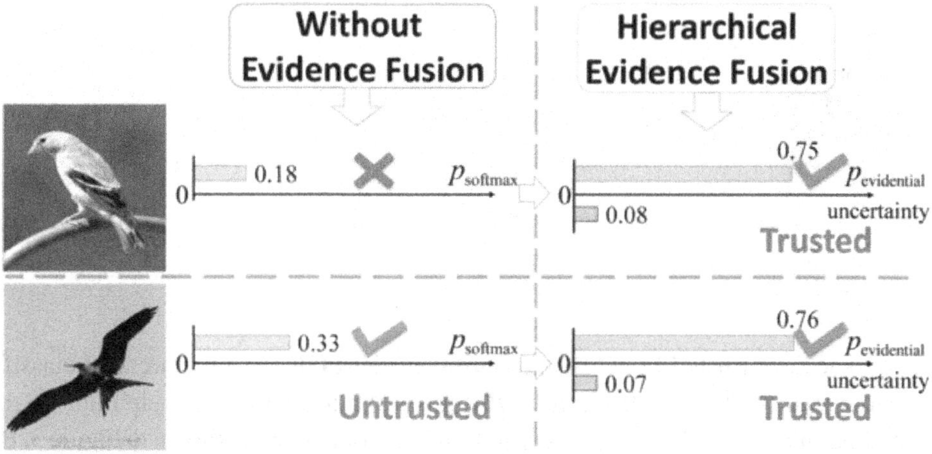

In this section, we give a detailed introduction of the proposed trusted FGMIC method. We first give an example to illustrate the merits of trust FGIC method by using evidence theory. For the first image of Figure 2, the traditional method, lacking evidence fusion, yields a low probability for the ground-truth class using softmax, resulting in a false classification. In contrast, by employing evidence fusion, our trusted FGIC method generates a higher probability belonging to ground-truth class, thereby correcting the predictive error. In the second image, while the traditional method accurately identifies the ground-truth class of the image, the low probability reflects significant uncertainty, rendering the classification untrusted. In contrast, our method delivers a classification result with higher probability that is considered trustworthy.

Figure 3. Framework of the trusted FGIC. In each classification layer (granularity), an evidence extractor (classifier) is constructed to extract evidence from input images. Then, we can hyper dirichlet distribution to formulate the fusion of multi-layer classification evidence.

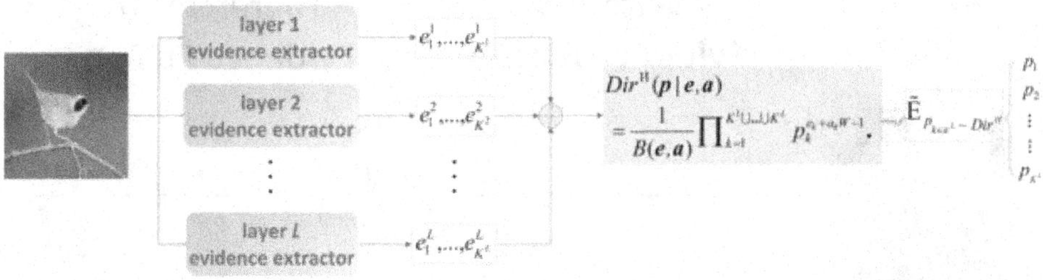

To achieve trusted FGIC method, we consider FGIC as a hierarchical classification process where multi-layer (multi-grained) information can help improve the accuracy and reduce the uncertainty. The overall framework is shown in Figure 3. By utilizing evidence theory, we construct an evidential classifier (evidence extractor) in each classification layer. For each image sample, the evidential classifier is used to obtain classification evidence values that represent belonging to different classes and is used to compute the uncertainty of classification. Then, evidence extracted from all layers forms multi-grained evidence. Assuming that classes of all layers are conditional independent, evidence of all classes in the label hierarchy can be fused through Dirichlet hyper probability distribution (Dir HPDF). Therefore, coarse-grained classification evidence can be decomposed into corresponding fine-grained classes to enhance fine-grained classification performance and reduce the overall prediction uncertainty.

Construction of Evidential Classifier in Each Classification Layer

We first give the definition of evidential classifier. Then we introduce the construction of evidential classifier in each classification layer.

Given that x denotes an image, and $\mathbf{p} = (p_1, ..., p_K)$ is a probability vector of belonging to class 1 to K and satisfies $\sum_{k=1}^{K} p_k = 1$. From the perspective of Bayesian estimation, $\mathbf{p}$ is considered as multivariate random variable. By using Bayes' theorem, we have

$$\pi(\mathbf{p}|x) = \frac{\pi(x|\mathbf{p})\pi(\mathbf{p})}{\int_{\mathbf{p}} \pi(x|\mathbf{p})\pi(\mathbf{p})}$$

. (1)

According to equation (1), we can obtain the posterior probability distribution of $\mathbf{p}$ given the input x. Assuming that $\pi(\mathbf{p})\sim Dir(\mathbf{p}|\widetilde{\boldsymbol{\alpha}})$ and $\pi(x|\mathbf{p})\sim Mult(\boldsymbol{\alpha}|\mathbf{p})$, by utilizing the conjugacy property of the distribution, we can derive

$$\pi(\mathbf{p}|x)\sim Dir(\mathbf{p}|\boldsymbol{\alpha}+\widetilde{\boldsymbol{\alpha}}) = \frac{1}{\mathbb{B}(\boldsymbol{\alpha}+\widetilde{\boldsymbol{\alpha}})}\prod_{k=1}^{K} p_k^{\alpha_k+\widetilde{\alpha}_k-1}$$

, (2)

where $\widetilde{\boldsymbol{\alpha}} > 0$ is the strength parameter vector of the prior distribution $\pi(\mathbf{p})$ and set as $\widetilde{\boldsymbol{\alpha}} = (1,...,1)$. So that$\pi(\mathbf{p})$ becomes a uniform distribution. Moveover, $\boldsymbol{\alpha} \in N$ is the strength parameter vector of the likelihood function $\pi(x|\mathbf{p})$, derived from the input x. Based on evidence theory, we employ neural network as the generalized likelihood function $\pi(x|\mathbf{p})$. Then, each image is input to the neural network and the output of the neural network is considered as generalized values of $\boldsymbol{\alpha}$, which is called classification evidence $\mathbf{e} \in R_{\geq 0}$.

Based on this, Equation (2) is tranformed as

$$\pi(\mathbf{p}|x)\sim Dir(\mathbf{p}|\mathbf{e}+1) = \frac{1}{\mathbb{B}(\mathbf{e}+1)}\prod_{k=1}^{K} p_k^{e_k+1-1}$$

. (3)

Therefore, the expected probability $\mathfrak{E}_{p_k}$ of belonging to class k can be obtained by computing the expectation of $\pi(\mathbf{p}|x)$

$$\mathfrak{E}_{p_k} = \frac{1+e_k}{K+\sum_{k=1}^{K} e_k}$$

. (4)

Furthermore, the predictive uncertainty u and the belief mass b_k of belonging to class k are obtained by decomposing $\mathfrak{E}_{p_k}$ as

$$\mathfrak{E}_{p_k} = \frac{e_k}{K+\sum_{k=1}^{K} e_k} + \frac{1}{K}\frac{K}{K+\sum_{k=1}^{K} e_k} = b_k + \frac{1}{K}u$$

, (5)

where

$$b_k = \frac{e_k}{K+\sum_{k=1}^{K} e_k}, \quad u = \frac{K}{K+\sum_{k=1}^{K} e_k}$$

. (6)

As can be seen from Equation (6), the larger the value of e, the smaller the value of u. We can utilize uncertainty u to measure the trustworthiness of the prediction, such that when the classifier is highly confident in its output, the prediction uncertainty u is small.

Then, at each classification layer, we can construct an evidential classifier. Specifically, as shown in Figure 4, evidential classifier is representated as a neural network with an additional activation function which ensures that the output evidence is non-negative.

Figure 4. Evidential classifier, including a general network and a non-negative activation function

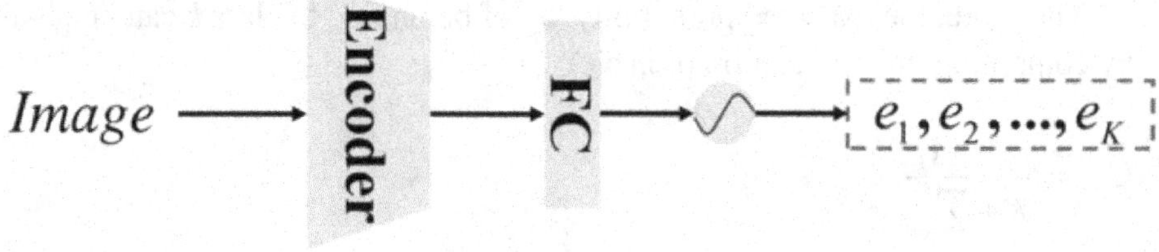

Hierarchical Evidence Fusion for Trusted FGIC

After extracting classification from all layers of label hierarchy, we further fuse all evidence. Assuming that the classes of different layers are independent of each other, evidence of all classes in the label hierarchy can be fused through Dirichlet hyper probability distribution (Dir HPDF), denoted as

$$Dir^{\mathrm{H}}(\widetilde{\mathbf{p}}|\widetilde{\mathbf{e}}+1) = \frac{1}{\mathbb{B}(\widetilde{\mathbf{e}}+1)}\prod_{k=1}^{|K^1\cup\ldots\cup K^L|} p_k^{e_k+1-1}$$

, (7)

where $K^1\cup\ldots\cup K^L$ is all the labels in the hierarchy. L is the total number of layers, and $\widetilde{\mathbf{p}} = \mathbf{p}^1 \cup \ldots \cup \mathbf{p}^L$ and $\widetilde{\mathbf{e}} = \mathbf{e}^1 \cup \ldots \cup \mathbf{e}^L$.

By using the generalized expectation formula of Dirichlet distribution, the expected probability of each fine-grained class k can be obtained by computing the expection value of Equation (7)

$$\begin{aligned}\widetilde{\mathfrak{E}}_{p_k} &= \frac{1+\sum_{k'\in\widetilde{K}}\delta(k',k)\cdot e_{k'}}{\left|K^L\right|+\sum_{k'\in\widetilde{K}} e_{k'}} \qquad (\forall k \in K^L)\\ &= \underbrace{\frac{e_k}{\left|K^L\right|+\sum_{k'\in\widetilde{K}} e_{k'}}}_{b_k^S} + \underbrace{\frac{\sum_{k'\in\widetilde{K},k'\neq k}\delta(k',k)e_{k'}}{\left|K^L\right|+\sum_{k'\in\widetilde{K}} e_{k'}}}_{b_k^V} + \underbrace{\frac{1}{\left|K^L\right|+\sum_{k'\in\widetilde{K}} e_{k'}}}_{u_k^F} \qquad (8)\\ &= b_k^S + b_k^V + u_k^F,\end{aligned}$$

where

$$\delta(k',k) = \begin{cases} 1/C_{k'}, & \text{if } k' \text{ is the ancestor class of } k,\\ 1, & \text{else if } k' = k,\\ 0, & \text{else.}\end{cases} \qquad (9)$$

By using Equation (8), coarse-grained classification evidence is decomposed into corresponding fine-grained classes to enhance fine-grained classification performance.

In addition, we can easily prove that the overall uncertainty can be reduced when evidence of coarse-grained classification are fused by using Equation (8). Assuming that in hierarchical classification process, the uncertainty value of fine-grained classification layer u_L (see Equation (3) and (6)) can be denoted as

$$u_L = \frac{|K^L|}{S} = \frac{|K^L|}{\sum_{k\in K^L} e_k^L + |K^L|} . \tag{10}$$

After using Equation (8) to perform multi-layer evidence fusion, the uncertainty value is

$$\begin{aligned} u'_L &= \frac{|K^L|}{\left|K^L\right| + \sum_{k=1}^{|K^L|}\sum_{k'=1}^{|\bar{K}|}\delta(k',k)\cdot e_{k'}} \\ &= \frac{|K^L|}{\sum_{k\in K^L} e_k^L + \left|K^L\right| + \sum_{k=1}^{|K^L|}\sum_{k'\in\bar{K},k'\neq k}^{|\bar{K}|}\delta(k',k)\cdot e_{k'}} . \end{aligned} \tag{11}$$

It is obvious that the uncertainty value u_L of fine-grained classification layer is reduced after fusing the evidence from coarse-grained layers, and thereby we can achieve trusted FGIC.

The training process of evidential classifier of each classification layer are performed separately. The loss function of each layer is denoted as

$$\mathbb{L}^l = \mathbb{L}^l_{CE} + \lambda_t \mathbb{L}^l_{KL} , \tag{12}$$

where $\lambda_t = \min\{1.0,\ t/T\}$ is the annealing coefficient and t is current training epoch.

$$\begin{aligned} \mathbb{L}^l_{CE} &= \int\left[\sum_{k=1}^{|K^l|} -y_k \log p_k\right] \frac{1}{\mathbb{B}(\mathbf{e}^l + 1)} \prod_{k=1}^{|K^l|} p_k^{e_k^l+1-1}\, dp \\ &= \sum_{k=1}^{|K^l|} y_k\left[\psi(S) - \psi(e_k^l + 1)\right], \end{aligned} \tag{13}$$

where $S = \sum_{k=1}^{|K^l|}(e_k^{l,i} + 1)$, $\psi(\cdot)$ is digamma function.

$$\mathbb{L}_{KL}^{l} = KL[Dir(\mathbf{p}^l|\tilde{\boldsymbol{\alpha}}^l)||Dir(\mathbf{p}^l|1)] \\ = \log\frac{\Gamma(\sum_{k=1}^{|K^l|}\tilde{\alpha}_k^l)}{\Gamma(|K^l|)\prod_{k=1}^{|K^l|}\Gamma(\tilde{\alpha}_k^l)} + \sum_{k=1}^{|K^l|}(\tilde{\alpha}_k^l - 1)[\psi(\tilde{\alpha}_k^l) - \psi(\sum_{k=1}^{|K^l|}\tilde{\alpha}_k^l)], \tag{14}$$

where $\Gamma(\cdot)$ is gamma function, and $\tilde{\boldsymbol{\alpha}}^l$ is

$$\tilde{\alpha}_k^{l,i} = \begin{cases} \alpha_k^{l,i}, & \text{if} k \neq \text{ground-truth}, \\ 1, & \text{otherwise}. \end{cases} \tag{15}$$

Trusted FGIC Extension for Fine-Grained Medical Image Classification

In medical image analysis, fine-grained medical image classification (FGMIC) aims to explore that the accurate classification model to identify disease subclasses within the corresponding metaclass, e.g., cancer subtype classification. However, due to insufficient medical images, the accuracy of FGMIC can be very limited, and the trustworthiness of the model can also be affected, which is crucial for practical clinical applications. Therefore, we expand the proposed trusted FGIC method to the medical image classification, and thereby improving the accuracy and trustworthiness of the model.

Figure 5. Framework of the trusted medical image classification

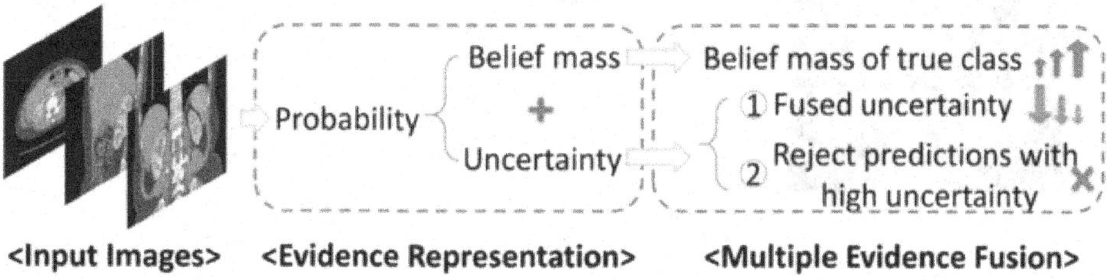

As shown in Figure 6, medical images are usually 3D. Directly transferring FGIC model developed for 2D images to this domain can present certain challenges. Thus, we decompose 3D image to three 2D views based on the different viewing angles.

Figure 6. An example of 3D medical image and its corresponding three 2D image views. Different 2D image views contain different information of lesion area. In general, clinicians diagnose disease by analyzing all 2D image views comprehensively.

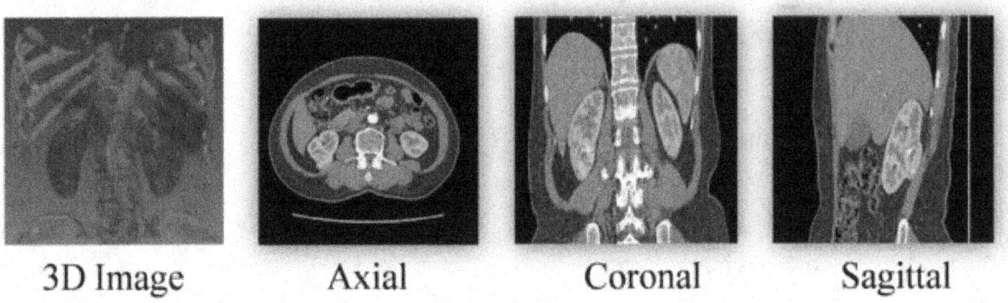

In addition, we can also view fine-grained medical image classification as a hierarchical classification process. As shown in Figure 7, we take bladder tumor staging as an example. In layer 1, tumor staging can be roughly divided into two classes,'≤ T1' and '≥ T2'. As the number of classification layers increases, the granularity of the classification becomes finer and the semantics of each class becomes more specific.

Figure 7. Construction of label hierarchical for bladder tumor staging task

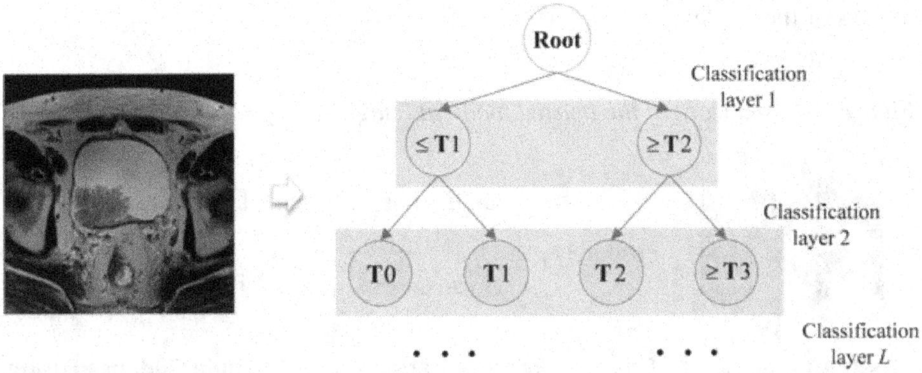

Then, on each 2D medical image view, we can construct a trusted FGIC model. Moreover, considering that the lesion regions in the image have different pathological manifestations under different 2D image views. After obtaining the classification results at each 2D view, we perform a multi-view classification evidence fusion based on the uncertainties at different 2D views.

$$\mathbf{e}^{l} = \sum_{v=1}^{V} \exp[(1 - u^{l,v})/\eta] \cdot \mathbf{e}^{l,v} \tag{16}$$

where l is classification layer, η is a hyperparameter.

EXPERIMENTS

In this section, we perform experiments on three natural FGIC datasets, CUB-200-2011 (CUB), FGVC Aircraft (AIR) and Stanford Cars (CAR), and two medical image datasets collected from our collaborating hospital, MRI Bladder tumor staging dataset and CT Renal tumor classification dataset. We employ ResNet50 as the backbone of evidential classifier of each classification layer.

As shown in Table 1, compared with other 14 state-of-the-art FGIC methods, our Trusted FGIC method achieves competitive performance across three natural image datasets, which well validate the effectiveness of the proposed method.

Table 1. Trusted FGIC method

	CUB	**AIR**	**CAR**
CIN	87.5	92.8	94.4
Cross-X	87.7	92.6	94.6
DCL	87.8	93.0	94.8
API-Net	87.7	93.0	94.8
ACNet	88.1	92.4	94.6
GCL	88.3	93.2	94.0
S3N	88.5	92.8	94.7
FDL	88.6	93.4	94.3
DF-GMM	88.8	93.8	94.8
CSC-Net	89.2	93.8	<u>94.9</u>
PMG	<u>89.6</u>	93.4	**95.1**
GHORD	<u>89.6</u>	<u>94.3</u>	**95.1**
MGDR	86.8	92.8	94.3
HSE	88.1	-	-
Trusted FGIC	**89.9**	**94.8**	<u>94.9</u>

Moveover, as shown in Table 2, compared with other 8 state-of-the-art methods, our extension of Trusted FGIC method achieves competitive performance across two medical image classification datasets.

Table 2. Trusted FGIC method

	Method	Renal	Bladder
Multi-view based methods	CCA	84.9	-
	DCCA	83.8	-
	TMV	92.0	-
	TMC	91.6	-
FGIC based methods	MMM	89.4	76.5
	PMG	91.2	78.7
	TransFG	87.2	77.9
	T-FGIC	87.6	75.7
	Trusted FGIC	**93.1**	**80.9**

Except improvement of classification accuracy, we also give some representative examples to illustrate the trustworthiness of the proposed method. As shown in Figure 8, the trustworthiness of the proposed method can be manifested in three aspects.

Firstly, as shown in the first row, all images have significant features or distinct backgrounds. However, baseline method incorrctly classifies these samples into wrong classes with high confidence. In contrast, the proposed trusted FGIC methods successfully identifies the ground-truth classes of these samples and generate low uncertainty values, representing that the predictions are trustworthy.

Secondly, the samples in the second row, in contrast to those in the first row, contain significant noise. This factor leads the baseline method to incorrectly classify these samples into the wrong classes with high confidence. Conversely, our method enhances the confidence of assigning these samples to the ground-truth classes through hierarchical evidence fusion and effectively identifies these untrustworthy classifications.

Finally, in the last row, the baseline method is capable of identifying the ground-truth classes for the samples, but the confidence associated with these correct classifications is low. This low confidence can result in the predictions being untrustworthy. In contrast, our method enhances the prediction confidence by incorporating hierarchical evidence fusion.

Figure 8. Three kinds of representative cases to illustrate the trustworthiness of the proposed trusted FGIC method

CONCLUSION

In this chapter, we introduce a general framework of trusted fine-grained image classification, and its extension to the fine-grained medical image classification tasks. Based on evidence theory, we view FGIC as a hierarchical classification and achieve trusted classification by fusing hierarchical evidence into fine-grained classification. In addition to improving the classification performance, the proposed framework can also reduce predictive uncertainty. Moreover, the proposed framework can be easily integrated on the top of the extant state-of-the-art FGIC methods.

REFERENCES

Chang, D., Ding, Y., Xie, J., Bhunia, A. K., Li, X., Ma, Z., Wu, M., Guo, J., & Song, Y. Z. (2020). The devil is in the channels: Mutual-channel loss for fine-grained image classification. *IEEE Transactions on Image Processing*, 29, 4683–4695. 10.1109/TIP.2020.297381232092002

Chu, G., Potetz, B., Wang, W., Howard, A., Song, Y., Brucher, F., & Adam, H. (2019). Geo-aware networks for fine-grained recognition. *Proceedings of the IEEE/CVF International Conference on Computer Vision Workshops*, 247-254.

Du, R., Chang, D., Bhunia, A. K., Xie, J., Ma, Z., Song, Y. Z., & Guo, J. (2020). Fine-grained visual classification via progressive multi-granularity training of jigsaw patches. *European Conference on Computer Vision,* 153-168. 10.1007/978-3-030-58565-5_10

Gao, Y., Han, X., Wang, X., Huang, W., & Scott, M. (2020). Channel interaction networks for fine-grained image categorization. *Proceedings of the AAAI Conference on Artificial Intelligence*, 34(7), 10818–10825. 10.1609/aaai.v34i07.6712

He, J., Chen, J. N., Liu, S., Kortylewski, A., Yang, C., Bai, Y., & Wang, C. (2022). Transfg: A transformer architecture for fine-grained recognition. *Proceedings of the AAAI Conference on Artificial Intelligence*, 36(1), 852–860. 10.1609/aaai.v36i1.19967

He, K., Zhang, X., Ren, S., & Sun, J. (2016). Deep residual learning for image recognition. *Proceedings of the IEEE conference on computer vision and pattern recognition*, 770-778.

Hu, J., Shen, L., & Sun, G. (2018). Squeeze-and-excitation networks. *Proceedings of the IEEE conference on computer vision and pattern recognition*, 7132-7141.

Huang, G., Liu, Z., Van Der Maaten, L., & Weinberger, K. Q. (2017). Densely connected convolutional networks. *Proceedings of the IEEE conference on computer vision and pattern recognition*, 4700-4708.

Ji, R., Wen, L., Zhang, L., Du, D., Wu, Y., Zhao, C., & Huang, F. (2020). Attention convolutional binary neural tree for fine-grained visual categorization. *Proceedings of the IEEE/CVF Conference on Computer Vision and Pattern Recognition*, 10468-10477. 10.1109/CVPR42600.2020.01048

Liu, K., Chen, K., & Jia, K. (2022). Convolutional fine-grained classification with self-Supervised target relation regularization. *IEEE Transactions on Image Processing*, 31, 5570–5584. 10.1109/TIP.2022.319793135981063

Simonyan, K., & Zisserman, A. (2014). Very deep convolutional networks for large-scale image recognition. *arXiv preprint arXiv:1409.1556.*

Song, J., & Yang, R. (2021). Learning granularity-aware convolutional neural network for fine-grained visual classification. *arXiv preprint arXiv:2103.02788.*

Sun, H., He, X., & Peng, Y. (2022). Sim-trans: Structure information modeling transformer for fine-grained visual categorization. *Proceedings of the 30th ACM International Conference on Multimedia*, 5853-5861. 10.1145/3503161.3548308

Sun, M., Yuan, Y., Zhou, F., & Ding, E. (2018). Multi-attention multi-class constraint for fine-grained image recognition. *Proceedings of the european conference on computer vision*, 805-821. 10.1007/978-3-030-01270-0_49

Wang, D., Shen, Z., Shao, J., Zhang, W., Xue, X., & Zhang, Z. (2015). Multiple granularity descriptors for fine-grained categorization. *Proceedings of the IEEE international conference on computer vision,* 2399-2406.

Wang, Q., Wang, J., Deng, H., Wu, X., Wang, Y., & Hao, G. (2023). Aa-trans: Core attention aggregating transformer with information entropy selector for fine-grained visual classification. *Pattern Recognition*, 140, 109547. 10.1016/j.patcog.2023.109547

Yang, S., Liu, S., Yang, C., & Wang, C. (2021). Re-rank coarse classification with local region enhanced features for fine-grained image recognition. *arXiv preprint arXiv:2102.09875.*

Zhang, F., Li, M., Zhai, G., & Liu, Y. (2021). Multi-branch and multi-scale attention learning for fine-grained visual categorization. *MultiMedia Modeling: 27th International Conference, MMM*, 136-147.

Zhang, N., Donahue, J., Girshick, R., & Darrell, T. (2014). Part-based R-CNNs for fine-grained category detection. *Computer Vision–ECCV 2014: 13th European Conference*, 834-849.

Zhang, X., Zhou, F., Lin, Y., & Zhang, S. (2016). Embedding label structures for fine-grained feature representation. *Proceedings of the IEEE Conference on Computer Vision and Pattern Recognition,* 1114-1123. 10.1109/CVPR.2016.126

Zhao, Y., Li, J., Chen, X., & Tian, Y. (2021). Part-guided relational transformers for fine-grained visual recognition. *IEEE Transactions on Image Processing*, 30, 9470–9481. 10.1109/TIP.2021.312649034780327

Zheng, H., Fu, J., Mei, T., & Luo, J. (2017). Learning multi-attention convolutional neural network for fine-grained image recognition. *Proceedings of the IEEE international conference on computer vision*, 5209-5217. 10.1109/ICCV.2017.557

Zhou, F., & Lin, Y. (2016). Fine-grained image classification by exploring bipartite-graph labels. *Proceedings of the IEEE Conference on Computer Vision and Pattern Recognition,* 1124-1133. 10.1109/CVPR.2016.127

Zhuang, P., Wang, Y., & Qiao, Y. (2020). Learning attentive pairwise interaction for fine-grained classification. *Proceedings of the AAAI Conference on Artificial Intelligence*, 34(7), 13130–13137. 10.1609/aaai.v34i07.7016

Compilation of References

Anton, H., Bivens, I., & Davis, S. (2008). *Calculus*. Higher Education Press.

Apolloni, B., Bassis, S., Rota, J., Galliani, G. L., Gioia, M., & Ferrari, L. (2016). A neurofuzzy algorithm for learning from complex granules. *Granular Computing*, 1(4), 225–246. Advance online publication. 10.1007/s41066-016-0018-1

Atanassov, K. T. (1986). Intuitionistic fuzzy sets. *Fuzzy Sets and Systems*, 20(1), 87–96. 10.1016/S0165-0114(86)80034-3

Atanassov, K. T., & Gargov, G. (1989). Interval valued intuitionistic fuzzy sets. *Fuzzy Sets and Systems*, 31(3), 343–349. 10.1016/0165-0114(89)90205-4

Bai, L., Cheng, X., Liang, J., & Guo, Y. (2017). Fast graph clustering with a new description model for community detection. *Information Sciences*, 388, 37–47. 10.1016/j.ins.2017.01.026

Bai, X. L., Yun, Z. Q., Xuan, D., Lai, T. H., & Jia, W. J. (2009). Optimal patterns for four-connectivity and full coverage in wireless sensor networks. *IEEE Transactions on Mobile Computing*, 9(3), 435–448.

Barman, B., & Patra, S. (2019). A novel technique to detect a suboptimal threshold of neighborhood rough sets for hyperspectral band selection. *Soft Computing*, 23(24), 13709–13719. 10.1007/s00500-019-03909-4

Beliakov, G., Bustince, H., James, S., Calvo, T., & Fernandez, J. (2012). Aggregation for Atanassov's intuitionistic and interval valued fuzzy sets: The median operator. *IEEE Transactions on Fuzzy Systems*, 20(3), 487–498. 10.1109/TFUZZ.2011.2177271

Beliakov, G., Pradera, A., & Calvo, T. (2007). *Conjunctive and Disjunctive Functions*. Springer. 10.1007/978-3-540-73721-6_3

Blondel, V. D., Guillaume, J. L., Lambiotte, R., & Lefebvre, E. (2008). *Fast unfolding of communities in large networks*. 10.1088/1742-5468/2008/10/P10008

Boeut, S., Laowattanabandit, P., & Fujii, Y. (2017), Extracting residual coal by auger highwall mining at Mae Tan Coal Mine, Thailand. *Proceedings of Spring Meeting of MMIJ Hokkaido Branch,* 59-60.

Bonikowski, Z., Brynirski, E., & Wybraniec, U. (1998). Extensions and intentions in the rough set theory. *Information Sciences*, 107(1-4), 149–167. 10.1016/S0020-0255(97)10046-9

Bustince, H., Barrenechea, E., Calvo, T., James, S., & Beliakov, G. (2014). Consensus in multi-expert decision making problems using penalty functions defined over a Cartesian product of lattices. *Information Fusion*, 17, 56–64. 10.1016/j.inffus.2011.10.002

Cai, B., Liu, Y., Fan, Q., Zhang, Y., Liu, Z., Yu, S., & Ji, R. (2014). Multi-source information fusion based fault diagnosis of ground-source heat pump using Bayesian network. *Applied Energy*, 114, 1–9. 10.1016/j.apenergy.2013.09.043

Cai, B., Wang, Y., Zeng, L., Hu, Y., & Li, H. (2020). Edge classification based on convolutional neural networks for community detection in complex network. *Physica A*, 556, 124826. 10.1016/j.physa.2020.124826

Cai, B., Zeng, L. N., Wang, Y. P., Li, H. J., & Hu, Y. M. (2019). Community detection method based on node density, degree centrality, and *k*-means clustering in complex network. *Entropy (Basel, Switzerland)*, 21(12), 1145. 10.3390/e21121145

Chang, D., Ding, Y., Xie, J., Bhunia, A. K., Li, X., Ma, Z., Wu, M., Guo, J., & Song, Y. Z. (2020). The devil is in the channels: Mutual-channel loss for fine-grained image classification. *IEEE Transactions on Image Processing*, 29, 4683–4695. 10.1109/TIP.2020.297381232092002

Chen, C., Huang, H., Zhao, B., Shu, D., & Wang, Y. (2023). The research of AHP-based credit rating system on a blockchain application. *Electronics (Basel)*, 12(4), 887. 10.3390/electronics12040887

Chen, H., Guo, Q., Wang, L., & Meng, X. (2023). Evaluation of slope stability within the influence of mining based on combined weighting and finite cloud model. *Energy Exploration & Exploitation*, 41(2), 636–655. 10.1177/01445987221134638

Chen, J., Li, H., Hu, Z., Liu, K., & Hou, Y. (2022). Evaluation Index for IVIS Integration Test under a Closed Condition Based on the Analytic Hierarchy Process. *Electronics (Basel)*, 11(22), 3830. 10.3390/electronics11223830

Chen, S. M., Cheng, S. H., & Lan, T. C. (2016a). Multicriteria decision making based on the TOPSIS method and similarity measures between intuitionistic fuzzy values. *Information Sciences*, 367-368, 279–295. 10.1016/j.ins.2016.05.044

Chen, S. M., Cheng, S. H., & Tsai, W. H. (2016b). Multiple attribute group decision making based on interval-valued intuitionistic fuzzy aggregation operators and transformation techniques of interval-valued intuitionistic fuzzy values. *Information Sciences*, 367-368, 418–442. 10.1016/j.ins.2016.05.041

Chen, Y., Shimada, H., Sasaoka, T., Hamanaka, A., & Matsui, K. (2013). Research on exploiting residual coal around final end-walls by highwall mining system in China. *International Journal of Mining, Reclamation and Environment*, 27(3), 166–179. 10.1080/17480930.2012.678768

Che, X. Y., Mi, J. S., & Chen, D. G. (2018). Information fusion and numerical characterization of a multi-source information system. *Knowledge-Based Systems*, 145, 121–133. 10.1016/j.knosys.2018.01.008

Chien, E., Lin, C. Y., & Wang, I. H. (2018). Community detection in hypergraphs: optimal statistical limit and efficient algorithms. *International Conference on Artificial Intelligence and Statistics*. https://proceedings.mlr.press/v84/chien18a/chien18a-supp.pdf

Chu, G., Potetz, B., Wang, W., Howard, A., Song, Y., Brucher, F., & Adam, H. (2019). Geo-aware networks for fine-grained recognition. *Proceedings of the IEEE/CVF International Conference on Computer Vision Workshops*, 247-254.

Chu, J. F., Liu, X. W., Wang, Y. M., & Chin, K. S. (2016). A group decision making model considering both the additive consistency and group consensus of intuitionistic fuzzy preference relations. *Computers & Industrial Engineering*, 101, 227–242. 10.1016/j.cie.2016.08.018

Clauset, A., Newman, M. E. J., & Moore, C. (2004). Finding community structure in very large networks. *Physical Review. E*, 70(6 Pt 2), 066111. 10.1103/PhysRevE.70.06611115697438

Cui, Y. E. H., Pedrycz, W., & Li, Z. (2021). Designing distributed fuzzy rule-based models. *IEEE Transactions on Fuzzy Systems*, 29(7), 2047–2053. 10.1109/TFUZZ.2020.2984971

Dai, J. H., Hu, H., Wu, W. Z., Qian, Y. H., & Huang, D. B. (2013). Maximal discernibility pairs based approach to attribute reduction in fuzzy rough sets. *IEEE Transactions on Fuzzy Systems*, 219, 151–167.

Dai, J. H., Wei, B. J., Zhang, X. H., & Zhang, Q. L. (2017). Uncertainty measurement for incomplete interval-valued information systems based on α-weak similarity. *Knowledge-Based Systems*, 136, 159–171. 10.1016/j.knosys.2017.09.009

Dai, J. H., & Xu, Q. (2013). Attribute selection based on information gain ratio in fuzzy rough set theory with application to tumor classification. *Applied Soft Computing*, 13(1), 211–221. 10.1016/j.asoc.2012.07.029

Deng, Z., Li, T., Deng, D., Liu, K., Zhang, P., Zhang, S., & Luo, Z. (2022). Feature selection for label distribution learning using dual-similarity based neighborhood fuzzy entropy. *Information Sciences*, 615, 385–404. 10.1016/j.ins.2022.10.054

Deng, Z., Li, T., Liu, K., Zhang, P., & Deng, D. (2023). Feature selection based on probability and mathematical expectation. *International Journal of Machine Learning and Cybernetics*, 1–15.

Deschrijver, G., & Kerre, E. E. (2002). A generalization of operators on intuitionistic fuzzy sets using triangular norms and conorms. *Notes on IFS*, 8(1), 19–27.

Ding, X., Zhang, J., & Yang, J. (2018). A robust two-stage algorithm for local community detection. *Knowledge-Based Systems, 152*, 188-199. 10.1016/j.knosys.2018.04.018

Ding, X., Li, F., & Fu, T. (2021). Overburden movement and failure law of coalface in end slope and the slope stability control method. *Meitan Xuebao*, 46(9), 2883–2894.

Doluca, O., & Oguz, K. (2021). APAL: Adjacency propagation algorithm for overlapping community detection in biological networks. *Information Sciences*, 579, 574–590. 10.1016/j.ins.2021.08.031

Domiingos, P. (1999). MetaCosts: A general method for making classifiers cost-sensitive. *ACM SIGKDD International Conference on Knowledge Discovery and Data Mining*. ACM.

Dong, G., Wei, W., Xia, X., Woźniak, M., & Damaševičius, R. (2020). Safety risk assessment of a Pb-Zn mine based on fuzzy-grey correlation analysis. *Electronics (Basel)*, 9(1), 130. 10.3390/electronics9010130

Dou, H. L., Yang, X. B., Song, X. N., Yu, H. L., Wu, W. Z., & Yang, J. Y. (2016). Decision-theoretic rough set: A multi-cost strategy. *Knowledge-Based Systems*, 91, 71–83. 10.1016/j.knosys.2015.09.011

Duan, L., Guo, S., Han, L., & Wei, H. (2022). Research on optimal selection of steep slope mining based on AHP-TOPSIS method. *Coal Technology*, 41(9), 18–22.

Duan, Z., Sun, X., Zhao, S., Chen, J., Zhang, Y. P., & Tang, J. (2020). Hierarchical community structure preserving approach for network embedding. *Information Sciences*, 546, 1084–1096. 10.1016/j.ins.2020.09.053

Dubois, D., & Prade, H. (1992). Putting rough sets and fuzzy sets together. In R. Słowin´ski (Ed.), *Intelligent decision support: Handbook of applications and advances of the rough sets theory* (pp. 203–232). Dordrecht: Kluwer Academic Publishers. 10.1007/978-94-015-7975-9_14

Dubois, D., & Prade, H. (1990). Rough fuzzy sets and fuzzy rough sets. *International Journal of General Systems*, 17(2–3), 191–209. 10.1080/03081079008935107

Du, R., Chang, D., Bhunia, A. K., Xie, J., Ma, Z., Song, Y. Z., & Guo, J. (2020). Fine-grained visual classification via progressive multi-granularity training of jigsaw patches. *European Conference on Computer Vision,* 153-168. 10.1007/978-3-030-58565-5_10

Du, Y. J., Zhou, Q., Luo, J. X., Li, X. Y., & Hu, J. R. (2021). Detection of key figures in social networks by combining harmonic modularity with community structure-regulated network embedding. *Information Sciences*, 570, 722–743. 10.1016/j.ins.2021.04.081

E, H., Cui, Y., Pedrycz, W., Li, Z. (2022). Fuzzy Relational Matrix Factorization and Its Granular Characterization in Data Description. *IEEE Transactions on Fuzzy Systems, 30*(3), 794–804.

E, H., Cui, Y., Pedrycz, W., Li, Z. (2023). Design of Distributed Rule-Based Models in the Presence of Large Data. *IEEE Transactions on Fuzzy Systems, 31*(7), 2479–2486.

E, H., Cui, Y., Pedrycz, W., & Li, Z. (2022). Fuzzy relational matrix factorization and its granular characterization in data description. *IEEE Transactions on Fuzzy Systems*, 30(3), 794–804. 10.1109/TFUZZ.2020.3048577

E, H., Cui, Y., Pedrycz, W., & Li, Z. (2023). Design of distributed rule-based models in the presence of large data. *IEEE Transactions on Fuzzy Systems*, 31(7), 2479–2486. 10.1109/TFUZZ.2022.3226250

Elmouttie, M., & Karekal, S. (2017). A framework for geotechnical hazard analysis in highwall mining entries. *Procedia Engineering*, 2017(191), 1203–1210. 10.1016/j.proeng.2017.05.296

Fan, B. J., Tsang, E. C. C., Xu, W. H., & Yu, J. H. (2017). Double-quantitative rough fuzzy set based decisions. *Information Sciences*, 378, 264–281. 10.1016/j.ins.2016.05.035

Fan, B., Tsang, E. C. C., & Xu, W. (2016). Double-quantitative rough fuzzy set based decisions: A logical operations method. *Information Sciences*.

Fang, Y., & Min, F. (2019). Cost-sensitive approximate attribute reduction with three-way decisions. *International Journal of Approximate Reasoning*, 104, 148–165. 10.1016/j.ijar.2018.11.003

Fan, S. D., & Zhi, T. Y. (2001). The algebraic property of rough sets [in Chinese]. *Journal of Shanxi University*, 24, 116–119.

Fan, W., & Xiao, F. (2022). A complex Jensen–Shannon divergence in complex evidence theory with its application in multi-source information fusion. *Engineering Applications of Artificial Intelligence*, 116, 105362. 10.1016/j.engappai.2022.105362

Fayaz, M., Ullah, I., Park, D. H., Kim, K., & Kim, D. (2017). An integrated risk index model based on hierarchical fuzzy logic for underground risk assessment. *Applied Sciences (Basel, Switzerland)*, 7(10), 1037. 10.3390/app7101037

Feng, T., Fan, H. T., & Mi, J. S. (2017). Uncertainty and reduction of variable precision multigranulation fuzzy rough sets based on three-way decisions. *International Journal of Approximate Reasoning*, 85, 36–58. 10.1016/j.ijar.2017.03.002

Ferone, A. (2018). Feature selection based on composition of rough sets induced by feature granulation. *International Journal of Approximate Reasoning*, 101, 276–292. 10.1016/j.ijar.2018.07.011

Gao, Y., Han, X., Wang, X., Huang, W., & Scott, M. (2020). Channel interaction networks for fine-grained image categorization. *Proceedings of the AAAI Conference on Artificial Intelligence*, 34(7), 10818–10825. 10.1609/aaai.v34i07.6712

Garg, H. (2016a). A new generalized improved score function of interval-valued intuitionistic fuzzy sets and applications in expert systems. *Applied Soft Computing*, 38, 988–999. 10.1016/j.asoc.2015.10.040

Garg, H. (2016b). Generalized intuitionistic fuzzy interactive geometric interaction operators using Einstein t-norm and t-conorm and their application to decision making. *Computers & Industrial Engineering*, 101, 53–69. 10.1016/j.cie.2016.08.017

Girvan, M., & Newman, M. E. J. (2002). Community structure in social and biological networks. *Proc Natl Acad, USA, 99*(12), 7821-7826. 10.1073/pnas.122653799

Gong, Z., & Chai, R. (2016). Covering multigranulation trapezoidal fuzzy decision-theoretic rough fuzzy set models and applications. *Journal of Intelligent & Fuzzy Systems*, 31(3), 1–13. 10.3233/JIFS-151684

Greco, S., Matarazzo, B., & Slowinski, R. (1999). Rough approximation of a preference relation by dominance relations. *European Journal of Operational Research*, 117(1), 63–83. 10.1016/S0377-2217(98)00127-1

Greco, S., Matarazzo, B., & Slowinski, R. (2002). Rough approximation by dominance relations. *International Journal of Intelligent Systems*, 17(2), 153–171. 10.1002/int.10014

Green, O., & Bader, D. A. (2013). Faster betweenness centrality based on data structure experimentation. *Procedia Computer Science*, 18, 399–408. 10.1016/j.procs.2013.05.203

Guo, K., & Zhang, L. (2021). Multi-source information fusion for safety risk assessment in underground tunnels. *Knowledge-Based Systems*, 227, 107210. 10.1016/j.knosys.2021.107210

Guo, Y., Tsang, E. C., & Xu, W. (2017, July). A weighted multi-granulation decision-theoretic approach to multi-source decision systems. In *2017 International Conference on Machine Learning and Cybernetics (ICMLC)* (Vol. 1, pp. 202-210). IEEE. 10.1109/ICMLC.2017.8107765

Gupta, P., Mehlawat, M. K., & Grover, N. (2016). Intuitionistic fuzzy multi-attribute group decision-making with an application to plant location selection based on a new extended VIKOR method. *Information Sciences*, 370-371, 184–203. 10.1016/j.ins.2016.07.058

Hall, D. (1992). *Mathematical Techniques in Multisenor Data Fusion*. Artech House Publisher.

Hall, D. (2001). *Handbook of Multisenor Data Fusion*. CRC Press. 10.1201/9781420038545

Hamachar, H. (1978), Uber logische verknunpfungenn unssharfer Aussagen undderen Zugenhorige Bewertungsfunktione, *Progress in Cybernatics and Systems Research, 3*, 276-288.

Hao, C., Li, J., Fan, M., Liu, W., & Tsang, E. C. C. (2017). Optimal scale selection in dynamic multi-scale decision tables based on sequential three-way decisions. *Information Sciences*, 415, 213–232. 10.1016/j.ins.2017.06.032

He, D. X., You, X. X., Feng, Z. Y., Jin, D., Yang, X., & Zhang, W. (2018). A Network-Specific Markov Random Field Approach to Community Detection. *Proceedings of the 32th AAAI Conference on Artificial Intelligence.* 10.1609/aaai.v32i1.11281

He, J., Chen, J. N., Liu, S., Kortylewski, A., Yang, C., Bai, Y., & Wang, C. (2022). Transfg: A transformer architecture for fine-grained recognition. *Proceedings of the AAAI Conference on Artificial Intelligence*, 36(1), 852–860. 10.1609/aaai.v36i1.19967

He, K., Zhang, X., Ren, S., & Sun, J. (2016). Deep residual learning for image recognition. *Proceedings of the IEEE conference on computer vision and pattern recognition*, 770-778.

Huang, W., & Wang, Z. (2017), Comprehensive evaluation model of fuzzy analytic hierarchy process with variable weight for underground coal gasification. *Journal of Xi'an University Of Science and Technology*, *37*(54), 500-507.

Huang, G., Liu, Z., Van Der Maaten, L., & Weinberger, K. Q. (2017). Densely connected convolutional networks. *Proceedings of the IEEE conference on computer vision and pattern recognition*, 4700-4708.

Huang, J. Y. (2014). Intuitionistic fuzzy Hamacher aggregation operators and their application to multiple attribute decision making. *Journal of Intelligent & Fuzzy Systems*, 27(1), 505–513. 10.3233/IFS-131019

Huang, Y. Y., Li, T. R., Luo, C., Fujita, H., & Horng, S. J. (2018). Dynamic fusion of multi-source interval-valued data by fuzzy granulation. *IEEE Transactions on Fuzzy Systems*, 26(6), 3403–3417. 10.1109/TFUZZ.2018.2832608

Hu, J., Shen, L., & Sun, G. (2018). Squeeze-and-excitation networks. *Proceedings of the IEEE conference on computer vision and pattern recognition*, 7132-7141.

Hung, W. L., & Wu, J. W. (2002). Correlation of intuitionistic fuzzy sets by centroid method. *Information Sciences*, 144(1), 219–225. 10.1016/S0020-0255(02)00181-0

Hu, Q. H., Liu, J. F., & Yu, D. R. (2008b). Mixed feature selection based on granulation and approximation. *Knowledge-Based Systems*, 21(4), 294–304. 10.1016/j.knosys.2007.07.001

Hu, Q. H., Yu, D. R., Liu, J. F., & Wu, C. X. (2008a). Neighborhood rough set based heterogeneous feature subset selection. *Information Sciences*, 178(18), 3577–3594. 10.1016/j.ins.2008.05.024

Inaba, K., Inagaki, T., Igarashi, K., Utsunomiya, S., & Takesue, H. (2021). Potts model solver based on hybrid physical and digital architecture. *Communications on Physics*, 5(1), 1–8. 10.21203/rs.3.rs-464366/v1

Ivannikova, E., Park, H., Hmlinen, T., & Lee, K. (2018). *Revealing community structures by ensemble clustering using group diffusion*. Elsevier. 10.1016/j.inffus.2017.09.013

Jackson, T., & Green, K. P. (2015). *Fraser Institute Annual Survey of Mining Companies: 2015[EB/OL]*. https://www.fraserinstitute.org/studies/annual-survey-of-mining-companies-2015

Jia, X., Zheng, K., & Li, W. (2012). Three-way decisions solution to filter spam email: an empirical study. *International Conference on Rough Sets and Current Trends in Computing*. Springer Berlin Heidelberg.

Jiang, J., Lu, Y., Cao, L., Fu, T., Wang, D., Wang, L., & Li, L. (2023). Parameter design of coal pillar in highwall mining under the action of dynamic-static load. *Coal Science and Technology*, 51(5), 53–62.

Jia, Y. T., Zhang, Q. Q., Zhang, W. N., & Wang, X. B. (2019). CommunityGAN: Community Detection with Generative Adversarial Nets. *Proceedings of the WWW '19: The World Wide Web Conference*, 784-794. 10.1145/3308558.3313564

Jin, D., Wang, K., Zhang, G., Jiao, P., & Huang, X. (2019). Detecting communities with multiplex semantics by distinguishing background, general and specialized topics. *IEEE Transactions on Knowledge and Data Engineering*, 32(11), 2144–2158. 10.1109/TKDE.2019.2937298

Jing, B., Li, T., Ying, N., & Yu, X. (2021). Community detection in sparse networks using the symmetrized Laplacian inverse matrix (slim). *Statistica Sinica*, 32(1), 1–22. 10.5705/ss.202020.0094

Ji, Q. B., Li, D. Y., & Jin, Z. (2020). Divisive algorithm based on node clustering coefficient for community detection. *IEEE Access : Practical Innovations, Open Solutions*, 8, 142337–142347. 10.1109/ACCESS.2020.3013241

Ji, R., Wen, L., Zhang, L., Du, D., Wu, Y., Zhao, C., & Huang, F. (2020). Attention convolutional binary neural tree for fine-grained visual categorization. *Proceedings of the IEEE/CVF Conference on Computer Vision and Pattern Recognition*, 10468-10477. 10.1109/CVPR42600.2020.01048

Ju, Y. B., Zhang, W. K., & Yang, S. H. (2014). Some dual hesitant fuzzy Hamacher aggregation operators and their applications to multiple attribute decision making. *Journal of Intelligent & Fuzzy Systems*, 27(5), 2481–2495. 10.3233/IFS-141222

Kaminski, B., Pralat, P., & Theberge, F. (2020). Community Detection Algorithm Using Hypergraph Modularity. *International Workshop on Complex Networks and Their Applications*. Springer.

Karrer, B., & Newman, M. E. J. (2011). Stochastic blockmodels and community structure in networks. *Physical Review. E*, 83(1 Pt 2), 016107. 10.1103/PhysRevE.83.01610721405744

Khan, M. A., & Banerjee, M. (2008). Formal reasoning with rough sets in multiple-source approximation systems. *International Journal of Approximate Reasoning*, 49(2), 466–477. 10.1016/j.ijar.2008.04.005

Kong, L. S., Ren, X. F., & Fan, Y. J. (2019). Study on assessment method for computer network security based on rough set. In *2009 IEEE International Conference on Intelligent Computing and Intelligent Systems*, Shanghai, China.

Kong, Q. Z., & Chang, X. E. (2022a). Number characteristics of information granules in information tables. *Journal of Engineering*, 12, 1208–1218.

Kong, Q. Z., & Chang, X. E. (2022b). Rough set model based on variable universe. *CAAI Transactions on Intelligence Technology*, 7(3), 503–511. 10.1049/cit2.12064

Kong, Q. Z., Xu, W. H., & Zhang, D. X. (2022b). A comparative study of different granular structures induced from the information systems. *Soft Computing*, 26(1), 105–122. 10.1007/s00500-021-06499-2

Kong, Q. Z., Zhang, X. W., Xu, W. H., & Long, B. H. (2022a). A novel granular computing model based on three-way decision. *International Journal of Approximate Reasoning*, 144, 92–112. 10.1016/j.ijar.2022.01.015

Kryszkiewicz, M. (1998). Rough set approach to incomplete information systems. *Information Sciences*, 112(1-4), 39–49. 10.1016/S0020-0255(98)10019-1

Krzakala, F., Moore, C., Mossel, E., Neeman, J., Sly, A., Zdeborova, L., & Zhang, P. (2013). Spectral redemption in clustering sparse networks. *Proceedings of the National Academy of Sciences of the United States of America*, 110(52), 20935–20940. 10.1073/pnas.131248611024277835

Liang, D. C., Pedrycz, W., Liu, D., & Hu, P. (2015). Three-way decisions based on decision-theoretic rough sets under linguistic assessment with the aid of group decision making. *Applied Soft Computing*, 29(C), 256–269. 10.1016/j.asoc.2015.01.008

Liang, J., & Qian, Y. (2008). Information granules and entropy theory in information systems. *Science in China Series F: Information Sciences*, 51(10), 1427–1444. 10.1007/s11432-008-0113-2

Liao, H. C., & Xu, Z. S. (2014). Intuitionistic fuzzy hybrid weighted aggregation operators. *International Journal of Intelligent Systems*, 29(11), 971–993. 10.1002/int.21672

Liao, H. C., & Xu, Z. S. (2015). Extended hesitant fuzzy hybrid weighted aggregation operators and their application in decision making. *Soft Computing*, 19(9), 2551–2564. 10.1007/s00500-014-1422-6

Li, B., Pi, D., Lin, Y., Khan, I. A., & Cui, L. (2020). Multi-source information fusion based heterogeneous network embedding. *Information Sciences*, 534, 53–71. 10.1016/j.ins.2020.05.012

Li, F., Hu, B. Q., & Wang, J. (2017). Stepwise optimal scale selection for multi-scale decision tables via attribute significance. *Knowledge-Based Systems*, 129, 4–16. 10.1016/j.knosys.2017.04.005

Li, H. (1995). Factor spaces and mathematical frame of knowledge representation—Variable weights analysis. *Fuzzy Systems and Mathematics*, 9(3), 1–9.

Li, H., Huang, H. Z., Li, Y. F., Zhou, J., & Mi, J. (2018). Physics of failure-based reliability prediction of turbine blades using multi-source information fusion. *Applied Soft Computing*, 72, 624–635. 10.1016/j.asoc.2018.05.015

Li, H., Zhang, L., Huang, B., & Zhou, X. (2016). Sequential three-way decision and granulation for cost-sensitive face recognition. *Knowledge-Based Systems*, 91(C), 241–251. 10.1016/j.knosys.2015.07.040

Li, H., Zhang, L., Zhou, X., & Huang, B. (2017). Cost-sensitive sequential three-way decision modeling using a deep neural network. *International Journal of Approximate Reasoning*, 85(C), 68–78. 10.1016/j.ijar.2017.03.008

Li, J., Deng, C., Xu, J., Ma, Z., Shuai, P., & Zhang, L. (2023). Safety risk assessment and management of Panzhihua Open Pit (OP)-Underground (UG) Iron Mine based on AHP-FCE, Sichuan Province, China. *Sustainability (Basel)*, 15(5), 4497. 10.3390/su15054497

Li, J., Huang, C., Qi, J., Qian, Y., & Liu, W. (2017). Three-way cognitive concept learning via multi-granularity. *Information Sciences*, 378(1), 244–263. 10.1016/j.ins.2016.04.051

Li, M., & Zhang, X. (2017). Information fusion in a multi-source incomplete information system based on information entropy. *Entropy (Basel, Switzerland)*, 19(11), 570. 10.3390/e19110570

Lin, G. P., Liang, J. Y., & Qian, Y. H. (2013). Multigranulation rough sets: From partition to covering. *Information Systems*, 241, 101–118.

Lin, G. P., Liang, J. Y., & Qian, Y. H. (2015). An information fusion approach by combining multi-granulation rough sets and evidence theory. *Information Sciences*, 314, 184–199. 10.1016/j.ins.2015.03.051

Lin, G. P., Liang, J. Y., Qian, Y. H., & Li, J. J. (2016). A fuzzy multi-granulation decision-theoretic approach to multi-source fuzzy information systems. *Knowledge-Based Systems*, 91, 102–113. 10.1016/j.knosys.2015.09.022

Lin, G. P., Qian, Y. H., & Li, J. J. (2012). NMGRS: Neighborhood-based multi-granulation rough sets. *International Journal of Approximate Reasoning*, 53(7), 1080–1093. 10.1016/j.ijar.2012.05.004

Lingras, P. J., & Yao, Y. (1998). Data mining using extensions of the rough set model. *Journal of the American Society for Information Science*, 49(5), 415–422. 10.1002/(SICI)1097-4571(19980415)49:5<415::AID-ASI4>3.0.CO;2-Z

Lin, T. Y. (2004). Granular computing: From rough sets and neighborhood systems to information systems. *International Journal of Uncertainty, Fuzziness and Knowledge-based Systems*, 12, 651–672.

Liu, D., Li, T., & Liang, D. C. (2013). Fuzzy interval decision-theoretic rough sets. *Ifsa World Congress and Nafips Meeting*. IEEE.

Liu, D., Li, T. R., & Liang, D. C. (2014). Incorporating logistic regression to decision-theoretic rough sets for classifications. *International Journal of Approximate Reasoning*, 55(1), 197–210. 10.1016/j.ijar.2013.02.013

Liu, F., Xue, S., Wu, J., Zhou, C., Hu, W., Paris, C., Nepal, S., Yang, J., & Yu, P. S. (2020). Deep learning for community detection: progress, challenges and opportunities. http://arxiv.org/abs/2005.0822510.24963/ijcai.2020/693

Liu, K., Chen, K., & Jia, K. (2022). Convolutional fine-grained classification with self-Supervised target relation regularization. *IEEE Transactions on Image Processing*, 31, 5570–5584. 10.1109/TIP.2022.319793135981063

Liu, K., Li, T., Yang, X., Yang, X., Liu, D., Zhang, P., & Wang, J. (2022). Granular cabin: An efficient solution to neighborhood learning in big data. *Information Sciences*, 583, 189–201. 10.1016/j.ins.2021.11.034

Liu, P. D. (2014). Some Hamacher aggregation operators based on the interval-valued intuitionistic fuzzy numbers and their application to group decision making. *IEEE Transactions on Fuzzy Systems*, 22(1), 83–97. 10.1109/TFUZZ.2013.2248736

Liu, W. (1997). Balanced function and its application to variable weight synthesizing. *System Engineering Theory & Practice*, 17(4), 58–64.

Liu, W., Wang, L., & Fu, Q. (2012). SHM highwall mining technology and key issues of application. *Coastal Engineering*, 2012(6), 1–4.

Li, W. T., Pedrycz, W., Xue, X. P., Xu, W. H., & Fan, B. J. (2018). Distance-based double-quantitative rough fuzzy sets with logic operations. *International Journal of Approximate Reasoning*, 101, 206–233. 10.1016/j.ijar.2018.07.007

Li, W. T., & Xu, W. H. (2015). Double-quantitative decision-theoretic rough set. *Information Sciences*, 316, 54–67. 10.1016/j.ins.2015.04.020

Li, W. W., Jia, X. Y., Wang, L., & Zhou, B. (2019). Multi-objective attribute reduction in three-way decision-theoretic rough set model. *International Journal of Approximate Reasoning*, 105, 327–341. 10.1016/j.ijar.2018.12.008

Li, W., Deng, C., Pedrycz, W., Castillo, O., Zhang, C., & Zhan, T. (2023). Double-quantitative feature selection approach for multi-granularity ordered decision systems. *IEEE Transactions on Artificial Intelligence*. Advance online publication. 10.1109/TAI.2023.3319301

Li, W., Pedrycz, W., Xue, X., Xu, W., & Fan, B. (2019). Fuzziness and incremental information of disjoint regions in double-quantitative decision-theoretic rough set model. *International Journal of Machine Learning and Cybernetics*, 10(10), 2669–2690. 10.1007/s13042-018-0893-7

Li, W., Wei, Y., & Xu, W. (2022). General expression of knowledge granularity based on a fuzzy relation matrix. *Fuzzy Sets and Systems*, 440, 149–163. 10.1016/j.fss.2022.01.007

Li, W., & Xu, W. (2015). Multi-granulation decision-theoretic rough set in ordered information system. *Fundamenta Informaticae*, 139(1), 67–89. 10.3233/FI-2015-1226

Li, W., Xu, W., Zhang, X., & Zhang, J. (2022). Updating approximations with dynamic objects based on local multigranulation rough sets in ordered information systems. *Artificial Intelligence Review*, 55(8), 1821–1855. 10.1007/s10462-021-10053-9

Li, W., Zhai, S., Xu, W., Pedrycz, W., Qian, Y., Ding, W., & Zhan, T. (2023). Feature selection approach based on improved Fuzzy C-Means with principle of refined justifiable granularity. *IEEE Transactions on Fuzzy Systems*, 31(7), 2112–2126. 10.1109/TFUZZ.2022.3217377

Li, W., Zhang, X., & Sun, W. (2014). Further study of multigranulation T-fuzzy rough sets. *TheScientificWorldJournal*, 2014, 1–18.25215336

Li, W., Zhou, H., Xu, W., Wang, X., & Pedrycz, W. (2022). Interval dominance-based feature selection for interval-valued ordered data. *IEEE Transactions on Neural Networks and Learning Systems*, 34(10), 6898–6912. 10.1109/TNNLS.2022.318412035737612

Li, W., Zhu, H., Li, S., Wang, H., & Jin, Q. (2021). Evolutionary community discovery in dynamic social networks via resistance distance. *Expert Systems with Applications*, 171, 114536. 10.1016/j.eswa.2020.114536

Li, Z., Zhang, P., Ge, X., Xie, N., & Zhang, G. (2019b). Uncertainty measurement for a covering information system. *Soft Computing*, 23(14), 5307–5325. 10.1007/s00500-018-3458-5

Li, Z., Zhang, P., Ge, X., Xie, N., Zhang, G., & Wen, C. F. (2019a). Uncertainty measurement for a fuzzy relation information system. *IEEE Transactions on Fuzzy Systems*, 27(12), 2338–2352. 10.1109/TFUZZ.2019.2898158

Li, Z., Zhang, P., Xie, N., Zhang, G., & Wen, C. F. (2020). A novel three-way decision method in a hybrid information system with images and its application in medical diagnosis. *Engineering Applications of Artificial Intelligence*, 92, 103651. 10.1016/j.engappai.2020.103651

Llinas, J., & Waltz, E. (1990). *Multisensor Data Fusion*. Artech Housse publisher.

Lu, C., Xu, P., & Cong, L. H. (2020). Fault diagnosis model based on granular computing and echo state network. *Engineering Applications of Artificial Intelligence*, 94, 103694. 10.1016/j.engappai.2020.103694

Luo, K., Ma, L., Liu, C., Lv, G., Shi, L., Xu, T., & Xue, F. (2022). Feasibility analysis of end slope and steep mining technology in Hequ Open-pit Mine. *Coastal Engineering*, 54(5), 19–25.

Luo, W. J., Zhang, D. F., Jiang, H., Ni, L., & Hu, Y. M. (2018). Local community detection with the dynamic membership function. *IEEE Transactions on Fuzzy Systems*, 26(5), 3136–3315. 10.1109/TFUZZ.2018.2812148

Mahabadi, A., & Hosseini, M. (2020). SLPA-based parallel overlapping community detection approach in large complex social networks. *Multimedia Tools and Applications*, 80(5), 6567–6598. 10.1007/s11042-020-09993-1

Ma, J. (2021). Study on feasibility evaluation of continuous mining of residual coal based on variable weight fuzzy theory. *Coal Science and Technology*, 49(8), 30–37.

Ma, J., & Song, D. (2023). Mathematical evaluation on the applicability of bolter miners based on variable weight fuzzy theory. *Journal of China Coal Sociey*, 48(6), 2579–2589.

Marcel, S., & Jones, J. H. (2010). Dynamics and control of diseases in networks with community structure. *PLoS Computational Biology*, 6(4), e1000736. Advance online publication. 10.1371/journal.pcbi.100073620386735

Marek, V. W., & Pawlak, Z. (1976). Information storage and retrieval systems: Mathematical foundations. *Theoretical Computer Science*, 1(4), 331–354. 10.1016/0304-3975(76)90077-3

Marek, V. W., & Truszczynski, M. (1999). Contributions to the theory of rough sets. *Fundamenta Informaticae*, 39(4), 389–409. 10.3233/FI-1999-39404

Ma, X.-A., & Zhao, X. R. (2019). Cost-sensitive three-way class-specific attribute reduction. *International Journal of Approximate Reasoning*, 105, 153–174. 10.1016/j.ijar.2018.11.014

Mcguire, M. P., & Nguyen, N. P. (2014). Community structure analysis in big climate data. *2014 IEEE International Conference on Big Data (Big Data) IEEE*, 38-46. https://ieeexplore.ieee.org/document/7004442

Mendel, J. M. (2016). A comparison of three approaches for estimating (synthesizing) an interval type-2 fuzzy set model of a linguistic term for computing with words. *Granular Computing*, 1(1), 59–69. 10.1007/s41066-015-0009-7

Miguel, L. D., Bustince, H., Fernandez, J., Induráin, E., Kolesárová, A., & Mesiar, R. (2016). Construction of admissible linear orders for interval-valued Atanassov intuitionistic fuzzy sets with an application to decision making. *Information Fusion*, 27, 189–197. 10.1016/j.inffus.2015.03.004

Min, F., He, H. P., Qian, Y. H., & Zhu, W. (2011). Test-cost-sensitive attribute reduction. *Information Sciences*, 181(22), 4928–4942. 10.1016/j.ins.2011.07.010

Min, F., Zhang, Z. H., & Dong, J. (2018). Ant colony optimization with partial-complete searching for attribute reduction. *Journal of Computational Science*, 25, 170–182. 10.1016/j.jocs.2017.05.007

Min, F., & Zhu, W. (2012). Attribute reduction of data with error ranges and test costs. *Information Sciences*, 211(211), 48–67. 10.1016/j.ins.2012.04.031

Molontay, R., & Nagy, M. (2019). Two decades of network science: as seen through the co-authorship network of network scientists. *Proceedings of the 2019 IEEE/ACM international conference on advances in social networks analysis and mining*, 578-583. 10.1145/3341161.3343685

Mu, C., Mele, A., Hao, L., Cape, J., Athreya, A., & Priebe, C. E. (2022). On spectral algorithms for community detection in stochastic blockmodel graphs with vertex covariates. *IEEE Transactions on Network Science and Engineering*, (5). https://doi.org//arXiv.2007.0215610.48550

Newman, M. E. J. (2006). Finding community structure in networks using the eigenvectors of matrices. *Physical Review. E*, 74(3), 036104. 10.1103/PhysRevE.74.03610417025705

Newman, M. E. J. (2010). *Networks: An Introduction*. Oxford Univ. Press. 10.1093/acprof:oso/9780199206650.001.0001

Newman, M. E. J. (2012). Communities, modules and large-scale structure in networks. *Nature Physics*, 8(1), 25–31. 10.1038/nphys2162

Newman, M. E. J., & Girvan, M. (2004). Finding and evaluating community structure in networks. *Physical Review. E*, 69(2 Pt 2), 026113. 10.1103/PhysRevE.69.02611314995526

Nezarat, H., Sereshki, F., & Ataei, M. (2015). Ranking of geological risks in mechanized tunneling by using Fuzzy Analytical Hierarchy Process (FAHP). *Tunnelling and Underground Space Technology*, 50, 358–364. 10.1016/j.tust.2015.07.019

Palla, Derényi, Farkas, & Vicsek. (2005). Uncovering the overlapping community structure of complex networks in nature and society. *Nature, 435*(7043), 814-818. https://arxiv.org/PS_cache/physics/pdf/0506/0506133v1.pdf

Pal, S. K., Shankar, B. U., & Mitra, P. (2005). Granular computing, rough entropy and object extraction. *Pattern Recognition Letters*, 26(16), 2509–2517. 10.1016/j.patrec.2005.05.007

Pan, S., Hu, R., Fung, S. F., Long, G., Jiang, J., & Zhang, C. Q. (2020). Learning Graph Embedding with Adversarial Training Methods. *IEEE Transactions on Cybernetics*, 2020(50), 2475–2487. 10.1109/TCYB.2019.293209631484146

Pawlak. (1982). Rough sets. *International Journal of Computer Information Sciences, 11*(5), 341-356.

Pawlak, Z. (1973). Mathematical Foundations of Information Retrieval, Research Report CC. *PAS Reporter*, 101.

Pawlak, Z. (1981). Information systems, theoretical foundations. *Information Systems*, 6(3), 205–218. 10.1016/0306-4379(81)90023-5

Pawlak, Z. (1982). Rough sets. *International Journal of Computer Information Sciences*, 11(5), 341–356. 10.1007/BF01001956

Pawlak, Z. (1982). Rough sets. *Journal of Information Science*, 11, 341–356.

Pawlak, Z. (1984). Rough classification. *International Journal of Man-Machine Studies*, 20(5), 469–483. 10.1016/S0020-7373(84)80022-X

Pawlak, Z. (1991). *Rough sets: theoretical aspects of reasoning about data*. Kluwer Academic Publishers. 10.1007/978-94-011-3534-4

Pawlak, Z., Rough sets. (1982). International Journal of Computer &. *Information Sciences*, 11, 34–356.

Pedrycz, W., Alhmouz, R., Morfeq, A., & Balamash, A. (2013). The design of free structure granular mappings: The use of the principle of justifiable granularity. *IEEE Transactions on Cybernetics*, 43(6), 2105–2113. 10.1109/TCYB.2013.224038423757519

Pedrycz, W., & Bargiela, A. (2002). Granular clustering: A granular signature of data. *IEEE Transactions on Systems, Man, and Cybernetics. Part B, Cybernetics*, 32(2), 212–224. 10.1109/3477.99087818238121

Pedrycz, W., & Bargiela, A. (2012). An optimization of allocation of information granularity in the interpretation of data structures: Toward granular fuzzy clustering. *IEEE Transactions on Systems, Man, and Cybernetics. Part B, Cybernetics*, 42(3), 582–590. 10.1109/TSMCB.2011.217006722067434

Pedrycz, W., & Chen, S. M. (2015). *Granular Computing and Decision-Making: Interactive and Iterative Approaches*. Springer. 10.1007/978-3-319-16829-6

Pedrycz, W., & Homenda, W. (2013). Building the fundamentals of granular computing: A principle of justifiable granularity. *Applied Soft Computing*, 13(10), 4209–4218. 10.1016/j.asoc.2013.06.017

Pedrycz, W., & Skowron, A. (2008). *Handbook of granular computing*. Wiley-Interscience. 10.1002/9780470724163

Peng, S. (2017). *Advances in coal mine ground control*. Woodhead Publishing.

Perry, K., Raffaldi, M., & Harris, K. (2015). Influence of highwall mining progression on web and barrier pillar stability. *Mining Engineering*, 67(3), 59–67.

Pomykala, J. A. (1987). Approximation operations in approximation space. *Bulletin of the Polish Academy of Sciences*, 9-10, 653–662.

Porathur, J. L., Roy, P., Shen, B., & Karekal, S. (2017). *Highwall mining: Applicability, design & safety*. CRC Press/Balkema. 10.1201/9781315171234

Porathur, J., Karekal, S., & Palroy, P. (2013). Web pillar design approach for highwall mining extraction. *International Journal of Rock Mechanics and Mining Sciences*, 64(12), 73–83. 10.1016/j.ijrmms.2013.08.029

Pothen, A., Simon, H. D., & Liou, K. P. (1990). Partitioning sparse matrices with eigenvectors of graphs. *SIAM Journal on Matrix Analysis and Applications*, 11(3), 430–452. 10.1137/0611030

Prakash, A., Kumar, A., & Singh, B. (2015). Highwall mining: A critical appraisal. *Minetech*, 36(3), 17–30.

Pulgar-Rubio, F., Rivera-Rivas, A. J., Pérez-Godoy, M. D., González, P., Carmona, C. J., & Del Jesus, M. J. (2017). Multi-objective evolutionary fuzzy algorithm for subgroup discovery in big data environments - A MapReduce solution. *Knowledge-Based Systems*, 2017(117), 70–78. 10.1016/j.knosys.2016.08.021

Qian, J., Dang, C., Yue, X., & Zhang, N. (2017). Attribute reduction for sequential three-way decisions under dynamic granulation. *International Journal of Approximate Reasoning*, 85, 85. 10.1016/j.ijar.2017.03.009

Qian, J., Liu, C. H., & Yue, X. D. (2019). Multi-granulation sequential three-way decisions based on multiple thresholds. *International Journal of Approximate Reasoning*, 105, 396–416. 10.1016/j.ijar.2018.12.007

Qian, Y. H., Liang, J. Y., Yao, Y. Y., & Dang, C. Y. (2010). MGRS: A multi-granulation rough set. *Information Sciences*, 180(6), 949–970. 10.1016/j.ins.2009.11.023

Qian, Y. H., Liang, X. Y., Wang, Q., Liang, J. Y., Liu, B., Skowron, A., Yao, Y. Y., Ma, J. M., & Dang, C. Y. (2018). Local rough set: A solution to rough data analysis in big data. *International Journal of Approximate Reasoning*, 97, 38–63. 10.1016/j.ijar.2018.01.008

Qian, Y. H., Zhang, H., Sang, Y. L., & Liang, J. Y. (2014). Multi-granulation decision-theoretic rough sets. *International Journal of Approximate Reasoning*, 55(1), 225–237. 10.1016/j.ijar.2013.03.004

Qian, Y., Liang, J., & Pang, C. (2010). Incomplete multigranulation rough set, *IEEE Transactions on Systems. IEEE Transactions on Systems, Man, and Cybernetics. Part A, Systems and Humans*, 20(2), 420–431. 10.1109/TSMCA.2009.2035436

Qian, Y., Liang, X., Lin, G., Guo, Q., & Liang, J. (2017). Local multigranulation decision-theoretic rough sets. *International Journal of Approximate Reasoning*, 82, 119–137. 10.1016/j.ijar.2016.12.008

Qin, J., Liu, Y., & Grosvenor, R. (2018). Multi-source data analytics for AM energy consumption prediction. *Advanced Engineering Informatics*, 38, 840–850. 10.1016/j.aei.2018.10.008

Radicchi, F., Castellano, C., Cecconi, F., Loreto, V., & Parisi, D. (2004). Defining and identifying communities in networks. *National Academy of Sciences, 101*(9), 2658-2663. http://arxiv.org/PS_cache/cond-mat/pdf/0309/0309488v2.pdf

Raghavan, U. N., Réka, A., & Kumara, S. (2007). Near linear time algorithm to detect community structures in large-scale networks. *Physical Review. E*, 76(3 Pt 2), 036106. 10.1103/PhysRevE.76.03610617930305

Randall Wilson, D., & Martinez, T. R. (1997). Improved heterogeneous distance functions. *Journal of Artificial Intelligence Research*, 6, 1–34. 10.1613/jair.346

Raza, M. S., & Qamar, U. (2018). Feature selection using rough set-based direct dependency calculation by avoiding the positive region. *International Journal of Approximate Reasoning*, 92, 175–197. 10.1016/j.ijar.2017.10.012

Ross, C., Conover, D., & Baine, J. (2019). Highwall mining of thick, steeply dipping coal a case study in geotechnical design and recovery optimization. *International Journal of Mining Science and Technology*, 29(5), 777–780. 10.1016/j.ijmst.2017.12.022

Roychowdhury, S., & Wang, B. H. (1998). On generalized Hamacher families of triangular operators. *International Journal of Approximate Reasoning*, 19(3), 419–439. 10.1016/S0888-613X(98)10018-X

Rubner, Y. (1997). The earth mover's distance, multi-dimensional scaling, and color-based image retrieval. *Proceedings of the Arpa Image Understanding Workshop*, 661-668.

Rubner, Y., Tomasi, C., & Guibas, L. J. (2000). The earth mover's distance as a metric for image retrieval. *International Journal of Computer Vision*, 40(2), 99–121. 10.1023/A:1026543900054

Saaty, T. L. (2003). Decision-making with the AHP: Why is the principal eigenvector necessary. *European Journal of Operational Research*, 145(1), 85–89. 10.1016/S0377-2217(02)00227-8

Saberi, M., Mirtalaie, M. S., Hussain, F. K., Azadeh, A., Hussain, O. K., & Ashjari, B. (2013). A granular computing-based approach to credit scoring modeling. *Neurocomputing*, 122, 100–115. 10.1016/j.neucom.2013.05.020

Sang, B. B., Guo, Y. T., Shi, D. R., & Xu, W. H. (2017). Decision-theoretic rough set model of multi-source decision systems. *International Journal of Machine Learning and Cybernetics*, 9, 1–14.

Sang, B., Guo, Y., Shi, D., & Xu, W. (2018). Decision-theoretic rough set model of multi-source decision systems. *International Journal of Machine Learning and Cybernetics*, 9(11), 1941–1954. 10.1007/s13042-017-0729-x

Sasaoka, T., Karian, T., Hamanaka, A., Shimada, H., & Matsui, K. (2016). Application of highwall mining system in weak geological condition. *International Journal of Coal Science & Technology*, 3(3), 311–321. 10.1007/s40789-016-0121-6

Schweizer, B., & Sklar, A. (1960). Statistical metric spaces. *Pacific Journal of Mathematics*, 10(1), 313–334. 10.2140/pjm.1960.10.313

Sharmila, M., Chitra, P., Jeba, G. S., Priyanka, N., & Mirunalini, K. (2020). Community Detection in Social Networks based on Local Edge Centrality and Adaptive Thresholding. *2020 4th International Conference on Trends in Electronics and Informatics (ICOEI),* 751-756. 10.1109/ICOEI48184.2020.9142897

Shen, H., Cheng, X., Cai, K., & Hu, M. B. (2008). Detect overlapping and hierarchical community structure in networks. *Physica A Statal Mechanics & Its Applications, 388*(8), 1706-1712. 10.1016/j.physa.2008.12.021

Shen, B., & Duncan Fama, M. E. (2001). Review of highwall mining experience in Australia and a case study. *Australian Geomechanics*, 36(2), 25–32.

Shimada, H., Chen, Y., Hamanaka, A., Sasaoka, T., Shimada, H., & Matsui, K. (2013). Application of highwall mining system to recover residual coal in End-walls. *Procedia Earth and Planetary Science*, 2013(6), 311–318. 10.1016/j.proeps.2013.01.041

Simonyan, K., & Zisserman, A. (2014). Very deep convolutional networks for large-scale image recognition. *arXiv preprint arXiv:1409.1556.*

Skowron, A., Jankowski, A., & Dutta, S. (2016). Interactive granular computing. *Granular Computing*, 1(2), 95–113. 10.1007/s41066-015-0002-1

Skowron, A., & Stepaniuk, J. (2001, January). Information granules: Towards foundations of computing. *International Journal of Intelligent Systems*, 16(1), 57–85. 10.1002/1098-111X(200101)16:1<57::AID-INT6>3.0.CO;2-Y

Skowronabcd, A. (2012). Modeling rough granular computing based on approximation spaces. *Information Sciences*, 184(1), 20–43. 10.1016/j.ins.2011.08.001

Song, J., & Yang, R. (2021). Learning granularity-aware convolutional neural network for fine-grained visual classification. *arXiv preprint arXiv:2103.02788.*

Song, M. L., & Wang, Y. B. (2016). A study of granular computing in the agenda of growth of artificial neural networks. *Granular Computing*, 1(4), 247–257. Advance online publication. 10.1007/s41066-016-0020-7

Souravlas, S., Anastasiadou, S., & Katsavounis, S. (2021). A survey on the recent advances of deep community detection. *Applied Sciences (Basel, Switzerland)*, 11(16), 7179. 10.3390/app11167179

Strogatz, S. H. (2001). Exploring complex networks. *Nature*, 410(6825), 268–276. 10.1038/3506572511258382

Sun, B. Z., Ma, W. M., & Chen, X. T. (2019). Variable precision multi-granulation rough fuzzy set approach to multiple attribute group decision-making based on λ-similarity relation. *Computers & Industrial Engineering*, 127, 326–343. 10.1016/j.cie.2018.10.009

Sun, B. Z., Ma, W. M., Li, B. J., & Li, X. N. (2018). Three-way decisions approach to multiple attribute group decision making with linguistic information- based decision-theoretic rough fuzzy set. *International Journal of Approximate Reasoning*, 93, 424–442. 10.1016/j.ijar.2017.11.015

Sun, B. Z., Ma, W. M., & Zhao, H. (2014). Decision-theoretic rough fuzzy set model and application. *Information Sciences*, 283(5), 180–196. 10.1016/j.ins.2014.06.045

Sun, H., He, X., & Peng, Y. (2022). Sim-trans: Structure information modeling transformer for fine-grained visual categorization. *Proceedings of the 30th ACM International Conference on Multimedia*, 5853-5861. 10.1145/3503161.3548308

Sun, M. F., Chen, J. T., Zhang, Y., & Shi, S. Z. (2012). A new method of feature selection for flow classification. *Physics Procedia*, 24, 1729–1736. 10.1016/j.phpro.2012.02.255

Sun, M., Yuan, Y., Zhou, F., & Ding, E. (2018). Multi-attention multi-class constraint for fine-grained image recognition. *Proceedings of the european conference on computer vision*, 805-821. 10.1007/978-3-030-01270-0_49

Sun, S. L., Luo, C., & Chen, J. Y. (2017). A review of natural language processing techniques for opinion mining systems. *Information Fusion*, 36, 10–25. 10.1016/j.inffus.2016.10.004

Su, X., Xue, S., Liu, F. Z., Wu, J., Yang, J., Zhou, C., Hu, W. B., Paris, C., Nepal, S., Jin, D., Sheng, Q. Z., & Yu, P. S. (2022). A comprehensive survey on community detection with deep learning. *IEEE Transactions on Neural Networks and Learning Systems*. Advance online publication. 10.1109/TNNLS.2021.313739635263257

Tan, C. Q., Yi, W. T., & Chen, X. H. (2015). Hesitant fuzzy Hamacher aggregation operators for multicriteria decision making. *Applied Soft Computing*, 26, 325–349. 10.1016/j.asoc.2014.10.007

Tang, X., Peng, Z., Zhang, Q., Pedrycz, W., & Yang, S. (2020a). Consistency and consensus-driven models to personalize individual semantics of linguistic terms for supporting group decision making with distribution linguistic preference relations. *Knowledge-Based Systems*, 189, 105078. 10.1016/j.knosys.2019.105078

Tang, X., Zhang, Q., Peng, Z., Pedrycz, W., & Yang, S. (2020b). Distribution linguistic preference relations with incomplete symbolic proportions for group decision making. *Applied Soft Computing*, 88, 106005. 10.1016/j.asoc.2019.106005

The Nobel Committee for Physics. (2021). *Data snapshot: Scientific Background on the Nobel Prize in Physics 2021*. https://www.nobelprize.org/prizes/physics/2021/advanced-information

Thillaigovindan, N., Shanthi, S. A., & Naidu, J. V. (2016). A better score function for multiple criteria decision making in fuzzy environment with criteria choice under risk. *Expert Systems with Applications*, 59, 78–85. 10.1016/j.eswa.2016.04.023

Tian, Y., Tu, L., Lu, X., Zhou, W., Jiskani, I. M., Liu, F., & Cai, Q. (2023). Stability analysis of multi-layer highwall mining: A sustainable approach for thick-seam open-pit mines. *Sustainability (Basel)*, 15(4), 3603. 10.3390/su15043603

Torra, V. (2010). Hesitant fuzzy sets. *International Journal of Intelligent Systems*, 25(6), 529–539.

Vespignani, A. (2018). Twenty years of network science. *Nature*, 558(7711), 528–529. 10.1038/d41586-018-05444-y29941900

Wang, Z., Li, Z., Yuan, G., Sun, Y., Rui, X., & Xiang, X. (2018). Tracking the evolution of overlapping communities in dynamic social networks. *Knowledge-Based Systems, 157*, 81-97. 10.1016/j.knosys.2018.05.026

Wang, C. Y. (2017). Topological characterizations of generalized fuzzy rough sets. *Fuzzy Sets and Systems*, 312, 109–125. 10.1016/j.fss.2016.02.005

Wang, C. Z., Huang, Y., Shao, M. W., & Chen, D. G. (2019). Uncertainty measures for general fuzzy relations. *Fuzzy Sets and Systems*, 360, 82–96. 10.1016/j.fss.2018.07.006

Wang, C., Pan, S., Hu, R., Long, G., Jiang, J., & Zhang, C. (2019). Attributed Graph Clustering: A Deep Attentional Embedding Approach. *Proceedings of the Twenty-Eighth International Joint Conference on Artificial Intelligence (IJCAI-19),* 3670–3676. 10.24963/ijcai.2019/509

Wang, D., Li, T., Deng, P., Wang, H., & Zhang, P. (2022b). Dual graph-regularized sparse concept factorization for clustering. *Information Sciences*, 607, 1074–1088. 10.1016/j.ins.2022.05.101

Wang, D., Li, T., Deng, P., Zhang, F., Huang, W., Zhang, P., & Liu, J. (2023). A generalized deep learning clustering algorithm based on non-negative matrix factorization. *ACM Transactions on Knowledge Discovery from Data*, 17(7), 1–20. 10.1145/3584862

Wang, D., Li, T., Huang, W., Luo, Z., Deng, P., Zhang, P., & Ma, M. (2023). A multi-view clustering algorithm based on deep semi-NMF. *Information Fusion*, 99, 101884. 10.1016/j.inffus.2023.101884

Wang, D., Shen, Z., Shao, J., Zhang, W., Xue, X., & Zhang, Z. (2015). Multiple granularity descriptors for fine-grained categorization. *Proceedings of the IEEE international conference on computer vision,* 2399-2406.

Wang, F. L., Wang, J. X., Cao, J. Z., Chen, C., & Ban, X. G. J. (2019). Extracting trips from multi-sourced data for mobility pattern analysis: An app-based data example. *Transportation Research Part C, Emerging Technologies*, 105, 183–202. 10.1016/j.trc.2019.05.02832764848

Wang, G. (2017). DGCC: Data-driven granular cognitive computing. *Granular Computing*, (1), 1–13.

Wang, G., Li, T., Zhang, P., Huang, Q., & Chen, H. (2021). Double-local rough sets for efficient data mining. *Information Sciences*, 571, 475–498. 10.1016/j.ins.2021.05.007

Wang, G., Yang, J., & Xu, J. (2017). Granular computing: From granularity optimization to multi-granularity joint problem solving. *Granular Computing*, 2(3), 1–16. 10.1007/s41066-016-0032-3

Wang, H. J., Zhao, X. F., & Wei, G. W. (2014). Dual hesitant fuzzy aggregation operators in multiple attribute decision making. *Journal of Intelligent & Fuzzy Systems*, 26(5), 2281–2290. 10.3233/IFS-130901

Wang, L., Shen, Q. G., & Zhu, L. (2016). Dual hesitant fuzzy power aggregation operators based on Archimedean t-conorm and t-norm and their application to multiple attribute group decision making. *Applied Soft Computing*, 38, 23–50. 10.1016/j.asoc.2015.09.012

Wang, M., Lin, Y., Min, F., & Liu, D. (2019). Cost-sensitive active learning through statistical methods. *Information Sciences*, 501, 460–482. 10.1016/j.ins.2019.06.015

Wang, P., Zhang, P., & Li, Z. (2019). A three-way decision method based on Gaussian kernel in a hybrid information system with images: An application in medical diagnosis. *Applied Soft Computing*, 77, 734–749. 10.1016/j.asoc.2019.01.031

Wang, Q., Qian, Y. H., Liang, X. Y., Guo, Q., & Liang, J. (2018). Local neighborhood rough set. *Knowledge-Based Systems*, 153, 53–64. 10.1016/j.knosys.2018.04.023

Wang, Q., Wang, J., Deng, H., Wu, X., Wang, Y., & Hao, G. (2023). Aa-trans: Core attention aggregating transformer with information entropy selector for fine-grained visual classification. *Pattern Recognition*, 140, 109547. 10.1016/j.patcog.2023.109547

Wang, R., Yan, S., Bai, J., Chang, Z., & Zhao, T. (2019). Theoretical analysis of damaged width & instability mechanism of rib pillar in open-pit highwall mining. *Advances in Civil Engineering*, 2019(2), 1–15. 10.1155/2019/6328702

Wang, S., Liu, F., & Hu, G. (2022). Study on end slope shearer mining feasibility in Xinjiang Open-pit Mine. *Opencast Mining Technology*, 37(6), 22–26.

Wang, T., Liu, R., & Qi, G. (2022). Multi-classification assessment of bank personal credit risk based on multi-source information fusion. *Expert Systems with Applications*, 191, 116236. 10.1016/j.eswa.2021.116236

Wang, Z., Chen, H., Yuan, Z., Yang, X., Zhang, P., & Li, T. (2022a). Exploiting fuzzy rough mutual information for feature selection. *Applied Soft Computing*, 131, 109769. 10.1016/j.asoc.2022.109769

Wan, S. P., Xu, G. L., & Dong, J. Y. (2016). A novel method for group decision making with interval-valued Atanassov intuitionistic fuzzy preference relations. *Information Sciences*, 372, 53–71. 10.1016/j.ins.2016.08.019

Wei, M., & Ahnert, S. E. (2020). Neutral components show a hierarchical community structure in the genotype-phenotype map of RNA secondary structure. *Journal of the Royal Society, Interface*, 20200608(171), 20200608. 10.1098/rsif.2020.0608

Wei, W., & Liang, J. (2019). Information fusion in rough set theory: An overview. *Information Fusion*, 48, 107–118. 10.1016/j.inffus.2018.08.007

Wei, W., Liang, J. Y., & Qian, Y. H. (2012). A comparative study of rough sets for hybrid data. *Information Sciences*, 190, 1–16. 10.1016/j.ins.2011.12.006

Wen, S. D., & Bao, Q. H. (2017). Dominance-based rough fuzzy set approach and its application to rule induction. *European Journal of Operational Research*, 261(2), 690–703. 10.1016/j.ejor.2016.12.004

Wilke, G., & Portmann, E. (2016). Granular computing as a basis of human–data interaction: A cognitive cities use case. *Granular Computing*, 1(3), 181–197. 10.1007/s41066-016-0015-4

Wu, W. Z., & Leung, Y. (2011). Theory and applications of granular labelled partitions in multi-scale decision tables. *Information Sciences*, 181(18), 3878–3897. 10.1016/j.ins.2011.04.047

Wu, W. Z., & Leung, Y. (2013). Optimal scale selection for multi-scale decision tables. *International Journal of Approximate Reasoning*, 54(8), 1107–1129. 10.1016/j.ijar.2013.03.017

Wu, W. Z., Qian, Y., Li, T. J., & Gu, S.-M. (2017). On rule acquisition in incomplete multi-scale decision tables. *Information Sciences*, 378, 282–302. 10.1016/j.ins.2016.03.041

Wu, Y. X., Min, X. Y., Min, F., & Wang, M. (2019). Cost-sensitive active learning with a label uniform distribution model. *International Journal of Approximate Reasoning*, 105, 49–65. 10.1016/j.ijar.2018.11.004

Xia, M. M., & Xu, Z. S. (2011). Hesitant fuzzy information aggregation in decision making. *International Journal of Approximate Reasoning*, 52(3), 395–407. 10.1016/j.ijar.2010.09.002

Xia, M. M., Xu, Z. S., & Zhu, B. (2012). Some issues on intuitionistic fuzzy aggregation operators based on Archimedean t-conorm and t-norm. *Knowledge-Based Systems*, 31, 78–88. 10.1016/j.knosys.2012.02.004

Xiao, L., Li, F., Niu, C., Dai, G., Qiao, Q., & Lin, C. (2023). Evaluation of water inrush hazard in coal seam roof based on the AHP-CRITIC composite weighted method. *Energies*, 16(1), 114. 10.3390/en16010114

Xiao, S. (2014). Induced interval-valued intuitionistic fuzzy Hamacher ordered weighted geometric operator and their application to multiple attribute decision making. *Journal of Intelligent & Fuzzy Systems*, 27(1), 527–534. 10.3233/IFS-131021

Xie, X., Li, Z., Zhang, P., & Zhang, G. (2019). Information structures and uncertainty measures in an incomplete probabilistic set-valued information system. *IEEE Access : Practical Innovations, Open Solutions*, 7, 27501–27514. 10.1109/ACCESS.2019.2897752

Xin, W., & Chaokun, B. (2017). Deep community detection in topologically incomplete networks. *Physica A*, 469, 342–352. 10.1016/j.physa.2016.11.029

Xiu, Z., Nie, W., Cai, P., Chen, D., & Zhang, X. (2022). Study on intelligent adaptability evaluation of intelligent coal mining working face based on ANP and matter-element extension model. *Journal of Mining and Strata Control Engineering*, 5(2), 023037.

Xu, G., Guo, J., & Yang, P. (2020). Tns-LPA: an improved label propagation algorithm for community detection based on two-level neighbourhood similarity. *IEEE Access*, 23526-23536. 10.1109/ACCESS.2020.3045085

Xu, W. H., & Guo, Y. T. (2016). Generalized multi-granulation double-quantitative decision-theoretic rough set. *Knowledge-Based Systems*, 105, 190–205. 10.1016/j.knosys.2016.05.021

Xu, W. H., Li, M. M., & Wang, X. Z. (2016). Information fusion based on information entropy in fuzzy multi-source incomplete information system. *International Journal of Fuzzy Systems*, 19, 1–17.

Xu, W. H., & Yu, J. H. (2017). A novel approach to information fusion in multi-source datasets: A granular computing viewpoint. *Information Sciences*, 378, 410–423. 10.1016/j.ins.2016.04.009

Xu, W. H., Zhang, X. T., & Wang, Q. R. (2012). A generalized multi-granulation rough set approach. *International Conference on Intelligent Computing*, 681–689.

Xu, W., Huang, X., & Cai, K. (2023). Review of multi-source information fusion methods based on granular computing. *Journal of Data Acquisition & Processing*, 38(2), 245–261.

Xu, W., & Li, W. (2016). Granular computing approach to two-way learning based on formal concept analysis in fuzzy datasets. *IEEE Transactions on Cybernetics*, 46(2), 366–379. 10.1109/TCYB.2014.236177225347892

Xu, W., Li, W., & Zhang, X. (2017). Generalized multigranulation rough sets and optimal granularity selection. *Granular Computing*, 2(4), 271–288. 10.1007/s41066-017-0042-9

Xu, W., Sun, W., Zhang, X., & Zhang, W. (2012). Multiple granulation rough set approach to ordered information systems. *International Journal of General Systems*, 41(5), 475–501. 10.1080/03081079.2012.673598

Xu, Z. S. (2000). On consistency of the weighted geometric mean complex judgement matrix in AHP. *European Journal of Operational Research*, 126(3), 683–687. 10.1016/S0377-2217(99)00082-X

Xu, Z. S., & Liao, H. C. (2015). A survey of approaches to decision making with intuitionistic fuzzy preference relations. *Knowledge-Based Systems*, 80, 131–142. 10.1016/j.knosys.2014.12.034

Xu, Z. S., & Wang, H. (2016). Managing multi-granularity linguistic information in qualitative group decision making: An overview. *Granular Computing*, 1(1), 21–35. 10.1007/s41066-015-0006-x

Xu, Z. S., & Yager, R. R. (2006). Some geometric aggregation operators based on intuitionistic fuzzy sets. *International Journal of General Systems*, 35(4), 417–433. 10.1080/03081070600574353

Yager, R. R. (2004). A framework for multi-source data fusion. *Information Sciences*, 163(1-3), 175–200. 10.1016/j.ins.2003.03.018

Yan, C. (2022). Nestedness interacts with subnetwork structures and interconnection patterns to affect community dynamics in ecological multilayer networks. *Journal of Animal Ecology*, 91(4), 738–751. 10.1111/1365-2656.1366535061910

Yang, F., & Zhang, P. (2021). Using 2-tuple Linguistic Model for Multi-source Set-valued Information Fusion. In *2021 16th International Conference on Intelligent Systems and Knowledge Engineering (ISKE)* (pp. 557-560). IEEE.

Yang, S., Liu, S., Yang, C., & Wang, C. (2021). Re-rank coarse classification with local region enhanced features for fine-grained image recognition. *arXiv preprint arXiv:2102.09875.*

Yang, X., Qi, Y., & Yu, H. (2014). Want More? Pay More! *International Conference on Rough Sets and Current Trends in Computing*. Springer.

Yang, F., & Zhang, P. (2023). MSIF: Multi-source information fusion based on information sets. *Journal of Intelligent & Fuzzy Systems*, 44(3), 4103–4112. 10.3233/JIFS-222210

Yang, J., & Leskovec, J. (2012). Defining and evaluating network communities based on ground-truth. *Knowledge and Information Systems*, 42(1), 181–213. 10.1007/s10115-013-0693-z

Yang, J., & Leskovec, J. (2013). Overlapping community detection at scale: A nonnegative matrix factorization approach. *ACM International Conference on Web Search & Data Mining*. ACM. 10.1145/2433396.2433471

Yang, L., Wang, Y., Gu, J., Wang, C., Cao, X., & Guo, Y. (2020). JANE: Jointly Adversarial Network Embedding. *Proceedings of the Twenty-Ninth International Joint Conference on Artificial Intelligence (IJCAI-20)*, 1381–1387. 10.24963/ijcai.2020/192

Yang, T., Wang, H., Dong, X., Liu, F., Zhang, P., & Deng, W. (2020). Current situation, problems and countermeasures of intelligent evaluation of slope stability in open pit. *Meitan Xuebao*, 45(6), 2277–2295.

Yang, X., Chen, H., Li, T., Zhang, P., & Luo, C. (2022). Student-t kernelized fuzzy rough set model with fuzzy divergence for feature selection. *Information Sciences*, 610, 52–72. 10.1016/j.ins.2022.07.139

Yang, X., Li, T. R., Fujita, H., & Liu, D. (2019). A sequential three-way approach to multi-class decision. *International Journal of Approximate Reasoning*, 104, 108–112. 10.1016/j.ijar.2018.11.001

Yang, X., Li, T. R., Liu, D., & Fujita, H. (2019). A temporal-spatial composite sequential approach of three-way granular computing. *Information Sciences*, 486, 171–189. 10.1016/j.ins.2019.02.048

Yang, X., Li, T., Fujita, H., Liu, D., & Yao, Y. (2017). A unified model of sequential three-way decisions and multilevel incremental processing. *Knowledge-Based Systems*, 134, 172–188. 10.1016/j.knosys.2017.07.031

Yang, Y., Shi, P., Wang, Y., & He, K. (2020). Quadratic optimization based clique expansion for overlapping community detection. http://arxiv.org/abs/2011.01640

Yao, Y. Y. (2007). Decision-theoretic rough set model. *International conference on rough sets and knowledge technology*. Springer-Verlag.

Yao, Y., & Deng, X. (2011). Sequential three-way decisions with probabilistic rough sets. *IEEE International Conference on Cognitive Informatics & Cognitive Computing*. IEEE.

Yao, J. T., Raghavan, V. V., & Wu, Z. (2008). Web information fusion: A review of the state of the art. *Information Fusion*, 9(4), 446–449. 10.1016/j.inffus.2008.05.002

Yao, J., Vasilakos, A. V., & Pedrycz, W. (2013). Granular computing: Perspectives and challenges. *IEEE Transactions on Cybernetics*, 43(6), 1977–1989. 10.1109/TSMCC.2012.223664823757594

Yao, Y. (2009). Interpreting concept learning in cognitive informatics and granular computing. *IEEE Transactions on Systems, Man, and Cybernetics. Part B, Cybernetics*, 39(4), 855–866. 10.1109/TSMCB.2009.201333419342352

Yao, Y. Y. (2007). Decision-theoretic rough set models. *Lecture Notes in Computer Science*, 178, 1–12.

Yao, Y. Y. (2010). Three-way decisions with probabilistic rough sets. *Information Sciences*, 180(3), 341–353. 10.1016/j.ins.2009.09.021

Yao, Y. Y. (2011). The superiority of three-way decisions in probabilistic rough set models. *Information Sciences*, 181(6), 1080–1096. 10.1016/j.ins.2010.11.019

Yao, Y. Y. (2013). Granular computing and sequential three-way decisions. *International Conference on Rough Sets and Knowledge Technology*, 16–27. 10.1007/978-3-642-41299-8_3

Yao, Y. Y. (2015). The two sides of the theory of rough sets. *Knowledge-Based Systems*, 80, 67–77. 10.1016/j.knosys.2015.01.004

Yao, Y. Y. (2016). A triarchic theory of granular computing. *Granular Computing*, 1(2), 145–157. 10.1007/s41066-015-0011-0

Yao, Y. Y. (2018). Three-way decision and granular computing. *International Journal of Approximate Reasoning*, 103, 107–123. 10.1016/j.ijar.2018.09.005

Yao, Y. Y., & Lin, T. Y. (1996). Generalization of rough sets using modal logics. *Intelligent Automation & Soft Computing*, 2(2), 103–120. 10.1080/10798587.1996.10750660

Yao, Y. Y., Wong, S. K. M., & Lingras, P. (1990). *A Decision-Theoretic Rough Set Model, Methodologies for Intelligent Systems*. North-Holland.

Yao, Y. Y., & Yao, B. X. (2012). Covering based rough set approximations. *Information Sciences*, 200(1), 91–107. 10.1016/j.ins.2012.02.065

Yao, Y. Y., & Zhao, Y. (2008). Attribute reduction in decision-theoretic rough set models. *Information Sciences*, 178(17), 3356–3373. 10.1016/j.ins.2008.05.010

Ye, J. (2014). Correlation coefficient of dual hesitant fuzzy sets and its application to multiple attribute decision making. *Applied Mathematical Modelling*, 38(2), 659–666. 10.1016/j.apm.2013.07.010

Yi, J., & Guo, L. (2023). AHP-Based network security situation assessment for industrial internet of things. *Electronics (Basel)*, 12(16), 3458. 10.3390/electronics12163458

Yi, Y., Jin, L. H., Yu, H., Juo, H. R., & Cheng, F. (2021). Density sensitive random walk for local community detection. *IEEE Access : Practical Innovations, Open Solutions*, 9, 27773–27782. 10.1109/ACCESS.2021.3058908

Yu, M. (2018). *Stability mechanism study of coal pillar and slope body under strip mining of end-slope coal* [PhD Dissertation]. China University of Mining and Technology.

Yuan, Z., Chen, H. M., Li, T. R., Sang, B. B., & Wang, S. (2022). Outlier detection based on fuzzy rough granules in mixed attribute data. *IEEE Transactions on Cybernetics*, 52(8), 8399–8412. 10.1109/TCYB.2021.305878033750721

Yuan, Z., Chen, H., Xie, P., Zhang, P., Liu, J., & Li, T. (2021a). Attribute reduction methods in fuzzy rough set theory: An overview, comparative experiments, and new directions. *Applied Soft Computing*, 107, 107353. 10.1016/j.asoc.2021.107353

Yuan, Z., Chen, H., Zhang, P., Wan, J., & Li, T. (2021b). A novel unsupervised approach to heterogeneous feature selection based on fuzzy mutual information. *IEEE Transactions on Fuzzy Systems*, 30(9), 3395–3409. 10.1109/TFUZZ.2021.3114734

Yu, H., Liu, Z., & Wang, G. Y. (2014). An automatic method to determine the number of clusters using decision-theoretic rough set. *International Journal of Approximate Reasoning*, 55(1), 101–115. 10.1016/j.ijar.2013.03.018

Yu, H., Zhang, C., & Wang, G. Y. (2015). A tree-based incremental overlapping clustering method using the three-way decision theory. *Knowledge-Based Systems*, 91(C), 189–203.

Yu, J. H., Zhang, B., Chen, M. H., & Xu, W. H. (2018). Double-quantitative decision-theoretic approach to multi-granulation approximate space. *International Journal of Approximate Reasoning*, 98, 236–258. 10.1016/j.ijar.2018.05.001

Yu, J., Zhu, L., & Xu, G. (2019). Safety and high efficiency adaptability evaluation of coal mine intelligent fully-mechanized mining face. *Coal Science and Technology*, 47(3), 60–65.

Zachary, W. W. (1977). An information flow model for conflict and fission in small groups. *Journal of Anthropological Research*, 33(4), 452–473. 10.1086/jar.33.4.3629752

Zadeh, L. A. (1979). Fuzzy sets and information granularity. *Fuzzy sets, fuzzy logic, and fuzzy systems: Selected papers*, 433-448.

Zadeh, L. A. (1965). Fuzzy sets. *Information and Control*, 8(3), 338–353. 10.1016/S0019-9958(65)90241-X

Zadeh, L. A. (1979). Fuzzy sets and information granularity. In *Advances in Fuzzy Set Theory and Applications* (pp. 3–18). North-Holland.

Zadeh, L. A. (1997). Toward a theory of fuzzy information granulation and its centrality in human reasoning and fuzzy logic. *Fuzzy Sets and Systems*, 90(2), 111–127. 10.1016/S0165-0114(97)00077-8

Zadeh, L. A. (1998). Some reflections on soft computing, granular computing and their roles in the conception, design and utilization of information/intelligent systems. *Soft Computing*, 2(1), 23–25. 10.1007/s005000050030

Zakowski, W. (1983). Approximations in the space (μ,π). *Demonstratio Mathematica*, 16(3), 761–769. 10.1515/dema-1983-0319

Zeng, J., & Yu, H. (2018). A Distributed Infomap Algorithm for Scalable and High-Quality Community Detection. *Proceedings of the 47th International Conference on Parallel Processing*. 10.1145/3225058.3225137

Zeng, J., Li, Z., Zhang, P., & Wang, P. (2020). Information structures and uncertainty measures in a hybrid information system: Gaussian kernel method. *International Journal of Fuzzy Systems*, 22(1), 212–231. 10.1007/s40815-019-00779-8

Zhang, F., Li, M., Zhai, G., & Liu, Y. (2021). Multi-branch and multi-scale attention learning for fine-grained visual categorization. *MultiMedia Modeling: 27th International Conference, MMM*, 136-147.

Zhang, N., Donahue, J., Girshick, R., & Darrell, T. (2014). Part-based R-CNNs for fine-grained category detection. *Computer Vision–ECCV 2014: 13th European Conference*, 834-849.

Zhang, Q. H., Xu, K., & Wang, G. (2016). Fuzzy equivalence relation and its multigranulation spaces. *Information Sciences,* 346–347. (http://archive.ics.uci.edu/ml/)

Zhang, G., Li, Z., Zhang, P., & Xie, N. (2021). Information structures and uncertainty in an image information system. *Journal of Intelligent & Fuzzy Systems*, 40(1), 295–317. 10.3233/JIFS-191628

Zhang, P., Li, T., Luo, C., & Wang, G. (2022a). AMG-DTRS: Adaptive multi-granulation decision-theoretic rough sets. *International Journal of Approximate Reasoning*, 140, 7–30. 10.1016/j.ijar.2021.09.017

Zhang, P., Li, T., Wang, G., Luo, C., Chen, H., Zhang, J., Wang, D., & Yu, Z. (2021). Multi-source information fusion based on rough set theory: A review. *Information Fusion*, 68, 85–117. 10.1016/j.inffus.2020.11.004

Zhang, P., Li, T., Wang, G., Wang, D., Lai, P., & Zhang, F. (2023a). A multi-source information fusion model for outlier detection. *Information Fusion*, 93, 192–208. 10.1016/j.inffus.2022.12.027

Zhang, P., Li, T., Yuan, Z., Deng, Z., Wang, G., Wang, D., & Zhang, F. (2023b). A possibilistic information fusion-based unsupervised feature selection method using information quality measures. *IEEE Transactions on Fuzzy Systems*, 31(9), 2975–2988. 10.1109/TFUZZ.2023.3238803

Zhang, P., Li, T., Yuan, Z., Luo, C., Liu, K., & Yang, X. (2022c). Heterogeneous feature selection based on neighborhood combination entropy. *IEEE Transactions on Neural Networks and Learning Systems*.35925855

Zhang, P., Li, T., Yuan, Z., Luo, C., Wang, G., Liu, J., & Du, S. (2022b). A data-level fusion model for unsupervised attribute selection in multi-source homogeneous data. *Information Fusion*, 80, 87–103. 10.1016/j.inffus.2021.10.017

Zhang, Q. H., Wang, J., & Wang, G. Y. (2015). The approximate representation of rough-fuzzy sets. *Chinese Journal of Computer*, (7), 1484–1496.

Zhang, Q. H., Zhang, P., & Wang, G. Y. (2017). Research on approximation set of rough set based on fuzzy similarity. *Journal of Intelligent & Fuzzy Systems*, 32(3), 2549–2562. 10.3233/JIFS-16533

Zhang, W. S., Zhang, Y. J., Zhai, J., Zhao, D. H., Xu, L., Zhou, J. H., Li, Z. W., & Yang, S. (2018). Multi-source data fusion using deep learning for smart refrigerators. *Computers in Industry*, 95, 15–21. 10.1016/j.compind.2017.09.001

Zhang, W., Kong, F., Yang, L., Chen, Y. F., & Zhang, M. Y. (2018). Hierarchical community detection based on partial matrix convergence using random walks. *Tsinghua Science and Technology*, 23(1), 35–46. 10.26599/TST.2018.9010053

Zhang, X., Mei, C. L., Chen, D. G., & Li, J. H. (2016). Feature selection in mixed data: A method using a novel fuzzy rough set-based information entropy. *Pattern Recognition*, 56, 1–15. 10.1016/j.patcog.2016.02.013

Zhang, X., Zhou, F., Lin, Y., & Zhang, S. (2016). Embedding label structures for fine-grained feature representation. *Proceedings of the IEEE Conference on Computer Vision and Pattern Recognition,* 1114-1123. 10.1109/CVPR.2016.126

Zhang, Y. B., Miao, D. Q., Wang, J. Q., & Zhang, Z. F. (2019). A cost-sensitive three-way combination technique for ensemble learning in sentiment classification. *International Journal of Approximate Reasoning*, 105, 85–97. 10.1016/j.ijar.2018.10.019

Zhang, Y., Zhang, H., Nasrabadi, N. M., & Huang, T. S. (2013). Multi-metric learning for multi-sensor fusion based classification. *Information Fusion*, 14(4), 431–440. 10.1016/j.inffus.2012.05.002

Zhang, Y., & Zhou, Z. H. (2010). Cost-sensitive Face Recognition. *IEEE Transactions on Pattern Analysis and Machine Intelligence*, 32(10), 1758–1769. 10.1109/TPAMI.2009.19520724754

Zhao, H., Wang, P., & Hu, Q. (2016). Cost-sensitive feature selection based on adaptive neighborhood granularity with multi-level confidence. *Information Sciences*, 366, 134–149. 10.1016/j.ins.2016.05.025

Zhao, H., & Zhu, W. (2014). Optimal cost-sensitive granularization based on rough sets for variable costs. *Knowledge-Based Systems*, 65(4), 72–82. 10.1016/j.knosys.2014.04.009

Zhao, W., Luo, J., Fan, T., Ren, Y., & Xia, Y. (2021). Analyzing and visualizing scientific research collaboration network with core node evaluation and community detection based on network embedding. *Pattern Recognition Letters*, 144(10), 54–60. 10.1016/j.patrec.2021.01.007

Zhao, X. F., & Wei, G. W. (2013). Some intuitionistic fuzzy Einstein hybrid aggregation operators and their application to multiple attribute decision making. *Knowledge-Based Systems*, 37, 472–479. 10.1016/j.knosys.2012.09.006

Zhao, Y., Li, J., Chen, X., & Tian, Y. (2021). Part-guided relational transformers for fine-grained visual recognition. *IEEE Transactions on Image Processing*, 30, 9470–9481. 10.1109/TIP.2021.312649034780327

Zheng, H., Fu, J., Mei, T., & Luo, J. (2017). Learning multi-attention convolutional neural network for fine-grained image recognition. *Proceedings of the IEEE international conference on computer vision*, 5209-5217. 10.1109/ICCV.2017.557

Zhou, B. (2011). A New Formulation of Multi-category Decision-Theoretic Rough Sets. *Rough Sets and Knowledge Technology.* Springer Berlin Heidelberg.

Zhou, F., & Lin, Y. (2016). Fine-grained image classification by exploring bipartite-graph labels. *Proceedings of the IEEE Conference on Computer Vision and Pattern Recognition,* 1124-1133. 10.1109/CVPR.2016.127

Zhou, L. Y., Zhao, X. F., & Wei, G. W. (2014). Hesitant fuzzy Hamacher aggregation operators and their application to multiple attribute decision making. *Journal of Intelligent & Fuzzy Systems*, 26(6), 2689–2699. 10.3233/IFS-130939

Zhuang, P., Wang, Y., & Qiao, Y. (2020). Learning attentive pairwise interaction for fine-grained classification. *Proceedings of the AAAI Conference on Artificial Intelligence*, 34(7), 13130–13137. 10.1609/aaai.v34i07.7016

Zhu, B., Xu, Z. S., & Xia, M. M. (2012). Dual hesitant fuzzy sets. *Journal of Applied Mathematics*, 2012, 1–13. Advance online publication. 10.1155/2012/879629

Zhu, W. (2009). Relationship among basic concepts in covering-based rough sets. *Information Sciences*, 179(14), 2478–2486. 10.1016/j.ins.2009.02.013

Zhu, W., & Wang, F. Y. (2012). The fourth type of covering-based rough sets. *Information Sciences*, 201, 80–92. 10.1016/j.ins.2012.01.026

Zipf, R., & Bhatt, S. (2004). Analysis of practical ground control issues in highwall mining. *Proceedings of the 23rd International Conference on Ground Control in Mining*, 210-219.

About the Contributors

Chao Zhang, Professor of Institute of Intelligent Information Processing, Shanxi University, his main study interests include data mining, granular computing and intelligent decision making. In recent years, he has published more than 80 papers including IEEE Transactions on Computational Social Systems, IEEE Transactions on Fuzzy Systems, IEEE Transactions on Consumer Electronics, Information Sciences, Information Fusion, International Journal of Approximate Reasoning. Among them, one paper has been selected as "ESI highly cited paper". He has published 3 academic monographs in national publishers. He has published 2 national invention patents. He has been awarded the first prize of Outstanding Achievements in Scientific Research in Institutions of Higher Learning in Shanxi Province, the second prize of Outstanding Achievement Award in Social Sciences in Shanxi Province, two Excellent Academic Paper Awards in Taiyuan City, ACM Excellent Doctoral Dissertation Award in Taiyuan Chapter.

Wentao Li received the Ph.D. degree from the Department of Mathematics, Harbin Institute of Technology in 2019. From 2016 to 2018, he was a joint Ph. D student with the University of Alberta, Edmonton. He is currently working at the College of Artificial Intelligence, Southwest University. He has published over 50 articles in international journals, such as: IEEE TCYB, IEEE TNNLS, IEEE TFS, IEEE TSMC, IEEE TAI, IEEE TCE, IEEE TETCI, INS, FSS, IJAR, etc. His current research interests include fuzzy sets, rough sets, feature selection, and granular computing.

* * *

Qingbin Ji received his Ph.D. degree from the School of Computer and Information Technology, Shanxi University, and is currently working at the School of Mathematics, North University of China. His research interests include both technical and scientific fields, with a focus on complex network analysis and community detection.

Tao Jiang, as a Professor of the School of Intelligent Medicine, Chengdu University of Traditional Chinese Medicine. His research interests include artificial intelligence, smart medical care, special intelligent robots, and driverless cars. He has published more than 60 papers including Information Fusion, Pattern Recognition, Frontiers in Micriobiology, Artificial Intelligence Review, etc.

Ying Lv, received his Ph.D. from Shanghai University. His main study interests include deep learning and transfer learning. In recent years, he has published more than 20 papers including Expert Systems with Applications, IEEE BIBM, CIKM and AAAI.

Xiaoan Tang received the Ph.D. degree from the School of Management, Hefei University of Technology in 2019. From 2017 to 2018, he was a joint Ph. D student with the University of Alberta, Edmonton. He is current an Associate Professor with the School of Management, Hefei University of Technology. He has published over 30 articles in international journals, such as: IEEE TFS, INF, INS, EJOR, FSS, KBS, etc. His current research interests include group decision-making, fuzzy sets, feature selection, and granular computing.

Dexian Wang is an associate professor in the College of Intelligent Medicine, Chengdu University of Traditional Chinese Medicine, with main research interests in data mining , intelligent analysis of TCM information. He has published more than 20 papers in recent years, including IEEE Transactions on Systems, Man, and Cybernetics-Systems, IEEE Transactions on Big Data, IEEE Transactions on Computational Social Systems, IEEE Transactions on Fuzzy Systems, ACM Transactions on Knowledge Discovery from Data, ACM Transactions on Intelligent Systems and Technology, Information Science, Information Fusion, Knowledge-Based Systems, International Journal of Information Science, etc. Two of them were selected as "ESI Highly Cited Papers". He has published 1 national invention patent. Won the national third prize of the 7th CCF Big Data and Computer Intelligence Competition.

Zhikang Xu, Lecturer of Institute of Intelligent Information Processing, Shanxi University, his main study interests include deep learning and computer vision. In recent years, he has published more than 20 papers including AAAI, IEEE BIBM, Medical Image Analysis, MICCAI, International Journal of Machine Learning and Cybernetics.

Xiaodong Yue a professor in the school of future technology at Shanghai University. The major research interests of Dr. Yue include the theories and applications of Machine Learning, in which he has the special focus on Soft Computing, Image Analysis and Data Mining. He has published more than 60 academic papers in these areas, including prestigious journals and international conferences. In the past five years, Dr. Yue served as a PC member for a number of international conferences such as AAAI, PAKDD, ICONIP and also served as a publication chair for ICME2012, DSAA2014 and RSKT2014. He is an area editor of International Journal of Approximate Reasoning (IJAR) and an associate editor of the Elsevier journal Array. He also served as a reviewer for several international journals such as 'Pattern Recognition', 'Information Sciences' and 'Knowledge-based Systems'.

Tao Zhan received her Ph.D. degree in School of Mathematics, Shandong University. She is currently working at the School of Mathematics and Statistics, Southwest University, Chongqing. Her current research interests include nonlinear fractional order systems, singular system and impulsive control.

Pengfei Zhang, as an Associate Professor of the School of Intelligent Medicine, Chengdu University of Traditional Chinese Medicine. His research interests include granular computing, rough set theory, data mining and information fusion. He has published over 30 papers in prestigious journals, including IEEE TNNLS, IEEE TFS, ACM TKDD, ACM TIST, Information Fusion, Information Sciences, Applied Soft Computing, Engineering Applications of Artificial Intelligence, International Journal of Approximate Reasoning, etc. Among them, one paper has been selected as "ESI highly cited paper". He has been awarded the ACM Chengdu Chapter Outstanding Doctoral Dissertation Award, Southwest Jiaotong University Outstanding Doctoral Dissertation Award. He also serves as a Reviewer for a number of prestigious journals, such as the IEEE TFS, Information Fusion, Pattern Recognition, International Journal of Approximate Reasoning, Artificial Intelligence Review, etc.

Index

Symbols

A

B

C

D

E

F

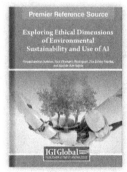

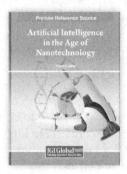

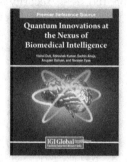

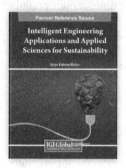

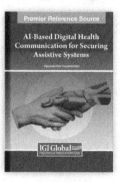

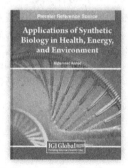

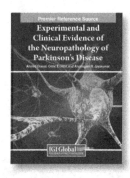

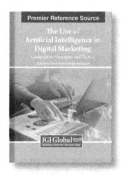

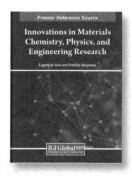

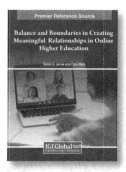

Printed in the United States
by Baker & Taylor Publisher Services